# Frontiers of Medicine
# in the Anglo-Egyptian Sudan
## 1899–1940

Heather Bell

CLARENDON PRESS · OXFORD

1999

Oxford University Press, Great Clarendon Street, Oxford OX2 6DP
Oxford New York
Athens Auckland Bangkok Bogotá Buenos Aires Calcutta
Cape Town Chennai Dar es Salaam Delhi Florence Hong Kong Istanbul
Karachi Kuala Lumpur Madrid Melbourne Mexico City Mumbai
Nairobi Paris São Paulo Singapore Taipei Tokyo Toronto Warsaw
and associated companies in Berlin Ibadan

Oxford is a registered trade mark of Oxford University Press

Published in the United States
by Oxford University Press Inc., New York
© Heather Bell 1999
The moral rights of the author have been asserted
First published 1999

British Library Cataloguing in Publication Data
Data available

Library of Congress Cataloging in Publication Data
Bell, Heather.
Frontiers of medicine in the Anglo-Eqyptian Sudan, 1899–1940
Heather Bell.
p. cm.–(Oxford historical monographs)
Revised and extended version of the author's doctoral thesis.
Includes bibliographical references and index.
1. Medicine–Sudan–History–20th century. 2. Imperialism–Health
aspects–Sudan–History–20th century. 3. Public health–Sudan–
History–20th century. 4. Medical care–Sudan–History–20th
century. 5. Communicable diseases–Sudan–History–20th century.
I. Title. II. Series.
[DNLM: 1. History of Medicine, 19th Cent.–Sudan. 2. History of
Medicine, 20th Cent.–Sudan. 3. Colonialism. WZ 70 HS86 1999]
R651.B44 1999
610'.9624'09041–dc21
DNLM/DLC
for Library of Congress                                98-40976

ISBN 0-19-820749-2

1 3 5 7 9 10 8 6 4 2

Typeset in Monotype Ehrhardt
by Best-set Typesetter Ltd., Hong Kong
Printed in Great Britain
on acid-free paper by
Biddles Ltd., Guildford & King's Lynn

For my parents
*Alexander*
and
*Virginia Bell*

# ACKNOWLEDGEMENTS

THIS study, a revised and extended version of my doctoral thesis, would not have been possible without the generous help of many individuals and institutions. In this age of shrinking budgets for research in the humanities, I gratefully acknowledge indispensable financial support from the Commonwealth Scholarship Commission, Nuffield College, the University of Oxford Beit Fund, the Rockefeller Archive Center, the Social Sciences and Humanities Research Council of Canada, and the Rhodes Trust.

I have been fortunate in having congenial places in which to research. I would like to thank Jane Hogan and Lesley Forbes at the University of Durham Library, Ali Salih Karrar at the National Records Office, Khartoum, Tom Rosenbaum at the Rockefeller Archive Center, John Davies at Glaxo Wellcome, and Shirley Dixon at the Wellcome Institute for the History of Medicine Library, for guiding me through the archives in their care. I have become something of a regular in Durham and at the Rockefeller Archive Center and would like to particularly thank Jane, Tom, and the staff of the Palace Green Library for their warm hospitality, and for their patience with copyright queries.

I am delighted to thank Josephine Street for permission to quote from the papers of her grandfather, Sir F. R. Wingate; Janet Cropley for permission to quote from the papers of her father, T. R. H. Owen; Mary Macdonald for permission to quote from her unpublished notes on the Spence letters; Dr T. P. Ormerod for permission to quote from the papers of his uncle, Dr J. B. Christopherson; and Max Ward for permission to quote from the papers of his grandfather, Sir Basil Neven-Spence. I am grateful to the Rockefeller Archive Center for permission to quote from the Rockefeller Foundation papers and to reproduce Plate 3; to Glaxo Wellcome for permission to quote from the Wellcome papers; to the University of Durham Library for permission to reproduce Plates 1, 2, 4, and 5; and to Prof. Hassen Osman Abdel Nour, State Minister in Sudan's Ministry of Agriculture and Forestry, for permission to reproduce the irrigation data in Table 4.1, from W. N. Allan, 'Irrigation in the Sudan', in J. D. Tothill, *Agriculture in the Sudan* (London: Oxford University Press, 1948), table opposite p. 608. An early version of Chapter 7 appeared in the *Journal of African History*, 39/2 (1998) under the title 'Midwifery

Training and Female Circumcision in the Inter-war Anglo-Egyptian Sudan'; I am grateful to Cambridge University Press for permission to publish an extended version of this article here.

I am indebted to the many people who helped to make my Sudan trip a success. Lutfi Radwan provided indispensable assistance before I left, and along with his family, companionship while I was in Khartoum. Dr Mahassin Hag Al Safi welcomed me to the Institute of African and Asian Studies at the University of Khartoum. The organizational skills of the incomparable George Pagoulatos at the Acropole Hotel enabled me to squeeze the most out of my stay. Dr Ahmed Abdel-Hameed helped me to access records at the National Medical Research Laboratories Library and kindly showed me documents from Wad Medani.

My intellectual debts are numerous. The material in this book has been greatly improved by the comments of my thesis examiners, Paul Weindling and Shula Marks. It has also benefited from the comments of participants in seminars at the Universities of Oxford and London, and at conferences in Boston, Nottingham, Oxford, and San Francisco. I thank Peter Buck, Douglas Johnson, Laura Newby, and Katherine Rake for helpful discussions and astute readings. I am grateful to Harriet Deacon, Thorsten Körner, Ilana Löwy, Helen Power, Molly Sutphen, and Luise White for sharing unpublished work with me and to Luise for allowing me to quote from her unpublished paper. Megan Vaughan, my supervisor reincarnated as sub-editor, knew what this book was about long before I did, and has been infinitely patient in allowing me to make my way in my own good time. Her insights, and her example, have been invaluable to me.

Robert Bickers, the most outstanding of colleagues and the most de-voted of friends, has read every draft of every chapter of this manuscript at least twice. I can never thank him enough. I cannot articulate what Neil Shephard's care and support have meant, and continue to mean to me: he has sustained me throughout this project. My brothers have insisted on seeing their names in print, so I will say that Derek and Scott Bell provided essential comic relief during the writing of this book. Our parents have always believed that we could do anything and it is with great pride, heartfelt thanks, and much love that I dedicate this book to them.

H. B.

*Oxford*
*August 1997*

# CONTENTS

# ILLUSTRATIONS

# MAP

# TABLES

# ABBREVIATIONS

| | |
|---|---|
| *ARED* | *Annual Report of the Education Department* |
| *ATMP* | *Annals of Tropical Medicine and Parasitology* |
| BCGA | British Cotton Growing Association |
| *BMJ* | *British Medical Journal* |
| BNP | Blue Nile province; also designates files on this province held at the National Records Office, Khartoum |
| *BOIHP* | *Bulletin mensuel, Office international d'hygiène publique* |
| *BSSB* | *Bulletin of the Sleeping Sickness Bureau* |
| BW&Co | Burroughs Wellcome and Company |
| CBPH | Central Board of Public Health (1940 onward) |
| CIVSEC | Files of the Civil Secretary, held at the National Records Office, Khartoum |
| CMS | Church Missionary Society |
| CSB | Central Sanitary Board (1905–40) |
| EA | Egyptian Army |
| EAMC | Egyptian Army Medical Corps |
| ECGC | Empire Cotton Growing Corporation |
| GMC | Gordon Memorial College, Khartoum |
| *GMCRA* | *The Gordon Memorial College at Khartoum, Report and Accounts* |
| GWGA | Glaxo Wellcome Group Archive |
| IHD | International Health Division of the Rockefeller Foundation |
| ISC | International Sanitary Convention on Aerial Navigation |
| *JRAMC* | *Journal of the Royal Army Medical Corps* |
| *JTMH* | *Journal of Tropical Medicine and Hygiene* |
| KASSALA | Files on Kassala province held at the National Records Office, Khartoum |
| LANDS | Files of the Department of Lands held at the National Records Office, Khartoum |
| LB | Letter book |
| MOH | Medical Officer of Health |
| MONGALLA | Files on Mongalla province, held at the National Records Office, Khartoum |
| MTS | Midwifery Training School |
| NMRLL | National Medical Research Laboratories Library, Khartoum |
| NRO | National Records Office, Khartoum |
| PMO | Principal Medical Officer |
| RAC | Rockefeller Archive Center, North Tarrytown, New York |
| RAMC | Royal Army Medical Corps |

| | |
|---|---|
| RF | Rockefeller Foundation |
| RFA | Rockefeller Foundation Archive |
| *RFACS* | *Report on the Finances, Administration and Condition of the Sudan* |
| RG | Record group |
| *RSMS* | *Report of the Sudan Medical Service* |
| *RWRL* | *Report of the Wellcome Research Laboratories* |
| *RWTRL* | *Report of the Wellcome Tropical Research Laboratories* |
| SAD | Sudan Archive, University of Durham Library |
| SDF | Sudan Defence Force |
| SEH | Secretary for Education and Health |
| *SGG* | *Sudan Government Gazette* |
| *SIR* | *Sudan Intelligence Report* |
| SMO | Senior Medical Officer |
| SMS | Sudan Medical Service (1924 onward) |
| *SNR* | *Sudan Notes and Records* |
| *TRSTMH* | *Transactions of the Royal Society of Tropical Medicine and Hygiene* |
| WA | Wellcome Archive, Contemporary Medical Archives Centre, Wellcome Institute for the History of Medicine Library |
| WRL | Wellcome Research Laboratories (1903–11) |
| WTRL | Wellcome Tropical Research Laboratories (1911–35) |

# GLOSSARY

| | |
|---|---|
| *abu ashrin* | feeder channel |
| *benge* | Zande poison oracle which operates through the administration of strychnine to fowls |
| *dawaran* | scour pit |
| *daya* | traditional midwife |
| *dura* | millet (sorghum vulgare) |
| *feddan* | unit of land measurement = 1.038 acres |
| *fetwa* | legal opinion issued by a *mufti* |
| *habl* | rope |
| *hallaq* | traditional barber-surgeon |
| *jebel* | hill or mountain |
| *kantar* | unit of weight = 100 lbs of ginned cotton or 315 lbs of unginned cotton |
| *khor* | water course |
| *lubia* | bean crop used for fodder |
| *lugud* | natural depression |
| *mamur* | district official |
| *mek* | chief or king |
| *merissa* | beer |
| *mufti* | expert in Islamic law |
| *nazir* | leader of a tribe or section of a tribe |
| *omda* | headman of a town or a group of villages |
| *qadi* | judge of an Islamic religious court |
| *tariqa* | *sufi* order or brotherhood |
| *terebai* | perversion of the French word *travailleur* (worker) |
| *tumargi* | hospital attendant/untrained nurse |
| *zaraib* | armed camps (plural of *zariba*) |

N.B. £E1 (one Egyptian pound) = £1. 0s. 6d. = 100 Pt (piastres)

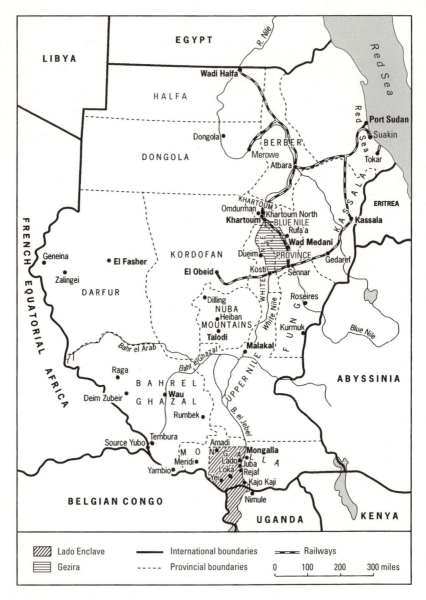

MAP 1.   The Anglo-Egyptian Sudan, showing province divisions and railway lines from 1928 and present-day borders. Based on map by Sudan Survey Department, Khartoum, April 1928.

# I

# The Boundaries of Colonial Medicine

This book is about colonial medicine. While tropical medicine and imperial medicine stress the tropics and the empire as units of analysis, colonial medicine emphasizes the colony. It suggests that we should understand overseas medical practice during the age of imperialism in the context of the interwoven political, economic, and social institutions and interests that constituted each different colonial regime. Such an emphasis is particularly important because colonialism, even within the British empire, took on a wide range of forms. But the term 'colonial medicine' also presents analytical challenges, not least because what it meant for an institution or a medical practice or a form of power to be 'colonial'—beyond the literal sense of 'occurring in a colony'—continues to be ill-defined. What is clear is that new scholarship is remaking the terms in which we conceptualize the colonial encounter. The general literature on the 'tensions of empire' that is growing up around the intersection of history and anthropology has emphasized that the category of 'colonizer' cannot be regarded monolithically: it has shown that significant divisions of race, gender, class, and outlook existed between, for example, missionaries, policemen, district commissioners, and prostitutes.[1] Certainties about the binary division between colonizer and colonized are being challenged as we come to appreciate the roles played by members of the 'colonized' population in colonial administrations. While many analyses of the operation of colonial medical power in Africa are, for example, predicated on the assumption that white European doctors treated black African patients—indeed this is the standard image that the term 'colonial medicine' conjures up—the reality was that the great majority of the practitioners of Western medicine in Africa during the colonial period were not European doctors, but non-Europeans, usually trained African auxiliaries. Recognizing and investi-

[1] Frederick Cooper and Ann Laura Stoler (eds.), *Tensions of Empire: Colonial Cultures in a Bourgeois World* (Berkeley: University of California Press, 1997); Jean Comaroff and John Comaroff, *Of Revelation and Revolution: Christianity, Colonialism, and Consciousness in South Africa*, i (Chicago: University of Chicago Press, 1991); Nicholas Thomas, *Colonialism's Culture: Anthropology, Travel, and Government* (Oxford: Polity Press, 1994).

gating this reality is essential if we are to understand the way in which colonial medicine functioned; this book contributes to the growing literature on this subject.

The growth of area studies has overturned the notion that 'colonial' must always denote a subordination of the periphery to the imperial centre. In the same spirit, recent work has undermined the view that colonial medicine and colonial science were always applied rather than pure, and were consistently derivative of metropolitan knowledge and practice.[2] Mark Harrison has shown that far from being a subsidiary of metropolitan medicine, the Indian Medical Service formed a distinctive medical community with its own medical tradition, which 'emphasized the distinctiveness of the Indian disease environment'.[3] Doctors and scientists working in the colonies generated their own scientific knowledge and propagated their own medical discourses.

While the meaning of 'colonial' is elusive and shifting, defining 'medicine', strange as it may seem, is not so simple either. The microscopic investigation of helminths in a floating laboratory, the filling-in of puddles in which anopheline mosquitoes might breed, the mass administration of atoxyl injections in a sleeping sickness settlement, and the teaching of episiotomies on rubber tyres to student midwives are not activities which, at first glance, appear to have much in common. Though they all took place in Sudan between 1899 and 1940, it is hard to know by what other independent criteria these activities belong together. Only one of these 'medical' activities actually involved sick people. These activities were performed by an array of different people, of different nationalities, with varying amounts of training. British researchers based in the Wellcome Tropical Research Laboratories performed helminthic studies; Sudanese sanitary personnel and labourers filled in puddles, supervised by British sanitary inspectors; military doctors, predominantly Syrian, though a few were British, provided sleeping sickness treatment; British nurse-midwives, assisted by Sudanese staff midwives, taught episiotomy lessons. The concerns of disease-obsessed male medical researchers seem a world away from those of the women midwives involved in the apparently much more culture-bound activity of training Sudanese midwives. Each activity dealt with a distinct project—scientific research, disease

---

[2] For this view, see Michael Worboys, 'Science and British Colonial Imperialism, 1895–1940', D.Phil. thesis (University of Sussex, 1979), esp. the conclusion.

[3] Mark Harrison, *Public Health in British India: Anglo-Indian Preventive Medicine 1859–1914* (Cambridge: Cambridge University Press, 1994), chs. 2 and 4, quote 58; see also Mark Harrison, 'Tropical Medicine in Nineteenth-Century India', *British Journal for the History of Science*, 25 (1992), 299–318.

prevention, disease cure, and medical education—and all were ultimately aimed at distinct groups of people.

This book seeks to describe and define the 'colonial' and the 'medical' in Sudan between 1899 and 1940. Properly defining the 'colonial' would require an extended comparison with the 'metropolitan', namely British medicine, a study which I have chosen not to undertake. But we can begin by identifying some general features which seem distinctive to the colonial context that shaped the development of medicine. Colonialism in Africa started with conquest: a foreign government through military force took charge of a territory essentially unknown to it, in parts of which its control remained only nominal for some years; where the identity and location of the colony's peoples, never mind its diseases, remained a mystery; and where the country's borders, if fixed on a map, in reality remained indeterminate. Conquest and administration were accomplished with few resources: perhaps the defining feature of colonialism was that in order to avoid burdening taxpayers at home, colonial regimes were run on shoestring budgets, and were chronically underfunded and undermanned. Threatened violence, on both sides, underwrote the colonial encounter, particularly as colonial administrations had a tendency to regard indigenous populations as primitive and dangerous. As colonized peoples never had representative and responsible government, public and political life was always much more potentially volatile than that in the metropole, if not actually so. These conditions meant that colonialism was characterized both by extreme exertions of power by the colonial state and by the extreme tenuousness of control by that state; evidence of the colonial state's simultaneous strength and vulnerability runs throughout this book.

This book argues that colonial medicine was centrally concerned with boundaries and frontiers of all kinds, physical and psychological, natural and imposed, real and imagined. Colonial officials, including doctors, worked at physical frontiers, between provinces, nations, peoples, and zones of infection and non-infection. Colonialism in Sudan, as elsewhere in Africa, was partly the struggle to create and maintain borders. Most fundamental was the task of defining a country as territory by translating lines on maps, often arbitrarily drawn, into physical realities on the ground. But there were also borders to be created within the country: keeping tribal groups separate and their distinct cultures intact, and protecting the 'pagan' areas of southern Sudan from the influence of northern Sudanese Arab and Islamic culture were among the hallmarks of government policy in the inter-war period. Declaring parts of southern Sudan to be 'closed districts', to be entered only by individuals with appropriate authorization, was in effect implementing a sanitary cordon against political and cultural infection from neighbouring colonies and from northern Sudan. In their control of schistosomiasis and sleeping sickness in particular, discussed in Chapters 4 and 5, doctors in Sudan also embraced a spatial conception of infection, seeking to protect a territory, rather than specific individuals, from disease by controlling inward and outward movement, and by targeting particular groups of outsiders as disease carriers. These disease control efforts gave a physical presence to international borders between Sudan and Egypt, Uganda, French Congo, and Belgian Congo, and to internal divisions between parts of southern Sudan, and between northern and southern Sudan; such efforts also helped to mark off the cotton-growing Gezira irrigation scheme, already distinctive, as a protected site of production. Such borders could of course never be impermeable: most were too long for an under-resourced administration to control effectively; African communities, often artificially divided, continued to trade and interact across them; some Africans crossed them in search of less oppressive colonial rule; and though often in contradiction of health considerations, the colonial economy demanded the free flow of labourers, Sudanese and foreign, into and within the country. In the 1930s, the start of commercial air travel made conventional international borders irrelevant, relocating them to aerodromes in the hearts of countries; as the discussion of yellow fever in Chapter 6 shows, Sudan, like the rest of the international community, then had to find ways of reinventing those borders as effective barriers to disease spread. Recourse to a new type of international medicine was one solution.

In addition to working on physical frontiers, colonial officials also worked on frontiers of knowledge: they worked in areas where they often knew little about the indigenous population and the local environment. Colonial doctors, moreover, often worked on diseases whose epidemiology was poorly understood and constructed control measures out of knowledge which was only recently acquired, and was sometimes contested, by the medical community. This ignorance was one of the reasons that such great stress was laid on knowing, defining, and ordering the country's territory, a project partly accomplished, I argue, through scientific research and disease control. The Wellcome Tropical Research Laboratories, discussed in Chapter 3, organized and supported scientific expeditions which collected and classified specimens, and catalogued the Sudanese natural environment for the benefit of the Western scientific community and for use in planning future economic exploitation. Chapter

5 argues that it was largely through the study and control of sleeping sickness that the government came to know, order, and administer the border regions of southern Sudan: before serious disease control could begin, roads had to be built, maps made, and censuses conducted. Medical knowledge also produced and reproduced generalizations about the strength, weakness, and general capacity of different racial or social groups in Sudan. Such generalizations served colonial ideologies, particularly about different labouring groups, as Chapter 4 shows in its discussion of disease control in the Gezira scheme. Chapter 2, which looks at medical policy and medical personnel, demonstrates that racial stereotypes also structured training programmes for Sudanese medical personnel, and political considerations, in which racial characteristics played a significant role, influenced which personnel were posted to different parts of Sudan. The heightened importance of race as an ordering category was of course another distinctly colonial feature. If the civilian and military medical services in Sudan seemed inclusive in their employment of non-European personnel—if the professional boundaries around medicine at times seemed fluid—this book demonstrates that British doctors disciplined that inclusiveness through hierarchies of race, gender, class, and occupation. These hierarchies emerge most clearly in Chapter 2, and in Chapter 7, which discusses efforts to train Sudanese women as Western midwives.

Many of the boundaries explored in this book are in fact professional. One way of defining 'medicine' and determining where 'medicine' ended, and 'society' or 'politics' began, is to look at the boundary, often contested, that historical actors themselves drew around medical activity.[4] The diversity of the medical activities outlined earlier may be puzzling to us, but it was not so to the British doctors working in Sudan: if anything united those activities, it was the practitioners' belief, usually shared by their political colleagues, that these were all 'medical' activities, performed to further medical knowledge and to use medical knowledge to improve the public health. Doctors in Sudan—and many auxiliary medical practitioners—would have agreed with the four traditional assumptions about medicine that Peter Wright and Andrew Treacher outline as having characterized the history and sociology of medicine until the 1960s. The first assumption was that 'the identification of medicine

[4] Barry Barnes and Steven Shapin appeal for such an approach in Barry Barnes, *Scientific Knowledge and Sociological Theory* (London: Routledge & Kegan Paul, 1974), 99–124, and Steven Shapin, 'Discipline and Bounding: The History and Sociology of Science as Seen through the Externalism–Internalism Debate', *History of Science*, 30 (1992), 351–4.

or medical knowledge posed no difficulties; indeed it was self-evident: medicine was what doctors and their ancillary workers did' and medical knowledge was transmitted through classes at medical schools and textbooks. Secondly, 'medical knowledge was distinctive' because it was 'built upon the foundations of modern science; and because it was effective'. Thirdly, diseases were 'natural objects which existed prior to and independently of their isolation or designation by doctors'. And finally, social forces 'were assumed to be self-evidently distinct from medicine'.[5]

If doctors (and lay people) gave the general impression that medical work was self-defining, the reality was rather more complicated. Some divisions between the medical and the non-medical, and within medicine itself, mattered enormously. Nor did these divisions simply exist naturally: they were constructed, contested, and policed. Transplanting Western medicine to Sudan involved managing the Wellcome Tropical Research Laboratories, a significant scientific research institution. Chapter 3 argues that the central problem for this institution throughout its existence was negotiating the division between scientific research and scientific practice. Colonial doctors had to choose disease control measures on the basis of new technology such as the mouse protection test, crucial to identifying yellow fever immunity. Chapter 6 shows doctors policing the external boundary of medicine in judging whether this test produced legitimate, accepted medical knowledge. Colonial medicine in Sudan also involved employing non-European doctors and training African medical personnel, discussed in Chapters 2 and 7. Here again we see British medical practitioners guarding medicine's professional prestige by defining who constituted a legitimate practitioner of Western medicine. While I argue that midwifery training and practice involved considerable exchange between Sudanese and British cultures and Western and traditional medicine, this did not mean that the British women who taught midwifery viewed the situation similarly. They defended the boundaries of Western medicine by demanding the highest standards of personal character from their pupils and by defending certain key medical practices.

As much of this discussion about the 'colonial' and the 'medical' suggests, the relationship between medicine and politics—or between medicine and colonial administration—lies at the heart of this book,

[5] Peter Wright and Andrew Treacher, 'Introduction', in Peter Wright and Andrew Treacher (eds.), *The Problem of Medical Knowledge: Examining the Social Construction of Medicine* (Edinburgh: Edinburgh University Press, 1982), 3–5.

which has been written largely from unpublished official sources from an explicitly political archive, namely the medical files of the Sudan government's civil secretariat. Jean Comaroff has written of the 'dialectical interplay' of nineteenth-century medicine and the colonizing project in South Africa:

> The two were in many senses inseparable. Both were driven by a global sense of man that had emerged out of the enlightenment. Both concerned the extension of 'rational' control over domains of nature that were vital and dangerous. Although ostensibly an autonomous field of knowledge and practice, medicine both informed and was informed by imperialism, in Africa and elsewhere. It gave the validity of science to the humanitarian claims of colonialism, while finding confirmation for its own authority in the living laboratories enclosed by expanding imperial frontiers.[6]

Such comments apply equally well to Sudan between 1899 and 1940, where the identification between medicine and colonial administration was often extremely strong. Political officials and doctors were aware of the benefits that colonialism and medicine each had to offer to the other. From the political official's vantage point: medico-scientific research and practice would make Sudan safe for its white rulers; create a body of knowledge that would allow them to understand those they ruled; assess the country's natural resources and allow for their exploitation; solve the sometimes man-made disease problems that might inhibit economic development; provide intellectual and humanitarian justification for colonial rule; and secure a good relationship with the Sudanese population by providing popular treatments, thus assisting pacification, civilization, and the extension of colonial rule. At the dedication of the Kitchener Memorial School of Medicine at Khartoum on 29 February 1924, Governor-General Lee Stack declared: 'I am convinced that medical work is of the highest value to administration. . . . The first essential of successful administration is mutual confidence, and one of the surest ways of obtaining that confidence is by medical assistance.'[7] Medicine could be used for genuine humanitarian purposes; it could also be a 'tool of empire' and an instrument for social control.

But empire was also a tool of medicine, a vehicle through which doctors could promote their professional interests, most notably through the

---

[6] Jean Comaroff, 'The Diseased Heart of Africa: Medicine, Colonialism, and the Black Body', in Shirley Lindenbaum and Margaret Lock (eds.), *Knowledge, Power, and Practice: The Anthropology of Medicine and Everyday Life* (Berkeley: University of California Press, 1993), 324.
[7] *Report, Kitchener School of Medicine 1924–1925*, 9.

creation of the new discipline of tropical medicine at the turn of this century.[8] Work in Sudan allowed British doctors to assume a wide range of medical responsibilities at a young age, to make their names in this new field of research and practice, and to accumulate capital away from a competitive medical market at home. Doctors and other medical personnel discussed in this book obviously had an interest in the persistence of the colonial state: most were state employees. The vast majority of doctors in Sudan were either civilian employees of the colonial government or were members of the army created to defend Sudanese territory: members of the civilian Sudan medical service were both doctors and government officials; members of the medical corps of the Egyptian Army and the Sudan Defence Force were both doctors and soldiers. Their writings and their biographies underline the importance of these dual identities and the fluidity of the boundary between them. For at least two doctors in the Egyptian Army, political work appealed so greatly that they left the medical corps to work as political officials. For doctors who remained in medical service, the 'medical' and the 'administrative' at times virtually dissolved into one another: as Chapter 5 demonstrates, colonial administration in parts of southern Sudan *was* sleeping sickness control, carried out by military doctors. Most marked in the case of sleeping sickness, the assumption of multiple roles by doctors—magistrate, administrator, engineer, gardener, town planner, medic—was a function of the complexity of the diseases confronted and of the thinness of the colonial administration on the ground. To even consider controlling disease, colonial doctors had to be renaissance men.

The existence of this mutual self-interest and this periodic identity of medicine and administration did not, however, mean that medical and political interests were always identical, that medical services were regarded by other government officials as unequivocally worthy, or that medical personnel were always allowed to assume political roles. Chapter 5 also shows the dialectical nature of the medical–political relationship: the fact that disease control allowed, even required, doctors to assume an administrative role did not eliminate their calls for administrative support, nor did it guarantee them delivery of that support. The medical–administrative boundary had not completely dissolved for them. If the

[8] Michael Worboys, 'The Emergence of Tropical Medicine: A Study in the Establishment of a Scientific Specialty', in Gerard Lemaine, Roy MacLeod, Michael Mulkay, and Peter Weingart (eds.), *Perspectives on the Emergence of Scientific Disciplines* (Chicago: Aldine, 1976), 75–98; Michael Worboys, 'Manson, Ross and Colonial Medical Policy: Tropical Medicine in London and Liverpool, 1899–1914', in Roy Macleod and Milton Lewis (eds.), *Disease, Medicine and Empire* (London: Routledge, 1988), 21–37.

boundary between medicine and politics was fluid at some times and in some places, it was also rigidly drawn at others, most markedly in the context of government debate over the charged issue of female circumcision, discussed in Chapter 7. Circumcision was defined as a political matter, which could therefore not be handled by medical personnel.

That political and economic considerations influenced medical policy is clear, but the disease control campaigns discussed in this book show that political and economic determinism cannot be carried too far. My comments here are directed at the 'political economy of health' literature, which encompasses several different approaches. Most such analyses argue that capitalist development had health costs, which fell disproportionately on the working class. With this, I have little argument: in Chapter 4, I highlight some of the health costs of irrigated agriculture. However, some of these analyses, in addition to too readily equating colonialism with capitalism, too readily equate medicine with capitalist interests, and do not take medicine seriously enough as its own enterprise.[9] In their radical critique of modern medicine and capitalism, Leslie Doyal and Imogen Pennell argued from the British and East African cases that the capitalist mode of production creates illness, differentially distributed amongst the population, and that capitalist interests have played, and continue to play, a crucial role in the development of modern medicine, with a resulting bias towards cure rather than prevention.[10] In her work on Tanzania, Meredeth Turshen has also emphasized the way in which the political economy under colonial rule generated ill health. But her analysis has little to say about colonial medical intervention, which she views as both misdirected, since it concentrates on cure rather than prevention, and impotent, given the massive epidemiological changes being caused by other aspects of colonial administration.[11] To say that colonial doctors concentrated on cure is simply wrong: the ambitious disease campaigns described in this book, which were the backbone of colonial

---

[9] The notable exception is Randall M. Packard, *White Plague, Black Labor: Tuberculosis and the Political Economy of Health and Disease in South Africa* (Berkeley: University of California Press, 1989), who offers a nuanced view of the relationship between medicine, health, and capitalism. Packard shows how the specific historical context of developing industrial capitalism in South Africa influenced changes in the epidemiology of tuberculosis, medical explanations of the disease's distribution, and efforts to control the disease.

[10] Leslie Doyal with Imogen Pennell, *The Political Economy of Health* (London: Pluto, 1979).

[11] Meredeth Turshen, 'The Impact of Colonialism on Health and Health Services in Tanzania', *International Journal of Health Services*, 7 (1977), 7–35; Meredeth Turshen, *The Political Ecology of Disease in Tanzania* (New Brunswick, NJ: Rutgers University Press, 1984).

medicine in Sudan, were primarily efforts in disease prevention. The distinction between medicine and health, which I discuss later in this chapter, is an important one. But to dismiss doctors reductively as the handmaidens of colonialism or capitalism ignores the more complex, and more interesting, reality. To take one example: the use of sanitary cordons to contain disease in Sudan put into sharp focus the tension between the public health need for impermeable boundaries and the socio-economic need for porous ones. Medical and political officials did not always divide neatly in these debates: if doctors sometimes argued for changes in policy on the basis of labour needs, it is also true that political officials sometimes made arguments solely in the interests of public health. Moreover, the decisions to lift quarantines or to blame disease on foreigners were never made solely on the basis of economic and political considerations, such as the need to keep labour moving in the first instance or the political need to keep foreign influence at bay in the second. Medical knowledge, epidemiological evidence, and local disease history also shaped these decisions, and although admittedly socially influenced and often racist in interpretation, such knowledge, evidence, and history were never simply designed to serve capitalist interests. Particularly in Chapters 4 through 6, I argue that medical factors—I am here drawing my own boundary around 'medicine' which doctors in Sudan may or may not have recognized—joined political and economic factors in influencing the choice of disease control measures in Sudan.

## COLONIALISM IN SUDAN

Exploring these themes requires an understanding of the distinctive form of colonialism created in Sudan. From 1899 until 1956, Sudan was governed by an Anglo-Egyptian Condominium. In theory, Britain and Egypt ruled jointly over Sudan; in practice, while Egypt's involvement remained an important political consideration, British officials made policy and determined the character of the administration. Although under the jurisdiction of the Foreign Office, Sudan was very much a part of the British empire. A British governor-general, who also acted as sirdar (commander-in-chief) of the Egyptian Army, was the highest military and civil authority in Sudan and was appointed by Khedivial decree on the recommendation of the British government; the governor-general communicated with the Foreign Office through the British agent and consul-general, later the high commissioner, in Egypt. The extent to which Cairo involved itself in Sudan's affairs depended on the individuals involved.[12] For our purposes, it is sufficient to say that the ambiguous legal status of a Condominium and placement under the Foreign Office at times provided Sudan government officials with more administrative independence than their explicitly colonial or protectorate counterparts. Condominium status made Egyptians and Syrians an integral, if junior part of the Sudan government. It also meant that the Sudan government was staffed by its own, self-consciously elite medical and political services, recruited independently of other colonial services, which in the political realm developed an inward-looking, uncritical mentality and a suspicion of intervention by London and Cairo.[13]

There were other important ways in which Sudan was distinct from Britain's other African colonies. Broadly speaking, it was divided between an Arab, Islamic, arid northern region that seemed part of North Africa, even the Middle East, and a Nilotic, 'animist' south, whose swamps, tropical vegetation, and inhabitants seemed recognizably Central African: in other words, it contained internally significant regional frontiers. Aside from colonial officials and missionaries, there were no white settlers in Sudan, making for a racialized society quite different from those in Kenya and southern Africa. Although the colonial state resettled some Sudanese and restricted Sudanese movement, massive land alienation was not part of the colonial experience in Sudan; land shortages and accompanying rural proletarianization came only after independence in 1956, with the expansion of large-scale, rain-fed mechanized farming first started in the 1940s.[14] Sudan was also poor in mineral wealth: industrialization and urbanization of the kind prompted by mining development in South Africa and the Rhodesias were unknown, although the urbanization and 'detribalization' of Africans were concerns of the government in Sudan as elsewhere in colonial Africa.

Sudan government revenues depended heavily on annual subventions and other capital investments from the Egyptian government.[15] Agricultural production, mainly of grains such as *dura* (millet), increased until the First World War, but there were significant periods of shortage, most

[12] M. W. Daly, *Empire on the Nile: The Anglo-Egyptian Sudan, 1898–1934* (Cambridge: Cambridge University Press, 1986), 11–18, 42–54.

[13] M. W. Daly, *Imperial Sudan: The Anglo-Egyptian Condominium, 1934–1956* (Cambridge: Cambridge University Press, 1991), 14.

[14] Abdalla Mohammed Elhassan, 'The Encroachment of Large Scale Mechanized Agriculture: Elements of Differentiation among the Peasantry', in Tony Barnett and Abbas Abdelkarim (eds.), *Sudan: State, Capital and Transformation* (London: Croom Helm, 1988), 161–79.

[15] Daly, *Imperial Sudan*, 3.

notably the famine of 1913–14. Sesame, cotton, live animals, animal products, and particularly gum arabic became Sudan's chief exports. The
opening of the Gezira irrigation scheme in 1925 refocused the country's
economy almost entirely on cotton and on indirect revenues from the
export of cotton, such as customs duties and railway freight. Although
necessary to development, outside private capital was regarded warily by
the Sudan government, which was concerned to avoid intervention that
could upset relations with the Sudanese and interfere in government
policy-making.[16] The Gezira scheme was the most significant site of outside investment: it was built and run by the government and a private
British company, the Sudan Plantations Syndicate, with the Sudanese
tenants cultivating the land in the scheme as (nominal) third 'partners'.
(The operation and financing of the Gezira scheme are discussed in more
detail in Chapters 3 and 4.)

For the first two decades of the Condominium, the Sudan government
avoided using taxation and other conventional methods of creating a wage
labour force, fearing revolt: high taxes were known to be unpopular and
were thought to have brought the downfall of the Turco-Egyptian regime
(1821–85) in Sudan.[17] Jay O'Brien argues that in the inter-war period, the
'colonial regime mobilised all its powers to meet the large demand for
wage labour in the Gezira Scheme', but these powers do not seem overwhelming. The main measures involved in stimulating a flow from labour
supply areas were propaganda, a higher level of taxation, collected more
rigorously at an appropriate point in the Gezira labour cycle, and the
aggressive marketing of consumption goods.[18] According to Martin Daly,
Egyptian subventions allowed the Sudan government to pursue a policy of
comparatively low taxation throughout the inter-war period.[19] Overall,
this was a much less extractive, exploitative colonial regime than those
elsewhere in colonial Africa, for example in the Belgian Congo and
Northern Rhodesia. Collectively, these circumstances influenced which
health problems were prevalent and which medical interventions were
undertaken.

[16] Daly, *Empire*, 215–30, 420–33.
[17] Jay O'Brien, 'The Formation and Transformation of the Agricultural Labour Force in
Sudan', in Norman O'Neill and Jay O'Brien (eds.), *Economy and Class in Sudan* (Aldershot:
Avebury, 1988), 138; Daly, *Empire*, 197.
[18] O'Brien, 'Formation and Transformation', 140; see also John James O'Brien III, 'Agricultural Labor and Development in Sudan', Ph.D. thesis (University of Connecticut,
1980), 163–7, 170–1.
[19] Daly, *Imperial Sudan*, 3.

The vast majority of these medical interventions were made by the colonial state. In other parts of British Africa, missions were often the leaders in medical development, and the state came to rely on them for the provision of medical services to the indigenous population, particularly in rural areas; it was usually missionaries who, in the inter-war period, treated lepers, campaigned against the spread of sexually transmitted diseases, and took charge of maternal and child welfare.[20] Missions never constituted this kind of medical force in Sudan. Concerned not to provoke a Muslim backlash, the government from the start of the Condominium confined missionary activity to non-Muslim southern Sudan, assigning spheres to the different missionary organizations.[21] Most missions provided first aid such as dressing of wounds and ulcers, but there were only a handful of specifically medical missions: proselytization and education remained the focus for missionaries, who often had a great deal of difficulty in establishing their stations. According to H. C. Squires, at the peak of medical mission work around 1935, there were eight missionary doctors and eight missionary nurses in the country.[22] As Table 1.1 indicates, the most successful southern medical mission was the Church Missionary Society (CMS) station at Lui, Mongalla (later Equatoria), opened in 1921. Much admired by government officials for their work at Lui,[23] Dr Kenneth and Mrs Eileen Fraser built a hospital which provided general medical services, treated lepers, and trained local men to staff their own regional dispensary network.[24] The one exception to the ban on missions in Muslim areas was the CMS Gordon Memorial Mission at Omdurman, founded at conquest; after an uncertain start, the medical side of the mission moved to permanent hospital premises in 1914. Starting in the 1920s, the CMS administered the Omdurman leper hostel on behalf of the Sudan medical service (SMS) and during the 1930s, it opened several satellite dispensaries and child welfare clinics. Medical missions delivered important medical services to limited areas of (mainly southern) Sudan.[25]

---

[20] Megan Vaughan, *Curing their Ills: Colonial Power and African Illness* (Oxford: Polity Press, 1991), chs. 3, 4, and 6.

[21] On government policy towards missions, see Daly, *Empire*, 250–9; Lilian Passmore Sanderson and Neville Sanderson, *Education, Religion & Politics in Southern Sudan, 1899–1964* (London: Ithaca Press, 1981).

[22] H. C. Squires, *The Sudan Medical Service: An Experiment in Social Medicine* (London: William Heinemann, 1958), 119.

[23] See e.g. *RFACS 1926*, 76.

[24] Eileen Fraser, *The Doctor Comes to Lui* (London: Church Missionary Society, 1938).

[25] Information on medical missions from Ahmed Bayoumi, *A History of Sudan Health Services* (Nairobi: Kenya Literature Bureau, 1979), 111–18; Squires, *Sudan Medical Service*, 119–22.

TABLE 1.1. *Medical mission attendances in 1939*

| Mission Station | Inpatients | Outpatients | Operations |
|---|---|---|---|
| Church Missionary Society | | | |
| Omdurman (Khartoum) | 1,283 | 79,608 | 239 |
| Lui (Equatoria) | 671 | 168,957 | 196 |
| Zeraf Island (Upper Nile) | 617 | 6,854 | 238 |
| Sallara (Nuba Mountains) | 199 | 10,229 | — |
| Sudan United Mission | | | |
| Abri (Nuba Mountains) | 86 | 2,932 | — |
| Tabanya (Nuba Mountains) | — | 1,515 | — |
| Rom (Upper Nile) | 27 | 3,680 | — |
| American Presbyterian Mission | | | |
| Nasir (Upper Nile) | — | 10,233 | 56 |
| Doleib Hill (Upper Nile) | — | 13,548 | — |

*Source*: *RSMS 1939*, 78.

But comparison of Table 1.1 and Table 2.1 demonstrates that missions provided a small fraction of overall medical services in Sudan. It is for this reason that they barely feature in this book.

There were other ways in which Sudan's development was more typical of British colonies in Africa. Before the First World War, the administration remained essentially military in terms both of personnel and of orientation. Sudan was run by the men of the Egyptian Army: British officers seconded from the British Army and Egyptians and Syrians hired directly to the junior ranks. The slaughter of the Mahdists at Karari in September 1898 reconquered Sudan in the name of Britain and Egypt, but it was only the first step in a long process of bringing British authority and effective British administration to a vast country. Before 1914, the regime's main priority was pacification. Serious economic development, mainly in the form of the Gezira scheme, started only in the inter-war period. While civilians had been recruited to the civil service in Sudan since 1901, the military ethos and a preference for soldiers over civilians prevailed under Governor-General F. R. Wingate (1899–1916); the dominance of civilian officials was only established by the departure of soldiers for military duty elsewhere during the First World War and the intake, post-war, of large numbers of civilian recruits.[26] Each province had a governor, with several inspectors, later called district commissioners, stationed in the field in charge of local affairs. Egyptian *mamurs* (district officials) filled the junior ranks in the provinces until they were expelled in

[26] Daly, *Empire*, 82–91, 271–2.

1924; starting in 1912, they were joined by the first Sudanese sub-*mamurs*.[27] It was only during the inter-war period that the Sudan government developed an effective, centralized, bureaucratic structure, built around the dominant department of the civil secretary. Other senior administrators included the financial secretary, the legal secretary, the Sudan agent who represented the government in Cairo, and the director of intelligence. A governor-general's council, composed largely of these office-holders, was established in 1910 and was used primarily as an advisory committee by Wingate; it only became a significant power, 'in effect, a cabinet', under his successors. Personality played an important role in the formulation of policy throughout the Condominium.[28]

Before and during the First World War, the Sudan government pursued a dual policy of ruling through traditional leaders where possible and educating some Sudanese for employment in the government. Like other British colonies in Africa, it embraced indirect rule during the inter-war period, reflecting official fear of educated elites and the desire for inexpensive administration. Such fear was brought to its peak in 1924, a year of political unrest which can be read as a nationalist uprising: protests led by the pro-Egyptian White Flag League and unrest in Sudanese battalions of the army in the summer and autumn seriously unsettled the government, which was thrown into crisis in November by the assassination of Governor-General Lee Stack (1919–24, acting from 1917) by Egyptian nationalists in Cairo. Though not without a revolt by Sudanese soldiers, Stack's death resulted in the expulsion of all Egyptian soldiers and officials from Sudan.[29] The events of 1924 had a lasting influence on education policy, discussed in Chapter 2, and were used to justify the adoption of indirect rule. A series of inter-war laws—the Powers of Nomad Sheikhs Ordinance 1922, the Powers of Sheikhs Ordinance 1927, the Native Courts Ordinance 1932—served to invest judicial and administrative power in the nomad and sedentary sheikhs of northern Sudan.[30] In southern Sudan, the government attempted to reinforce, often re-create, traditional authority throughout the 1920s. Through Southern Policy, formally adopted in 1929–30 and in effect the southern version of indirect rule, the government sought to promote the creation of independent tribal units whose structure and organization were based on indigenous custom. Im-

[27] On early provincial administration, see ibid. 71–82.

[28] Ibid. 54–67, 70–1, 272–8, quote 271.

[29] Tim Niblock, *Class and Power in Sudan: The Dynamics of Sudanese Politics, 1898–1985* (London: Macmillan, 1987), 163–9; Daly, *Empire*, 287–98, 306–12.

[30] On native administration in northern Sudan, see Daly, *Empire*, 360–79.

plementation of this policy involved the removal of foreign influence—defined mainly as Muslim and Arab—through the expulsion of northern Sudanese traders and officials, prohibitions on southern Sudanese using northern Sudanese names and styles of dress, promotion of vernacular languages, even an attempt to create, through forced relocation, a no man's land between Muslim Darfur and the western district of the Bahr-el-Ghazal.[31] While there was some return to a dual policy in the mid- to late 1930s, considerable damage had been done to relations with educated Sudanese and to the development of the southern part of the country.

## HEALTH AND MOBILITY

This was the administrative context in which medicine operated in Sudan. There was also a health context. A bifurcation persists in the historical literature between the history of medicine, and the history of health and disease.[32] 'What role did medical institutions and personnel play within empire?' and 'What impact did the colonial enterprise have on the health of indigenous populations?', though not unrelated, are two different questions, that tend to send the researcher to two different sets of sources. Western medicine, residing with doctors, dispensaries, and disease control, can be tracked through medical reports. Health in the colonial world, as in Europe, particularly before the advent of antibiotics and sulphonamides, often had less to do with medicine than with standards of living, nutrition, sanitation, and in colonial Africa where insects transmitted tropical diseases, patterns of land and water use. African healing systems were also crucial to the preservation and restoration of 'health' in the colonial period; therapeutic pluralism was and continues to be a feature central to African management of illness.[33]

Although medicine rather than health is my primary focus, an analysis of colonial medicine is incomplete without some sense of the broader

[31] Douglas H. Johnson, 'Criminal Secrecy: The Case of the Zande "Secret Societies"', *Past & Present*, 130 (1991), 180; Daly, *Empire*, 410, 413–19; R. O. Collins, *Shadows in the Grass: Britain in the Southern Sudan, 1918–1956* (New Haven: Yale University Press, 1983), 172–8, 181–96.
[32] For a fuller discussion of this point, see Megan Vaughan, 'Healing and Curing: Issues in the Social History and Anthropology of Medicine in Africa', *Social History of Medicine*, 7 (1994), 287–90.
[33] Steven Feierman, 'Change in African Therapeutic Systems', *Social Science and Medicine*, 13B (1979), 277–84.

disease environment within which it was operating. The health branch of the literature has amply demonstrated that colonialism changed disease patterns, which often had severe consequences for indigenous populations. The most famous example of such epidemiological change is still the introduction of new diseases into the 'virgin soil' of the Americas by conquering armies,[34] an analysis which has been shown to be less applicable to Africa, because of the continent's long history of contact with the outside world.[35] Marc Dawson's careful studies of colonial Kenya have shown how new infrastructure, such as railways and roads, mass labour migrancy, the concentration of people in new urban centres, the development of land for cash crops, and the expansion of trade combined to alter disease patterns.[36] Maryinez Lyons has argued that in the Belgian Congo, colonial conquest, economic exploitation, and punitive taxation forced Africans into greater contact with the tsetse fly that carries trypanosomiasis;[37] Chapter 5 discusses other explanations for the turn of the century sleeping sickness epidemics more fully. Randall Packard has shown how the specific economic, political, and social conditions created by industrialization, urbanization, and labour migrancy in late nineteenth- and twentieth-century South Africa changed the epidemiology of tuberculosis.[38] Using a range of diseases and demographic measures, Rita Headrick has investigated what she terms 'the demographic crisis which occurred in French Equatorial Africa with the imposition and consolidation of colonial rule'.[39] In colonial Malaya, adult, infant, and maternal mortality rates, and infectious diseases generally declined between the late nineteenth century and the Second World War. Lenore

[34] A. W. Crosby, *The Columbian Exchange: Biological and Cultural Consequences of 1492* (Westport, Conn.: Greenwood Press, 1972), 35–63; A. W. Crosby, 'Hawaiian Depopulation as a Model for the Amerindian Experience', in Terence Ranger and Paul Slack (eds.), *Epidemics and Ideas: Essays on the Historical Perception of Pestilence* (Cambridge: Cambridge University Press, 1992), 175–201.

[35] See John Iliffe, *Africans: The History of a Continent* (Cambridge: Cambridge University Press, 1995).

[36] Marc H. Dawson, 'Socioeconomic Change and Disease: Smallpox in Colonial Kenya, 1880–1920', in Steven Feierman and John M. Janzen (eds.), *The Social Basis of Health and Healing in Africa* (Berkeley: University of California Press, 1992), 90–103; Marc H. Dawson, 'Socio-economic and Epidemiological Change in Kenya: 1880–1925', Ph.D. thesis (University of Wisconsin-Madison, 1983).

[37] Maryinez Lyons, *The Colonial Disease: A Social History of Sleeping Sickness in Northern Zaire, 1900–1940* (Cambridge: Cambridge University Press, 1992).

[38] Packard, *White Plague*.

[39] Rita Headrick, *Colonialism, Health, and Illness in French Equatorial Africa, 1885–1935*, ed. Daniel R. Headrick (Atlanta: African Studies Association Press, 1994), 2.

Manderson argues, however, that this decline masked important regional, class, race, and gender differences: her discussion of poor health and living conditions among those living in cities and on plantation estates amply illustrates the health costs of colonial rule.[40] Donald Denoon has described colonialism as 'literally a health hazard'.[41]

It is not my intention to reconstruct overall demographic and health trends in Sudan, a mammoth task greatly complicated by the poverty of the available data. The first census of Sudan was conducted only in 1956 and earlier population figures are clearly speculative and unreliable. But in their focus on disease control campaigns, the middle chapters of this book discuss the possible origins, and the changing morbidity and mortality impact, of endemic and epidemic schistosomiasis, malaria, sleeping sickness, and yellow fever, and in so doing, reinforce the arguments in the above literature about epidemiological change. The Gezira irrigation scheme, with its hundreds of miles of stagnant water, lack of alternative water supplies, poor housing, and dependence on thousands of labour migrants in poor health, created the ideal conditions for the amplification of schistosomiasis and malaria, as well as other epidemic diseases such as relapsing fever and cerebrospinal meningitis. Colonial doctors knew that colonial rule was changing epidemiology: it was largely for this reason that they poured so many resources into disease prevention and control in the Gezira, and spent more than five years in remote parts of Sudan trying unsuccessfully to locate cases of sleeping sickness and yellow fever, diseases clinically unknown in the country until they erupted in epidemic form.

Colonial doctors recognized that one of the main ways in which colonial rule changed epidemiology was by influencing patterns of population movement. Colonial rule intensified some existing patterns of movement and also created new ones. One of the first significant population movements after conquest was the return to the provinces of the tens of thousands who had gathered in Omdurman and the Gezira under the Khalifa; a government eager to disperse Mahdists, restore pre-Mahdiya tribal geography, and boost agricultural production encouraged such movements through loans and grants of grain.[42] Throughout the colonial period, population movement within Sudan was

[40] Lenore Manderson, *Sickness and the State: Health and Illness in Colonial Malaya, 1870–1940* (Cambridge: Cambridge University Press, 1997).
[41] Donald Denoon, *Public Health in Papua New Guinea: Medical Possibility and Social Constraint, 1884–1984* (Cambridge: Cambridge University Press, 1989), 52.
[42] Gabriel Warburg, *The Sudan Under Wingate* (London: Frank Cass, 1971), 142.

generally from west to east, and from the north to the centre of the country. Poor communications and poor education meant that the three southern provinces contributed comparatively little to inter-provincial migration.[43] Government centres, especially Khartoum, Atbara, and Port Sudan, and to a lesser extent all provincial capitals and garrisons, served as magnets for migrants. Railroads built by the Anglo-Egyptian regime before the First World War, from Wadi Halfa to Khartoum, the Gezira, and Sennar, and then out to El Obeid, and from the Nile to the Red Sea, increased internal communications; crucial extensions made in the 1920s completed the Gezira's link to Port Sudan and reached the Gash delta.[44] The start of cotton-growing in the Gezira and the Gash delta in Kassala in the inter-war period attracted migrants from around northern Sudan. Nomads moved seasonally from Darfur and Kordofan down into the Bahr-el-Ghazal, and across to Upper Nile province, in search of water for their cattle; similar seasonal migration of pastoralists occurred within the southern provinces.

Most immigrants to Sudan during the colonial period were Westerners, a non-racial category that refers to all those coming from parts west of Sudan such as Nigeria and French Equatorial Africa, as well as from Darfur. Because of their significance as labourers and disease carriers, discussed in Chapter 4, this section briefly discusses the origins of their migration. The link between Westerners and Sudan was the pilgrimage to Mecca: the route from West Africa via Chad to Darfur, running through central Sudan to the Red Sea, along the savannas between the Sahara to the north and the tsetse fly belt to the south, dated to at least the seventeenth century.[45] The pilgrimage took years to complete—even in the 1970s, with access to lorries and trains, the average journey time was eight years[46]—which meant that pilgrims often settled temporarily in Sudan. But as Mark Duffield has argued, the pilgrimage alone cannot adequately account for the scale—it is estimated that Nigerian settlers and their descendants account for 10 per cent of Sudan's present population—and

---

[43] K. M. Barbour, 'Population Shifts and Changes in Sudan Since 1898', *Middle Eastern Studies*, 2 (1966), 114–17.

[44] Daly, *Empire*, 202–6, 432.

[45] Barbour, 118–19; J. S. Birks, 'Migration, a Significant Factor in the Historical Demography of the Savannas: The Growth of the West African Population of Darfur, Sudan', in *African Historical Demography* (Edinburgh, 1977), 197. On the ongoing centrality of the pilgrimage to West Africans in Sudan, many of whom are third to fifth generation residents of Sudan, see C. Bawa Yamba, *Permanent Pilgrims: The Role of Pilgrimage in the Lives of West African Muslims in Sudan* (Edinburgh: Edinburgh University Press, 1995).

[46] J. S. Birks, 'The Mecca Pilgrimage by West African Pastoral Nomads', *Journal of Modern African Studies*, 15 (1977), 47.

the timing of Westerner migration to Sudan. Duffield has demonstrated that the different Nigerian groups who migrated to Sudan did so in response to social, economic, and political changes arising from colonial administration in Nigeria. The British defeat of the Fulani emirates in 1900–3 combined with drought and famine to prompt thousands of Fulani to undertake the *hijra* (religiously ordained flight) from Nigeria; heading east towards Mecca, many settled in their own quarters of Sudanese towns such as Gedaref and El Obeid, and in new settlements along the Blue Nile between Sennar and Singa. From 1914 onwards, they were joined by Fulani fleeing political turbulence in the Hedjaz. Other Westerners went to Sudan to avoid military service or forced labour in French Equatorial Africa.[47] By the start of the 1920s, the number of Hausa settling in Sudan outnumbered the Fulani. These migrants were peasants from the poorest section of Hausa society who, lacking craft skills and capital, and facing land and food shortages, and exploitation as free labour by the Fulani aristocracy under native administration, undertook the *hajj* (pilgrimage) eastwards, settling in Sudan, in order to escape their poverty and assert their independence.[48]

The government harboured a certain ambivalence about Westerners: many had joined Mahdist armies and the Khalifa's following in Omdurman during the Mahdiya, and Fulani Mahdists were involved in various militant Mahdist uprisings in Sudan during the 1910s. But it encouraged Nigerians to settle in Sudan through tax concessions, grants of land, building materials, and even money, in order to increase its labour pool and replenish a peasantry that was seriously depleted in some areas. As it attempted to build towns and the infrastructure of a state in the early years of the Condominium, the colonial government was confronted by a labour shortage: essentially self-sufficient, most Sudanese had no interest in engaging in wage labour and to preserve political stability, the government avoided using taxation and other common methods to force them to do so. Westerners, along with freed Sudanese slaves, socialized by their vulnerability into a dependence on wage labour, formed the core of Sudan's unskilled labour force from the early 1900s onward.[49] During the

[47] Mark Duffield, *Maiurno: Capitalism & Rural Life in Sudan* (London: Ithaca Press, 1981), 26–9; Birks, 'Migration', 199; D. B. Mather, 'Migration in the Sudan', in R. W. Steel and C. A. Fisher (eds.), *Geographical Essays on British Tropical Lands* (London: George Philip, 1956), 121, 126–7.
[48] Mark R. Duffield, 'Hausa and Fulani Settlement and the Development of Capitalism in Sudan: With Special Reference to Maiurno, Blue Nile Province', Ph.D. thesis (Centre of West African Studies, University of Birmingham, 1978), 88–106.
[49] Mark Duffield, 'Change among West African Settlers in Northern Sudan', *Review*

inter-war period, as discussed in Chapter 4, Westerner labourers became an integral part of cotton-growing schemes in the Gezira. Large numbers of Egyptians were brought to Sudan during the colonial period, to work as skilled and experienced labourers on construction projects such as the building of Port Sudan and the Sennar Dam. But for political reasons, they were usually obliged to return to Egypt after the expiration of their contracts and in the long term, Westerners have been a much more important category of immigrants.

The movement of people spreads disease, changing the accepted boundaries of infection. Labourers headed to the Gezira carried schistosomiasis with them; Westerners brought epidemic smallpox and relapsing fever as they moved eastwards into Sudan; returning pilgrims arriving at Suakin and travelling westward brought whichever disease was prevalent at Mecca. Troop movements, and renewed and increased trade, local and long distance, also provided new avenues for disease transmission. Freed women slaves and divorced and abandoned women turned to prostitution in brothels and *merissa* (beer) shops during the colonial period, meeting the sexual and social needs of Sudanese, Egyptian, and European men, including government officials and soldiers.[50] The result was the spread of syphilis and gonorrhoea, feared by the Sudan government partly for their negative impact on the Sudanese birthrate but mainly for their effect on the health and efficiency of Egyptian Army troops and Sudanese government employees: venereal disease was a major cause of admissions to military hospitals and of work days lost due to illness.[51]

Colonial medicine in Sudan developed against, and in constant interaction with, this changing political and epidemiological background. This development—the expanding boundaries of colonial medicine between 1899 and 1940, and the identity and training of those chosen to be colonial medical practitioners—is the subject of Chapter 2.

---

*of African Political Economy*, 26 (1983), 48–50; Duffield, *Maiurno*, 29, 31, 41; O'Brien, 'Agricultural Labor', 132–4; Daly, *Empire*, 237–8.

[50] Jay Spaulding and Stephanie Beswick, 'Sex, Bondage, and the Market: The Emergence of Prostitution in Northern Sudan, 1750–1950', *Journal of the History of Sexuality*, 5 (1995), 528–31.

[51] *RFACS 1902*, 126–30; *RFACS 1906*, 387.

# 2

# *Medical Policy and Medical Practitioners*

This chapter provides an overview of the medical administration in the Anglo-Egyptian Sudan between 1899 and 1940, arguing that the distinctive form of colonialism developed in Sudan, and outlined in Chapter 1, shaped the medical services provided. The chapter begins by charting the shifting goals of the medical department/service, showing how they paralleled the changing ambitions of the colonial state, and goes on to highlight the colonial financial and human resource limitations that constrained medical activity. The second half of the chapter discusses the different categories of personnel who practised Western medicine on behalf of the colonial state. Analysis of biographical information about British military and civilian doctors and their terms of service suggests that both groups were middle class, well educated, and enjoyed financial and social standing comparable to their political counterparts. A discussion of Syrian and Sudanese medical personnel demonstrates clearly the way in which political and economic policies influenced who delivered which medical services in different parts of the country at particular points in time. It also shows that British doctors' perception of racial difference, and their class, gender, and occupation hierarchies structured the training of Sudanese medical personnel and the medical service, counterbalancing the fluidity of the boundary drawn around the profession of medicine in Sudan.

## MEDICAL ADMINISTRATION

The development of the Sudan medical department, renamed the Sudan medical service in 1924, mirrored the development of political administration and broadly reflected the government's political priorities. Military staffing and military leadership of civil medicine in Sudan remained a fact of life until the First World War, and military control over civilian medical care persisted into the 1920s in some provinces. As in the political realm, senior doctors were British men, seconded from the Royal Army Medical Corps to the Egyptian Army Medical Corps (EAMC), while junior doctors were mainly Syrian, but also Egyptian, men hired directly to the EAMC. The governmental intention from the start of the Condominium was to establish an entirely independent civil medical department, but personalities, finances, and the fact that 'pacification' was not achieved in some parts of the country until the 1920s meant that military influence persisted longer than expected. This is the history, then, of the slow, uneven expansion of civilian responsibility for civil medical services.

While the first civilian doctors arrived in Sudan in 1901 and a medical department report appeared as early as 1902, civil medicine secured its first real foothold on 15 March 1904, with the appointment of three doctors to exclusively civil government posts. This fairly tentative beginning in fact created lasting personal and interdepartmental antipathies, which had a significant influence on institutional development in a small place like Khartoum. Dr J. B. Christopherson and Dr E. S. Crispin had both been approached to be the first director of the medical department, with the result that neither could be appointed. But Christopherson was given a senior posting in Khartoum, making him director in all but name, which prompted Crispin to resign in protest, though he was eventually persuaded to stay on. The third doctor, Dr Andrew Balfour, already director of the Wellcome Research Laboratories, was appointed medical officer of health (MOH) for Khartoum and insisted that his post be under the sole jurisdiction of the Khartoum province administration, with no connection to the nascent medical department.[1] The start to civil medicine was not particularly 'civil' in at least one other respect: the first officially named director of the Sudan medical department, appointed 1 March 1905, was in fact a military doctor, G. D. Hunter, principal medical officer of the Egyptian Army (PMO).[2] The civil and the military medical departments were split as of 1 November 1905, giving medical responsibility for Khartoum, Khartoum North, Omdurman, Halfa, Dongola, Berber, White Nile province, Port Sudan, Suakin, and the railways administration to the acting head of the medical department, Christopherson. Where the organization of the department was considered 'incomplete', in reality non-existent, namely in the rest of Sudan, medical administration was to remain in the charge of the PMO. At the same time, a Central Sanitary Board of senior medical and political officials was established to address sanitation, quarantine, and other issues of medical policy as they affected the entire country. While this established separate civil and military medical staff, offices, drugs, stores, equipment,

[1] *RFACS 1902*, 117–22; Squires, *Sudan Medical Service*, 4–7; *SGG*, no. 60, 1 Mar. 1904, 181.
[2] *SGG*, no. 76, 1 May 1905, 326.

and hospitals for the first time,[3] the PMO in fact acted as director-general
of the Sudan medical department until 1916, save for one brief, divisive
experiment in civilian leadership under Christopherson in 1907–8.[4] Conflict among doctors can only have undermined their credibility within the
government, but there does not seem to have been a resulting scepticism
in the value of medicine to the governmental project. Such conflict may
have impeded the development of an independent civil medical department with exclusively civilian personnel, but there were other reasons for
maintaining military control of medicine: it suited the military character
of the wider adminstration and EAMC salaries were paid by the Egyptian
government, while the Sudan government paid for civilians.

   Overall, whether civilian or military doctors were providing medical
services seems to have made little difference to what actually got done
before the First World War. Both military and civilian doctors concentrated on preserving the health of British officials and of military men of
all nationalities: they were engaged in the project of safeguarding the
colonizing elite and the indigenous manpower employed to build and
defend a new colonial regime. As Ellen Gruenbaum has observed, it was
no accident that the first civilian doctors were concentrated in Khartoum,
the capital, Atbara, the headquarters of the Sudan Railways, and Port
Sudan, where a new town and port were being constructed.[5] Early medical
initiatives, executed in government stations by military and civilian
doctors, focused on urban sanitation (clean water supply, waste disposal,
food hygiene), anti-malarial mosquito control, and the inspection of prostitutes for venereal disease. Designed to protect those who ruled Sudan by
creating 'safe' environments and part of the larger colonial project of
civilizing, refreshing, and ordering Sudan after Mahdist rule,[6] these meas-

---

[3] *RFACS 1905*, 102, 117, 129. The Central Sanitary Board usually consisted of the
director of the medical department/service, the PMO of the Egyptian Army, the director of
the WTRL, the MOH for Khartoum, the civil secretary, the legal secretary, and from 1927
to 1934, the secretary for education and health (SEH).

[4] Christopherson was not popular among his colleagues. Governor-General Wingate
observed that although he showed great skill as a doctor and surgeon, there 'can be no doubt
that he has altogether failed to obtain the friendship or the confidence of any of his Profession, including even those actually in his own Department' (F. R. Wingate to T. D. Acland,
29 Nov. 1908, SAD 284/3/68–70). See also P. R. Phipps to Wingate, 17 Mar. 1908, SAD
282/3/80–2.

[5] Ellen Ruth Gruenbaum, 'Health Services, Health, and Development in Sudan: The
Impact of the Gezira Irrigated Scheme', Ph.D. thesis (University of Connecticut, 1982), 96,
193.

[6] Heather Bell, 'Cleaning Up the Anglo-Egyptian Sudan: Water, Mosquitoes, and
Venereal Disease, 1899–1914', paper presented to the Sudan Studies Association Conference, Boston, Mass., Apr. 1994; Daly, *Empire*, 18–28.

ures automatically implicated Sudanese civilians, and they did not go uncontested. In Kassala in 1909–10, malaria control meant examining children for enlarged spleens, inspecting wells, and if necessary, treating them with potassium permanganate; the cooperation of local sheikhs and headmen was secured by inviting them to a reception where Dr Asad Malouf gave a talk on malaria transmission and eradication. By contrast, attempts to ensure a clean meat supply by requiring all butchers to pass a medical examination incited great opposition—butchers resented being classed with prostitutes, the only other social group required to submit to 'such indignity'—and culminated in one butcher attacking members of the crowd assembled for the opening of the new slaughterhouse with his sword.[7]

Simple, comparatively inexpensive, and proven, smallpox vaccination was the first public health measure directed on a large scale at Sudanese. Poor technique, and deterioration in lymph quality due to heat and age meant that vaccination was often ineffective, but doctors and officials in various northern Sudanese towns commented repeatedly in the early 1900s that Sudanese understood the value of vaccination, and cooperated in presenting their children for the procedure.[8] The other significant pre-1914 medical initiative was the building of civil hospitals in towns. Often no more than grass huts, these were overseen by military and civilian doctors, depending on the province. While officials believed that hospitals helped to inspire Sudanese confidence in the government and that medical treatment would help to civilize the Sudanese, most women stayed away, reluctant to come into contact with unfamiliar men. Many Sudanese seem to have regarded hospitals as places of last resort for serious illness. At Omdurman Civil Hospital in 1903, the most common complaints were broken and injured limbs, pneumonia, tuberculosis, and chest pains. In 1913, inpatients in all civil hospitals, both military- and civilian-run, numbered 9,776; outpatient figures, 'the test of appreciation of the people of the hospital' according to Christopherson, totalled 200,891.[9] If progress was being made, pre-World War I state medicine was still a fairly minimalist affair, and in its confinement to

---

[7] William Byam, *The Road to Harley Street* (London: Geoffrey Bles, 1963), 62–6.

[8] Resumé of J. B. Christopherson's report on smallpox in Omdurman for Cromer's bluebook, 21 Nov. 1903, SAD 407/1/68–71; *RFACS 1903*, 68; *RFACS 1906*, 581, 643, 654, 768; *RFACS 1907*, 231, 330. See also Gerald W. Hartwig, 'Smallpox in the Sudan', *International Journal of African Historical Studies*, 14 (1981), 5–33.

[9] Quote from *RFACS 1905*, 119; figures from *RFACS 1913*, ii. 351, 373; *RFACS 1902*, 118; *RFACS 1906*, 558; J. B. Christopherson, Omdurman Civil Hospital manuscript diary 1903, SAD 406/5/1–104.

colonial enclaves reflected the limited aims of the pre-war colonial state.[10]

Sudan as a territory was only peripherally involved in the First World War: its one campaign, only nominally linked to the main action, was the 1916 defeat of Sultan Ali Dinar, which added Darfur to Condominium territory.[11] There was certainly no comparable experience in wartime Sudan to the devastating mortality from disease and exhaustion inflicted on African troops, labourers, and porters in East Africa.[12] The war did, however, give civilians the upper hand in the administration of medicine, as in the wider political administration. The boundaries between military and civilian medicine blurred. With military personnel recalled for duty elsewhere, civilian doctors were assigned military medical duties; medical activities concentrated on serving the troops, staffing hospitals, and controlling epidemic disease. Leadership of the medical department reverted to a civilian—Crispin became acting director in 1915 and full director in 1916—and Blue Nile (1915), Fung, Kordofan, and Kassala provinces (1917), all came under the department's jurisdiction, although they remained staffed by military doctors.[13]

The medical department emerged from the war under civilian control; the medical department director's presence on the governor-general's council from 1919 was recognition of medicine's importance to the wider colonial administrative enterprise.[14] Under O. F. H. Atkey (director 1922–33), the medical department sought to extend civil medical services to the Sudanese population throughout the country. This shift in the aim of the medical department—from a pre-war concern with protecting Europeans, to an inter-war concern with catering to the African population—was typical in colonial Africa.[15] In Sudan, it reflected a shift in governmental

[10] On medical control in Indian colonial enclaves, see David Arnold, *Colonizing the Body: State Medicine and Epidemic Disease in Nineteenth-Century India* (Berkeley: University of California Press, 1993), ch. 2.

[11] Daly, *Empire*, 171–91.

[12] Iliffe, *Africans*, 208.

[13] [Director, SMS], 'Unification of Control of Civil Medical Work in the Sudan', [1926], p. 31, CIVSEC 1/51/138, NRO; Squires, *Sudan Medical Service*, 47–8; *RFACS 1914/1919*, 134.

[14] Medical interests on the council were represented by the SEH from 1927, but the director of the SMS rejoined the council when the secretariat was retrenched in 1934 (Ahmed Bayoumi, 'Medical Administration in the Sudan 1899–1970', *Clio Medica*, 11 (1976), 107–8; Daly, *Imperial Sudan*, 122).

[15] Marc H. Dawson, 'The 1920s Anti-Yaws Campaigns and Colonial Medical Policy in Kenya', *International Journal of African Historical Studies*, 20 (1987), 417–19; Colin Baker, 'The Government Medical Service in Malawi, 1891–1974', *Medical History*, 20 (1976), 296–303; Judith N. Lasker, 'The Role of Health Services in Colonial Rule: The Case of the Ivory

priorities from pacification towards development, a concern for the health of indigenous labour connected to the opening of the Gezira scheme, and perhaps, especially after 1924, the need to legitimize the colonial adminis- tration in face of nationalist and Egyptian criticism.[16] As in other colonies, the institutional framework for achieving greater medical provision in Sudan was a network of rural dispensaries, staffed by trained indigenous auxiliaries, variously known as sanitary hakims, dispensary hakims, and assistant medical officers.[17] On an outpatient basis, these men adminis- tered primary care and dispensed drugs to the local community; they were expected to refer serious cases to the nearest hospital and to notify any outbreaks of disease. Through local dispensaries, the medical department hoped to attract more Sudanese to Western medical treatment, and to decrease the number and length of stay of hospital inpatients, by encourag- ing early treatment and providing community-based post-operative care. There were also professional and implicitly racial rationales for the estab- lishment of such a system, as Sir Alfred Webb-Johnson, a British doctor who visited Sudan in 1939, observed: 'The Service of qualified medical men is supplemented by a host of subsidiary officers working in native villages where, for economic, social and psychological reasons, no qualified medical man could be expected to sojourn for longer than is necessary for inspection and supervision.'[18] Table 2.1 shows the sizeable increase in the number of Sudan medical service dispensaries, hospitals, and attendances between 1920 and 1940.

Sorting out the relationship between the civil and military medical establishments was obviously central to the development of medical ad- ministration. In 1924, a medical committee of Atkey, Wellcome Tropical Research Laboratories Director R. G. Archibald, and PMO Benjamin Biggar was established to review medical policy and plan future medical work.[19] Their report, filed in May, recognized that all civil medical work

Coast', *Culture, Medicine and Psychiatry*, 1 (1977), 280–5; K. David Patterson, *Health in Colonial Ghana: Disease, Medicine, and Socio-economic Change, 1900–1955* (Waltham, Mass.: Crossroads Press, 1981), 12–13.

[16] This latter possibility is from Gruenbaum, 'Health Services', 48.

[17] Ann Beck, *Medicine, Tradition, and Development in Kenya and Tanzania, 1920–1970* (Waltham, Mass.: Crossroads Press, 1981), 15–18; Maryinez Lyons, 'The Power to Heal: African Medical Auxiliaries in Colonial Belgian Congo and Uganda', in Dagmar Engels and Shula Marks (eds.), *Contesting Colonial Hegemony: State and Society in Africa and India* (London: British Academic Press, 1994), 206–10.

[18] Examining Board in England by the Royal College of Physicians of London and the Royal College of Surgeons of England, Report, dated 16 June 1939, of the Committee of Management, p. 2, SAD 676/5/25.

[19] Minutes of the first meeting of the Medical Committee, p. 1a, CIVSEC 1/51/138.

TABLE 2.1. *Sudan medical department/service provision*

|              | 1920    | 1925    | 1930      | 1935      | 1940      |
|--------------|---------|---------|-----------|-----------|-----------|
| Outpatients  | 292,932 | 470,697 | 3,840,923 | 6,112,303 | 6,649,335 |
| Inpatients   | 15,527  | 18,637  | 49,911    | 89,083    | 104,422   |
| Operations   | 1,544   | 2,565   | 6,110     | 11,124    | 11,139    |
| Hospitals    | n.a.    | 20      | 47        | 40        | 39        |
| Dispensaries | 11      | 65      | 146       | 296       | 375       |

n.a. = not available

Sources: *RSMS 1925*, 5–6; *RSMS 1930*, 125; *RSMS 1935*, 103; *RSMS 1940*, 61.

in Sudan would eventually be carried out by the medical department alone and initiated a period of transition. Jurisdiction over Nuba Mountains province was turned over to the renamed Sudan medical service (SMS), although medical work there was still executed by military medical personnel. For the first time, the PMO started receiving funds and auxiliary staff such as assistant medical officers specifically earmarked for civil medical work in Darfur, and in the southern provinces of Mongalla and Bahr-el-Ghazal.[20]

But the events of the summer and autumn of 1924—Sudanese protests, military unrest, and the assassination of Governor-General Stack—upset all planning and demanded new arrangements. Stack's assassination had three immediate consequences for medical development. The first involved personnel: the Sudan government responded to Stack's death by expelling all Egyptian soldiers and many Egyptian civilian officials from the country, including doctors. The opening of the Kitchener Memorial School of Medicine in February 1924 had been Stack's last official act in Sudan;[21] the loss of Egyptian doctors made the decision to train Sudanese doctors, discussed in more detail below, seem particularly enlightened. The second consequence was financial: the SMS was the single largest beneficiary of the £500,000 indemnity paid by the Egyptian government to the Sudan government. Capital grants totalling £E64,000 from the Lee Stack Indemnity Fund paid for new medical facilities, including travelling and permanent hospitals, particularly for southern Sudan, a travelling railway laboratory car, and lorries and instruments for use on disease campaigns. From 1927 until at least 1934, the SMS also received an annual grant of between £13,400 and £18,400 for work on

[20] [Director, SMS], 'Unification of Control of Civil Medical Work in the Sudan', [1926], p. 32, CIVSEC 1/51/138.
[21] Squires, *Sudan Medical Service*, 65.

schistosomiasis, sleeping sickness, ophthalmia, and other endemic diseases.[22] These expenditures reflected the inter-war SMS's concern to strengthen the ties between medical research and medical practice, to expand proper medical services to the south, and to combat disease with a campaign approach.

The third consequence was organizational. The formation of the Sudan Defence Force (SDF) in place of the withdrawn Egyptian Army probably delayed the amalgamation of military and civil medicine. A medical corps was considered essential to the new force and the PMO of the Egyptian Army was asked, for the sake of continuity, to stay on as PMO of the SDF; many other British and Syrian doctors stayed on as well, and were joined by directly hired recruits. The military/civilian division of medical labour remained as it had following the 1924 report.[23] But amid growing concern about the general level of medical expenditure,[24] claims of wasteful duplication of administration and of the dangers of three border provinces being compartmentalized under military control forced the issue.[25] On 15 December 1928, all civil medical work in Sudan finally came under the control of the SMS director. The PMO became assistant director of the SMS in charge of the border provinces of Darfur, Mongalla, and Bahr-el-Ghazal but remained in exclusive charge of a separate SDF medical corps,[26] disbanded only under the financial pressures of the depression on 1 May 1931. The medical needs of the SDF were thenceforth met entirely by the SMS.[27]

Given that military responsibilities had first call on the time of military medical officers, it may seem inevitable that civil medicine in the border provinces was retarded by military control. While considerable medical resources were concentrated in parts of Mongalla and Bahr-el-Ghazal, these were designed to control sleeping sickness, not to provide a general medical infrastructure. Indeed, in 1927, in spite of the 1924 changes, the

[22] Lee Stack Indemnity Fund, Annual Reports of the Supervisory Committee, Annexes to *RFACS 1927* through *RFACS 1934*.

[23] [Director, SMS], 'Unification of Control of Civil Medical Work in the Sudan', [1926], pp. 33–4, CIVSEC 1/51/138.

[24] [Financial Secretary], 'Note on the Medical Service', [1926], pp. 21–7, CIVSEC 1/51/138.

[25] SEH to Secretary, Governor-General's Council, 17 Mar. 1928, pp. 94–7, CIVSEC 1/51/138.

[26] Atkey, 'Unity of Direction in Civil Medical Work', p. 85; Atkey to all heads of departments and governors, p. 139, CIVSEC 1/51/138.

[27] S. S. Butler, Kaid el 'Amm, to Financial Secretary, 14 Dec. 1930, pp. 197–8; Minutes of the 340th meeting of the Governor-General's Council, 11 Jan. 1931, p. 209; Military Secretary, SDF to SEH through PMO, 4 Apr. 1931, pp. 210–11, CIVSEC 1/51/138.

acting PMO thought that civil medicine in the border provinces did not receive the attention it deserved because of the small size of his staff.[28] But the progress of civil medical services in Upper Nile province, which came under medical department control and was first assigned a medical inspector in 1921, was only slightly more rapid than in the other two southern provinces. From 1922, the focus in Upper Nile province was on injections for yaws, administered from the floating hospital ship, the Lady Baker, and later from dispensaries on land. But it was only in the late 1920s that the SMS had the funds, the equipment, the personnel, and the requisite administrative control to seriously start a yaws eradication campaign (1927) in the province and to conduct medical surveys of its different ethnic groups (the Shilluk (1928–9), the Dinka (1929), the Nuer (1929), and the northern and Twi Dinkas (1931)).[29] Darfur was put on the medical map by the outbreak of epidemic relapsing fever in 1926; delousing stations and dispensaries were established to prevent the spread of the disease to the Gezira.[30] Regardless, then, of whether the personnel or the control was civilian or military, the general medical needs of people in the south and Darfur only started receiving concerted attention in the late 1920s. The persistence of military control over civil medicine in the border provinces reflected Khartoum's perception that they were backward, economically irrelevant, and politically unstable. Only when pacification was complete, and development deemed a possibility, was civil medical provision in the south increased. The rationale, as explained by the governor of Upper Nile province in 1927, was clear: 'not only is it one of the few things that the natives want and appreciate but the serious development of the economic possibilities of the province must depend partially on the improvement of general health'.[31] Consisting of a few hospitals and the sleeping sickness campaign until the late 1920s, civil medicine in southern Sudan expanded to comprise injections for syphilis and yaws, leper settlements, and a network of dispensaries that grew from one in Mongalla and Bahr-el-Ghazal in 1930 to seventy-eight in the amalgamated province of Equatoria in 1937.[32] Accompanying the relative medical neglect of the border provinces was a disproportionate concentra-

---

[28] W. Hunt, Acting PMO, to Financial Secretary, 22 Feb. 1927, pp. 1–4, CIVSEC 44/13/54.

[29] *RSMS 1927*, 19, 26; *RSMS 1928*, 34–43; *RSMS 1929*, 44–53; *RSMS 1931*, 68–9.

[30] Gerald W. Hartwig, 'Louse-Borne Relapsing Fever in Sudan, 1908–51', in Gerald W. Hartwig and K. David Patterson (eds.), *Disease in African History: An Introductory Survey and Case Studies* (Durham, NC: Duke University Press, 1978), 224.

[31] C. A. Willis to Civil Secretary, 17 Mar. 1927, p. 15, CIVSEC 44/13/54.

[32] *RSMS 1930*, 125; *RSMS 1937*, 108.

tion of medical resources in the Gezira irrigation scheme, for economic and political reasons discussed in Chapter 4. As Gruenbaum has observed, the colonial regime established the pattern that persists in Sudan today, whereby those living in urban areas have higher availability of health institutions than those living in rural areas, as do those living in the central part of the country around the northern Nile valley, relative to those living in the southern, western, and eastern provinces.[33]

All medical expenditure came from a limited pool of government money. The Sudan government did not spend as much of its annual budget on the medical department as its counterparts elsewhere in colonial Africa. Sudan allocated 4 to 6 per cent of its inter-war budgets to medicine, as shown in Table 2.2, while Ghana allocated 8 to 13 per cent, Nyasaland on average 8 per cent, French Equatorial Africa between 4 and 9 per cent, and Kenya and Tanganyika between 8 and 9 per cent in the late 1930s.[34] The Sudan percentages are, however, somewhat deceptive, and should be higher for the period before 1935: they do not appear to include any medical expenditure from the Stack Indemnity Fund; before 1929 they do not include the civil medical services performed by military doctors; and before 1935, they omit expenditure on medical research. Such additions to the budget discourage us from reading too much into the increase in SMS expenditure as a proportion of total expenditure from 1926 to 1938. I would nonetheless suggest that there was some increase in the budgetary proportion allocated to medicine in this period and that the Sudan government regarded medical expenditure as a relative priority: expenditure on medicine greatly exceeded that on education, the other main social service, and in 1929, the SMS overtook posts and telegraphs as the government department with the highest expenditure. The more significant point, however, is that the Sudan medical department, like all departments of colonial administrations, was in absolute terms short of funds for the tasks that it was expected to perform. For a country with an estimated population of 5.7 million in 1936 and covering a vast geographical area, £200,000 per annum was a miserly sum.[35] Limited funds and the difficulties in organizing medical services to reach a predominantly rural population in a large country with poor internal communications appear constantly in this book as constraints on medical activity.

[33] Gruenbaum, 'Health Services', 90, 187.
[34] Patterson, *Health*, 27, 112; Baker, 'Malawi', 302; Headrick, *Colonialism*, 224; Ann Beck, *A History of the British Medical Administration of East Africa, 1900–1950* (Cambridge, Mass.: Harvard University Press, 1970), 216–17, 224.
[35] Population estimate from Barbour, 'Population Shifts', 107.

TABLE 2.2. *Medical service expenditure, 1926–1939*

| Year | Expenditure (£E) | % of total government expenditure | Year | Expenditure (£E) | % of total government expenditure |
|---|---|---|---|---|---|
| 1926 | 147,006 | 3.9 | 1933 | 213,213 | 5.9 |
| 1927 | 180,803 | 4.8 | 1934 | 219,963 | 5.9 |
| 1928 | 177,576 | 4.4 | 1935 | 255,812 | 6.4 |
| 1929 | 219,581 | 4.9 | 1936 | 256,173 | 6.1 |
| 1930 | 254,239 | 5.4 | 1937 | 272,050 | 6.1 |
| 1931 | 263,566 | 6.0 | 1938 | 283,630 | 5.8 |
| 1932 | 219,176 | 5.7 | 1939 | 285,731 | n.a. |

n.a. = not available

*Sources*: Sudan government, *Financial and Trade Statistics 1926–1938*; *RSMS 1939*, 83.

The depression joined the First World War as a significant turning point for the development of medical services. The failure of the cotton crop, combined with the collapse of the cotton market, threatened to ruin the Gezira scheme, and placed the Sudan government in a precarious financial position. The result was a British Treasury-appointed financial secretary, salary cuts of between 5 and 10 per cent for all personnel, and staff retrenchment at all levels of government.[36] In medicine, the depression prompted the disbanding of the SDF medical corps, the closing of at least ten hospitals between 1930 and 1932, and the slowing down of dispensary construction; in later chapters, we will see its impact on the organization of research and on disease control in the Gezira. As Table 2.2 indicates, retrenchment brought a sharp decrease in medical expenditure from 1931 to 1932, and 1931 levels of expenditure were only recovered in 1937. Staffing levels either stayed the same or increased during the 1930s (see Table 2.5), with the exception of Syrian doctors, whose planned replacement was hastened by the depression: they were retired in favour of Sudanese doctors who worked for lower salaries and had lower career expectations.[37] But the depression did not bring medical work to a standstill: as Table 2.1 shows, the number of outpatients, inpatients, and dispensaries continued to increase.

The absorption of medical research into the SMS after the dismantling of the Wellcome Tropical Research Laboratories meant that in 1935, all state medical work finally resided within one department. Under the direction of E. D. Pridie (director 1933–45), three assistant directors—

[36] Daly, *Empire*, 435–9.
[37] SEH to Assistant Financial Secretary, 17 Dec. 1930, pp. 3–4, CIVSEC 44/3/18.

one each for laboratory services, public health, and hospitals—managed research, preventive medicine, and curative medicine, respectively. By 1937, the SMS was visibly embracing the rhetoric of social medicine:

It is likely that the medical service as a whole is now as fully developed in all its branches as is necessary and that the interests of public health in the near future may be better served by spending any additional funds available not directly on medical and public health administration, but indirectly on the improvement of urban and rural water supplies, sanitation and drainage, housing and food.[38]

As later chapters demonstrate, there was a significant gap between this rhetoric and the reality on the ground, but there was a greater institutional commitment to public health and preventive medicine in the 1930s. In 1931 the SMS started a three-year course to train Sudanese sanitary officers to replace British sanitary inspectors and in 1935 the training and employment of sanitary overseers, previously left to provincial staff, was overhauled, standardized, and centralized.[39] Such training programmes, discussed in more detail below, were arguably the greatest achievement of the medical service. While the SMS's unclassified staff, mainly labourers, had always been exclusively Sudanese, by 1939 over 90 per cent of its male classified officials, ranging from doctors to hospital orderlies and including eight senior medical post holders, were Sudanese.[40]

## BRITISH DOCTORS

This observation offers a convenient entry point to a more detailed discussion of the medical personnel who defined, administered, and/or delivered medical services in Sudan. At the top of the hierarchy, on grounds of race and education, were British doctors. Recent studies of the professionalization, educational backgrounds, and economic security of colonial doctors have provided a better sense of their ambitions, their heterogeneity, and their often precarious positioning within the colonial order, which in turn affected their ability to influence policy.[41] With similar aims, this section discusses the available information on the previous experience and training which British doctors brought with them to

[38] *RSMS 1937*, 97.
[39] Squires, *Sudan Medical Service*, 89–90; *RSMS 1935*, 34; *RSMS 1937*, 96.
[40] *RSMS 1939*, 75.
[41] E. B. van Heyningen, 'Agents of Empire: The Medical Profession in the Cape Colony, 1880–1910', *Medical History*, 33 (1989), 450–71; Anne Digby, ' "A Medical El Dorado?" Colonial Medical Incomes and Practice at the Cape', *Social History of Medicine*, 8 (1995), 463–79; Harriet Deacon, 'Cape Town and "Country" Doctors in the Cape Colony during the First Half of the Nineteenth Century', *Social History of Medicine*, 10 (1997), 25–52.

Sudan, and the terms of employment and type of work they engaged in once there. Mark Harrison has argued that Indian Medical Service doctors occupied a marginal position in Anglo-Indian society, above the police, but below the members of the Indian Civil Service and of the British and Indian armies. This low status, a lack of legal protection for the medical profession, and poor terms of service translated into professional insecurity, a resistance to innovation, and conflict with India's political administration.[42] Comprehensive data like Harrison's on the social and ethnic background of Sudan's doctors are not available. The evidence that we do have, however, indicates that for military doctors, secondment to the Egyptian Army was a prize posting; that Sudan's civilian doctors did not suffer from a marginal position relative to other civilian services, most notably the vaunted Sudan political service; and that there were significant differences in the training and previous experience of civilian and military doctors.[43]

Until the First World War, military doctors in Sudan vastly outnumbered the civilian doctors hired directly to the Sudan medical department. Between 1899 and 1940, more British military doctors than British civilian doctors served in Sudan. Including the doctors who were seconded to the Egyptian Army at the time of conquest in September 1898, a total of one hundred and three members of the Royal Army Medical Corps were seconded to the Egyptian Army and the SDF between conquest and the disbanding of the SDF medical corps in 1931, as Table 2.3 indicates.[44] The Sudan medical department/service hired seventy-eight British civilian doctors between 1904 and 1940, fifty-two of them between 1924 and 1933.

When Dr William Byam was approached about secondment to the Egyptian Army in 1908, he knew that such secondment was 'regarded as an honour' and 'that there was a long waiting list of men anxious to join'. The initial secondment was for two years, with the possibility of subse-

---

[42] Harrison, *Public Health*, ch. 1.

[43] The information about the number and lives of military and civilian doctors who served in Sudan that follows was compiled from the following sources: *RSMS 1925* to *1940*; the British *Army List*, 1899–1934; the Sudan government *Quarterly List*, 1914–40; *The Medical Directory*, 1880–1940; A. Peterkin, William Johnston, and R. Drew, *Commissioned Officers in the Medical Services of the British Army 1660–1960*, 2 vols. (London: Wellcome Historical Medical Library, 1968); autobiographies and obituaries in medical journals of some of the doctors in question. Such information has been loosely assembled in what I have labelled Heather Bell, 'A Directory of Military and Civilian Doctors in Sudan', unpublished paper, 1997.

[44] Four doctors given temporary posts in the EAMC during the First World War are not included in this tally.

TABLE 2.3. *Hiring and secondment of British civilian and military doctors*

| Date of hiring / secondment | Number of civilian doctors | Number of military doctors | Average length of military secondment in years |
| --- | --- | --- | --- |
| Seconded at conquest | n.a. | 9 | 5.8 |
| Conquest–1903 | n.a. | 11 | 7.7 |
| 1904–8 | 8 | 17 | 5.9 |
| 1909–13 | 1 | 17 | 6.8 |
| 1914–18 | 0 | 11 | 5.9 |
| 1919–23 | 10 | 23 | 4.8 |
| 1924–8 | 27 | 10 | 4.2 |
| 1929–33 | 25 | 5 | 2.0 |
| 1934–8 | 7 | n.a. | n.a. |
| TOTAL to 1940 | 78 | 103 | 5.6 |

n.a. = not applicable

*Notes*: The last military doctor was seconded in 1931.

*Source*: Bell, 'A Directory'.

quent contracts for two years, three years, and three years, for a total possible tour of duty of ten years. Three months annual leave were granted in the first year, four months in the second. Byam viewed his new monthly pay of forty-five pounds as a 'lordly sum'. Men who married would be retransferred to the British Army, as Sudan was not considered a suitable place for women. Those seconded had to learn conversational Arabic. Doctors seconded to the Egyptian Army worked primarily in Sudan but there were also some Egyptian postings, mainly in Cairo.[45] The period of secondment does not therefore necessarily correspond to the amount of time served in Sudan. This was particularly true during the First World War. At least thirteen of the twenty-nine military doctors seconded to the Egyptian Army for all or part of the war spent part of their secondments elsewhere, many at Gallipoli and in Egypt, but also in France, in Palestine, and with the Egyptian Expeditionary Force.

The standard position for the military doctor was senior medical officer of a Sudanese province, which involved acting as senior physician and surgeon at the military and civil hospitals in the province's main government station and as local MOH, and performing tours of the province to inspect conditions in subsidiary towns and hospitals. Military doctors were also attached to military patrols sent to 'pacify' recalcitrant

[45] Byam, *The Road*, 50–1, 172, quote 50; see also 'Memorandum on Service of British Officers in the Egyptian Army', Oct. 1912, SAD 152/7/4.

indigenous populations; they manned the sleeping sickness and kala-azar commissions sent to determine the extent of these two diseases in southern and eastern Sudan; and for part or all of their secondment, six military doctors were assigned to work in the bacteriological section of the Wellcome Tropical Research Laboratories. Table 2.3 indicates that on average, doctors seconded to the Egyptian Army and the SDF filled at least two contracts; one-third of those seconded through 1913 served the full ten years. The move towards greater integration of military and civilian medical administrations after 1924 probably accounts for the decrease in average length of service after the First World War. These figures suggest that there was some coherence and continuity to the military medical corps as a corporate body; turnover does not appear to have been unduly high. But there was rapid turnover of posts within Sudan. According to Byam:

> The usual practice was to appoint a successor when a Senior Medical Officer of a province went on leave. This, admittedly, was a bad plan, but it saved expense. Leave was granted alternately after nine and twelve months' work; schemes inaugurated had seldom matured in those short periods and a new man not infrequently failed to complete them, either because he did not grasp their significance or because he decided to carry out some scheme of his own.[46]

These sentiments were echoed elsewhere: the 1906 annual report for Kordofan commented that Sudanese would use the hospital more if the doctor did not change every year, observing that as soon as a doctor was known, he was transferred.[47] Death was another cause of turnover: at least nine military doctors died in Egypt and Sudan during the period of their secondment. The assignment of responsibility for civil medical services in remote areas to military doctors meant that they were consistently posted to stations reached only through hard travel, and that usually lacked insect-proof housing, a safe water supply, proper sanitation, and access to advanced medical care. This left them particularly vulnerable to injury and infectious disease.

A compilation of places of births confirms that like other colonial services, the military medical service in Sudan was disproportionately staffed by men from Ireland and Scotland, the so-called Celtic fringe: 39 per cent were born in Scotland and Ireland compared with 33 per cent in England (the country of birth remains unknown for 13 per cent). Similarly complete information is not available for civilian doctors. The small minority of military doctors born overseas (13 per cent), particularly in

[46] Byam, *The Road*, 93.        [47] *RFACS 1906*, 704.

TABLE 2.4. *Country of training of British doctors*

| Country of training | To 1913 | | 1914–31 | | Total | |
|---|---|---|---|---|---|---|
| | Military | Civilian | Military | Civilian | Military | Civilian |
| England | 29 (54%) | 9 (100%) | 19 (39%) | 48 (69%) | 48 (47%) | 57 (73%) |
| Scotland | 11 (20%) | 0 | 22 (45%) | 15 (22%) | 33 (32%) | 15 (19%) |
| Ireland | 14 (26%) | 0 | 8 (16%) | 6 ( 9%) | 22 (21%) | 6 ( 8%) |

*Source*: Bell, 'A Directory'.

parts of the British empire such as India, suggests that by choosing to work in the Anglo-Egyptian Sudan, at least some men were upholding a family tradition. Precise information about their father's occupation—a reasonable gauge of social background—is available only for a handful (fifteen) of civilian and military doctors. This slender evidence suggests that the British military and civilian doctors who worked in Sudan generally came from middle-class backgrounds, ranging from the modest to the highly comfortable.

As Table 2.4 shows, an overall majority of military doctors had trained in Scotland and Ireland.[48] The shift from English-trained to Scottish-trained doctors during and after the First World War was really a shift away from the products of London hospitals towards graduates of Scottish universities, mainly Edinburgh. This in turn corresponded to a shift away from medical licences awarded by the English, Scottish, and Irish colleges of physicians and surgeons towards university medical degrees as the primary professional qualification. The proportion of military doctors holding licences fell from 59 per cent before 1914 to 41 per cent between 1914 and 1931; for the same periods, the fraction holding university medical degrees rose from 48 to 63 per cent.

By contrast, the civil medical service was dominated by doctors trained in England. The nine men who worked for the medical department before the First World War came from the cream of London's medical elite: five had Oxbridge arts degrees, six had medical degrees from Oxbridge and London, all trained in London hospitals, and four held the prestigious Fellowship of the Royal College of Surgeons when they joined. The men recruited between 1919 and 1923 continued this pattern, though with fewer post-graduate qualifications. With its 1924–38 recruits, three-quarters of whom had university medical degrees, the Sudan medical

[48] Some men trained in several locations, but with two exceptions, multiple listings did not cross national boundaries.

service expanded recruitment out of England, and beyond the old universities and historic medical centres: 50 per cent of these sixty men had degrees from universities other than Oxbridge and London and 35 per cent from institutions other than the latter, Edinburgh, and Dublin, such as Bristol, Liverpool, and Glasgow. Ties to London remained strong, however, with 47 per cent of this cohort trained at London hospitals. Although they had, proportionately, far fewer prestigious postgraduate qualifications than their predecessors, the 1924–38 recruits included the first ten men to hold the diploma of tropical medicine and hygiene; by 1926, all new appointees had to take a three-month course at either the London or Liverpool School of Tropical Medicine.[49] Civilian doctors had much less non-British experience before arriving in Sudan than their military counterparts: only 19 per cent of civil recruits had previous military and/or overseas medical experience, while 76 per cent of military doctors had previous foreign experience when seconded to the Egyptian Army, in Egypt, India, East Africa, West Africa, South Africa (usually Boer War experience), and in the European and Mediterranean military theatres of the First World War.

Precisely what impact these differences in training location, qualifications, and experience had on the medical cultures of the military and civilian medical services remains as yet unclear. No obvious clashes between military and civilian doctors, or among differently trained military or civilian doctors, that can be traced to these differences emerge in the chapters to come. The secondary literature on medical education has only just started to outline the differences in training between the United States, France, Germany, and Britain;[50] for the late nineteenth and early twentieth centuries, it has yet to provide the kinds of distinctions among and between English, Scottish, and Irish medical schools that would allow me to make more meaningful observations on the above information. The comparative records on overseas experience suggest that military doctors newly arrived in Sudan worked with more confidence in the colonial, tropical setting than their civilian colleagues. As in the civil political service, the strong and sole attachment to Sudan of civilian doctors may have fostered a certain insularity and the conviction, which surfaces in the disease control efforts discussed in later chapters, that only they could understand Sudan's unique situation. Overall, civilian doctors were more elite in terms of qualifications than their military counterparts, particu-

---

[49] O. F. H. Atkey, 'The Sudan Medical Service', 1 Jan. 1926, p. 6, CIVSEC 44/3/16.
[50] Thomas Neville Bonner, *Becoming a Physician: Medical Education in Britain, France, Germany and the United States, 1750–1945* (Oxford: Oxford University Press, 1995).

larly before the First World War. Civilian doctors were paid, pre-war, a higher starting salary (£E600) than seconded military doctors of captain rank (£540). But the Sudan government was dominated by military men before 1914. Civilians may have needed elite qualifications and higher pay to earn military respect.

Medical service in Sudan seems to have been regarded as an honour and an opportunity by both sets of doctors, and with reason. The medical department/service offered excellent terms of service, superior to those of the West African Medical Service,[51] and on a par with those of the famously elite Sudan political service. Serving in Sudan offered the possibility of capital accumulation and a pension, as well as the shift to a second career in middle age. The increased recruitment of civilian doctors from newer, provincial universities during the inter-war period might have been expected to marginalize members of the medical service, particularly when the political service was recruited primarily from Oxford and Cambridge, and never hired a graduate of an English provincial university.[52] But throughout our period, members of the medical and political services were offered similar and excellent terms of employment. The salaries of both services operated on approximately the same age scale, with political officers receiving a lower starting salary (£E420 before 1914; £E480 by 1924) than doctors (£E600 before 1914; £E720 by 1926) on the (accurate) assumption that recruited political officials were younger than recruited medical inspectors. By the inter-war period, as in the political service, doctors had to pass a medical exam and an Arabic test after completing their two-year probationary period in order to receive their first pay increase. For political, military, and medical officials alike, each year of work earned a generous ninety days leave. In contrast to the pre-1914 Indian Medical Service, opportunities for promotion were good: pay increases of £E72 could be awarded every two years; medical inspectors could be promoted to senior medical inspector after seven years and usually were, from which level they were eligible for appointment to senior specialist posts which carried higher salaries. Retirement was mandatory at 50. This was a service that valued professional development and as subsequent chapters make clear, encouraged publication and research:

---

[51] See Squires, *Sudan Medical Service*, 15, and Ralph Schram, *A History of the Nigerian Health Services* (Ibadan: Ibadan University Press, 1971), 134–5.

[52] Daly, *Imperial Sudan*, 14. On the political service, see Robert Collins, 'The Sudan Political Service: A Portrait of the "Imperialists"', *African Affairs*, 71 (1972), 293–303; A. H. M. Kirk-Greene, 'The Sudan Political Service: A Profile in the Sociology of Imperialism', *International Journal of African Historical Studies*, 15 (1983), 21–48; A. H. M. Kirk-Greene, *The Sudan Political Service: A Preliminary Profile* (Oxford, 1982).

study leave provision allowed five doctors to obtain the diploma of public health; six men acquired MD (doctor of medicine) degrees, some on the basis of research conducted in Sudan, during their service; others took advanced qualifications such as the Fellowship of the Royal College of Surgeons and the Membership of the Royal College of Physicians.[53] This background suggests that there is no case for tensions between medical and political officials arising from differences in terms of service or social status. As in the political service, the recruitment process and the terms of employment in the medical service were intended to attract an elite and largely did.

## SYRIAN DOCTORS

While colonial medical administrations in Africa often relied on non-European personnel, comparison of Sudan to other colonies shows that its colonial regime was among the most progressive in training indigenous medical personnel: in the 1930s, Sudan trained more African personnel at all levels than Uganda and Ghana, and more doctors and midwives, though fewer dispensary attendants, than the Belgian Congo.[54] The Sudan government's willingness to train and employ non-European practitioners of Western medicine, documented in Table 2.5, suggests that British doctors in Sudan believed in the universalism of scientific and medical discourse: by following appropriate standards of behaviour and by mastering the correct techniques, Sudanese, Syrians, and Egyptians too could become practitioners of Western medicine. But this was never simply an enlightened gesture of inclusion. As this section demonstrates, the training and employment of non-European medical personnel emerged from, and was structured by, practical economic and political considerations, and was always informed by racial perceptions. Moreover, the apparent fluidity of the professional boundary drawn around medicine in this model was in fact disciplined by hierarchies of race, gender, class, training, and occupation. Conflicting hierarchies could produce tensions, but sometimes, as with the midwives discussed in Chapter 7, these different hierarchies simply reinforced one another. The colonial setting accentuated, rather than created, this professional stratification: Eliot Freidson describes similar hierarchies for post-war American medicine.[55]

---

[53] Squires, *Sudan Medical Service*, 15; O. F. H. Atkey, 'The Sudan Medical Service', 6 Jan. 1926, pp. 3–7, CIVSEC 44/3/16; 'The Sudan Political Service Information for Candidates', Apr. 1924, SAD 534/1/1–3.

[54] Lyons, 'Power', 208; Patterson, *Health*, 16–17.

[55] Eliot Freidson, *Profession of Medicine: A Study of the Sociology of Applied Knowledge* (New York: Harper and Row, 1970), 52–7.

TABLE 2.5. *Selected Sudan medical service staffing levels*

| Position | 1925 | 1930 | 1935 | 1940 |
|---|---|---|---|---|
| British doctors | 24 | 32 | 44 | 44 |
| Syrian doctors | 30 | 41 | 8 | 2 |
| Sudanese doctors | 0 | 14 | 53 | 67 |
| Sudanese assistant medical officers[a] | 41 | 70 | 227 | 274 |
| Sudanese sanitary hakims | 25 | 98 | — | — |
| Sudanese trained midwives | 54 | 109 | 205 | 290 |
| Sudanese laboratory assistants | 8 | 10 | 10 | 35 |
| British nurses | 7 | 13 | 15 | 17 |
| British sanitary inspectors | 15 | 22 | 15 | 12 |

[a] Assistant medical officers were renamed dispensary hakims in 1927; in 1933 as part of depression retrenchment, dispensary and sanitary hakims were merged into one category of assistant medical officer.

*Notes*: These figures do not include British, Syrian, and Sudanese military medical personnel. The midwifery figures for 1925 and 1935 are only approximate. The nursing totals do not include the two British nurse-midwives who taught midwifery. Culled mainly from *RSMS* appointment lists, these figures often do not agree with *Quarterly List* numbers or with the totals given elsewhere in the annual reports.

*Sources*: *RSMS 1925*, 18; *RSMS 1930*, 105; Annual Report of the MTS 1930, SAD 581/1/43; *RSMS 1935*, 95; *RSMS 1940*, 40, 66–7; *Quarterly List 1940*, 9–11.

In Sudan, doctors outranked all other medical practitioners. In our period, British doctors controlled the medical division of labour and medical education, and positioned themselves at the top of the medical hierarchy, above Syrian and Sudanese doctors. Syrian doctors performed roughly the same medical and sanitary functions as their British counterparts. But while a British doctor may have had less relevant experience than his Syrian colleague—Dr Alexander Cruickshank recalled that for the first few months he 'leaned heavily on [the] experience' of Dr Audah, his Syrian colleague, when he took up his first post at Atbara in 1924, aged 24[56]—he could never be officially subordinate to him. Syrian doctors often ran military and civilian hospitals independently, but always subject to inspection by their British superiors. For medical auxiliaries, perhaps the central lesson of training was learning when to call in a medical superior. Female Sudanese midwives reported to Sudanese male dispensary hakims who in turn reported to male doctors of whatever nationality; Sudanese mosquito men reported to Sudanese sanitary overseers who reported to (usually British) sanitary inspectors.

British doctors provide the dominant voice in archival correspondence,

[56] Alexander Cruickshank, *Itchy Feet—A Doctor's Tale* (Devon: Arthur H. Stockwell, 1991), 39.

in annual reports, and in published and unpublished memoirs. Non-European and/or auxiliary personnel are much less visible in the historical record. Full listings of such personnel never appeared in the government's *Quarterly List*, which was thorough for British doctors; the annual reports of the SMS similarly fail to provide more than numbers, or incomplete lists of names, of non-European personnel; Syrian and Egyptian doctors were not listed in the British *Army List*. This means that even basic information about their terms of service, their backgrounds, and their experiences remains unknown. It also gives the impression that all medical activity was due to the energy and initiative of British doctors, an impression that was of course crucial to the operation of colonial medical power. As Celia Davies has argued, 'professions represent themselves as autonomous only by ignoring or misrepresenting the work of others'. The maintenance of the appearance of professional autonomy, in which doctors took on an 'active, agentic and distant and controlling character', in fact depended on the work, and the comparatively low profile, of subordinate staff, in Sudan's case, non-European, usually auxiliary personnel.[57] Indeed, colonial control more generally depended on the appearance of great and independent authority being vested in British officials, but such an appearance was possible only because of the invisible work of a range of Sudanese, Syrian, and Egyptian agents.

The Syrian doctors who filled the junior ranks of the medical corps of the Egyptian Army and the Sudan Defence Force, and the civilian Sudan medical department/service were graduates of two medical schools in Beirut. The American Presbyterian Mission opened the Syrian Protestant College in 1866 and started its first medical course in 1867; in 1920, the College became the American University of Beirut. By the mid-1880s, English had replaced Arabic as the language of instruction. Students followed what would seem to have been an American medical curriculum, but successful graduates also had to pass further examinations administered by the only authority legally empowered to grant a medical diploma in the Ottoman Empire, the Imperial School of Medicine.[58] The Université Saint Joseph, opened in 1875 by the French Jesuit mission in part to counter the influence of the Syrian Protestant College, started its

[57] Celia Davies, *Gender and the Professional Predicament in Nursing* (Buckingham: Open University Press, 1995), 60.

[58] A. L. Tibawi, 'The Genesis and Early History of the Syrian Protestant College', in Fûad Sarrûf and Suha Tamim (eds.), *American University of Beirut Festival Book* (Beirut: American University of Beirut, Centennial Publications, 1967), 276, 279, 281–2, 285–8; see also Bayard Dodge, *The American University of Beirut: A Brief History of the University and the Lands which it Serves* (Beirut: Khayat's, 1958).

faculty of medicine in 1883. The Université appears to have always pursued a French medical curriculum, using French as the language of instruction. Such an orientation can only have increased under the French mandate which began after the First World War.[59] The overwhelming majority of the students at the College and at the Université Saint Joseph were Christian, mainly Presbyterian and Catholic, respectively, though also Greek Orthodox and Maronite. Determining the social background of the Syrian doctors employed in Sudan beyond the circular labelling of 'educated elite' is impossible, but they may have had more diverse social origins than this labelling suggests. Missionary rivalries, as well as the desire of local religious communities not to leave education solely to foreign establishments, meant that educational provision in late nineteenth-century Syria was substantial, particularly in comparison with its Middle Eastern neighbours. According to Thomas Philipp, 'To the gifted, regardless of social background, secondary education was accessible and could lead to college and professional education.'[60]

The model for employing Syrian Christians in government administration came from Egypt. The modernization of the Egyptian state initiated by Khedive Ismail, in its expansion of government activity and its shift from Turkish to Arabic as the administrative language, required the services of more Arabic-speaking educated officials than Egypt's education system could then provide. Increasing European intervention in Egyptian affairs, culminating in the British occupation of 1882, meant that such officials had also to be versed in European languages.[61] For the Englishman in Egypt in search of a subordinate, Muslims and Copts were not educated enough; for political and economic reasons, Europeans were not an option. According to Lord Cromer, 'Under these circumstances, the Syrian was a godsend.'[62] He credited Syrians with standing 'on a distinctly high level' from 'a moral, social, or intellectual point of view'. A high-class Syrian 'can do more than copy the European': 'He is not by any means wanting in the logical faculty. It would, in a word, be wholly incorrect to say that he merely apes civilization. It may be said with truth that he really is civilized. In this respect, he is probably superior, not only to the Copt, but also to the Europeanised Egyptian, who is but too often

---

[59] Roderic D. Matthews and Matta Akrawi, *Education in Arab Countries of the Near East: Egypt, Iraq, Palestine, Transjordan, Syria, Lebanon* (Washington, DC: American Council on Education, 1949), 471–4.

[60] Thomas Philipp, *The Syrians in Egypt 1725–1975* (Stuttgart: Franz Steiner Verlag Wiesbaden GMBH, 1985), 84.

[61] Ibid. 97–9.

[62] [Lord] Cromer, *Modern Egypt*, ii (London: Macmillan, 1908), 216.

a mere mimic.'[63] The inability to think creatively or to do more than mimic the colonizer was the standard, dismissive charge levelled at Western-educated non-Europeans by Britons throughout the empire, so these comments were high praise indeed; here was the race-based rationale for employing Syrians.

Conditions similar to those described by Cromer existed in Sudan at the start of the Condominium. British officials were expensive to employ. The only available Western education for Sudanese was at the Gordon Memorial College in Khartoum, where primary education started in 1902, and secondary education to train engineers, land surveyors, and teachers started in 1905–6.[64] Egyptians could be and were employed in the Egyptian Army and by the Sudan government. But according to Byam, they were reluctant to work in Sudan, 'largely through fear and ignorance of living conditions in the country from which their forbears had been forcibly expelled'.[65] The fact that Egyptians were Muslim and from the other Condominium partner meant that their involvement would always be politically charged. With growing nationalism in Egypt, the Sudan government increasingly feared that Egyptian officials working in Sudan would spread nationalist propaganda among the Sudanese. Government officials, perhaps naively, regarded Syrians, as Christians and non-Egyptians, as politically safer and felt that they could be posted to southern Sudan without worry that they would spread Islamic influence. For Syrian Christians, the situation at home—the lack of professional opportunities, perceived political oppression, and religious strife—spurred migration to these foreign posts.[66]

It remains unclear what differences, if any, in medical practice and culture emerged from the American and French training of Syrian doctors on the one hand and the British training of British doctors on the other. But it is clear that British doctors did not consider Syrian doctors to be perfectly trained: to the distress of the Ottomans, many Syrian doctors eager to serve in the Egyptian Army were rejected. Byam blamed the medical examiners: 'Syrian-trained doctors were well-versed in rare conditions but were often ignorant of the more common complaints, since examiners were bent on exposing gaps in students' knowledge rather than attempting to find out how much they knew about conditions with which they might expect to be called upon to cope.' At the

[63] Cromer, *Modern Egypt*, ii 218.     [64] Daly, *Empire*, 243–5.

[65] Byam, *The Road*, 174.

[66] Philipp, *Syrians*, xii, 83–4, 97; Edward Atiyah, *An Arab Tells His Story: A Study in Loyalties* (London: John Murray, 1946), esp. 25–6, 132.

request of Ottoman officials, Byam and Dr Asad Malouf, trained at the Université Saint Joseph, were sent to Beirut in 1913 to explain the Egyptian Army's requirements more fully.[67] Despite the critiques, the 'shutting off absolutely' of the supply of doctors from Beirut during the First World War made a substantial impression in Khartoum, and spurred efforts to found a Sudanese medical school in memory of Kitchener.[68] Hiring of Syrian doctors resumed after the war and continued throughout the 1920s.

British doctors' opinions of their Syrian colleagues, as detailed in their memoirs, were mixed, and focused on character as much as medical ability. As discussed in Chapter 5, most of the military doctors who worked to control sleeping sickness in southern Sudan between 1910 and 1931 were Syrian. Far away from the hierarchies of Khartoum, these Syrian doctors carved out a sphere of influence and expertise; praise was universal for this work. Drs Yusef Derwish and Nesib Baz were Sudan's sleeping sickness experts and were much respected by their British colleagues. When Baz diagnosed the sleeping sickness epidemic at Tembura, officials in Khartoum thought he had made a mistake. But according to his colleague, Lt. Col. G. K. Maurice, 'Baz did not made [*sic*] mistakes.' 'Imperturbable, methodical and resourceful, liking primitive people and, therefore, easily gaining their confidence, he was fitted beyond most men for the task in hand.' Maurice 'learned much from Derwish'. 'Thorough, concientious [*sic*] beyond most men in detail and routine, fearless and far seeing in councils, he had proved himself more than the weighty ally I had expected him to be.' Derwish left Tembura in June 1924, and Maurice later commented: 'Through him very largely we had already broken the back of the epidemic.'[69] Derwish received the OBE for his efforts. Dr Alexander Cruickshank described Dr Negib Yunis, a Syrian doctor awarded the MBE for his sleeping sickness work, as 'a tower of strength in administration, building and agricultural pursuits' who applied his 'dynamic personality and great energy and initiative' to the operation of the Li Rangu leper settlement, started in 1929.[70] While Dr Leonard Bousfield considered the Egyptian and Syrian doctors working in Sudan to be of 'varying calibre; it is only fair to record', he went on, 'that these were both worthy and conscientious'.[71] Byam agreed that the Syrian

[67] Byam, *The Road*, 174–6, quote 174–5.   [68] *GMCRA 1916*, 10.

[69] Lt. Col. G. K. Maurice, 'Sleeping Sickness', SAD 627/7/2, 12 on Baz and Derwish, respectively.

[70] Quotes from Alexander Cruickshank, 'The Birth of a Leper Settlement—Li-Rangu, Equatoria', *SNR* 29 (1948), 187, and Alexander Cruickshank, *The Kindling Fire: Medical Adventures in the Southern Sudan* (London: Heinemann, 1962), 72, respectively.

[71] Leonard Bousfield, *Sudan Doctor* (London: Christopher Johnson, 1954), 71.

doctors who worked under him 'varied greatly in ability and character'.
He felt that some, like Ibrahim Abu Haidar, who performed excellent
work on the ill-fated Anuak patrol of 1912, were 'capable and trustworthy'. Others he seems to have regarded as entertaining juvenile
delinquents, suggesting that he had lower expectations of Syrian doctors:
'Mousa Zacharia was a scoundrel who knew I knew he was a scamp. All
the same, he amused me and I liked him though I never trusted him as far
as I could see him.'[72] Dr Eric Pridie wrote that one of his Druse colleagues
in Kassala became his 'friend and a very loyal colleague with the highest
ethical standards'.[73] The formation of friendships and regular socializing
between Syrian and British doctors would have been easier outside of
Khartoum, where social life was highly stratified, and where the different
ethnic communities rarely mixed. The scarcity of foreign personnel in
smaller towns such as Kassala and in remote, rural postings such as the
Source Yubo sleeping sickness settlement broke down social barriers.[74]

We know little about Syrian doctors' views of their work experience.
Edward Atiyah, a Syrian Christian educated at Oxford, has provided a
dismaying description of his tenure as a history lecturer at Gordon College in 1926–7. He had hoped to find intellectual companionship, but soon
discovered, to his growing anger, that the British tutors, like him recent
Oxbridge graduates, showed no interest in the Syrian and Sudanese
teachers, who were treated like second-class citizens, assigned a group
common room rather than individual offices, and kept out of the way
when the governor-general came to visit. At his next job in the intelligence
department, however, Atiyah felt that his race was irrelevant: he was
treated as an individual, and judged on his ideas and abilities. It remains
unclear which type of work environment most hospitals provided.
Edward's father, Dr Selim Atiyah worked at the military hospital at
Omdurman before the First World War, and according to his son, developed 'a lasting professional friendship' with some of his British colleagues. But sensitive to any suggestion of racial or social inferiority, he
did not see these men privately, 'to avoid unpleasant complications'.[75] A
Dr Malhamé resigned from government employ 'after a few years, mainly
from resentment at the way he was treated by his British superiors' and set
up private practice. According to Atiyah, disillusionment with the British

---

[72] Byam, *The Road*, 175.

[73] Eric Pridie, 'Travels in Peace and War', unpublished memoir, 1968, SAD 720/7/19.

[74] On the warm personal relationship between Baz and Maurice, see Lt. Col. G. K.
Maurice, 'Sleeping Sickness', SAD 627/7/1–14, esp. 6.

[75] Atiyah, *An Arab*, 137–40, 147, 158–9, quote 42.

was widespread in the Syrian community in Sudan in the inter-war period, and was regularly voiced in informal conversation at the Syrian Club in Khartoum.[76]

While their services were essential to the colonial state, discussion regarding the eligibility of Syrian doctors for pension suggests that their position within the colonial order was far from secure. When the Egyptian Army was expelled from Sudan in 1924, many Syrian medical officers stayed and transferred their service to the SDF, continuing to serve under the Egyptian pension law. To replace the evacuated Egyptian doctors, other Syrian doctors were hired directly to the SDF. In 1929, the PMO pressed for a decision on whether the ten of these latter doctors whom he considered 'really good' (of a total of twenty-six) could come on to the pension list, as they had been 'practically promised pension during the past six years'.[77] Eleven civilian doctors hired by the SMS were, by similarity of contract, also affected.[78] But the secretary for education and health and the director of the SMS decided that no decision could be taken until the precise dates of retirement of the pensionable and non-pensionable doctors had been worked out.[79] When the director of the SMS raised the issue again in 1931, in the context of depression retrenchment and the amalgamation of the civil and military medical establishments, only six of the military doctors in question remained. His account put the matter even more strongly: when their contracts expired, these doctors had refused to renew them 'without an assurance that they would be taken on pension. This assurance was given definitely.' He did not feel that the claim could be 'honourably disregard[ed]' by the government.[80] The six doctors were finally made pensionable under the Sudan Government Pension Ordinance 1919, but were required to forfeit any gratuities to which they were eligible under their SDF contracts in respect of the back service that could be counted towards their pensions.[81] Such a requirement was doubtless designed to reduce the total pension paid. Syrian doctors were essential in ensuring the continuity of medical services in the wake of the Egyptian Army withdrawal. But the inept handling of the pension issue—and in particular, the fact that the honouring of verbal

[76] Ibid. 149–52, quote 149.

[77] G. K. Maurice, PMO to Headquarters, SDF, through Director, SMS, 25 Mar. 1929, pp. 10–11, CIVSEC 44/3/17.

[78] O. F. H. Atkey, Director, SMS, Memorandum, 27 May 1929, p. 7, CIVSEC 44/3/17.

[79] J. G. Matthew to Director, SMS, 26 May 1929, p. 6, CIVSEC 44/3/17.

[80] Atkey to A. J. C. Huddleston, 22 Jan. 1931, p. 20, CIVSEC 44/3/17.

[81] For Financial Secretary to Headquarters, SDF, 25 June 1931, p. 213, CIVSEC 1/51/138.

assurances made to Syrian doctors about their livelihood was a matter of lengthy negotiation, rather than a matter of course—indicates that the Sudan government did not value the service of Syrian doctors enough to deal with them straightforwardly and in good faith.

## SUDANESE PERSONNEL

Sudanese personnel had been part of the medical department from the time of conquest, working primarily as *tumargis* (hospital attendants) and as sanitary barbers. But it was the First World War that prompted the systematization and proliferation of training programmes for Sudanese. The war accentuated the limitations of any medical system that relied on military personnel when British doctors seconded to the Egyptian Army were recalled for military duty elsewhere. More civilian British doctors were hired by the medical department immediately after the war, but such men would always be costly to employ. In addition to highlighting the vulnerability of the supply of Syrian doctors, the war raised questions about continuing to employ Egyptians in the government and the army: the support of some Egyptians for the Ottoman side during the war, the Egyptian revolution of 1919, and the granting of independence to Egypt in 1922 increased British mistrust of Egyptians, whom they feared would foment nationalist feeling among the Sudanese.[82] The extension of medical services to the Sudanese population would have to rely on Sudanese trained medical personnel, who were less of a political risk than Egyptians, easily accessible, potentially numerous, and cheap to employ.

Inter-war medical department training programmes can be placed into three categories.[83] The Sudanese doctors trained at the Kitchener Memorial School of Medicine from 1924 constitute the first category. These men were the best students to graduate from Sudan's only secondary school, the Gordon Memorial College; they were the elite products of Sudan's small Western education system. They underwent four to six years of medical training (the course changed over the inter-war period) and their language of instruction was English. Upon graduation, they were issued with the diploma of the Kitchener School of Medicine which licensed them to practise medicine within Sudan, and were considered to be medical officers, the same term used for Syrian doctors. This contrasts markedly with inter-war South Africa and the Belgian Congo, where only

[82]  Daly, *Empire*, 269–70.
[83]  For further details on medical training programmes, see *RSMS 1925* through *RSMS 1940*; Squires, *Sudan Medical Service*, 61–91; Bayoumi, *Health Services*, 142–61.

the training of African medical aids and medical assistants could be coun-
tenanced; with Uganda, where Makerere College graduates were called
'assistant medical officers' rather than 'doctors'; and with Nigeria where
the Yaba Medical Training College, only started issuing diplomas to
'assistant medical officers' in 1940, after a decade of training medical
assistants.[84] The SMS sought from the start to maintain high standards
among Sudanese medical students by bringing in outside assessors from
Britain and Cairo for examinations.[85] In 1939, the Kitchener School received partial recognition from the London Conjoint Board: graduates
with two years of hospital experience and the recommendation of the
SMS director could, after a further year of study at a hospital in Britain,
take the final conjoint licence examination.[86] In 1946, the Conjoint Board
fully recognized the School.[87]

The Sudan government's greater willingness to train doctors can be
traced to several factors. The presence of Egyptian and Syrian doctors in
Sudan's medical administration provided a strong precedent for a junior
tier of non-European doctors. It was only a small step from employing
these men to training Sudanese. Moreover, all of the doctors trained in
this period were northern Sudanese and therefore came from an Arab,
Islamic culture that had its own traditions of medicine and scholarship.
While the British in Sudan still regarded this culture as inferior, northern
Sudanese were considered more advanced than southern Sudanese, or
indeed other East and Central Africans, and thus more capable of handling medical education and responsibilities: the 'Arab race' of northern
Sudan was considered 'quick, intelligent, and eager for education'.[88] In
the Belgian Congo and Uganda, many European doctors were reluctant to
train even African medical auxiliaries: preventing Africans, considered
racially and morally inferior, from practising medicine would safeguard

---

[84] Karin A. Shapiro, 'Doctors or Medical Aids—The Debate over the Training of Black
Medical Personnel for the Rural Black Population in South Africa in the 1920s and 1930s',
*Journal of Southern African Studies*, 13 (1987), 234–55; Lyons, 'Power', 210–15; N. R. E.
Fendall, 'A History of the Yaba School of Medicine, Nigeria', *West African Medical Journal*,
Aug. 1967, 120.

[85] See e.g. *RSMS 1928*, 100–1.

[86] Examining Board in England by the Royal College of Physicians of London and the
Royal College of Surgeons of England, Report, dated 16 June 1939, of the Committee of
Management, p. 8, SAD 676/5/24–7.

[87] Information on the Kitchener School from Squires, *Sudan Medical Service*, 64–78. On
the content of the medical course, see e.g. *Report, Kitchener School of Medicine 1924–1925*,
18–37.

[88] 'Notes on the Kitchener Memorial Medical School', appendix III, in M. O. Beshir,
*Educational Development in the Sudan* (Oxford: Clarendon Press, 1969), 218.

their limited professional prestige. In South Africa, many white doctors opposed the training of African doctors out of fear that this new competition would jeopardize their incomes.[89] The professional standing and security enjoyed by British doctors in Sudan meant that they did not share these preoccupations; state-employed, they did not have private practices to safeguard.

A second category comprises Sudanese trained auxiliaries, such as assistant medical officers, sanitary hakims, and sanitary overseers. Although previous formal education was not a prerequisite for this group, all were required to be literate. Depending on the particular course, training ranged from six months to two years, and was always in Arabic. To take one example: sanitary hakims were selected from the most able hospital orderlies for one year of intensive training. Capable of reading and writing well, they were taught basic anatomy and physiology, to recognize common diseases, to give treatment and intravenous injections, to identify bilharzia ova under the microscope, and to perform some sanitary work.[90] Trained midwives and trained sanitary barbers fall into a third category of trained personnel, created out of, and in rivalry to, existing classes of traditional medical practitioners, known as *dayas* (midwives) and *hallaqs* (barber-surgeons).[91] As discussed in Chapter 7, midwifery pupils had rarely had any formal education, were usually illiterate and remained so, and were trained in Arabic for three to six months. Outside these three categories lies a group of people who were essentially labourers—mosquito men, hospital assistants, tsetse fly catchers—on whose work the medical department depended, but whose training was minimal and usually conducted on the job. Literacy was not required; low wages reflected the large pool of potential candidates for such work. The length of training, lan-

[89] Lyons, 'Power', 210–11; Shapiro, 'Doctors', 246–7.

[90] *RSMS 1928*, 93.

[91] With the exception of midwives, this book does not discuss traditional Sudanese medical practitioners or Sudanese healing systems. For northern Sudan, the reader is referred to J. B. Christopherson, 'Medical and Surgical Customs in the Sudan', 29 Mar. 1908, SAD 407/6/1–28; Hassan Effendi Zeki, 'The Healing Art as Practised by the Dervishes in the Sudan During the Rule of the Mahdi and of the Khalifa', *Third RWRL*, 269–72; Leonard Bousfield, 'The Native Methods of Treatment of Diseases in Kassala and Neighbourhood', *Third RWRL*, 273–5; R. G. Anderson, 'Medical Practices and Superstitions Amongst the People of Kordofan', *Third RWRL*, 281–322; E. J. R. Hussey, 'A Fiki's Clinic', *SNR* 6 (1923), 35–9; Ahmed Abdel Halim, 'Native Medicine and Ways of Treatment in the Northern Sudan', *SNR* 22 (1939), 27–48; Ahmad al-Safi, *Native Medicine in the Sudan: Sources, Concepts and Methods* (Khartoum: University of Khartoum, 1970); Susan M. Kenyon, *Five Women of Sennar: Culture and Change in Central Sudan* (Oxford: Clarendon Press, 1991), 137–221; Janice Boddy, *Wombs and Alien Spirits: Women, Men and the Zar Cult in Northern Sudan* (Madison: University of Wisconsin Press, 1989).

PLATE I. An assistant medical officer examining patients outside a block dispensary in the Gezira, *c.*1937. (Courtesy of the University of Durham Library.)

guage of training, the prerequisite education, and the level of remuneration once employed served as indicators of the status of trained personnel within the medical hierarchy, and within government more generally.

The way in which medical personnel were trained and the areas to which they were posted reflected political and economic considerations and British racial stereotypes. In the inter-war period, the dogma of indirect rule politicized education policy: particularly after 1924, the government turned away from modern, higher, and technical education to promote traditional village schools.[92] In this context, the founding of the Kitchener School, the only institution of higher education in Sudan before the late 1930s, seems strange, and suggests that the need for Sudanese doctors overrode the potential political liabilities of such a step. In fact, the Kitchener School had much to commend it from the indirect rule perspective. It created a highly educated elite, but a small one: no more than nine doctors graduated annually. Small classes were intended to ensure close rapport between students and teachers, and therefore a greater success rate, crucial for establishing the international credibility of

[92] Daly, *Empire*, 379–87.

the Kitchener School diploma. A scientific training seems to have been considered much less likely to lead to politicization than a higher education in the arts: 'there is no safer or more desirable channel into which the energies of the mentally active and intellectually restless can be directed than that of medical work and medical research, a sphere of work and line of thought that leads away from a narrow territorial and racial outlook to a wide humanitarian view of life.' Moreover, a cadre of Sudanese doctors would preclude the need for more expensive Syrian doctors and the existence of a local medical school meant that Sudanese did not have to be sent abroad to study, 'removing them from the influence of their homes, customs and traditions and exposing them to intellectual and moral influences which they are not yet ready to meet'.[93]

Only in the mid- to late 1930s was there some return to a dual policy in administration and a recognition that educated Sudanese had a place in the future governance of Sudan. The start, in 1937, of postgraduate training for select Sudanese doctors in London can therefore be seen as a reflection of this policy shift as much as an indication of the higher medical standards reached at the Kitchener School. But there was an important distinction between medical and political spheres: while Sudanese doctors continued to be outranked by their British counterparts, by 1937, they occupied the specialist posts of assistant ophthalmic surgeon, assistant bacteriologist, and medical sub-inspector, and were therefore entrusted with much greater responsibility than Sudanese working in political administration.[94]

Mastering the appropriate Western medical practices—such as examining slides under the microscope, sterilizing equipment, delivering babies in the the semi-reclining position—was clearly important for Sudanese in medical training programmes. But if they did not show the right character and adopt appropriate standards of behaviour, they could never be proper practitioners of Western medicine. Stereotypes about race, gender, and caring were deeply embedded in British attitudes towards non-British colleagues. Elaine Hills-Young, director of the Nursing Training School in Omdurman from 1930, observed that no matter how able some Sudanese nurses seemed, some abstract quality escaped them: 'As in the case of boys, it is difficult to instil into these girls and women the true spirit of service for others. Very few of the trained or untrained are nurses in the real sense of the word, although some can do excellent

---

[93] *Report, Kitchener School of Medicine 1924–1925*, 10.
[94] *RSMS 1937*, 100; Squires, *Sudan Medical Service*, 115–16; Daly, *Imperial Sudan*, 15–19, 25–38.

work.'[95] The outside assessors for the Kitchener School final examination in 1928 commented on the 'production of so capable, practical and adaptable young doctors'. Appearance obviously had something to do with this impression, though the assessors' observations both praised and infantilized the Sudanese medical students: 'Their appearance and deportment seemed to us comparable to those of the English public schoolboy. It is difficult to realise that eight or ten years ago these candidates were completely illiterate children.'[96] Assumptions about how different races learned structured teaching: assessor Douglas G. Derry recommended 'constant reference to the living body' during anatomy dissecting classes, considering such a teaching method 'all the more essential where the habit of mind is not naturally deductive' as in the Sudanese.[97]

The influence of indirect rule can be seen in other aspects of staffing. The incorporation of *dayas* into the medical service, for example, was consistent with the wider reliance on traditional figures. The desire to protect southern Sudan from allegedly subversive northern Arab and Islamic influence and from detribalization, encapsulated in Southern Policy, meant that a class of chiefs' dressers was created in the late 1920s to extend medical services to less accessible southern Sudanese communities. Chosen from 'among the untaught, unsophisticated tribesmen', nominated by the chiefs themselves, and approved by the local medical inspector, chiefs' dressers were trained 'in such places and in such manner as to prevent them from adopting the habits and dress of the townsmen', namely during short periods at the nearest hospital or dispensary. Taught 'to dress wounds, to treat inflammatory conditions of the eye, to treat ulcers, to vaccinate and to administer simple stock mixtures', they remained under the authority of the chief for discipline and were usually paid out of the native administration budget.[98] Chiefs' dressers, and other trained southern Sudanese, obviated the need for outside personnel, specifically northern Sudanese, to be posted to southern Sudan. By 1928, the governor of Mongalla and the secretary for education and health were calling for the replacement of northern Sudanese assistant medical officers with locally trained southern Sudanese.[99] The same outlook led to the 1929 conclusion that Syrian doctors would be needed in the south for 'a

[95] E. Hills Young, 'Nursing in the Sudan', *International Nursing Review*, (1931/32), 179–83, SAD 631/3/4.

[96] *RSMS 1928*, 101.

[97] *RSMS 1929*, 106.

[98] Quotes from *RSMS 1928*, 1–2, 94, respectively; *RFACS 1930*, 108.

[99] Governor, Mongalla to Civil Secretary, 7 Mar. 1928, p. 118; J. G. Matthew, 'Medical Work in the Upper Nile Province', 13 Jan. 1928, p. 102, CIVSEC 44/13/54.

long time to come': replacing them with northern Sudanese doctors would be against government policy.[100] In the event, depression retrenchment and replacement by graduating Sudanese doctors greatly reduced the number of Syrian doctors, and by January 1938, at least three northern Sudanese doctors were working at Juba and Wau.[101] The south finally got a training school for local sanitary overseers at Juba in 1937, but programmes for other medical auxiliaries only came later.[102] In medicine as in the wider administration, indirect rule and Southern Policy were never as rigidly implemented as their most ardent proponents hoped.[103] But throughout our period the distinctiveness of the south and the political desire to keep it separate exerted a significant influence on the medical policy and disease control efforts pursued there.

## CONCLUSION

Between 1899 and 1940, military and civilian medical services in Sudan were constrained by limited resources and by political considerations, which shaped the structure and timing of medical service provision to different parts of the country and the choice of personnel to staff medical facilities. The incorporation of a range of different medical practitioners into the civil and military medical administrations nonetheless suggests a belief in the universality of medical science on the part of British doctors, as well as a conviction that medicine could civilize both the practitioner and the patient; it also reflects the self-confidence of a well-qualified, well-rewarded professional group. Despite this inclusiveness, colonial and professional order were maintained within the medical services by hierarchies of skill level, race, gender, and class. These hierarchies were partly generated by science itself, which provided knowledge of, and categories to describe, the Sudanese population through vehicles such as the Wellcome Tropical Research Laboratories, uneasy container of research of all kinds, to whose history we now turn.

---

[100] Quote from SEH to Director, SMS, 26 May 1929, p. 6; SEH to Military Secretary, SDF, 12 Apr. 1929, p. 5, CIVSEC 44/3/17.
[101] *Quarterly List*, 1 Jan. 1938, 10.
[102] *RSMS 1937*, 96; Squires, *Sudan Medical Service*, 91.
[103] Daly, *Imperial Sudan*, 29, 38–9.

# 3

# The Wellcome Tropical Research
# Laboratories and the Organization
# of Research

Sudan was identified as a rich field for exploring frontiers of scientific knowledge almost from the beginning of colonial rule. Before there was a civil medical department in the country, there were laboratories for bacteriological and chemical research. Opened in Khartoum in 1903 and soon housing an entomological laboratory as well, the Wellcome Tropical Research Laboratories (WTRL) constituted the primary institution for scientific research of all kinds in Sudan. By the standards of other British colonies in Africa, such a foundation, so soon after colonial conquest, was exceptionally early. While the French had their overseas Pasteur Institutes,[1] the more decentralized British empire, lacking a Pasteur and therefore a dominant scientific methodology to export, never had a network of metropolitan-affiliated research laboratories in its colonial territories. British tropical medicine remained a metropolitan-based discipline, centred around the Liverpool and London Schools of Tropical Medicine, sustained by overseas research and collection expeditions by scientists from these institutions.[2] Laboratories based in Britain's African colonies grew up, therefore, in an ad hoc

---

[1] See Anne Marie Moulin, 'Patriarchal Science: The Network of the Overseas Pasteur Institutes', in Patrick Petitjean, Catherine Jami, and Anne Marie Moulin (eds.), *Science and Empires* (Boston: Kluwer Academic, 1992), 307–22; Anne Marie Moulin, 'The Pasteur Institutes between the Two World Wars. The Transformation of the International Sanitary Order', in Paul Weindling (ed.), *International Health Organisations and Movements 1918–1939* (Cambridge: Cambridge University Press, 1995), 244–65; Kim Pelis, 'Pasteur's Imperial Missionary: Charles Nicolle (1866–1936) and the Pasteur Institute of Tunis', Ph.D. thesis (The Johns Hopkins University, 1995).

[2] Jennifer Beinart, 'The Inner World of Imperial Sickness: The MRC and Research in Tropical Medicine', in Joan Austoker and Linda Bryder (eds.), *Historical Perspectives on the Role of the MRC* (Oxford: Oxford University Press, 1989), 109–26; Worboys, 'Emergence of Tropical Medicine', 75–98; Worboys, 'Manson, Ross', 21–37; Helen Power, 'Keeping the Strains Alive and More: Trypanosomiasis Research at the Liverpool School of Tropical Medicine's Laboratory in Runcorn', paper presented at the Wellcome Unit for the History of Medicine, Oxford, 22 Feb. 1996.

way.[3] Colonial governments generally saw research as a luxury to be undertaken only when resources permitted and when a sufficiently developed medical department required. This meant that research—as opposed to routine analyses—usually started only in the inter-war period or even later: in East Africa, institutionalized research began in 1949 as part of post-war colonial development.[4] As we will see, Sudan's exceptionalism in the matter of laboratory research was due to its scientific patron, Henry Wellcome, his fascination with imperialism, and his expansive belief in unfettered research.

The WTRL was founded as an independent research institution, outside the control of the medical and agricultural departments. As a result, the fundamental problem for the WTRL throughout its history was negotiating the boundary between research and practice, in the context of changing visions of research, and changing demands on practice. In this process, the interests of capital, first in the form of Wellcome and later in the form of the British cotton industry, were crucial. While the founding of the WTRL was a sign of the perceived power of the laboratory, Andrew Balfour, first director of the WTRL, still had to persuade agricultural, medical, and political officials that the routine and research work of the laboratories could enhance their various practices. Borrowing Bruno Latour's analysis of the Pasteur Institute, I argue that Balfour situated his institution 'in such a way that all the interested commercial, colonial, and medical interests had to pass through [the] laboratories to borrow the technics, the gestures, the products, the diagnostic kits that were necessary to further their own desires'.[5] Balfour's efforts, and the publicity generated for them by Wellcome, meant not only that research became an integral part of medical and agricultural activity in Sudan, but also that research defined Sudan and the civilizing project of the Sudan government to government officials themselves, and to the wider world.

The work of Balfour and his successor, Albert Chalmers, established the relevance of research to practice so well that when government departments such as medicine and agriculture emerged from the First World

[3] For typical examples of the haphazard origins of these laboratories and their work, see Charles Tettey, 'A Brief History of the Medical Research Institute and Laboratory Service of the Gold Coast (Ghana) 1908–1957', *West African Medical Journal*, 9 (1960), 73–85; David F. Clyde, *History of the Medical Services of Tanganyika* (Dar Es Salaam: Government Press, 1962), 19–43, 75, 102–40.

[4] Ann Beck, 'Medical Administration and Medical Research in Developing Countries: Remarks on their History in Colonial East Africa', *Bulletin of the History of Medicine*, 46 (1972), 349–58; Beck, *A History*, 174–97.

[5] Bruno Latour, 'Give me a Laboratory and I will Raise the World', in Karin Knorr-Cetina and Michael Mulkay (eds.), *Science Observed: Perspectives on the Social Study of Science* (London: Sage, 1983), 159.

War under civilian administration and committed to socio-economic development, they started demanding research support tied more closely to their needs and crucially, under their control. The research priorities had shifted: the major patrons of scientific research in inter-war Sudan were the government and the Empire Cotton Growing Corporation, and what mattered most to them was agricultural research that would guarantee good, high-quality cotton crop yields and therefore a high return on their investments in the Gezira irrigation scheme. Conflict erupted not over the content of research, but its organization. In response to practitioners' demands for control over research, outside expert Sir John Farmer and Robert Archibald, third WTRL director, drew a firm boundary between the aims and styles of work of research scientists and of those of practical men. They argued that the WTRL should remain an independent institution, insisting that researchers needed a scientific community, and that practitioners could not be depended on to protect and foster the professional interests of research scientists. For practitioners, the decisive boundary lay elsewhere: they argued that the improved coordination of research and practice needed in Sudan could only be achieved by locating the research and the practice of a particular field, such as medicine or agriculture, in the same department, under the control of a practitioner. While the boundaries drawn by researchers held in the late 1920s and early 1930s, Sudan's experience of the depression meant that the practitioners' position ultimately triumphed. The constituent elements of the WTRL were divided between the departments of medicine and agriculture in 1935.

The chapter tells this story chronologically, and makes clear that research agendas at the WTRL shifted throughout the institution's existence, influenced by factors such as the preoccupations of patrons, the needs of practice, the intellectual interests of WTRL directors and researchers, and of the wider scientific community, and not least, the availability of funds, staff, scientific material, and transportation. Organizational changes, such as the 1935 dismantling, seem to have brought comparatively minor changes in the laboratories' activities, which I gauge by examining the laboratories' teaching function and bacteriological section research.

## WELLCOME AND HIS VISION
## OF SCIENTIFIC RESEARCH

An American based in London who introduced compressed or 'tabloid' medicines to Britain through his partnership with Silas Burroughs,

Henry Wellcome was commercially successful and socially prominent in 1901, when he offered to donate the equipment for research laboratories in Khartoum. Wellcome believed in the British imperial project, and followed the exploration and acquisition of Africa with intense personal interest. Through his close friend, May French-Sheldon, an American woman who travelled extensively in Africa, he became an intimate of famed explorer Henry M. Stanley and a member of French-Sheldon's de facto London salon for African travellers.[6] An astute publicist, Wellcome also exploited imperialism commercially. Seizing on the public fascination for explorers' travel, he produced magnificent Burroughs Wellcome and Company 'tabloid' medicine chests, designed to withstand rough treatment under extreme conditions; the first one, known as the Congo chest, accompanied Stanley on his mission to rescue Emin Pasha. The financial deal made for these chests varied, but Wellcome usually stipulated that they be returned to him:[7] appropriately battered, they appeared with testimonials in company advertisements.

Wellcome's decision to give laboratories to Khartoum was similarly driven by personal passion, accompanied by a keen sense of the commercial value of participating in such a well-known imperial venture. Kitchener's conquest of Sudan in 1898, which avenged the death of General Gordon at the hands of the Mahdists in 1885, captured the imagination of the British public and Wellcome's along with it: for their 1898 Christmas present, Wellcome gave all his employees two books, Rudolf von Slatin's *Fire and Sword in the Sudan* and G. W. Steevens's *With Kitchener to Khartoum*.[8] When Kitchener announced his intention to found a Gordon Memorial College to educate Sudanese boys, Wellcome sent in a subscription of 100 guineas and a promise to outfit a school dispensary.[9]

Wellcome's ties to the country became tangible in early 1901, when

---

[6] Robert Rhodes James, *Henry Wellcome* (London: Hodder and Stoughton, 1994), 134, 247.

[7] See e.g. BW&Co to Wellcome, 24 May 1901, Glaxo Wellcome Group Archive, Glaxo Wellcome Research and Development, Greenford, Middlesex (GWGA): LB15, 853–4.

[8] J. B. Fairley et al. to Wellcome, 21 Feb. 1899, File 2B; Alec Hector to H. F. Johnson, 21 Feb. 1899, File 8H, Box 35 miscellaneous correspondence 1898–1899, Wellcome Archive, Contemporary Medical Archives Centre, Wellcome Institute for the History of Medicine Library (WA).

[9] Draft letter Wellcome to Kitchener, 26 Nov. 1898, File H. S. Wellcome: Personal correspondence with Lord K (miscellaneous) 1898–1917, WA; see also various letters in GWGA: LB14, 953–6.

he formed part of the first group of European civilians to visit the 'Anglo-Egyptian' Sudan. 'Deeply impressed' by the visit, particularly by the poor health and living conditions of the Sudanese,[10] Wellcome decided to take part in the civilizing mission of the Sudan government by donating the 'complete equipment for Chemical and Bacteriological Laboratories for Analytical and Research work'. The Gordon Memorial College, the one authentically British and civilian institution in the country, seemed the obvious location for them. The only stipulation that Wellcome made was that the 'Authorities' 'maintain the laboratories and appoint and maintain an efficient Director and Staff for conducting the work'.[11] After due consideration, the government gratefully accepted the gift, said to be valued at £15,000.[12] Lord Cromer, British Agent and Consul-General in Egypt, expressed the prevailing view when he wrote: 'It is clear that this offer must be accepted . . . I do not make out clearly what the cost will be, but somehow I think the money will have to be found.'[13]

The establishment of the laboratory as the crucial scientific space was a nineteenth-century phenomenon, a by-product of the rise of modern industrialized society. Chemistry was the science first associated with the laboratory: in the early nineteenth century, a laboratory was defined by the presence of chemical apparatus. Prompted by technical and industrial demands, the re-siting of physics in institutional laboratories only occurred in Britain between 1865 and 1885.[14] The 'laboratory revolution' in medicine started with the German physiological laboratories of the 1830s and 1840s: the research and teaching of Claude Bernard in France and Karl Ludwig in Germany established a laboratory-based, experimental tradition of scientific medicine on the continent, though it was only in the 1870s under Michael Foster at Cambridge that English physiology emerged from stagnation. Pasteur's work on fermentation and his resulting 'microbiology' brought laboratory chemistry to work for medicine; along with Koch's microscope and his postulation of a strict

[10] A. R. Hall and B. A. Bembridge, *Physic and Philanthropy: A History of the Wellcome Trust 1936–1986* (Cambridge: Cambridge University Press, 1986), 11, 220; Rhodes James, *Wellcome*, 250–1.

[11] Wellcome to Wingate, 28 Sept. 1901, Gordon Memorial College (GMC) Minutebook, SAD 572/5/61–3.

[12] Minutes of the meeting of the trustees and executive committee of the GMC, 4 Oct. 1901, GMC Minutebook, SAD 572/5/43.

[13] Cromer to Wingate, 17 Sept. 1901, GMC Minutebook, SAD 572/5/63.

[14] Graeme Gooday, 'Precision Measurement and the Genesis of Physics Teaching Laboratories in Victorian Britain', *British Journal for the History of Science*, 23 (1990), 25–51.

bacteriological methodology, this created another kind of laboratory medicine.[15]

Scholars analysing nineteenth-century medicine have emphasized the contingency of the ascendance of scientific medicine and of the laboratory, arguing that this rise was not the inevitable result of obvious improvements in therapeutic and diagnostic technique. Rather they have shown that the incorporation of science into medical education and clinical practice was a highly contested process that varied depending on the local and national context. Some doctors turned to the laboratory and to science to enhance their professional and cultural authority, or to render medical administration more efficient.[16] Others, such as the London medical elite, long resisted making clinical practice scientific because this threatened their claims to superiority as gentlemen who had mastered the clinical art.[17] In late nineteenth-century Glasgow, surgeons who prided themselves on their scientific practice did not fully exploit the resources of the pathology department, because of their 'faith in the sufficiency of their clinical judgment'.[18] In our context, the laboratory and the microscope were unequivocally the hallmarks of the new discipline of tropical medicine forged in the late nineteenth and early twentieth centuries; indeed, the first task in any tropical field expedition was to create a laboratory space.[19] But while virtually all the doctors who worked in Sudan had trained in a post-germ theory world, the extent of their laboratory exposure during training and their attitudes towards the laboratory would have varied: according to Bonner, while the importance of the basic sciences to early medical training was fully accepted by 1910, precisely

[15] Andrew Cunningham and Perry Williams (eds.), *The Laboratory Revolution in Medicine* (Cambridge: Cambridge University Press, 1992); W. F. Bynum, *Science and the Practice of Medicine in the Nineteenth Century* (Cambridge: Cambridge University Press, 1994), 92–117; Gerald L. Geison, *Michael Foster and the Cambridge School of Physiology: The Scientific Enterprise in Late Victorian Society* (Princeton: Princeton University Press, 1978).

[16] John Harley Warner, 'The Fall and Rise of Professional Mystery: Epistemology, Authority and the Emergence of Laboratory Medicine in Nineteenth-Century America', in Cunningham and Williams (eds.), *Laboratory Revolution*, 110–41; Steve Sturdy, 'The Political Economy of Scientific Medicine: Science, Education and the Transformation of Medical Practice in Sheffield, 1890–1922', *Medical History*, 36 (1992), 125–59.

[17] Christopher Lawrence, 'Incommunicable Knowledge: Science, Technology and the Clinical Art in Britain, 1850–1914', *Journal of Contemporary History*, 20 (1985), 503–20.

[18] L. S. Jacyna, 'The Laboratory and the Clinic: The Impact of Pathology on Surgical Diagnosis in the Glasgow Western Infirmary, 1875–1910', *Bulletin of the History of Medicine*, 62 (1988), 384–406, quote 406.

[19] See e.g. the creation of Hong Kong plague laboratories by Yersin and Kitasato: Andrew Cunningham, 'Transforming Plague: The Laboratory and the Identity of Infectious Disease', in Cunningham and Williams (eds.), *Laboratory Revolution*, 228–30.

'how much science was needed, how it should be taught, and who should teach it' remained subjects of debate. The slow pace of laboratory building and the failure of English hospitals to apply laboratory findings to clinical cases remained serious criticisms of British medicine in the 1910s.[20]

The model for the Khartoum laboratories did not, however, come from academic institutions, the tropical medical world, or even the medical community: it came rather from the commercial research laboratories that Wellcome owned in London. Wellcome's decision to invest in laboratories as a means of improving the public health and the general standard of living in Sudan, rather than in institutions of curative care such as hospitals or dispensaries, highlights his strong belief in all forms of scientific research. Wellcome was the first in British pharmaceuticals to appreciate the commercial possibilities of laboratory research and its ability to produce marketable drugs. He founded his own research facilities in London in 1894 to produce diphtheria anti-toxin; the Wellcome Physiological Research Laboratories, as they became known, were joined by the Wellcome Chemical Research Laboratories in 1896. These institutions forged a link between science and commerce that was controversial and hotly contested by the medical community. While Wellcome always insisted that his laboratories were separate from Burroughs Wellcome and Company, the fact was that Wellcome Laboratories scientists were all company employees, and the Physiological Laboratories were created in order to produce a drug to be sold by the company. But these were not straightforward company laboratories either: the scientists were also paid to pursue independent, original research.[21]

The Khartoum laboratories were a gift from Wellcome to the Sudan government: Wellcome did not employ the Khartoum scientists, he did not own the Khartoum laboratories, and they were not part of the greater London research institution of laboratories, museums, and libraries that he was assembling. In fact, the designation as '*Wellcome* Research

[20] Bonner, *Becoming a Physician*, 260–4, 275–6, 278–9, 284, 288–90, 295–306, 330–2, quote 298; Charles Newman, *The Evolution of Medical Education in the Nineteenth Century* (London: Oxford University Press, 1957), 270–310.
[21] E. M. Tansey, 'The Wellcome Physiological Research Laboratories 1894–1904: The Home Office, Pharmaceutical Firms, and Animal Experiments', *Medical History*, 33 (1989), 1–41; E. M. Tansey, 'What's in a Name? Henry Dale and Adrenaline, 1906', *Medical History*, 39 (1995), 460–4; E. M. Tansey and Rosemary C. E. Milligan, 'The Early History of the Wellcome Research Laboratories, 1894–1914', in Gregory J. Higby and Elaine C. Stroud (eds.), *Pill Peddlers: Essays on the History of the Pharmaceutical Industry* (Madison: American Institute of the History of Pharmacy, 1990), 91–106.

Laboratories' (WRL) emerged out of Khartoum in 1903.[22] (The 'Tropical' was added in 1911.) But Wellcome's role in Khartoum, at least until 1913, was much more than that of a one-time donor, and the London laboratories clearly provided a powerful model for the Khartoum institution. Wellcome donated chemical and bacteriological laboratories because these were roughly the two kinds of laboratory he had in London. As in London, Wellcome's donation and continued support of the Khartoum laboratories were shrewd, self-promoting moves: he was allying himself with the new tropical medical experts. Although there was never any explicit agreement, any new drugs or vaccines to be developed in Khartoum would almost certainly have been offered to his company for production. The gift was possibly also intended to ingratiate Wellcome with the Egyptian Army Medical Corps, whose contracts Burroughs Wellcome and Company was bidding for at this time.[23] The decision to name the laboratories after Wellcome heightened the commercial dividends, spreading the Wellcome name in Egypt and the Middle East, where Wellcome had posted a company salesman following his visit to Sudan.[24] The new name also offered Wellcome free, targeted publicity: articles published by scientists from the Wellcome Research Laboratories, Khartoum appeared in the same medical journals in which Burroughs Wellcome and Company advertised its products.

But self-interested, if indirect, commercial incentives were only part of the motivation. The aims that Wellcome outlined for the Khartoum laboratories showed his belief that the laboratory had become fundamental not only to medicine but to the functioning of an ordered society:

To promote technical education;

To undertake the testing and assaying of agricultural, mineral and other substances of practical interest in the industrial development of the Soudan;

To carry out such tests in connection with water, food stuffs, and sanitary matters as may be found desirable;

To aid criminal investigation in poisoning cases (which are so frequent in the Soudan) by the detection and experimental determination of toxic agents, particularly those obscure potent substances employed by the natives;

To study bacteriologically and physiologically tropical disorders especially the infective diseases of both man and beast peculiar to the Soudan, and to render

---

[22] Currie to Wellcome, 3 Aug. 1903, File 3C, Box 42 miscellaneous correspondence 1903, WA.

[23] See e.g. BW&Co to J. A. Atkinson, 29 Jan. 1904, GWGA: LB25, 584–5.

[24] Correspondence in GWGA: LB15–26 with J. A. Atkinson, BW&Co's agent in the Middle East and Egypt, gives details of this business.

assistance to the officers of health and to the clinics of the civil and military hospitals.[25]

This was a broad mandate indeed. These were to be teaching laboratories because of their location in a school; economic development laboratories that would help to make the colonial enterprise profitable; public health laboratories that monitored food standards and sanitation; forensic laboratories (though Wellcome's fascination with poison seems a piece of imperial paranoia, born perhaps of stories of African witchcraft); and medical research laboratories. This was a classic, if expansive, statement of Chamberlain era constructive imperialism, in which colonial development would be achieved through the creation of infrastructure that would attract investors, and through research.[26] The systematic application of scientific research would transform the condition of Sudan,[27] achieving Wellcome's imperial vision: 'All central Africa is going to be made perfectly habitable for the white man. Its agricultural, industrial, and commercial resources will become available. The Niles and their tributaries will teem with the commerce of a numerous and happy people.'[28]

Wellcome contributed money, ideas, and considerable personal effort to the Khartoum laboratories. He worked with his own scientist employees to design, painstakingly, the most modern of tropical laboratories, complete with wood specially seasoned to withstand the hot climate, and sat on the committee that chose Dr Andrew Balfour to be the new institution's first director.[29] While Balfour trained at the London School of Tropical Medicine from 15 October to 14 November 1902 at Egyptian government expense,[30] Wellcome acted the role of

[25] Wellcome to Wingate, 28 Sept. 1901, GMC Minutebook, SAD 572/5/61–2.

[26] On the role of science in colonial development, see Michael Worboys, 'The Imperial Institute: The State and the Development of the Natural Resources of the Colonial Empire, 1887–1923', in John M. MacKenzie (ed.), *Imperialism and the Natural World* (Manchester: Manchester University Press, 1990), 164–86; Worboys, 'Science'; Robert V. Kubicek, *The Administration of Imperialism: Joseph Chamberlain at the Colonial Office* (Durham, NC: Duke University Press, 1969).

[27] For similar attitudes in India and Malaya, see Roy M. MacLeod, 'Scientific Advice for British India: Imperial Perceptions and Administrative Goals, 1898–1923', *Modern Asian Studies*, 9 (1975), 355–6; Manderson, *Sickness and the State*, 9–10.

[28] Quoted in 'In Search of Microbes', *Daily Mail*, 25 Sept. 1906, SAD 759/12/10.

[29] The other two members of the search committee were Colonel R. H. Penton, PMO of the Egyptian Army, and Dr Noel Paton, the eminent Edinburgh physiologist. See correspondence in GWGA: LB19, 571–2, 581, 726, 745, 810, 812; Wellcome to Currie, 28 Aug. 1902, GWGA: LB6, 171–2. On outfitting the laboratories, see correspondence in Files 5–8, Box 40 miscellaneous correspondence 1901–1902, WA.

[30] Findlay to Marquess of Lansdowne, 4 Jan. 1903, FO 78/5301, Public Record Office, London.

consummate patron to the young doctor, introducing him to useful contacts such as the editor of the *Lancet*.[31] These introductions culminated in
a widely publicized farewell dinner held in Balfour's honour on 8 December, with seventy-eight of London's most eminent medical and scientific
men in attendance.[32]

Wellcome's influence continued to be felt once Balfour arrived in
Khartoum and, joined by laboratory assistant John Newlove, opened the
laboratories in seven rooms on the second floor of Gordon College. The
installation of equipment kept the patron in touch with the early development of the laboratories: he had agreed to make good all breakages and to
consider other equipment requests. Wellcome's attention meant that the
efficiency of, and the price reductions available to, his firm's bureaucracy
were put at Balfour's disposal, allowing the director in some measure to
by-pass a Sudan government that was underfunded and more preoccupied with pacification than with regularized administration.[33] When most
of the initial equipment was seriously damaged by a fire that broke out in
the bacteriological laboratory on 21 May 1908, Wellcome promptly
donated a whole new outfit.[34]

Wellcome determined the structure of the laboratories and his patron-
age provided them with equipment, services, and a mandate. His decision
to locate the laboratories in Gordon College meant that the director of
education, James Currie, was in administrative charge, but his status as a
well-meaning layman meant that Balfour set his own agenda. This administrative situation allowed the laboratories to develop a firm identity as the
central organization for research of all kinds, institutionally independent
of the practical work of any related, applied government department, such
as the civil medical department that opened in 1904. The backing of their
patron also signalled the laboratories' apartness: Wellcome's ongoing involvement was encouraged by his warm relationship with Balfour and was
officially secured in 1905 when he joined the executive committee of the
Gordon College trust fund.[35]

---

[31] Wellcome to Thomas Wakley, 12 Nov. 1902, File 22W, Box 41 miscellaneous correspondence 1902, WA.
[32] 'Gordon Memorial College, Khartum', *The Times*, 9 Dec. 1902; *Daily Chronicle*, 9 Dec.
1902; 'Gordon Memorial College at Khartoum . . .', SAD 724/14/4; 'Dinner to Dr.
Andrew Balfour . . .', *Journal of Tropical Medicine*, 15 Dec. 1902, 390–1.
[33] See e.g. Bright to Balfour, 20 Jan. 1905, GWGA: LB8, 305–6.
[34] *Third RWRL*, 24–5.
[35] Minutes of the meeting of the trustees and executive committee of the GMC, 15 Dec.
1905, GMC Minutebook, SAD 572/5/67.

## ANDREW BALFOUR AND THE
## RELEVANCE OF RESEARCH

Working himself mercilessly, Andrew Balfour applied his wide-ranging abilities to establishing the relevance of the new laboratories to most activities of the colonial state: to making research central to a variety of different practices.[36] He did this by realizing Wellcome's vision, making public health and sanitation, economic development, and specimen collection the three main areas of WRL work, and with Wellcome's assistance, winning international fame for the laboratories through the publication of institutional reports.

In her study of the Hong Kong bacteriological laboratory, Molly Sutphen has examined the process by which clinicians agreed to work through the laboratory. She argues that trust was crucial to the establishment of collaboration between clinicians and laboratory scientists and that the development of such trust depended heavily on the character and respectability of the laboratory researcher.[37] Following this analysis, the success of the WRL depended largely on Balfour's professional and personal credibility among the small group of doctors and the larger community of European officials in Khartoum. They had every reason to have confidence in him. Balfour held numerous qualifications in medicine (MB, CM, MD) and public health (DPH, BSc) from the Universities of Edinburgh and Cambridge, and had received the gold medal for his MD thesis. His time at the London School of Tropical Medicine, and Wellcome, had secured him connections amongst the London medical elite. For those concerned with character, Balfour was educated at George Watson's College, one of Edinburgh's leading public schools; he played rugby for Edinburgh, Cambridge, and Scotland; he had received the Queen's medal with three clasps for his service as a civil surgeon during the South African War; and he was a witty, personable, dedicated man. Balfour had attended the right schools, excelled at sport, and fought for his country.

These personal and professional characteristics helped Balfour to foster warm relations with many of the doctors in Sudan. He involved them in

---

[36] Charles Nicolle, director of the Pasteur Institute of Tunis from 1902, was engaged in a similar enterprise, fostering connections between his institute and local doctors, hospitals, and the colonial government, in part through his involvement in a wide range of public health projects (Pelis, 'Pasteur's Imperial Missionary', 14, 54–61).

[37] Molly Sutphen, 'Culturing Trust: Practitioners, Laboratory Medicine, and the Importance of Character in Hong Kong, 1902–1914', unpublished paper, Mar. 1997.

the WRL project by allowing them to use the laboratory facilities for their own research and analyses, by publishing their articles in the *Reports of the Wellcome Research Laboratories*, and by participating in and equipping the Sleeping Sickness and Kala-Azar Commissions that they staffed. Doctors responded by providing Balfour with access to clinical cases in their care, sending in specimens of blood, urine, faeces, and tissue from patients for analysis, and helping to build up the WRL museum with donations of pathological material, insects, and photographs.[38] Not everyone was charmed. J. B. Christopherson, product of Cambridge and St Bartholomew's Hospital, holder of the most elite English medical qualifications on offer, privately considered Balfour an ambitious, 'canny' Scot, whom he thought 'bent on dragging me down by fair means or foul' and whom he blamed for the allegations of professional misconduct that led to his removal as director of the medical department on 1 January 1909.[39] Balfour's comment in 1911 that 'we need more facilities for seeing cases, though, so far as the Military Hospital in Khartoum goes, these are most generously afforded' suggests that Christopherson, in his new capacity as director of the Khartoum and Omdurman civil hospitals, denied the laboratories access to cases under his charge.[40] Such an interpretation accords with the view, expressed decades later, that 'In the early history of the laboratories, medical research was considerably handicapped by the lack of cooperation between the Sudan Medical Service and the bacteriological section'.[41] It is also consistent with the tenor of inter-war debates about the relationship between research and practice, discussed below.

But if the rift between Balfour and Christopherson handicapped medical research, it did not cripple the operation of the laboratories generally, as Balfour gathered a wide range of functions to them. His assumption of the post of MOH for Khartoum in 1904 meant that the sanitary reform of the capital occurred through the laboratory, and that despite the formal independence of his two posts, his achievements in one capacity enhanced his reputation in the other. Following Ross's model for malaria eradication, Balfour established mosquito brigades, which, supported by laboratory analyses of pupae and larvae and testing of larvicides, had practically

---

[38] *RWRL*, 9, 11; *Second RWRL*, 11–12; *Third RWRL*, 22; *Fourth RWTRL*, vol. A, 23–4.

[39] Quotes from Christopherson to Sir Said Pasha Shoucair, [1908], SAD 494/11/2–7. See also *SGG*, no. 147, 1 Jan. 1909, 2; P. R. Phipps, Private Secretary to Wingate, 11 June 1908, SAD 282/6/41–2.

[40] *Fourth RWTRL*, vol. A, 23.

[41] Archibald, 'A Note on the Future Organization of the Wellcome Tropical Research Laboratories', 7 Feb. 1934, p. 254, CIVSEC 1/55/152.

abolished anophelines and the risk of malaria infection from Khartoum by 1905–6.[42] The chemical section, which began serious work with the appointment of Dr William Beam as chemist in October 1904, performed tests on milk, foodstuffs, and water which played a crucial role in the establishment, inspection, and maintenance of health and trade standards in Khartoum.[43] As WRL director, Balfour could provide the facilities for the laboratory tests that allowed him to set high sanitary standards as MOH. Some, such as the Khartoum province governor and the director of the public works department, objected to the cost and inconvenience of Balfour's sanitary zeal: his insistence on rigorous chemical and bacteriological testing, for example, substantially delayed the laying on of Khartoum's new piped water supply in 1907–9. But Balfour's good relationship with Governor-General Wingate meant that he usually prevailed in inter-departmental confrontations.[44] While Balfour often complained that 'routine work'—diagnostic and public health analyses—infringed on research time, he recognized that routine tests often grew into research projects, as with the water supply, and that increased demand for laboratory services was one measure of the WRL's success:[45] the growing number of routine tests showed the increasing willingness of doctors and other officials to work through and with the laboratory.

The chemical and entomological sections worked primarily on economic problems. Entomologist Harold H. King, hired in 1906, spent most of his time in the field, studying the habits and distribution of, and seeking control methods for, pests of all kinds, including locusts, mosquitoes causing malaria at the Zeidab pump irrigation scheme, and the stem-borer and *Asal* fly that attacked Sudan's staple food crop, *dura*.[46] The chemical section conducted an extended investigation into the production and quality of gum arabic, Sudan's largest export, and by the early 1910s, was engaged in a preliminary soil study in the Gezira as part of planning for the proposed irrigation scheme.[47]

The scientific work conducted by the WRL under Balfour introduced some innovations in tropical laboratory technique but no major breakthroughs in scientific understanding. The bulk of the early research

[42] *RFACS 1905*, 119; *Second RWRL*, 18. See also Bell, 'Cleaning Up'.

[43] *Second RWRL*, 205–15; *Third RWRL*, 385–6.

[44] *Third RWRL*, 84–6; *RFACS 1908*, 562–3; Balfour to Wingate, 10 Jan. 1909, SAD 285/1/87, Wingate to Balfour, 11 Jan. 1909, SAD 285/2/5; Balfour to Wingate, 11 Jan. 1909, SAD 285/2/7.

[45] *RWRL*, 49; *Third RWRL*, 17; *Fourth RWTRL*, vol. B, 17–18.

[46] *Third RWRL*, 201–48; *Fourth RWTRL*, vol. B, 95–143.

[47] *Second RWRL*, 222–31; *Third RWRL*, 414–50; *Fourth RWTRL*, vol. B, 45–84.

conducted by the WRL consisted of pushing back the frontier of European knowledge about the previously unstudied territory of Sudan, by
gathering and distributing information about disease in humans, animals,
and plants, and their vectors, for the benefit of local doctors and administrators, and of the wider scientific community. Mosquitoes, biting flies,
and other insects were collected from the extreme periphery, studied in
Khartoum, and were then often sent back to Europe for classification by
experts there. It soon became clear that the central challenge of this work
was to maintain the controlled conditions required for the collection,
preservation, and study of specimens in the midst of uncontrolled nature.
The 1904–5 collecting trip to southern Sudan of Dr Sheffield Neave, first
holder of the travelling pathologist and naturalist post which Balfour
had persuaded Wellcome to fund, proved less than successful: hard travel
encroached on research days and the heat and insects made careful investigation extremely difficult. Neave was soon dismissed, but this episode
and his own experiences impressed upon Balfour the physical obstacles
to field research.[48] To effectively bring the laboratory into the field,
the WRL outfitted a floating laboratory in April 1907. Wellcome supplied
the scientific equipment, while the government provided the barge
and a steamer, christened the *Culex*, to pull it.[49] Through specimen collection and study, the WRL participated in the wider political project of
mapping, categorizing, and 'knowing' the newly conquered territory of
Sudan.

WRL definitions of Sudan as a natural environment were carried into
the international community by the four *Reports of the Wellcome Research
Laboratories* (*RWRL*; 1904, 1906, 1908, 1911). The wide dissemination of
the *Reports*—lavish volumes, complete with detailed drawings of insects
and photographic plates, dealing with comparatively obscure scientific
subjects—was due to Wellcome's marketing expertise. Wellcome eagerly
became Balfour's designer, administrator, and editor, applying all his
business genius for effective packaging to the books that had started as an
outgrowth of the modest reports Balfour submitted to the Gordon College
trustees. The full extent of Wellcome's involvement was never made clear
to the reader. Apparently concerned about the response of a British
medical community sceptical of alliances between science and commerce,

[48] Wellcome to Balfour, 17 June 1904, GWGA: LB7, 436; Wellcome to Wingate, 31 Aug.
1904, GWGA: LB8, 109–11; *Second RWRL*, 183–204; Wellcome to Balfour, 20 May 1905,
GWGA: LB8, 481; Wellcome to Balfour, 15 June 1905, GWGA: LB9, 54; Wellcome to
Currie, 15 June 1905, GWGA: LB9, 55.
[49] *Third RWRL*, 19; *Fourth RWTRL*, vol. A, 26.

he asked Balfour to remove from the introduction to the *Second RWRL* the statement that it had been prepared 'under the auspices of Mr Wellcome', explaining that 'The omission of these words will make the publication appear more like <u>what it is</u> viz the <u>independent report of the laboratories</u> through the Director.'[50]

The publication of each report was a public relations triumph. The first *RWRL* is exemplary. Two thousand copies were sent in late 1904 to a list of people compiled by Currie, Wingate, Balfour, and Wellcome. Recipients included politicians and government officials in Britain, the United States, and the colonies, tropical medical men and institutions, and businessmen.[51] Wellcome also sent copies to the medical, commercial, and popular press around Britain, the empire, and the world; a second print run of 600 had to be made to satisfy requests for copies.[52] The numerous published reviews were universally glowing. Many seized on Balfour's success in fighting malaria: 'They have killed 220,000 mosquitos!' exulted the *Western Mail*.[53] The beauty of the *Report*, the existence of the laboratories, and the accounts of highly scientific work defined the Sudan government as civilizing, benevolent, and progressive: according to *The Financier & Bullionist*, 'So excellent is the scientific work in hand that it requires a stretch of the imagination to realise that only a few years back Khartoum was one of the dark places of the earth and the abode of horrid cruelty.'[54] Wellcome and the Sudan government shared the cost of this first report and its distribution,[55] and it was a sound investment for all parties. The Sudan government received considerable public praise for its administration; the work of the WRL director and scientists was brought to the attention of all who mattered in tropical medicine; and the name of Henry Wellcome, of Burroughs Wellcome and Company, was sounded throughout the world as that of a benevolent

---

[50] Emphasis his. Wellcome to Balfour, 7 Mar. 1906, GWGA: LB32, 81–2. Wellcome's input was mostly aesthetic: he offered opinions on which artists to hire, the quality of drawings and photographs, and the choice of print type. There is no evidence that he challenged the content of papers, as he did in his own London laboratories, for example attempting to prevent Henry Dale's use of the word 'adrenalin' in a paper (Tansey, 'What's in a Name?').

[51] Wellcome to Balfour, 17 Aug. 1904, GWGA: LB8, 50; BW&Co per Bright to Wellcome, 5 Oct. 1904, GWGA: LB33, 27–9; Bright to Balfour, 4 Nov. 1904, GWGA: LB8, 194; BW&Co to Wellcome, 26 Nov. 1904, GWGA: LB33: 91–3; BW&Co to Wellcome, 30 Nov. 1904, GWGA: LB33: 94–8.

[52] BW&Co per Bright to Wellcome, 8 Feb. 1905, GWGA: LB33, 233.

[53] *Western Mail*, 24 Dec. 1904, SAD 724/14/6.

[54] *The Financier & Bullionist*, 10 Nov. 1904, SAD 724/14/6.

[55] Bright to Financial Secretary, 30 Dec. 1904, GWGA: LB8, 278; Wellcome to Balfour, 17 Aug. 1904, GWGA: LB8, 50.

imperial philanthropist, at a time of international expansion for his company.[56]

Always much more than a simple summary of the WRL's activities, but less than a full-fledged journal, the reports became an important means of involving the wider scientific community and Sudan government officials in the WRL's project. They featured articles discussing work done in the laboratories, such as the annual reports of the chemical and entomological sections, which would not have been published elsewhere, and reprinted articles by WRL bacteriologists originally published in the *British Medical Journal*, the *Lancet*, or the *Journal of Tropical Medicine*. They also included articles describing work not done by the WRL but with some connection to them. Detailed accounts of mosquito control and sanitary reform in Khartoum, written by Balfour as MOH, appeared in all four reports. British and European experts contributed descriptive articles about Sudanese insects and reptiles sent to them for analysis by the WRL. British military doctors wrote anthropological articles on Sudanese medical practices that greatly enhanced the appeal of the *Third RWRL*, the first to be offered to the public for sale.

The *Reports* represented Sudan as a land full of natural dangers such as biting and noxious insects, blood-sucking diptera, human, animal, and vegetal pests, tropical diseases, and primitive peoples, and simultaneously as a land full of natural resources such as the Nile, grain crops, gum arabic, and in some places, rich soil suited to cotton-growing. Implicit in these texts was the assumption that it was only through science that these dangers could be overcome and these resources exploited. Sudanese people were not usually the direct objects of classification in these *Reports* which, like the work of the laboratories, were much more focused on animals, insects, and crops.[57] But when the Carnegie Research Fund agreed to recognize the WRL as an eligible host institution for its fellows and neither a chemist nor a bacteriologist could be found, Balfour agreed to host anthropologist Dr A. MacTier Pirrie in 1906, 'for the more that

[56] Wellcome opened BW&Co associated houses in South Africa in 1902, Italy in 1905, Canada and the United States in 1906, China in 1908, Argentina in 1910, and India in 1912 (Gilbert Macdonald, *In Pursuit of Excellence* (London: The Wellcome Foundation, 1980), 29).

[57] This is in marked contrast to the Philippines where, Warwick Anderson has argued, the discourse generated by American laboratory medicine 'fabricated and rationalized images of the bodies of the colonized' (Warwick Anderson, '"Where Every Prospect Pleases and Only Man Is Vile": Laboratory Medicine as Colonial Discourse', *Critical Inquiry*, 18 (1992), 507.

is known concerning the natives of the Sudan the more enlightened and correct is the administration of their affairs likely to be'.[58] Pirrie's research, published posthumously in the *Third RWRL*, described men of Dinka, Shilluk, Burun, and other origin at the most basic level, by providing measurements of their heads, faces, noses, nostrils, and limbs. His research also provided the Sudan government with essential information about the physical location and the general condition of the little known Burun, whom he described as sheikhless, animal poor, infested with disease, particularly syphilis and smallpox, and addicted to *merissa*, a beer made from *dura*.[59]

Implicitly and explicitly, the anthropological articles about Sudanese medical practices contrasted the science of the colonizers described in the rest of the volume with the superstition of the colonized. In his article, 'Some Tribal Customs in their Relation to Medicine and Morals of the Nyam-Nyam and Gour People Inhabiting the Eastern Bahr-el-Ghazal', Dr R. G. Anderson commented that 'medical and surgical practices' among the 'savage' people of whom he wrote 'form as yet no exact science, and merge imperceptibly with the religious, social and moral usages of the community';[60] the unspoken comparison was with Western medicine, where such imperceptible mergings obviously did not occur. Sudanese also figured in the *Reports* as WRL employees. Balfour declared in 1906 that Sudanese laboratory assistants had 'so far proved to be broken reeds. They cannot be trusted beyond the bottle-washing stage.'[61] Two years later, he was reporting that the 'chief native laboratory attendant' could 'now be trusted to make excellent blood films and attend to the sterilisation of bacteriological media'. He went on to relate that this man used to be 'one of the fighting Dervishes of Kordofan, while the man who keeps the museum clean, served in the ranks of the Khalifa at the battle of Omdurman'.[62] Through articles and anecdotes such as these, the *Reports* defined colonial rule in Sudan—to its rulers and to the wider public—as the project of rescuing a superstitious, devastated land through Western science.

The supplements to the *Third* and *Fourth Reports*, *Review of Some of the Recent Advances in Tropical Medicine* and *Second Review* . . . , showed a concern to assist with practice. They emerged from Balfour's desire to produce something 'more of an educative nature', aimed particularly at

---

[58] *Third RWRL*, 18.     [59] Ibid. 325–75.
[60] *Fourth RWTRL*, vol. B, 239.     [61] *Second RWRL*, 12.
[62] *Third RWRL*, 16.

medical and veterinary officers in Sudan who did not have the time or the facilities to keep up with the latest developments in tropical research.[63] With Wellcome's approval and assistance, Balfour started work on a paper and in typical fashion ended up with a thick tome of eighty-seven entries over 251 pages.[64] Here again the WRL was establishing its usefulness to doctors in Sudan and around the world.

Balfour's resignation on account of his health in 1913 did not result in any change of status for the WTRL,[65] but his departure did signal the end of Wellcome's intimate involvement with the laboratories, probably because much of his interest had been sustained by his relationship with Balfour, whom he admired as a hard-working, like-minded visionary; indeed, Balfour returned to London to work for Wellcome, as the founding director of the Wellcome Bureau of Scientific Research. Moreover, Wellcome had become absorbed in his archaeological dig at Jebel Moya, Sudan; criticism from London and from the Sudan government in 1912 regarding Wellcome's alleged mistreatment of his workers there may have dampened his enthusiasm for the laboratories.[66] Balfour's contributions had been to public health and to administration, rather than to pure science. Under his direction, the WTRL had literally taken the laboratory out into the field. Through their sanitary, economic development, and specimen collection work, and their publications, the WTRL achieved international recognition and established the value of laboratory science to colonial administration. By 1913, the laboratories boasted a scientific staff of nine men, five in the bacteriological section. As Balfour wrote in 1911:

We have already grown from small beginnings to a respectable stature, are, I think, secure against extinction, and, so long as we proceed on practical lines which have a bearing on the development and progress of the country, should not fail to receive that support and consideration which the magnitude, scope and importance of the work that now falls to our share amply justifies.[67]

---

[63] Quote from Balfour to Wellcome, 15 Aug. 1907, GWGA: HSW/Friends/Balfour 1; Balfour and R. G. Archibald, *Review*, 6.

[64] Wellcome to Balfour, 17 Aug. 1907, GWGA: HSW/Friends/Balfour 1.

[65] Wingate to Balfour, 27 Mar. 1913, SAD 185/3/111; Wingate to Balfour, 29 Nov. 1913, SAD 188/2/168. Rhodes James (*Wellcome*, 398) is wrong to maintain that Wellcome handed over control of the WTRL to the Sudan government in 1913.

[66] On these allegations, see Rhodes James, *Wellcome*, 319–20; Wellcome to Wingate, 18 May 1912, SAD 181/2/167–8; Slatin to Wingate, 2 Mar. 1913, SAD 185/3/92–6; Currie to Wingate, 10 Mar. 1913, SAD 185/3/48; Wingate to Slatin, 3 Apr. 1913, SAD 186/1/59; Wingate to Currie, 4 Apr. 1913, SAD 186/1/61.

[67] *Fourth RWTRL*, vol. B, 22.

While Balfour's successor, Albert Chalmers (1913–20), also had numerous qualifications and a broad set of interests,[68] he immediately
reoriented the work of the bacteriological section to human disease, marking a retreat from the eclecticism of the Balfour years and the start of a
focused medical research programme.[69] But the WTRL under Chalmers
was defined above all by the choices made within the constraints provided
by the First World War: here we see the extent to which limitations on
personnel and supplies could influence research agendas, resulting in this
case in a focus on major epidemic disease, immediately necessary routine
analysis, and local agricultural problems.

With its supplies of reagents from Europe cut off by the war, the
chemical section essentially shut down its research function, limited to a
few hundred routine analyses of food, water, and milk per year.[70] While
the chemical section also experienced staffing difficulties, it was in the
bacteriological section that reductions in personnel were felt most acutely.
The medical researcher's skills were vital to modern warfare. Chalmers
faced substantial pressure from Wingate and Balfour, now a Lieutenant-
Colonel who needed bacteriologists in the Dardanelles, not to hamper the
war effort by recalling three of his bacteriological staff, two of whom were
members of the Royal Army Medical Corps. When in 1915 his remaining
staff, unsurprisingly, fell ill, Chalmers was left running the section
singlehandedly.[71] With a rapidly growing number of routine tests,
Chalmers declared that he was restricting research work to urgent diseases
occurring in Sudan,[72] which included cerebrospinal meningitis, enteric-
like fevers, and dysentery; though enthusiasm for vaccine therapy had
started to wane in Britain before the war,[73] vaccine development was an
essential part of this work. Studies were however made, often of single

[68]  Albert J. Chalmers: born 1870. MB, ChB Victoria 1890; MRCS 1891; FRCS 1895;
MD (gold medal) Victoria 1893; MD Liverpool 1905; DPH Cambridge 1905. West African
Medical Service 1897–1901; Ashanti Field Force (mentioned in despatches, medal and
clasp). Registrar, later lecturer in pathology and animal parasitology, Colombo Medical
College, Ceylon 1901–12. Pellagra Commission 1912–13. Author, with Aldo Castellani, of *A
Manual of Tropical Medicine* (1910). Director, WTRL 1913–20. Died 1920.

[69]  *GMCRA 1912*, 24–5; *GMCRA 1913*, 20–1.

[70]  *GMCRA 1915*, 18; *GMCRA 1916*, 18; *GMCRA 1917*, 12, 15; *GMCRA 1918*, 21.

[71]  Chalmers to Wingate, 23 June 1915, SAD 195/4/239–45; Wingate to Chalmers, 26
June 1915, SAD 195/4/263–4; Chalmers to Wingate, 3 July 1915, SAD 196/1/95; Balfour
to Wingate, 18 Sept. 1915, SAD 196/3/219; Wingate to Balfour, 6 Oct. 1915, SAD 197/1/
48–9; Wingate to Chalmers, 6 Oct. 1915, SAD 197/1/56–7.

[72]  *GMCRA 1915*, 17.

[73]  Michael Worboys, 'Vaccine Therapy and Laboratory Medicine in Edwardian Britain',
in John V. Pickstone (ed.), *Medical Innovations in Historical Perspective* (London: Macmillan,
1992), 101–3.

cases, of non-urgent diseases, such as mycetoma and skin diseases, and non-tropical diseases, such as heart disease and a scarlet fever-like condition, probably because the availability of cases at local hospitals meant that they could be clinically investigated, at a superficial level, with few resources. Despite the enormous strain on Chalmers, the bacteriological section found ways of continuing research, producing ten European journal articles a year.[74] Chalmers continued to serve as one of the editors of the *Journal of Tropical Medicine and Hygiene* and fostered contacts with universities around the world, helping the WTRL to maintain an international presence during the war.[75]

The most significant development for the long term was in the entomological section, which concentrated on safeguarding the food supply by killing locusts and other pests, and on studying and controlling cotton pests. Local conditions had always been the primary influence on the work of the entomological section, but it was during the war that the close links between entomological research and agricultural practice started to be institutionalized. Rather than publishing in European journals (though such publication resumed to some extent in the 1920s), the entomological section issued practical circulars or bulletins to lay people printed in English and/or Arabic during the war.[76] Communicating with agricultural inspectors, political officials, and Sudanese cultivators had come to matter more than communicating with other scientists. Institutional recognition that the laboratory and the field needed to be drawn closer together came in the proposal for three out-stations near cotton-growing schemes, made in 1917, the same year that the first one opened at Tokar. Although the Tokar station closed in 1919 because of staffing shortages, the proposed number of field laboratories soon rose to nine.[77]

An increase in staff at the end of the war was not enough to compel a weary Chalmers to remain in Sudan. In 1919, there was still no sign of his being given the requisite £500 to publish a 'full' report along Balfour lines, an ongoing problem which had angered him to the point of considering resignation in 1915.[78] Chalmers finally did resign in 1920; his death that year while on holiday in India was, as the director of education wrote

[74] *GMCRA 1915*, 18–20; *GMCRA 1916*, 16–18; *GMCRA 1917*, 14–15; *GMCRA 1918*, 18–20.

[75] Chalmers to Wingate, 20 June 1917, SAD 164/8/125.

[76] *GMCRA 1915*, 21–2; *GMCRA 1916*, 18–19; *GMCRA 1917*, 15–16; *GMCRA 1918*, 21–2.

[77] *GMCRA 1917*, 15; *GMCRA 1919*, 24.

[78] Wingate to Balfour, 26 May 1915, SAD 195/2/168–9; *GMCRA 1913*, 18; *GMCRA 1916*, 5, 15; *GMCRA 1917*, 12; *GMCRA 1918*, 5, 17.

at the time, 'peculiarly tragic' and a sad epilogue to his difficult years at the WTRL.[79]

## DECENTRALIZATION AND THE PROBLEM OF AGRICULTURAL RESEARCH

Finding the optimal organization for research in light of growing demands from practitioners was the central problem for new director Major Robert G. Archibald, who had been with the WTRL since 1908.[80] The issue of organization had been raised before: in 1913, Currie had asked Balfour to rethink the structure of the WTRL in the light of planning for the Gezira scheme, hoping that the committee overseeing the Gezira loan would fund new laboratory facilities. Balfour's memoranda outlined a centralized institution on a grand scale, staffed by a range of new specialists who would give the WTRL an even broader research function. To ensure coordination of agricultural research, many entomologists would be jointly appointed to the WTRL and a proposed new agricultural school and institute.[81] But the loan committee turned down the request, and the pressures of war derailed the possibility of change.

The Gordon College report for 1920 declared that

The times when the prophets of research had to clamour for a hearing are happily over: there is no longer any hesitation on the part of Government departments or private enterprises to appeal for whatever assistance is forthcoming, and we have now to consider what new measures are necessary to meet our enlarged responsibilities.[82]

These new responsibilities were medical and agricultural. As explained in Chapter 2, wartime evacuation of military personnel forced a maturation of civil administration throughout the Sudan government. Under civilian

[79] *GMCRA 1919*, 18. On the memorialization of Chalmers in Britain, see Ahmed Awad Abdel-Hameed, 'The Wellcome Tropical Research Laboratories in Khartoum (1903–1934): An Experiment in Development', *Medical History*, 41 (1997), 47–9.

[80] Robert G. Archibald: born India 1880. MB, ChB Edinburgh 1902. RAMC 1906–19; seconded EAMC 1908–15, 1916–18. Pathology Prize, Army Medical School, 1906. DSO 1917. MD Edinburgh 1918. Knighted 1934. Royal Society Commission on Sleeping Sickness, Uganda, 1907. Pathologist WTRL 1908–20. Director, bacteriological laboratory at Mudros, Mediterranean Expeditionary Force 1915–16. Director, WTRL 1920–35. Adviser in Medical Research, Sudan 1935–6. Co-editor, with William Byam, of *The Practice of Medicine in the Tropics*, 3 vols. (London, 1921–3). Died 1953.

[81] Balfour to Director of Education, 9 Feb. 1913, SAD 185/2/76–81; Balfour to Director of Education, 11 Mar. 1913, SAD 185/3/50–6; E. R. Sawer, Principal Agricultural School to Currie, 9 Mar. 1913, SAD 183/3/46.

[82] *GMCRA 1920*, 20.

control and with expanded territorial jurisdiction in the inter-war period, the medical department would require more routine tests for its new civil hospitals. By 1921, the WTRL was performing approximately 5,000 routine bacteriological tests, mostly medical in nature, a number which would triple by 1934.[83] The medical department would also expect more of medical research. The bigger problem was agriculture. Plans for the Gezira scheme were moving ahead: despite precarious financing, the government and the Sudan Plantations Syndicate signed the Syndicate Agreement to govern future Gezira development in 1919. The Gezira scheme meant that the department of agriculture and forests, poorly organized and ineffective in the early years of the Condominium, became increasingly important during the 1920s,[84] as did agricultural research.

Archibald initially settled on a policy of devolution to field laboratories as a means of meeting the more ambitious aims of the colonial state, following proposals first made during Chalmers's tenure: decentralization would allocate staff efficiently and make for effective study of local conditions in a large country with limited railway communications.[85] Despite widespread support for the policy, financial constraints slowed and eventually stopped implementation altogether. Archibald sent a bacteriologist and a laboratory assistant to Wadi Halfa in 1921 to oversee the medical examination of labourers travelling to the Sennar Dam construction site and he sent a chemist to join the entomologist already at the Gezira Research Farm, opened at Wad Medani in 1918, for two years.[86] New entomological stations established to study cotton pests in the Gezira and at Gendettu, Berber province were declared an 'unqualified success' in 1923, but fell far short of the nine laboratories initially envisioned.[87] Of the three chemical laboratories proposed in 1920, two finally opened in 1924, one at Atbara to serve the department of railways and steamers by studying the priming of boilers and the calorific value of different fuels, and the second in the Gezira to investigate soil chemistry. The majority of the routine chemical tests performed by the WTRL in the inter-war period, which grew from 1,146 in 1920 to a peak of 58,724 in 1931, were soil analyses.[88]

[83] *GMCRA 1921*, 22; *GMCRA 1934*, 35.

[84] Daly, *Empire*, 214–15, 420.

[85] *GMCRA 1920*, 20; Lee Stack to Balfour, 2 June 1920, GWGA: HSW/Friends/Balfour 2, 19.

[86] *GMCRA 1921*, 21; *GMCRA 1920*, 20.

[87] *GMCRA 1923*, 26–7.

[88] *GMCRA 1920*, 22; *GMCRA 1924*, 25–6; *GMCRA 1931*, 34.

Devolution did not remedy the chaotic state of agricultural research organization and anxiety about the matter grew in the early 1920s with the opening of the Gezira scheme scheduled for 1925. The government had staked Sudan's economic future and its own ability to govern on the success of the Gezira; the scheme in turn could not survive without the scientific research that structured crop rotations and waterings, and controlled plant pests. The Gezira therefore required the attention of a range of WTRL scientists, still under the department of education: chemists analysed the content of the soil and its behaviour under perennial irrigation; entomologists studied the bionomics of cotton pests and proposed control measures; bacteriologists investigated bacterial plant diseases. The department of agriculture employed botanists, plant breeders, and other more applied agricultural personnel, while the Syndicate had its own field personnel. But no one government organization coordinated all agricultural research personnel or directed the agricultural research programme. The Gezira Research Farm was run jointly, and not entirely happily, by the Syndicate and the government.[89] Friction developed between those meant to be working together: Archibald erupted at both the Syndicate and the director of agriculture in 1921–2, when the entomologist whom he had seconded to the Gezira for cotton research considered leaving Sudan after being given inadequate housing at the Farm.[90]

The organization of this research mattered not only to the Sudan government and to the Syndicate, but to interest groups in Britain such as the British Cotton Growing Association (BCGA), founded in 1902, and the Empire Cotton Growing Corporation (ECGC), founded in 1921; the ECGC's first director was James Currie, Sudan's former director of education, who had first-hand knowledge of Sudan's research organization. When the failure of the Egyptian and American long staple cotton crops in 1909 highlighted the British textile industry's need for alternative sources of cotton, the BCGA promoted Sudan's potential publicly and invested in the Syndicate; it was joined by the ECGC in lobbying the British government for the loans that allowed the Gezira scheme to be built and to stay afloat.[91] With a vested interest in the survival of the

---

[89] Managing Director, Syndicate to Director of Agriculture, 23 Dec. 1922, File no. Per/21, National Medical Research Laboratories Library, Khartoum (NMRLL).

[90] Correspondence in File no. Per/21, NMRLL.

[91] 'Empire Cotton Growing Corporation 1921 to 1950', *The Empire Cotton Growing Corporation Review*, 28 (1951), 2–11; Arthur Gaitskell, *Gezira: A Story of Development in the Sudan* (London: Faber and Faber, 1959), 54–8, 62. The BCGA dealt primarily with commercial affairs, while the ECGC concentrated on the agricultural and scientific problems involved in cotton production.

scheme, these groups joined the colonial state as patrons of scientific research, helping to pay for research staff in Sudan and for outside scientific experts to visit Sudan and make recommendations for improving the country's agricultural research programme.[92]

Partially funded by the ECGC, the advisory visit of Sir John Russell, director of the Rothamsted Experimental Station and Dr H. Martin-Leake, principal of the Imperial College of Tropical Agriculture in Trinidad to Sudan in 1924, institutionalized outside input.[93] Russell's report spurred the establishment of a committee for the coordination of agricultural research in the Sudan, known as the London advisory committee, consisting of representatives from the Syndicate, the ECGC, and the Sudan government; British experts acted as technical advisers to the committee.[94] The committee was one means of giving all the relevant parties input into the research programme, and can also be seen as part of a wider trend in Britain and the empire towards the coordination of scientific research.[95] The Russell report prompted settlement of the Syndicate's role in research. The Syndicate was designated to run and staff the newly established Gezira seed farm. Although the Syndicate agreed to pay £3,000 per year towards its budget, the Gezira Research Farm came under exclusive government control.[96] This still meant, however, the ambiguity of dual control by the director of the WTRL and the director of agriculture.

Economic imperatives meant that agricultural research came to dominate the WTRL's agenda in the 1920s, but the pressures on medical research also grew. While there were no outside interest groups involved, discussion about the relationship between the medical department and the bacteriological section was ongoing. The medical committee established in 1924 (see Chapter 2) made the radical recommendation that the bacteriological section be taken over by the medical department.[97] This was strongly supported by Archibald, who argued that a bacteriological sec-

[92] 'Empire Cotton', 10.

[93] G. E. Schuster, Financial Secretary to Currie, 23 Feb. 1923, p. 19; Extract minutes of ECGC meeting 6 Nov. 1923, pp. 44–5; 'Memorandum of Terms of Reference for Sir John Russell', pp. 36–41, BNP 1/56/387, NRO.

[94] *Agricultural Research Work in the Sudan. Reports for the Season 1928–29 and the Programme for the Season 1929–30.*

[95] Roy M. MacLeod and E. Kay Andrews, 'The Committee of Civil Research: Scientific Advice for Economic Development 1925–30', *Minerva*, 7 (1969), 680–705.

[96] Macintyre [Managing Director of Syndicate] to Financial Secretary, 15 July 1924, p. 64; 'Note on Discussion Held at London Office, 29 Sept. 1924', pp. 66–8; F. Eckstein [Chairman of Syndicate] to Schuster, 8 Oct. 1924, pp. 69–70; Schuster to Eckstein, 15 Oct. 1924, pp. 71–3, BNP 1/56/387.

[97] 'The Committee's Recommendations with regard to Medical Research', [1924], pp. 3–4, CIVSEC 1/55/151.

tion independent of the medical department was unable to obtain the necessary cooperation for systematic research, and unable to create sufficient understanding between the clinician and the laboratory worker.[98] But the committee's recommendations were only partially implemented. While the WTRL did not become part of the new Sudan medical service, capital expenditures from the Stack Indemnity Fund that would enable the two organizations to coordinate their work more carefully were made. Most significantly, most of the bacteriological section moved to the new Stack Medical Research Laboratories, located in the grounds of Khartoum Civil Hospital, in October 1928. The move freed up space at the Gordon College site and made it easier for WTRL bacteriological staff to teach at the neighbouring Kitchener School of Medicine, to perform postmortems at the civil hospital, and to see patients.[99] The medical service director's 1928 proposal that medical research and medical practice be united when Archibald retired was not, however, simply accepted.[100] By 1929, Archibald had reversed his 1924 position. Apparently still having difficulty in securing cooperation for research initiatives, he recommended that all research, agricultural and medical, should be placed under one organization: a non-technical secretariat with 'administrative powers to obtain departmental cooperation necessary for the research worker', 'divorced from departmental control'. If research was controlled by departments, research would be confined to 'water-tight compartments' and researchers would find 'their interests often rendered subservient to a majority representing the non-technical side of a department'.[101]

This discussion about research organization resurfaced in 1928 in large part because of the possibility of Archibald's retirement. No one expected to find a successor who could, as Archibald had done, hold the diverging medical and agricultural sides of the WTRL together through the breadth of his scientific interests; a 'centrifugal tendency' was feared.[102] Representatives of outside capital urged action: James Currie recommended an 'overhaul' for the department of agriculture and the procurement of outside advice.[103] The central problem, as the financial secretary recognized, was to ensure 'due co-operation between the research worker

---

[98] Archibald, 'Medical Research in the Sudan', 8 May 1924, pp. 5–7, CIVSEC 1/55/151.

[99] The Lee Stack Indemnity Fund, Third Annual Report for the Year 1929, Annex to *RFACS 1929*, 156; *GMCRA 1925*, 21; *ARED 1928*, 61.

[100] Atkey to J. G. Matthew, SEH, 13 Mar. 1928, pp. 1–2, CIVSEC 1/55/151.

[101] Emphasis his. Archibald to A. J. C. Huddleston, 24 Apr. 1929, pp. 22–3, CIVSEC 1/55/151.

[102] Matthew, 'Note on Research Organization', 14 May 1929, p. 35, CIVSEC 1/55/151.

[103] Extract from Currie to Matthew, 15 Apr. 1929, p. 31, CIVSEC 1/55/151.

and the practical man'.[104] Invited to offer an outside expert opinion, Sir John Farmer, professor of botany at Imperial College, London, visited Sudan during the winter of 1929–30. Farmer backed Archibald in support of a status quo that was producing high-quality results. Delineating the differences between scientists and practical men, he argued that the central organization provided real value and efficiency in giving scientists freedom from the pressure to produce quick results and a 'sense of security from interruption in [their] work'; in fostering 'the freshness of viewpoint and the relief from stagnation' central to successful research; and in creating a scientific community in which scientists worked with, and were supervised by, other scientific men.[105]

While Farmer opposed departmental control of research, he did concede the existence of administrative problems with Gezira research. He therefore recommended the creation of a Gezira Research Corps, to which relevant personnel would be seconded, and whose head would coordinate Gezira research in part by liaising with the WTRL and the department of agriculture, and the creation of new organizational and policy committees.[106] To preserve the distinctiveness of researchers and practitioners, Farmer recommended that technicians or routine workers be transferred to departments, as their work was 'not <u>scientific research</u>' but sought 'a short and quick guide to practice';[107] scientists, such as the plant physiologist and botanist, whose work was 'more remote from the <u>direct</u> practice of agriculture' should be transferred to the WTRL, where they would benefit from a less utilitarian environment.[108] Farmer's much briefer recommendations about the relationship between the medical service and the bacteriological section followed the same model, with the government bacteriologist acting as liaison between the WTRL and the SMS, while other bacteriologists and laboratory assistants were seconded to the medical service.[109]

Far from solving the problem, the Farmer report only intensified the debate. The secretary for education and health stressed the importance of the difference in outlook between scientific and practical men and considered that very strong arguments would be needed to change the

---

[104] [Huddleston], 'Research Organization', 30 Apr. 1929, p. 25, CIVSEC 1/55/151.

[105] J. Farmer, '*Report* On the Organization of Research in connection with the Departments and Services of the Sudan Government, with recommendations as to the future Organization of such Research', 18 Feb. 1930, pp. 3–4, CIVSEC 1/55/151.

[106] Ibid. 9–10, 15–16, 21–4.

[107] Emphasis his. Ibid. 16.

[108] Emphasis his. Ibid. 13.

[109] Ibid. 25–30.

status quo, given the 'world-wide reputation' of the WTRL: 'Why alter a good show merely because departments would naturally like their own research staff?'[110] The director of the SMS argued that only an efficient, specialist, medical laboratory service that was under medical service control would produce the kind of working conditions for bacteriologists, and the kind of the research, that Farmer favoured. To Farmer's claim that bacteriologists would prefer to form part of a larger scientific organization, he replied that the bond between a medical bacteriologist and a practising doctor, who shared the experience of scientific, hospital training and collaborated daily on patients and research, was much stronger than the bond between a medical bacteriologist and a non-medical laboratory scientist, such as a soil chemist.[111] Some of the researchers shared this view. By June 1930, the three assistant bacteriologists preferred transfer to the medical service when Archibald left, 'though a year or two ago the prospect of such a transfer was uncongenial to them'; they seem to have feared that in future the WTRL director and even the government bacteriologist might not be medical men.[112]

But medical research faded into the background: for most senior officials, research organization meant agricultural research organization. In the course of discussion over how to reorganize Gezira research, the director of agriculture, W. A. Davie, and his predecessor argued vehemently for department of agriculture control over agricultural research. They were certain that only this organization could maintain 'the closest relationship' between agricultural research and agricultural practice, and bridge the gap between scientific results and their application; they argued that farming experiments could not be relegated to the background if the Gezira scheme was to survive.[113] The mistrust between Archibald and Davie was evident. The agreement struck on Gezira research organization in early May 1930 fell apart when Davie wrote that this involved transferring all relevant junior WTRL staff to the Gezira Research Farm.[114] Archibald would only support secondment, for transfer created a dangerous precedent for senior staff: 'in fact I am

---

[110]   Matthew to Huddleston, 20 Mar. 1930, p. 84, CIVSEC 1/55/151.
[111]   Atkey, 'Note on Sir John Farmer's Report in so far as it Concerns the Medical Service', 10 Apr. 1930, pp. 87–95, CIVSEC 1/55/151.
[112]   J. G. Matthew to Sir Andrew Balfour, 14 June 1930, p. 108, CIVSEC 1/55/151.
[113]   W. A. Davie to Financial Secretary, 4 Apr. 1930, pp. 151–2; Davie to Huddleston, 22 July 1930, pp. 123–4; Davie to Financial Secretary, 17 Sept. 1930, pp. 149–50, CIVSEC 1/55/151.
[114]   Davie to Huddleston, 7 May 1930, p. 98; Davie to Huddleston, 14 May 1930, pp. 101–2, CIVSEC 1/55/151.

nervous of a situation in which the thin edge of the Agricultural wedge is already apparent.'[115]

After months of debate, a compromise organization was introduced over the strenuous objections of the department of agriculture, and a system that depended on one exceptional personality was replaced by another that did exactly the same thing. M. A. Bailey, an ECGC-funded plant breeder, respected as both a scientific and a practical man, would head a new Gezira agricultural research service, responsible only to an agricultural research policy committee.[116] Staff would either be recruited directly to this new service or be seconded from the WTRL or the department of agriculture; at the insistence of Archibald and Bailey, all files of seconded personnel would stay with their home departments, to protect scientists' promotion opportunities and to prevent their resignations. To ensure that scientists served under scientific men, the British scientific personnel from the department of agriculture, and all relevant Sudanese staff from the department of agriculture, would be transferred to the WTRL.[117] It seemed that this new plan safeguarded the working conditions of scientists and supported the researchers' conception of the organizational relationship between research and practice. But not all researchers were satisfied. Assistant entomologist H. B. Johnston argued that the new plan was unlikely to work 'either efficiently or economically': entomologists seconded to the Gezira would be cut off from their chief and the post of government entomologist would be devalued, for he would lose staff and control over cotton research.[118] Recognizing that the entomologists were in a 'jumpy state', J. G. Matthew, secretary for education and health, recommended reassuring them and the chemists by making it clear that the government entomologist and the government chemist would continue to shape the Gezira research programme.[119] This seems

[115] Archibald to Financial Secretary through SEH, 20 May 1930, p. 99, CIVSEC 1/55/151.

[116] This committee consisted of the financial secretary as president, the SEH, the director of agriculture, and the director of the WTRL; a representative of the Syndicate was either to be a member or to attend meetings.

[117] 'Gezira Agricultural Research Organization', 17 Sept. 1930, pp. 147–8; see also M. A. Bailey to Huddleston, 4 July 1930, pp. 114–15; J. L. Maffey, Governor-General to High Commissioner, Cairo, 15 Oct. 1930, pp. 161–3, CIVSEC 1/55/151; 'Agricultural Research Organization. Arrangements for the initiation, execution and coordination of Research work', [1930], pp. 170–93; 'Gezira Agricultural Research Service', 21 Mar. 1931, pp. 227–30, CIVSEC 1/55/152.

[118] H. B. Johnston, 'Note on the Proposed Organization of Agricultural Research', [1930], pp. 199–203, CIVSEC 1/55/152.

[119] Matthew to Huddleston, 1 Jan. 1931, p. 205, CIVSEC 1/55/152.

to have worked: the new plan took effect without incident on 1 April 1931.

## THE DISMANTLING OF WTRL AND
## ITS CONSEQUENCES

When Archibald's retirement really became imminent in late 1933, he abandoned his hard-fought position and consented to the break-up of the WTRL organization.[120] The Wellcome Tropical Research Laboratories ceased to exist as such on 1 April 1935.[121] The bacteriological section was transferred to the medical service. The entomological and chemical sections were transferred to the Gezira agricultural research service in Wad Medani, which took over responsibility for all agricultural research in Sudan and was formally affiliated with the department of agriculture. On the recommendation of the government chemist and entomologist, who to some extent continued to back the status quo,[122] a small non-agricultural part of the chemical section remained in Khartoum under the name of the Wellcome Chemical Laboratories to perform analytical work for various departments, and a medical entomology sub-section was created and seconded to the medical service. Initially placed under the agricultural research department, both of these sections were transferred to the medical service in July 1939.[123] The problems envisioned, which three years earlier had been enough to stop any such proposals, were tackled with hardline stances. In the (now apparently unlikely) event that WTRL staff protested against the transfer to the department of agriculture, replacements would be found. Syndicate objections to the Gezira agricultural research service being used for non-Gezira research would not be accepted, since the Syndicate only paid 10 per cent of the Gezira research budget. It was now deemed unlikely that the director of agriculture would neglect the professional prospects of his new research staff.[124]

What had changed? The depression was the crucial turning point.

[120] Archibald, 'A Note on the Future Organization of the Wellcome Tropical Research Laboratories', 7 Feb. 1934, pp. 252–5, CIVSEC 1/55/152.
[121] J. A. Gillan, Civil Secretary to Controller, Agricultural Research Service, 19 Feb. 1935, p. 299, CIVSEC 1/55/152.
[122] Government Entomologist, 'Wellcome Tropical Research Laboratories', 3 Apr. 1934, pp. 259–62; Note by Government Chemist, [1934], pp. 263–5, CIVSEC 1/55/152.
[123] Reorganization details from 'Note of a Conversation at the Palace', 22 Dec. 1934, pp. 272–4; R. K. Winter to H. A. Van de Linde, 15 Mar. 1935, pp. 318–21, CIVSEC 1/55/152; *RSMS 1939*, 58, 71.
[124] 'Note of a Discussion at Erkowit on 28th April, 1934 on Research', pp. 267–9, CIVSEC 1/55/152.

Cotton yield in the Gezira collapsed in the early 1930s due to two cotton diseases, leaf curl and black arm. Although present in the late 1920s, neither disease caused much damage: early yields were strong and revenues high (see Table 4.1). This changed in 1929–30, when black arm flared up throughout the scheme, and then leaf curl set in. Yield plummeted and dropped further in 1930–1, even as scientists and practical officials alike, building on research from the 1920s, scrambled to find ways of controlling the diseases. The fact that more than a decade of agricultural research failed to prevent disease from devastating the scheme accounts for the intensity of the debate about agricultural research organization; the creation of the Gezira agricultural research service in 1931 was partly a response to these low yields.[125] Yield recovered in 1931–2, but the 1932–3 crop, sown according to the research-based recommendations of the government botanist, again failed.[126] From 1930, these low yields joined with falling world cotton prices to cripple government revenues. It became increasingly difficult to sell the crop at any price; tenants were unable to pay off their seasonal cultivation debts and the government's ability to service its Gezira loans and keep the scheme running came into doubt.[127]

The result was severe retrenchment at the WTRL as in all government departments. The Atbara chemical laboratory was closed in 1932. Suppression of posts, resignations, and retirements brought a 40 per cent reduction in European staff in the core three sections between 1930 and 1932, from twenty-eight to seventeen personnel.[128] Archibald was left with a much smaller establishment to defend. Moreover, the experience of the early 1930s demonstrated the importance of having a coherent agricultural research organization in the Gezira that was integrated with practice. By 1933, it was extremely unlikely that the WTRL staff seconded to the Gezira agricultural research service—25 per cent of the core three sections scientific personnel, 50 per cent of staff if the transferred agricultural scientists are included, nearly 70 per cent of total British and Sudanese WTRL personnel—would ever be withdrawn from agricultural research.[129] The handful of chemists and entomologists remaining in Khartoum worked primarily on agricultural and cotton-growing problems. The work of the bacteriological section had become increasingly medical

[125]  *RFACS 1931*, 10.
[126]  Gaitskell, *Gezira*, 146, 150–1.
[127]  Ibid. 142–4; Daly, *Empire*, 435–9.
[128]  *GMCRA 1930*; *GMCRA 1931*; *GMCRA 1932*; *Quarterly List*, 1930–2.
[129]  *Quarterly List*, 1 July 1933, p. 5; R. K. Winter to H. A. Van de Linde, 15 Mar. 1935, p. 319, CIVSEC 1/55/152.

over time, particularly since the building of the Stack laboratories; Archibald returned to his previous view that 'complete cooperation can only be attained by making this section an integral part of the Medical Service'.[130] In this context, there was much less of a rationale for a central, multi-disciplinary research institution. The fact that former WTRL scientists would work under scientific men—the assistant director for laboratory services at the medical service and the director of agricultural research at the department of agriculture—would have made the institutional subordination of research to practice more palatable to Archibald.

Dismemberment of the WTRL put agricultural research on the 'sound footing' that the ECGC and senior Sudan government officials had been seeking, but the changes, imparted to Henry Wellcome as a fait accompli by the Governor-General, 'enfuriated [him] to the point of rabies'; he took 'serious umbrage at the changes in the laboratory organization without prior consultation with the Governing Body of the Gordon College'.[131] Wellcome was particularly offended since he felt that his offer to construct a grand new WTRL building was still on the table.[132] Although he had never made the promised trip to Khartoum to consider construction sites, he had guided the prospective architect through his new Wellcome Research Institution in Euston Road, London and they had discussed rough sketches of the proposed building.[133] When Archibald reconsidered the offer in 1933, it did not seem particularly attractive: the maintenance costs were prohibitive and a new building in Khartoum seemed unnecessary with the consolidation of agricultural research in the Gezira.[134] But no firm decision was ever relayed to Wellcome. Warned that he might initiate legal action over the dismantling of the WTRL, a worried Sudan government consulted its legal secretary and was assured that Wellcome had no case.[135] The matter dropped, but Wellcome regarded the episode as a sour and unforgivable note on which

[130] Archibald, 'A Note on the Future Organization of the Wellcome Tropical Research Laboratories', 7 Feb. 1934, pp. 253–4, CIVSEC 1/55/152.
[131] G. S. Symes to Wellcome, 13 Mar. 1935, pp. 315–17; quotes from Currie to Symes, 6 Apr. 1935, p. 353A and Currie to Symes, 11 Apr. 1935, p. 353B, CIVSEC 1/55/152, respectively.
[132] *GMCRA 1929*, 13; Hudson Lyall to Wingate, 3 Apr. 1935, p. 353D, CIVSEC 1/55/152.
[133] Francis, 'The Wellcome Research Institution Euston Road', 19 July 1932, p. 15, CIVSEC 9/5/16.
[134] Archibald, 'Note on Sir Henry Wellcome's proposal to build new Laboratories in the Sudan', 17 June 1933, p. 16, CIVSEC 9/5/16.
[135] J. P. Gorman to R. K. Winter, SEH, 7 May 1935, pp. 365–6, CIVSEC 1/55/152.

to abruptly conclude his long association with Sudan. Although he named the Khartoum laboratories as a potential beneficiary in his will, his trustees declined to give their support when approached in 1938 because the Wellcome name and the central organization had lapsed.[136]

It is instructive to look at WTRL involvement in training and education to gauge the impact that the debates about organization, and the actual dismantling of the WTRL, had on the relationship between researchers and practitioners. The WTRL started to engage in the promotion of technical education, as Wellcome had intended, during the First World War and the inter-war period. Chalmers sat on the committee that planned and raised funds for the Kitchener School of Medicine; the director of the WTRL, the government chemist, and the government entomologist were made members of the School council.[137] When the School opened in 1924, staff from the WTRL bacteriological section lectured on physiology, pathology, and bacteriology, and did demonstration post-mortems at Khartoum Civil Hospital; chemists lectured in chemistry and physics; entomologists taught biology.[138] Physics, chemistry, and biology teaching laboratories were installed at Gordon College in 1925; by 1928, the lecturers in these subjects were a WTRL chemist and biologist, seconded to the College.[139] The WTRL profited from this scientific education: in 1928 for example, nine of the Gordon College science section graduates went to the Kitchener School; the WTRL hired the remaining three to work as laboratory assistants.[140] Despite disagreements about who should control research, researchers cooperated with the medical service to educate a group of Sudanese medical practitioners.

While the WTRL was in existence, laboratory attendants were trained at the request of the medical service director, starting in 1926. Although shorter than assistant medical officer training, this targeted the same group of people: hospital attendants, usually with some education, studied elementary laboratory methods at the WTRL.[141] They learned how to 'prepare and examine blood films for malaria, to examine for urinary and intestinal parasites, to carry out the various urinary tests, and other simple laboratory work' and were then posted to provincial hospitals and to quarantine stations.[142] The director of the WTRL undertook such train-

[136] Rhodes James, *Wellcome*, 352–3; Hall and Bembridge, *Physic and Philanthropy*, 35.
[137] *GMCRA 1923*, 10; *Report, Kitchener School of Medicine 1924–1925*, 7.
[138] *GMCRA 1927*, 31.
[139] *GMCRA 1925*, 15; *ARED 1928*, 15–16.
[140] *ARED 1928*, 22.
[141] *GMCRA 1926*, 36.        [142] *RSMS 1928*, 94.

ing as a means of reducing the burden of routine testing on the central laboratories and as a favour to his medical service counterpart. But as long as research was his primary concern, this training to enhance the operation of government hospitals was never his priority. By contrast, the medical service director and his assistant director for laboratory services, who took over this training after the demise of the WTRL, regarded the creation of hospital laboratories as essential in providing modern medical services to the country. Under the medical service, the programme was reorganized and institutionalized, lasting a minimum of four months, with an emphasis on clinical pathology and dealing with infected materials.[143] As Table 2.5 indicates, the number of laboratory attendants tripled between 1935 and 1940.

It was these kinds of subtle, if significant, changes that occurred when the WTRL was dismantled. The transition from the WTRL to department-run and department-affiliated research branches was primarily a change in structure. It did not mark the end of scientific research in Sudan, but rather an adjustment to the institutional relationship between research and practice. The takeover of the bacteriological section by the medical service did bring a narrowing in the content of bacteriological research: bacteriologists no longer worked on outbreaks of anthrax in conjunction with veterinary officials, or studied the bacteria that caused black arm disease of cotton, as they had in the 1920s. But if bacteriologists were redefined as solely medical researchers in 1935, reorganization did not drastically change the work most performed. They continued to study major epidemic and endemic disease, and to publish their findings in European journals, to perform routine tests, to produce vaccines, to teach medicine and science, and to adapt laboratory technique to the tropics. The boundary around medical research continued to encompass a wide range of activities. Where the mid-1930s marked a turning point in the research component of SMS disease campaigns, it was because, ironically, the demise of the WTRL meant that the skills of entomologists were for the first time systematically applied to the problems of human disease. The promise of Wellcome's initial vision of bacteriologists, chemists, and entomologists working together on all kinds of tropical problems had previously gone largely unfulfilled for medicine, as the chemical and entomological sections had become increasingly tied to and defined by agricultural research in the Gezira.

[143] *RSMS 1935*, 70, 85.

## CONCLUSION

Negotiating the boundary between research and practice was the defining problem for the WTRL throughout its existence. The circumstances of the WTRL's founding gave it institutional independence, but this did not mean that WTRL scientists pursued research projects irrelevant to the colonial administration. On the contrary: one of the main achievements of the WTRL under Balfour was persuading government officials that research laboratories offered services of value to the colonial enterprise. One could argue that this strategy of showing the relevance of research to, in particular, the practice of medicine and agriculture succeeded too well. Research had come to be considered such an integral part of the 'medical' and the 'agricultural' in Sudan that inter-war departments sought sustained support for their ambitious new projects and control over research personnel and planning. The resulting debates showed that 'scientific' and 'practical' men were highly mistrustful of one another and conceptualized the organizational relationship between research and practice in different, if shifting, ways. Just as the First World War had prompted devolution to field laboratories, the depression years, which brought the collapse of the cotton crop and government-wide retrenchment, proved decisive in determining the demise of the WTRL.

If, at least on the medical side, reorganization brought only minor changes to routine, research, and educational work, and if researchers and practitioners continued to work together productively in spite of organizational debate, we may ask why the organizational structure was so fiercely contested. It may of course be that there was more tension over working together than the available sources reveal. But the question still remains: why, at this time and in this place, did the location of the organizational boundaries between research and practice become so important? Personalities undoubtedly had a great deal to do with it, but the fact that similar debates about the organization and control of medical and agricultural research, pitting researcher against practitioner, were being rehearsed in Britain at the same time, suggests that something broader was going on.[144] In Sudan, the debates emerged from the growing reach of the colonial state and the increasing responsibilities being placed on research-

---

[144] Joan Austoker, 'Walter Morley Fletcher and the Origins of a Basic Biomedical Research Policy', 23–33; Linda Bryder, 'Public Health Research and the MRC', 67–70; Celia Petty, 'Primary Research and Public Health: The Prioritization of Nutrition Research in Inter-War Britain', 89–90, all in Austoker and Bryder (eds.), *Historical Perspectives*; Timothy DeJager, 'Pure Science and Practical Interests: The Origins of the Agricultural Research Council, 1930–1937', *Minerva*, 31 (1993), 125–50.

ers and practitioners alike. With their departments assuming ever greater responsibilities for the public health and economic welfare of the country in the inter-war period, the directors of the medical and the agricultural departments must have regarded their lack of formal control over vital research in their fields as a serious affront. For scientists, the WTRL provided local and international prestige; the ability to work for other scientists and therefore a self-identity that was unquestionably professional and scientific; and a multidisciplinary ideal, physically embodied in Archibald, to cling to as their work grew increasingly specialized along medical and agricultural lines.

It is important to note the distinctly colonial dimensions to this story. Preserving the WTRL was so important to scientists and political officials because, in a world where European scientists often looked down on research performed in colonial institutions, the WTRL had an established identity and a respected international reputation. The relative poverty of the colonial government meant that outside patrons, such as Wellcome and the British cotton industry, could have a substantial impact on the development of local institutions. The stakes in the debate over research organization escalated so dramatically because of the nature of the colonial economy, dependent on one cash crop grown in a massive irrigation scheme that was a partnership between private and public capital. How different members of the government and the Sudan Plantations Syndicate conceptualized the disease threats to that irrigation scheme, and mobilized to meet them, is the subject of the next chapter.

# 4

# Disease, Quarantine, and Racial Categories in the Gezira Irrigation Scheme

As the main site of outside investment in Sudan and as the colonial government's major attempt at socio-economic development, the Gezira irrigation scheme throws into bold relief the complicated relationships between medicine, capital, and the health of labour. The Gezira scheme's financial and political importance to the Sudan government—between 1925 and 1956, it accounted for more than half of the country's exports and at least half of direct government revenues[1]—meant that virtually all policy was directed towards ensuring its success. The need to protect the Gezira from disease infection dominated inter-war medical policy and medical research. Doctors and political officials alike knew that the opening of a massive irrigation scheme would bring epidemiological change, potentially threatening the ability of tenants and labourers to cultivate cotton. Accordingly, and in conjunction with the Sudan Plantations Syndicate, the Sudan medical service mounted its most ambitious programme of preventive medicine, aimed particularly at the two diseases most closely associated with the presence of stagnant water, malaria, and schistosomiasis, also known as bilharzia.[2]

This chapter does not attempt to give a full account of medical service

---

[1] O'Brien, 'Agricultural Labor', 82.

[2] Schistosomiasis is in our context two diseases: intestinal schistosomiasis, caused by the eggs of *Schistosoma mansoni* inhabiting the veins of the intestines, and urinary schistosomiasis, caused by the eggs of *Schistosoma haematobium* inhabiting the veins of the urinary tract. Robert Leiper established the transmission cycle during research in Egypt in 1914–16: through excretion, humans expel schistosomal ova which hatch into miracidia in water, where they penetrate into intermediate snail hosts; the snails later release cercariae into the water which infect people by boring directly into their skin. The severity of the disease is related to the number of worms carried in the body. Many people with schistosomiasis do not know that they have the disease: its main symptoms are blood in the urine or faeces, occasional diarrhoea, and cramps. Chronic schistosomiasis can however have severe effects on the internal organs and the circulatory system. See John Farley, *Bilharzia: A History of Imperial Tropical Medicine* (Cambridge: Cambridge University Press, 1991), 5–10, 68–70.

provision in the Gezira or to examine in detail the changing array of measures adopted to control malaria and schistosomiasis there.[3] Instead, it adopts a more thematic approach to make three arguments. After outlining the structure of the scheme and the kinds of social transformations that it wrought, I argue first that, consistent with a political economy of health interpretation, this massive colonial project brought considerable health costs, specifically in increased rates of malaria and schistosomiasis. My second argument is that due attention must be paid to medical factors in any analysis of medical policy implemented for a capitalist enterprise such as the Gezira. This may sound a mild, even trivial statement. But it is less so given the nature of much of the writing about medicine, health, and capitalism, which I discussed in Chapter 1.[4] Here I start by showing how medical factors—such as preconceptions about disease epidemiology and assessments of disease severity—structured the way in which doctors thought about controlling these two, comparatively similar, diseases. I then address the essential tension in medical policy for the Gezira: the tension between the need to protect the scheme from disease infection that would jeopardize its operation, and the need to keep the scheme operating cheaply and efficiently, which depended in particular on a free flow of cheap labour. I explore this tension by examining debates about the establishment of a quarantine station for Egyptian labourers at Wadi Halfa, the installation of a drainage system to assist with malaria prevention, and the operation of schistosomiasis quarantine stations for Westerners in White Nile province. As the emphasis on quarantines suggests, the medical service's embrace of a spatial conception of disease meant that this tension often boiled down to conflict between the public health need for a boundary impermeable to infection to be maintained around the scheme, and the economic need for any such boundary to be extremely porous, if it existed at all.

At times, these debates confirm common assumptions. Concerns about cost and interfering with the flow of labour did mean that measures to prevent disease recommended by doctors were not implemented, with damaging consequences. Some doctors did identify with the interests of the state and of capital so completely that they made medical decisions solely on the basis of labour policy. But the Gezira example also shows the

[3] On these topics, see Gruenbaum, 'Health Services'; Heather Bell, 'Medical Research and Medical Practice in the Anglo-Egyptian Sudan, 1899–1940', D.Phil. thesis (Oxford University, 1996), ch. 3; Gerald W. Hartwig, 'Schistosomiasis in the Sudan', in K. David Patterson and Gerald W. Hartwig, *Schistosomiasis in Twentieth Century Africa: Historical Studies on West Africa and Sudan* (Los Angeles: Crossroads Press, 1984), 40–58.

[4] See e.g. Doyal with Pennell, *Political Economy*; Turshen, *Political Ecology*.

perils of blindly generalizing about the relationship between medicine and capitalism. The lifting of the Westerner quarantines in the middle of the depression, when anxiety about labour supply was at its peak, is easy to dismiss as an example of labour needs overriding health concerns. In fact, doctors backed the move on medical, as well as economic grounds. The policy of settling Westerners, labelled as the main carriers of schistosomiasis, in the Gezira might be thought another example of the need for an on-site reliable labour supply triumphing over health considerations. In fact, the medical service saw such settlement as the ultimate solution to the schistosomiasis problem. In our eagerness to see everywhere the negative impact of colonial capitalism, we must not ignore the practice, the logic, and the political claims of colonial medicine.

My third argument, built from the targeting of Westerners for schistosomiasis and the Gezira malariologist's analysis of malaria prevention, is that medical knowledge reflected, reinforced, even created images of different social and racial groups as strong or weak, diseased or healthy, susceptible or resistant to infection. Medical knowledge, in other words, contributed to what Maryinez Lyons has called 'a colonial discourse on "tribal traits"'.[5] Creating these categories was one of the ways in which medicine contributed to the wider colonial project of knowing, classifying, and ordering Sudan. I also argue that the labels of 'diseased' and 'fit' were essential features of the contradictory ideologies developed about Westerners by the Sudan government and the Sudanese people during the interwar period, ideologies which, as Mark Duffield has shown, were intended to ensure the reinforcement and the reproduction of the colonial economy.[6] The Westerner case, then, provides one example of how, as Megan Vaughan has argued, medicine 'elaborated classification systems and practices which have to be seen as intrinsic to the operation of colonial power'.[7]

## THE GEZIRA IRRIGATION SCHEME

Launched officially by the opening of the Sennar Dam in 1925, the Gezira irrigation scheme was in some ways the quintessentially colonial project: massive in scale, ambitious in its development aims, it also suffered from huge cost overruns and inefficiencies during building and heavily skewed

[5] Maryinez Lyons, 'Foreign Bodies: The History of Labour Migration as a Threat to Public Health in Uganda', in Paul Nugent and A. I. Asiwaju (eds.), *African Boundaries: Barriers, Conduits, and Opportunities* (London: Pinter, 1996), 136.

[6] Mark R. Duffield, 'The Fallata: Ideology and the National Economy in Sudan', in O'Neill and O'Brien (eds.), *Economy and Class*, 122–36.

[7] Vaughan, *Curing their Ills*, 8.

the colonial economy towards one cash crop. The Sudan government staked the economic future of the country, and its own ability to govern, on the success of the scheme, built with £14.9 million in loans guaranteed by the British government.[8] Created to serve the needs of the British cotton industry and to make Sudan economically self-supporting, the scheme was by far the most important site of investment by private (and public) capital in Sudan. The Syndicate and the government spoke of the scheme as a partnership. Net profits from the sale of the cotton crop, after deduction of marketing and ginning charges, were divided between three parties: 25 per cent (20 per cent from 1930) to the Sudan Plantations Syndicate, 35 per cent (40 per cent from 1930) to the government, and 40 per cent to the tenants. The Syndicate's main responsibility was to supervise and train the tenants and manage the agricultural side of the scheme; the agents of such supervision were three (British) Syndicate inspectors per 15,000 *feddan* block of the irrigated area. The Syndicate was also required to execute and finance the subsidiary canalization of the irrigated area and provide the houses, offices, and heavy machinery that it needed. In 1919, the government granted the Syndicate a concession lasting fourteen years from the completion of the dam; this was extended to twenty-five years in 1926. The government built the Sennar Dam, the major canals, and the railway extension that allowed the cotton to be exported; it rented irrigable land from its Sudanese owners for 10 Pt/*feddan* and purchased land needed for permanent works for £E1/*feddan*; it also assigned political and medical personnel to the area.[9]

As well as a money-making venture, this was also an exercise in transformative development, intended to create a class of independent male peasant farmers who lived on their tenancies and worked them with family labour. The government settled on a tenant system for political as much as economic reasons: it did not want to create either a powerful class of Sudanese landowners or a landless proletariat, but recognized that the country lacked a 'significant wage labour market'.[10] Tenants in the inter-war period were mostly local Sudanese men.[11] The scheme did not alienate Sudanese from the land, but ignored the pre-existing economy to

---

[8] Daly, *Empire*, 424.

[9] The Sudan Plantations Syndicate Ltd, 'Distribution of Profits and Expenses on the Gezira Scheme', [Nov. 1937], SAD 418/3/31; Gaitskell, *Gezira*, 80–1, 84–5, 99, 127–8.

[10] Jay O'Brien, 'The Formation of the Agricultural Labour Force in Sudan', *Review of African Political Economy*, 26 (1983), 18.

[11] Victoria Bernal, 'Cotton and Colonial Order in Sudan: A Social History with Emphasis on the Gezira Scheme', in Allen Isaacman and Richard Roberts (eds.), *Cotton, Colonialism, and Social History in Sub-Saharan Africa* (London: James Currey, 1995), 104.

impose a strict regimen that removed farmers' control over agricultural
production. Before the opening of the scheme, farmers along the Nile
exploited different ecological zones to grow a variety of grain and vege-
table crops; away from the Nile, cultivation was only possible during the
rainy season. The household was the unit of production, and most kept
cattle. Local and long-distance trade offered the possibility of accumulation. The cultivation season lasted three to six months. The scheme
introduced year-round agricultural work that was much more labour-
intensive, and constant intervention in the lives of Sudanese peasants to
ensure that this work got done.[12] Each tenant was assigned a thirty *feddan*
plot of land (forty from 1933–4), on which he grew ten *feddans* of cotton,
five *feddans* of *lubia* (a bean crop used for fodder), and five *feddans* of *dura*,
leaving the rest fallow.[13] Although the *dura* and *lubia* crops were not
'partnership' crops, the reliable growth of these crops was one of the
central attractions of the scheme for tenants.[14]

If the colonial regime was oppressive, it could never be all-powerful:
the colonial vision of the peasant farmer was quickly undone by Sudanese
action and by the structure of the scheme itself. The very regimentation of
cultivation meant that the tenant was 'not really a farmer at all but a
producer of agricultural commodities on a "conveyor belt of land" supplied to him by the management; and it is the management, not he, who
cares for the maintenance of its fertility'.[15] Though some built temporary
shelters on their tenancies for use during the picking season (January to
April), tenants remained based in existing villages.[16] Tenant demand for
outside labour,[17] and the number of man-hours involved in the production
of cotton, meant that the government forecast of 5,000–10,000 casual
labourers being needed to supplement family labour during weeding and
picking was vastly inadequate: at the peak of the picking season, the total
number of casual labourers in the scheme was 58,679 in 1928–9, rising to
102,673 in 1939–40.[18]

---

[12] Bernal, 'Cotton', 101–3, 105, 108.          [13] Gaitskell, *Gezira*, 152–4.

[14] Bernal, 'Cotton', 114–15.

[15] G. M. Culwick, 'Social Change in the Gezira Scheme', *Civilisations*, 5 (1955), 177.

[16] G. M. Culwick, *A Study of the Human Factor in the Gezira Scheme* (Barakat (reprint
from 1955 original): Sudan Gezira Board and Sudan Rural Television Project, 1975), 113–
14; Gaitskell, *Gezira*, 102.

[17] On the reasons for this demand, see Abbas Abdelkarim, 'Social Forms of Organization
of Labour in the Sudan Gezira', School of Development Studies, University of East Anglia,
discussion paper no. 171, Nov. 1984; O'Brien, 'Agricultural Labor', appendix 1, 513–16.

[18] Stack to Allenby, 18 Mar. 1924, p. 58, CIVSEC 2/13/57; 'A Review of the Casual
Labour Employed in the Gezira Scheme for the Season 1929–1930', appendix A, p. 24, BNP
1/20/125; O'Brien, Agricultural Labor', 149.

TABLE 4.1. *Gezira scheme area, cotton yield, and cotton price, 1925–1939*

| Year | Scheme area (*feddans*) | Cotton yield (*kantars/feddan*) | Cotton price (pence/lb) |
|---|---|---|---|
| 1925–6 | 241,928 | 4.8 | 18.0 |
| 1926–7 | 302,258 | 4.7 | 18.0 |
| 1927–8 | 305,022 | 3.3 | 19.7 |
| 1928–9 | 382,221 | 3.6 | 18.4 |
| 1929–30 | 511,775 | 2.3 | 7.9 |
| 1930–1 | 581,307 | 1.4 | 6.4 |
| 1931–2 | 666,579 | 4.1 | 8.5 |
| 1932–3 | 667,078 | 1.9 | 8.1 |
| 1933–4 | 698,226 | 2.3 | 8.6 |
| 1934–5 | 698,743 | 4.5 | 8.2 |
| 1935–6 | 753,251 | 3.7 | 7.9 |
| 1936–7 | 809,262 | 4.5 | 8.6 |
| 1937–8 | 842,341 | 4.6 | 5.9 |
| 1938–9 | 853,568 | 4.5 | 6.2 |

*Sources*: W. N. Allan, 'Irrigation in the Sudan', in J. D. Tothill (ed.), *Agriculture in the Sudan* (London: Oxford University Press, 1948), table opposite 608; Gaitskell, *Gezira*, 267.

The need to keep labour costs low, and the rapid growth of the irrigated area—it more than tripled in size during the inter-war period, as shown in Table 4.1—meant that there was usually considerable government and Syndicate anxiety about the labour supply, which had serious consequences for disease control. The size of the scheme presented its own challenges. In 1929–30, to take a snapshot, the SMS was trying to control malaria and schistosomiasis in an irrigated area of more than 500,000 *feddans*, harbouring canals stretching at least 720 miles, populated by 13,000 tenants and their families, and at least 60,592 casual and settled labourers at the peak of the picking season.[19]

The Gezira was privileged space in terms of medical provision: Gruenbaum has highlighted the concentration of medical facilities, personnel, and funds in the Gezira, as well as the absence of such facilities for villages even a few miles outside the scheme.[20] Medical work in the Gezira was overseen by three British medical inspectors, two based in Wad Medani and one at Makwar; two British sanitary inspectors, joined by a

[19] R. M. Humphreys, 'Vesical Schistosomiasis in the Gezira Irrigated Area of the Sudan', *TRSTMH* 26 (1932), 241; Gaitskell, *Gezira*, 270; 'A Review of the Casual Labour Employed in the Gezira Scheme for the Season 1929–1930', appendix A, p. 24, BNP 1/20/125.
[20] Gruenbaum, 'Health Services', 175, 187.

third in 1927, supervised sanitary work. Sanitary prevention and medical cure were administered in the irrigated area through dispensaries. Although built, maintained, and paid for by the Syndicate, the government owned and ran the dispensaries, and bought them back from the Syndicate in 1929, rather than wait, as initially agreed, until the end of the concession. Each dispensary served a 15,000 *feddan* block and was located at block headquarters, near the Syndicate office. Each was manned by a sanitary hakim, later known as an assistant medical officer, trained by the government, and a *tumargi* or *farrash* (cleaner) who served as his assistant, both paid for by the SMS. As elsewhere in the country, dispensaries were intended to provide primary medical care and to act as a filter for more serious cases: sanitary hakims tended minor ailments, administered first aid, gave medications such as Epsom salts, quinine, and novarsenobenzol, referred seriously ill individuals to the doctor or to the hospitals at Wad Medani and Abu Usher, and notified any epidemic. In addition to manning their dispensaries and touring their blocks, sanitary hakims were initially responsible for sanitary inspections: they were meant to check all canals, *abu ashrins* (feeder channels), and *dawarans* (scour pits) in their blocks for leaks, stagnant water, and mosquito breeding, and report any problems to the Syndicate block inspector who was expected to address them. Responsible for anti-malarial/sanitary measures on the canals it had constructed, the Syndicate had to ensure that tenants fulfilled their obligations of baling water out of the canals and filling in the seepage pools on their tenancies; similarly, the government was solely responsible for sanitary measures on government canals, namely the main canal and the upper reaches of some branch canals.[21]

Although privileged space, the Gezira was still in absolute terms under-resourced. To take one example, the organization assigned sanitary hakims too many responsibilities over too large an area and created dysfunctional hierarchies, problems made clear with the eruption of malaria epidemics in the late 1920s. The result was the SMS's attempt to rationalize the medical organization in 1930 by relieving sanitary hakims of their sanitary duties. This was intended to allow them to concentrate solely on curative care, especially for malaria;[22] to remove the need for dispensary

[21] Director, Medical Department, 'Memo on Gezira Irrigation', 29 Dec. 1923, pp. 75–9, LANDS 5/2/13, NRO; Governor, BNP to Managing Director, Syndicate, 30 May 1924, pp. 20–1, LANDS 5/8/86; Gruenbaum, 'Health Services', 139, 141–2; *RSMS 1927*, 69–70; Senior Medical Inspector, BNP, 'Instructions to Sanitary Hakims in Charge of Gezira Dispensaries', [1934], pp. 3–5, BNP 1/44/324.
[22] *RSMS 1930*, 59.

staff to 'inspect and report on other natives'—presumably tenants and irrigation staff—which was 'liable to grave abuse';[23] and to place sanitary hakims more firmly under the authority of the medical service, as opposed to the Syndicate. The fact that British sanitary inspectors and their sub-ordinate Sudanese staff took over responsibility for anti-malarial meas-ures, even on the smaller canals, in 1930, suggests that the government was less and less willing to rely on the Syndicate for disease prevention.[24] Tensions between the Syndicate and the government, the constant desire to save money, and poor organization and management of Sudanese staff all shaped disease control in the Gezira.

## THE HEALTH COSTS OF IRRIGATION

Common to the broad church of political economy of health analyses is the argument that capitalist development has damaging effects on health, which usually fall disproportionately on the labouring classes.[25] In provid-ing one example of what Steven Feierman has termed the 'social costs of production',[26] the Gezira supports this argument. Urinary and intestinal schistosomiasis, little known in the area prior to the start of irrigation, were entrenched in the scheme by 1943, possibly earlier. Irrigation also increased the prevalence of malaria, which debilitated the local population throughout the inter-war period, though its effect on the operation of the scheme does not seem to have ever been as great as it was in the late 1920s. The evidence for this, gleaned from SMS records, is not straightforward; it illuminates some of the preoccupations and the problems of the medical service and is therefore worth discussing in some detail.

Annual schistosomiasis surveys tested and treated local Sudanese and non-local migrant labourers; infection rates were highest in the latter group. Annual reports from 1933 onward, and Table 4.2, only record infection in local Sudanese, as this was considered the indicator for schistosomiasis entrenchment in the scheme. Preventing such entrench-ment, rather than preserving the health of individual labourers, was the SMS priority. The SMS regarded the Gezira as free of schistosomiasis in

---

[23] Dr E. D. Pridie, quoted in Gruenbaum, 'Health Services', 143.

[24] Gruenbaum, 'Health Services', 142–4.

[25] Doyal with Pennell, *Political Economy*; Turshen, 'Impact', 7–35; Turshen, *Political Ecology*; Manderson, *Sickness and the State*; Shula Marks and Neil Andersson, 'Issues in the Political Economy of Health in Southern Africa', *Journal of Southern African Studies*, 13 (1987), 177–86; Packard, *White Plague*.

[26] Steven Feierman, 'Struggles for Control: The Social Roots of Health and Healing in Modern Africa', *African Studies Review*, 28 (1985), 93–105.

TABLE 4.2. *Annual urinary schistosomiasis survey results*

| | Adults | | | Children | | | Total | | |
|------|--------|-------|------|--------|-------|------|--------|-------|------|
| Year | Exmd | Inftd | % | Exmd | Inftd | % | Exmd | Inftd | % |
| 1926 | 12,734 | 39 | 0.30 | 3,685 | 37 | 1.0 | 16,419 | 76 | 0.46 |
| 1929 | 9,431 | 71 | 0.75 | 2,341 | 37 | 1.6 | 11,772 | 108 | 0.92 |
| 1930 | 8,783 | 6 | 0.07 | 3,322 | 20 | 0.60 | 12,105 | 26 | 0.21 |
| 1931 | 11,102 | 84 | 0.76 | 6,895 | 51 | 0.74 | 17,995 | 135 | 0.75 |
| 1932 | 9,618 | 51 | 0.53 | 1,707 | 19 | 1.1 | 11,325 | 70 | 0.62 |
| 1933 | 14,188 | 28 | 0.20 | 3,288 | 27 | 0.82 | 17,476 | 55 | 0.31 |
| 1934 | 12,769 | 5 | 0.04 | 3,583 | 2 | 0.06 | 16,352 | 7 | 0.04 |
| 1935 | 13,902 | 8 | 0.06 | 2,945 | 12 | 0.41 | 16,847 | 20 | 0.12 |
| 1936 | 22,604 | 10 | 0.04 | 5,483 | 17 | 0.31 | 28,087 | 27 | 0.10 |
| 1937 | 30,768 | 26 | 0.08 | 10,038 | 63 | 0.62 | 40,806 | 89 | 0.22 |
| 1938 | 32,045 | 50 | 0.16 | 16,916 | 162 | 0.96 | 48,961 | 212 | 0.43 |
| 1939 | 17,044 | 30 | 0.18 | 10,877 | 174 | 1.6 | 27,921 | 204 | 0.73 |
| 1940 | 29,711 | 64 | 0.21 | 12,310 | 109 | 0.89 | 42,021 | 173 | 0.41 |
| 1941 | 19,588 | 17 | 0.09 | 14,243 | 37 | 0.26 | 33,831 | 54 | 0.16 |
| 1942 | 24,888 | 90 | 0.36 | 10,460 | 115 | 1.1 | 35,348 | 205 | 0.58 |
| 1943 | 32,320 | 321 | 0.99 | 11,929 | 143 | 1.2 | 44,249 | 464 | 1.0 |
| 1944 | 57,196 | 511 | 0.89 | 29,966 | 940 | 3.1 | 87,162 | 1,451 | 1.7 |
| 1945 | 22,681 | 399 | 1.8 | 12,133 | 632 | 5.2 | 34,814 | 1,031 | 3.0 |

Exmd = examined; inftd = infected

Sources: *RSMS 1933*, 8; *RSMS 1942*, 4; *RSMS 1945*, 27.

1925, and the annual survey figures suggest that their measures were successful in keeping it so throughout the inter-war period. Data collected during the Second World War, however, indicate that SMS confidence about the effectiveness of its control measures was misplaced. Posted as medical inspector to the northern district of the irrigated area in 1942, Dr R. W. Stephenson found infection rates of up to 5 per cent in some villages for *S. mansoni*, the more severe, intestinal form of schistosomiasis, for which annual surveys did not test because of local resistance to giving faecal samples. In dispensary records from 1941–4, he found 493 cases, including twenty-two deaths; in 45 per cent of the cases, the disease was acquired locally. Stephenson concluded that 'it can be definitely stated that [*S. mansoni*] occurs in the area, that it is probably widespread, and that in certain places there is a fairly high rate of infection.'[27] In addition, the annual survey figures did not, in his opinion, reflect the true situation regarding *S. haematobium* (urinary schistosomiasis). Examinations of the

[27] R. W. Stephenson, 'Bilharziasis in the Gezira Irrigated Area of the Sudan', *TRSTMH* 40 (1947), 488–9.

population in fifteen villages between 1942 and 1945 revealed an average infection rate with *S. haematobium* of 21 per cent in adults and 45 per cent in children.[28]

It is likely that the Second World War had a very immediate impact on the prevalence of schistosomiasis in the scheme: the redirection of personnel towards war duties and towards the control of epidemic relapsing fever resulted in a slackening of preventive and curative measures against schistosomiasis. Infection rates could grow rapidly in the absence of proper control, as Stephenson observed, and they probably did.[29] But this does not account for the difference in infection levels detected by Stephenson's special survey and the annual surveys during the war, nor for the feeling of Stephenson and his predecessor that the annual survey did not reflect the real position. Annual surveys were conducted by medical assistants, likely sanitary hakims, 'who went from village to village examining as many urines as they could'. Medical assistants also conducted Stephenson's special survey, though the most reliable were specifically chosen, and they examined 70 to 90 per cent of the residents of the chosen villages.[30] It may be that the annual surveys failed to provide a representative sample. Given the focal nature of the disease, it is possible that the annual surveyors simply missed important foci. Precisely which area was surveyed, and the basis on which villages were included in the survey, remains unclear: until 1932 at least, by which time the total irrigated area was 682,000 *feddans*, the survey was still confined to the original 300,000 *feddans*, because it was 'the only area found to harbour indigenous cases of this disease'.[31] Since control measures increasingly focused on existing areas of infection during the 1930s, there is a remote possibility that Stephenson was recording schistosomiasis that had simply not been looked for in the newer, northern part of the scheme. Overall, the Stephenson evidence suggests that there were problems with the design of the annual survey, the SMS's primary means of monitoring its control measures, and that in focusing solely on urinary schistosomiasis, the SMS completely missed the developing problem of *S. mansoni*. The result was the entrenchment of schistosomiasis that everyone feared; the health costs continue to be paid by people living in the Gezira today.

The sources for the SMS's handling of malaria in the Gezira are much less informative than those for schistosomiasis. Although annual malaria

[28] Ibid. 486–7.
[29] Hartwig, 'Schistosomiasis', 64; Gruenbaum, 'Health Services', 182 n. 1; Stephenson, 'Bilharziasis', 491.
[30] Ibid. 486–7, quote 482.    [31] *RSMS 1932*, 8.

surveys were conducted from 1928 to 1933, I have only been able to obtain one of the resulting reports. Survey results were not published in the SMS annual reports, allowing the SMS to appear more in control of malaria than it in fact was. As with schistosomiasis, there is some ambiguity surrounding the interpretation of those data that are available. Despite these difficulties, several points are worth making. First, irrigation undoubtedly increased the incidence of malaria in the Gezira. According to the malariologist's report for 1930, the incidence of malaria was higher in irrigated areas with low rainfall than in the southern unirrigated area with heavy rainfall; as he explained, 'Water is essential to cotton; where there is water, there will be mosquitoes.'[32] Second, whether or not it had been before the start of irrigation, malaria was endemic in the Gezira, and hyperendemic in some parts: in 1929, the malaria survey of 116 villages in the Gezira, both within and without the irrigated area, indicated that 60 per cent of children had malaria parasites in their blood and that 39 per cent of children had enlarged spleens, indicating chronic malaria.[33] Surveys of the splenic rate in Gezira schoolchildren, considered a gauge of endemicity, did however show an overall downward trend, from 43.7 per cent in 1933 to 14.8 per cent in 1940, suggesting increasing effectiveness of prevention and control measures.[34]

Third, regardless of terminology, malaria debilitated people in the irrigated area every rainy season throughout the inter-war period. No episode was spoken of with as much concern or was described as being as severe as the 1927 epidemic. Annual reports mentioned another epidemic in 1929 and the 'annual epidemic' in 1930, but thereafter referred only to increased incidence of malaria due to heavy rainfall or decreased incidence in drier years. By 1935, the SMS was reporting that the distribution of dispensaries in the irrigated area had 'eliminated the epidemics of acute malaria which used to rage, with heavy loss of life, before the country was irrigated'.[35] Without comparative data from the pre-irrigation period, and given the scarcity of inter-war statistics for mortality from malaria in the Gezira, it is impossible to say if this is accurate or not. The Gezira malariologist in 1930 referred to some deaths from cerebral malaria, but provided no figures; out of the malaria cases seen in hospitals and dispensaries in the Gezira, SMS annual reports registered an annual maximum of ten deaths.[36] The change between the late 1920s and the late 1930s

---

[32] Annual Report of the Gezira Malariologist, 12 June 1930, 4.
[33] *ARED 1929*, 82.
[34] *RSMS 1936*, 19; *RSMS 1938*, 21; *RSMS 1940*, 22.
[35] *RSMS 1935*, 18.
[36] Annual Report of the Gezira Malariologist, 12 June 1930, 3; *RSMS 1936*, 18; *RSMS 1938*, 20; *RSMS 1940*, 22.

TABLE 4.3. *Malaria cases in the Gezira*

|  | 1928 | 1935 | 1936 | 1937 | 1938 | 1939 | 1940 |
|---|---|---|---|---|---|---|---|
| Gezira dispensaries | 4,784 | 25,785 | 27,125 | 17,422 | 43,560 | 25,496 | 14,009 |
| Wad Medani hospital inpatients | n.a. | 798 | 1,177 | 465 | 2,042 | 1,017 | 620 |
| Wad Medani hospital outpatients | n.a. | n.a. | 5,033 | 3,095 | 11,056 | 1,369 | 821 |

n.a. = not available

*Sources*: Annual Report for the Period January 1st. to December 31st, 1928 [BNP], p. 2, BNP 1/27/201; *RSMS 1936*, 18; *RSMS 1938*, 20; *RSMS 1940*, 22.

seems to have been primarily in the SMS's choice of words to describe the situation. The later SMS reports downplayed the impact of malaria, commenting in 1938 for example that the 'incidence in Wad Medani and the Gezira showed a considerable increase compared with 1937 owing to the very heavy, badly spaced rainfall in the autumn'.[37] Gone is the word 'epidemic' or the horror with which the unexpected 1927 outbreak was greeted. But Table 4.3 shows the substantial increase in malaria admissions for 1938 and descriptions given elsewhere suggest little difference from 1927: malaria 'continued to devastate' people in the southern Gezira in November 1938, according to the Blue Nile province monthly diary.[38] In a 1933 article, the Gezira malariologist wrote that 'the disease becomes almost pandemic in the last three months of the year'.[39] Acute or chronic, dispensary and hospital returns indicate a persistently high incidence of malaria in the Gezira.

## BREAKING THE CYCLE

To control malaria and schistosomiasis, the SMS tried to break their transmission cycles at every possible point. A combination of control measures was always in use, designed to prevent human infection of the vector and vice versa, to eliminate the vector, and to destroy the parasite once in the human. Malaria control in the Gezira consisted of anti-mosquito measures, quinine and plasmochine prophylaxis and therapy, the provision of mosquito nets, and annual malaria surveys. Schistosomiasis control in the Gezira consisted of anti-snail measures,

[37] *RSMS 1938*, 20.
[38] BNP Province Monthly Diary, Nov. 1938, p. 6, CIVSEC 57/6/26.
[39] L. H. Henderson, 'Prophylaxis of Malaria in the Sudan, With Special Reference to the Use of Plasmoquine', *TRSTMH* 28 (1934), 157.

treatment with antimony tartrate administered at quarantine stations and dispensaries, propaganda against bathing and excretion in canals, latrine building, resettlement of villages away from canals, digging of wells to provide an alternative water supply, and annual schistosomiasis surveys. Anti-vector measures, based on scientific research into vector habits and the effectiveness of larvicides/molluscicides, were the staple of both campaigns. With schistosomiasis, there was a palpable shift towards social, sanitary solutions, such as the provision of latrines and wells and village relocation in the early to mid-1930s. With malaria control, the mid-1930s saw a redoubled emphasis on the study and destruction of mosquitoes. Both disease campaigns were run by the SMS doctors in Blue Nile Province and sanitary hakims administered treatment for both conditions. The growing sanitary wing of the SMS (sanitary inspectors, overseers, and labourers) and researchers affiliated to the WTRL and later to the SMS laboratory division were essential to both campaigns. Malaria did, however, have its own specialist doctor in the Gezira malariologist from 1928 until the position was abolished in 1933 due to depression retrenchment, and from 1935, the almost exclusive attention of a newly hired medical entomologist.

If there were similarities between efforts to control these diseases, the reality was that the SMS addressed them independently, consistent with its disease-based approach to medical intervention. Indeed, the annual surveys for malaria and schistosomiasis seem to have been conducted at different times, by different people. There were also fundamental differences in the way that doctors conceptualized these diseases, which led to important differences in the way that they were addressed. British doctors initially regarded schistosomiasis as an Egyptian disease foreign to Sudan. By the time the Gezira scheme opened in 1925, however, they knew that schistosomiasis existed in most of Sudan's provinces and had already attempted to control it through treatment in parts of Dongola, with reasonable success.[40] But they still considered the Gezira area to be essentially schistosomiasis-free in 1925: only sporadic cases had been found along the Blue Nile and a survey of children in twenty villages in the middle of the Gezira conducted the year before canalization started revealed no cases of urinary schistosomiasis.[41] The SMS hope that the Gezira might not become infested with snails proved short-lived. *Bullinus* snails, intermediates for urinary schistosomiasis, were found in six sets of canals in 1926 and throughout the scheme in large numbers by 1928;

---

[40] Bell, 'Medical Research', 117–19.
[41] Humphreys, 'Vesical Schistosomiasis', 241–2.

*planorbis* snails, intermediates for intestinal schistosomiasis, were found in two canal blocks in 1927, and twenty by 1928. Canals in an extension opened in August 1928 harboured both *planorbis* and *bullinus* snails by November. The first infected snails were found in four blocks in 1928, the year after snail destruction measures were started.[42] But the strong prior perception of non-infection encouraged the SMS to protect the Gezira by preventing the entry of humans who might infect snails into the scheme. The creation of quarantine stations external to the Gezira, which targeted and treated infected would-be labourers, was a critical, if controversial, element of the early schistosomiasis control strategy. By contrast, doctors regarded malaria as endemic in the Gezira before the opening of the scheme. Not considering the consequences of immigrants substantially increasing the local pool of parasite carriers or the impact on immigrants of entering a new disease environment,[43] they saw no point in erecting quarantines against outside groups. Besides, while schistosomiasis was apparently curable by injections of antimony tartrate, a treatment developed by Dr J. B. Christopherson during the First World War at Khartoum Civil Hospital, there was no lasting cure for malaria.[44]

There were other significant differences. Spread through bathing or working in contaminated water, schistosomiasis was a disease of tenants and labourers; the British in Sudan were rarely infected. Although Britons were much more likely to use mosquito nets and have access to quinine, the mobility and ubiquity of the mosquito meant that malaria was a disease that affected British, Sudanese, Egyptians, Chadians, and Nigerians alike. Schistosomiasis control was a major priority because doctors in Sudan, looking at the Egyptian experience, feared the health and labour consequences if the disease became endemic in the Gezira. They expected it to be impossible to eradicate and even if not deadly in itself, likely to

---

[42] *RSMS 1926*, 29; *RSMS 1928*, 20.

[43] R. Mansell Prothero, *Migrants and Malaria* (London: Longmans, 1965); Randall M. Packard, 'Maize, Cattle and Mosquitoes: The Political Economy of Malaria Epidemics in Colonial Swaziland', *Journal of African History*, 25 (1984), 189–212.

[44] J. B. Christopherson and J. R. Newlove, 'Laboratory and Other Notes on Seventy Cases of Bilharzia Treated at the Khartoum Civil Hospital by Intravenous Injections of Antimony Tartrate', *JTMH* 22 (1919), 129–44; J. B. Christopherson, 'Bilharzia Disease: The Sterilization of the Ova During the Course of Cure by Antimony (Tartrate)', *JTMH* 23 (1920), 165–7. I use the word 'apparently' because although Christopherson thought that antimony tartrate rendered infertile and/or killed schistosomal ova, the specific action of the drug was unknown until the Second World War. Research conducted then revealed that after four weeks of treatment with antimony tartrate, schistosome worms migrated to the liver and became smaller, and their ovaries degenerated. But at least half of the shrunken worms were still alive. Relapse frequently ensued when treatment stopped and the worms recovered (Farley, *Bilharzia*, 165).

lower an individual's resistance to malaria and other diseases.[45] But
throughout the inter-war period in the Gezira, it remained an apparently
mild disease, that often did not make those infected ill, and therefore did
not interfere with their ability to work. Malaria, by contrast, came in
acute, epidemic attacks. With both diseases, the SMS tried to make the
Gezira into an area free from the possibility of infection, mainly by
eliminating the disease vectors. But this was much more of a preoccupation with malaria, because it was the more immediately severe disease, it
affected everyone, and it could (and did) seriously impair the operation of
the scheme. The mildness of schistosomiasis, and the confinement of the
threat of infection to the non-British population, meant that it was much
easier for doctors to label it a disease of lifestyle and increasingly to seek to
change the behaviour of the at-risk population by issuing regulations
against excretion in canals, by building latrines, and by resettling villages.
The consequences of failed malaria control meant that control measures
were ultimately too important to be left entirely to individuals: the environment had to be made safe through mosquito destruction. This was
structured with increasing precision from 1935 by a new medical entomologist, who conducted careful studies of the bionomics of malaria-
transmitting mosquitoes and of the relative effectiveness of different
larvicides and of baling out canals. While great care was taken with snail
destruction, neither the SMS nor the WTRL ever employed a mycolo-
gist. The point of this comparative discussion is that medical factors—
which included medical preconceptions about disease epidemiology,
existing medical knowledge, the apparent efficacy of existing techniques
for control, and the comparative severity of the diseases—played an essential role in shaping the disease control measures implemented.

### ECONOMY AND DISEASE THREAT

There were other assumptions that underlay disease control efforts and
other factors that shaped disease control campaigns. Doctors, political
officials, and Syndicate employees alike agreed that the first priority in the
Gezira was to keep the scheme operating efficiently and profitably, but
this did not mean that all agreed on how this was best achieved. The
decisions to erect and to remove quarantine stations for labourers headed
to the Gezira show the tension between the need to protect the scheme
from outside infection that might imperil it and the need to ensure an
unimpeded flow of cheap labour to the scheme, first to build it, and then

[45] *RSMS 1925*, 1; *RSMS 1927*, 12.

to cultivate cotton. In providing insight into the interaction between medicine, politics, and economics, the Gezira case highlights the inadequacy of explanations which seek to pigeonhole colonial actors: the opinions of doctors, political officials, and Syndicate employees converged at some points and diverged at others. Sometimes doctors made arguments on economic grounds; sometimes political officials put forward the medical case.

As early as 1912, doctors such as William Byam, Robert Archibald, and Andrew Balfour were concerned about the health implications of importing Egyptian labourers to build the Sennar Dam, fearing that such labourers would bring hookworm, tuberculosis, and schistosomiasis. The latter in particular would spread throughout the scheme from the dam reservoir, infesting the 'peasant cultivators' who, 'instead of reaping the benefits they expected' would 'become miserable invalids, anaemic, slothful and degenerate, victims of the thoughtlessness of their paternal Government. Not actually killed by kindness but ruined, both physically and financially, by good intentions.'[46] When the building of the scheme was scheduled to start after the First World War, Dr E. S. Crispin, director of the medical department, pointed out the need for a station at which to screen Egyptian labourers destined for the building site. The civil engineer in charge of building replied that the only possible site for such a station was on Sudan's northernmost border, at Wadi Halfa. But as men would arrive there having travelled long distances, and possibly having disposed of most of their property, they would be unhappy to be rejected after a medical examination and on their return home, would spread bad publicity, making it harder for the government to obtain workers. Governor-General Lee Stack supported this position and so no station was planned.

Dismayed by this news, Byam, who had resigned from the Egyptian Army to take up private practice in Harley Street, drafted a letter to *The Times*. Recognizing that potential financial loss was usually a good incitement to action, he 'addressed [his] appeal to those who had subscribed to the recent Sudan Loan, advising them that their money would be jeopardized if the health of those who were to grow the crops, to which they looked for security and profit, deteriorated', and warned that 'disaster loomed large on the horizon'. When Crispin, doubtless fearing the end of his career, appealed to Byam not to send the letter, Byam instead showed it to Sir Walter Morley Fletcher of the Medical Research Council. Once

---

[46] Byam, *The Road*, 114.

Andrew Balfour and Lyle Cummins, professor and expert on tuberculosis, formerly of the EAMC, had backed Byam's position, Fletcher sent A. J. Balfour, Lord President of the Council, a revised version of the letter. A. J. Balfour's evaluation was political: if the Byam scenario materialized, the British 'would be presenting the Egyptians with the biggest stick they could wish for to chastise us as obviously unfit to rule the Sudan, which country, they would claim, should therefore be promptly handed over to their complete control'. Governor-General Stack was summoned and told to establish a quarantine station at Wadi Halfa immediately; Crispin's leave was cancelled so that he could supervise the project. Stack was not pleased by Byam's actions, asking him why he had made such a 'damaging attack on the Sudan' and if a knighthood would persuade him to keep his 'mouth shut in future'. Byam replied that he was concerned about the welfare of Sudan, and that his reputation, and the reputation of the British medical profession, would suffer if the British in Sudan, in contrast to the Americans in Panama, did not implement their knowledge of preventive medicine.[47]

Byam's is the only available account of this sequence of events but it is nonetheless revealing. Aside from highlighting the influence wielded by former Sudan officials and the national rivalries at work in tropical medicine, it shows medical considerations initially being subordinated to the need to ensure an adequate labour supply, and doctors appealing to financial and political, rather than primarily health and medical, grounds in order to make their argument for disease control heard. Although its origins were contested, the Wadi Halfa quarantine introduced a coercive regimen for examining the 45,029 Egyptian labourers who passed through between 1919 and 1925, employed on six-month contracts to build the Sennar Dam and canalize the Gezira. The quarantine provides one example of the extreme exertions of state power that characterized colonialism. Groups of up to 750 men spent four days, reduced to a maximum of forty-eight hours by 1925, in the station, where state control over them, embodied in a doctor, a laboratory assistant, and thirty local Sudanese, was absolute. With assigned numbers marked on their forearms in silver nitrate, all men were vaccinated, purged on the assumption that all carried parasites, had their clothes disinfected, their blood drawn, their urine and faeces examined, and *all* their body hair shaved off. The 20 per cent of men who could not urinate in a room full of other people were immediately catheterized: 'the granting of privacy would have resulted in

---

[47] Account from Byam, *The Road*, 112–117, quotes 115, 116, 117, respectively.

substitution of urines and . . . delay would have disorganized the whole routine . . .'[48]

Despite the success of Byam's campaign, the actual purpose of the quarantine was not to protect Sudan or the Gezira from outside infection. It was to ensure that the Gezira scheme got built, unhindered by out-breaks of epidemic disease or by unfit workers. Labourers were rejected and sent home if they were very old or very young, or if they suffered from conditions that would compromise their capacity to work, such as active syphilis, severe anaemia, and fevers.[49] Simple infection with schistosomiasis was not one of these conditions. The WTRL bacteriologist seconded from the EAMC who organized the quarantine station, Major B. H. H. Spence, recommended that all those infected with urinary schistosomiasis—18.5 per cent of labourers in 1920–1—should either be treated at Wadi Halfa or rejected.[50] But the Central Sanitary Board felt that rejecting such a high proportion of the prospective labour force was 'an impracticable proposition', particularly since schistosomiasis was already widespread in Sudan; it resolved to reconsider the issue when canalization work was further advanced.[51] Construction labour needs always won out. Until 1925, only those carriers of urinary schistosomiasis with 'poor physique, severe haematuria, marked anemia, or pyuria were rejected, as they would most probably have broken down under the stress of hard work if allowed to proceed to the Anglo-Egyptian Sudan'.[52] Spence's preferred policy only came into effect once the Gezira scheme had opened: from December 1925 onward all those infected with schistosomiasis who were proceeding to the irrigated area were either rejected or detained for treatment at Wadi Halfa.[53]

While Spence disagreed with political officials and other doctors about whether the function of the station was to protect Sudan from infection or to guarantee healthy labourers, he accepted the economic terms under which medical and health precautions in the Gezira should be discussed:

No doubt by the strict application of the knowledge we possess the Gezira could be kept entirely free from these diseases [ankylostomiasis and schistosomiasis]. But economy is a vital factor in ambitious schemes of development, and absolute perfection in hygienic matters may easily be attained at too high a price. It would,

---

[48] B. H. H. Spence, 'The Wadi Halfa Quarantine', *JRAMC* 43 (1924), 321–40, quote 336; *RSMS 1925*, 15. On the health of Egyptian labourers during construction, see *RSMS 1925*, 13–18.

[49] *RSMS 1925*, 15.

[50] Spence, 'Quarantine', 336–7

[51] *RFACS 1920*, 148.

[52] Spence, 'Quarantine', 336.    [53] *RSMS 1926*, 6, 60; *RSMS 1927*, 75–7.

in fact, be just as reprehensible to paralyse the scheme by taking too elaborate hygienic precautions as it would be to wreck it by taking none at all.[54]

As the debates about the necessity and the function of the Wadi Halfa quarantine indicate, different groups of political officials and doctors in London and Sudan had different opinions about the precise location of the happy medium between expensive, paralysing perfection, and cheap, destructive inaction.

Trade-offs between the need for economy and the need to prevent future disease occurred in the planning for malaria control as well, with damaging effect. Dr O. F. H. Atkey, senior medical inspector for Blue Nile province, asked in 1921 whether a drainage system was to be built alongside the canals. He argued that the success of the scheme from a sanitary point of view depended on adequate drainage; from rainy season experience, he considered it 'a matter of the greatest importance' that the drain for Barakat and the land behind Wad Medani be built at the same time as the irrigation canals and imagined that there were other drains of equal significance. 'It must be remembered', he wrote, 'that during good rains considerable parts of the Gezira are for all intents and purposes malarial swamps. The present inhabitants of the Gezirah [*sic*] are thoroughly malarialised. If the Gezirah [*sic*] is to support a considerable population healthy enough to work it must be drained.'[55] The director of lands and the director of agriculture replied that there was no plan to build a drainage system for the irrigation canals until it had been proven necessary. The director of agriculture felt that a complete drainage system for both canals and rainfall would be expensive and unlikely to be effective in preventing malaria; excess rainfall would be dealt with by confining it to small areas.[56]

The government paid a heavy price for the decision not to build a drainage system during the 1927 season, when the first 'good rains' since the scheme had opened and a warm winter combined to produce a long and widespread epidemic of malaria. The heavy rains combined with waterings, each one equivalent to three inches of rain, to soak the irrigated area. To save the crops from drowning, surface water was drained into the field channels and thence into the canals; the canals were emptied into *luguds* (natural depressions) in which weeds soon sprouted and mosquitoes bred. The rainy season (June to September) brought one cycle of

---

[54] Spence, 'Quarantine', 321.

[55] Atkey to President, CSB, 15 Jan. 1921, p. 63, LANDS 5/2/13.

[56] Director of Lands to Director of Agriculture, 20 Jan. 1921, p. 64; Director of Agriculture to Director of Lands, 8 Feb. 1921, p. 67, LANDS 5/2/13.

PLATE 2. The losing battle of malaria control in the Gezira: spraying oil on stagnant water, *c.*1937. (Courtesy of the University of Durham Library.)

malarial infection, and mosquitoes that bred out in *luguds*, which remained filled until October, brought another. The epidemic started a vicious cycle: tenants were too ill to bale out their field channels and Syndicate inspectors too ill to oversee anti-malaria precautions, leaving stagnant water in which more mosquitoes bred, increasing malarial transmission.[57] The epidemic impeded tenants' ability to tend their crops and deterred White Nile province labourers from going to the scheme. With the epidemic persisting into February 1928, a labour shortage during the picking season threatened, although it did not, in the end, materialize.[58]

Malaria had made its mark: as the Blue Nile province governor wrote in 1928, 'The epidemic of last year did good in that it showed what disorganization and disability could be caused by this disease and it has made everyone realise the importance of preventing a recurrence.'[59] The late 1920s epidemics prompted the changes in sanitary hakims' duties discussed above and convinced everyone of the need for a drainage system. The SMS annual report for 1930 identified surface drainage as 'the most important factor' in solving the problem of epidemic malaria. A basic system of drainage channels was in place by 1931, a decade after Atkey had

[57] *RSMS 1927*, 68.
[58] Annual Report for the Period January 1st. to December 31st, 1928 [BNP], pp. 1–2; Blue Nile Province, Annual Report for 1928, p. 28, BNP 1/27/201.
[59] Annual Report for the Period . . . 1928 [BNP], p. 2, BNP 1/27/201.

first raised the issue. Larger pumps were installed and the channels extended when the heavy rains of August 1932 again overwhelmed the existing system.[60] Superimposing a drainage system on existing canalization presented substantial engineering difficulties and, at a time of financial hardship, involved great expense.

## LABOUR AND QUARANTINE

The tension between the need for economy, specifically the need for an ample, cheap labour supply, and the need to prevent disease spread emerges most clearly in the targeting of Westerners, the most valued labourers in the Gezira scheme, as the primary disseminators of schistosomiasis infection. Imposing a quarantine to keep out such infection carried labour costs, but I will argue that there were medical as well as economic reasons for the eventual decision to lift the quarantines. This section, and the one on malaria that follows, also tell another, familiar story, of medical knowledge contributing to racial stereotypes of fitness and weakness, immunity and susceptibility, infection and health. Minority and immigrant communities around the world, marked by their race, class, gender distribution, and cultural otherness, have been common targets for such medical labelling.[61] In Uganda, immigrants from Rwanda known as the Banyaruanda have been blamed for introducing and spreading disease since the colonial period; like Westerners in Sudan, Banyaruanda in Uganda now account for a significant percentage of the population in some areas and their labour has been crucial in the creation of a modern economy.[62] While the Banyaruanda seem to have been labelled exclusively as sickly and starving, a more contradictory discourse grew up around Westerners in Sudan. This section concludes by showing how the simultaneous application of the labels of 'diseased' and 'fit' to Westerners reflected and reinforced the contradictory ideologies developed about Westerners by the Sudanese people and the colonial government during the inter-war period.

Westerner labour was central to the development of the Gezira scheme from its experimental beginnings in 1911. In 1921, 28 per cent of the labour force working on the Sennar Dam was 'Fellata', a term of changing definition (see discussion below) which at this time designated Nigerians;

---

[60] *RSMS 1930*, 60–1; *RSMS 1933*, 19; *RSMS 1932*, 27.

[61] Lara Marks and Michael Worboys (eds.), *Migrants, Minorities and Health: Historical and Contemporary Studies* (London: Routledge, 1997).

[62] Lyons, 'Foreign Bodies', 131–44.

several hundred 'Fellata' were settled on the Gezira area already under cultivation. By 1924, there were 2,000 Westerners in the scheme, mainly Hausa and Fulani.[63] Westerners were a diverse group: they comprised Fulani, Hausa, Fur, Borgu, Masalit, and others, and they worked in the irrigated area as residents of settlements within the Gezira, of villages outside the Gezira, such as Maiurno on the Blue Nile, and as unsettled migrants, usually single men. Westerner labour of all kinds was prized, particularly for weeding and cotton-picking. Government and Syndicate officials regarded Westerners as better, harder, more efficient workers than riverain Sudanese and once settled, as law-abiding people.[64] In the Gezira, their tools also made them superior labourers. The *kadanka*, the 'heavy, broad-bladed, short handled hoe' used by Westerners, was ideally suited to the heavy weeding of cotton performed during the rainy season; the *malod*, the long handled hoe used in northern Sudanese rainland agriculture, was only suitable for light surface weeding under dry conditions.[65] The majority of settled Westerner labourers in the Gezira were Nigerians, by the late 1920s mainly Hausa. As they had no farms of their own, in contrast to Arab Sudanese from Blue Nile and neighbouring provinces, they were available for year-round employment by Sudanese tenants. Settled Westerners also provided a pool of labour that allowed the Syndicate to discipline tenants. Under the Syndicate agreement, if a tenant fell behind in cotton operations, the Syndicate could hire so-called *tulba* labourers to work the land for wages as much as 50 to 100 per cent higher than normal, which were then charged to the tenant's account.[66] Arab Sudanese labourers usually brought animals with them for grazing, and therefore tended to remain on the edges of the scheme, and often had fixed arrangements to work for particular tenants. Westerners did not have these constraints, and therefore could and did work throughout the irrigated area. This last advantage applied particularly to Westerners from Chad and Darfur, who by the late 1920s formed a majority of the unsettled agricultural labour in the scheme. Unsettled labourers, usually single men, were a very flexible workforce, though they were more likely to drink, fight, and engage in petty crime than Nigerian pilgrims, who travelled in family units.[67]

It was their dependence on wage labour to survive that made

[63] Duffield, 'Hausa and Fulani', 116–17.

[64] Duffield, 'Fallata', 125–7.

[65] O'Brien, 'Agricultural Labor', 154.

[66] Tony Barnett and Abbas Abdelkarim, *Sudan: The Gezira Scheme and Agricultural Transition* (London: Frank Cass, 1991), 50–1; O'Brien, 'Agricultural Labor', 160.

[67] Duffield, 'Hausa and Fulani', 118–19.

Westerners so valuable to the scheme. This dependence meant that Westerners could be relied upon for the extremely hard labour involved in
canalization, opening up new land for irrigation, repairing canals, and
cotton-ginning.[68] It also meant that they could be depended on year after
year. Labour for cotton-picking had been ample during the scheme's first
two seasons, in part because severe drought resulting in famine conditions
throughout the rainland area of northern Sudan had prompted many
northern Sudanese to seek employment in the Gezira. In subsequent
seasons, the number of northern and central Sudanese rainland peasants
and herders who provided seasonal labour for cotton-picking in the
Gezira varied according to crop yields and animal prices.[69] Without farms
and animals, Westerners were much less vulnerable to these pressures.

If crucial to the operation of the Gezira scheme, Westerners also
presented difficulties, particularly as carriers of disease. The first
schistosomiasis survey in the Gezira, conducted in 1926, revealed 921
cases out of 27,285 men and boys examined. Over 90 per cent of these
cases were in non-local Sudanese and immigrants. Non-Sudanese Westerners (Borgowia from Chad, and Nigerians) accounted for 58 per cent of
these cases and at 14.6 per cent also showed the highest infection rate, by
a significant margin, of any one group. This was the source of some
concern to medical officials, since there were already signs that the disease
was becoming established in the scheme: of the seventy-six cases found
during the survey in local Sudanese, thirty-seven were found in boys, who
were presumed by their age to have acquired the disease locally.[70] Migrant
Westerners were also thought to be carriers of louse-borne relapsing fever,
which in the 1920s was sweeping eastward across Africa. While some
doctors traced the Darfur epidemic of 1926–7, which may have killed as
many as 200,000 Fur, to a small endemic centre in Darfur, others pointed
to West African pilgrims. Fearing that the Gezira scheme would be
crippled if the epidemic reached the irrigated area, the SDF medical corps
and the SMS implemented a series of coercive control measures. Quarantine and delousing stations were established in Darfur, Kordofan, the
Nuba Mountains, Bahr-el-Ghazal, and White Nile province for those
travelling eastward.[71] While these seem to have protected the Gezira from
significant infection, a relapsing fever epidemic did occur in the irrigated
area between August 1930 and June 1931. This epidemic, and the medical

[68] Duffield, 'Hausa and Fulami',118.
[69] O'Brien, 'Agricultural Labor', 147–8.
[70] *RSMS 1926*, 9, 29.
[71] Hartwig, 'Louse-Borne Relapsing Fever', 210–24; *RSMS 1927*, 2.

service's methods for controlling it, reinforced the diseased status of Westerners to British and Sudanese alike. The 492 cases that resulted in sixty-six deaths occurred mainly among Westerners; native administration authorities temporarily opened new quarantine and delousing stations in the irrigated area, aimed mainly at Westerners; the help of local people was enlisted in enforcing quarantine regulations on Westerners; and propaganda as to the 'danger of associating with western immigrants' was disseminated.[72]

One indication of the concern about the possible entrenchment of schistosomiasis in the Gezira was the fact that the SMS grafted schistosomiasis quarantines for Westerners onto four relapsing fever posts in Kordofan and White Nile province in 1926–7. This was never extended to all stations for fear that it would deflect people away from them and help to fuel the relapsing fever epidemic.[73] Once the epidemic abated, however, the delousing stations at Kosti and Dueim in White Nile province were converted into schistosomiasis quarantine stations. All pilgrims and all those headed for work in the Gezira were directed to these stations, where they were examined for urinary schistosomiasis. In theory, all those infected were detained, housed, fed, and treated with antimony tartrate until cured.[74]

This was a controversial measure, given the high value placed on Westerner labour: one doctor commented in 1928 that 'Much criticism has been levelled at the usefulness and efficacy of it.'[75] It became more controversial as time passed and the valuation of Westerner labour continued to rise. According to the Commissioner for the Gezira area in 1929:

Last year if one had asked a tenant or S.P.S. [Sudan Plantations Syndicate] official who was the best worker, I think that in nine cases out of ten, the answer would have been the Arab. This year there has been a tremendous swing of opinion in favour of the Westerner. The tenants admit that he steals, is hot headed and brawls, but they say they must have him. In Northern blocks where the season before his name was anathema, he has been received with open arms.[76]

The catastrophe of the depression made Westerners even more indispensable. As discussed in Chapter 3, cotton yield and cotton prices

---

[72] Quote from *RSMS 1931*, 7; see also correspondence, pp. 552–611, CIVSEC 44/3/24.
[73] President, Special Bilharzia Committee, 'Note on Bilharzia in the Gezira', 28 Mar. 1927, Bilharzia 2 File, NMRLL.
[74] *RSMS 1927*, 14.
[75] Annual Medical Report for 1928, Makwar, section 5, BNP 1/27/201.
[76] Commissioner Gezira Area, 'Report on Casual Labour in the Gezira 1928–1929', 7 July 1929, p. 5, BNP 1/20/125.

plummeted, threatening the government with financial ruin. Dismayed by
the disappearance of profits and by the destruction of *dura* crops by
locusts, over two thousand Sudanese tenants abandoned their tenancies
between 1930 and 1934. The government offered the vacant tenancies to
Westerners.[77] By 1933–4, 13 per cent (just under 2,000) of tenants were
Nigerians and French Equatorial Africans.[78] Granting Westerners tenancies ensured the continuation of production, and spurred the creation of
Westerner labour settlements as Westerner tenants acted as magnets for
Westerner labourers.[79] The number of settled Westerners in the Gezira
increased from 5,734 in 1928–9 to 10,203 in 1931–2.[80] Government and
Syndicate anxiety about labour supply climbed as the scheduled expansion of the irrigated area continued (see Table 4.1) and the start of the
construction of the Jebel Aulia dam in White Nile province in 1932
provided competition for labour.[81] The anxiety sprang, as Jay O'Brien has
argued, from the fact that the government and the Syndicate were concerned to attract 'not simply an "adequate" supply of labor in any general
sense, but a sufficient supply of labor which would work at rock bottom
wages'.[82] One measure of this anxiety was the fact that conscript labour
was used during the 1931–2 season.[83] Another was the launch during the
1932–3 season of what Duffield describes as a 'recruitment programme for
casual labour in the Gezira'. District commissioners in key towns in
Kordofan, Blue Nile province, and Kassala, many of them centres of
Westerner labour, were asked to spread propaganda about cotton-picking
work in the Gezira, and about improvements in conditions—a slight
increase in the piece rate for picking, the introduction of weighing ma-
chines to prevent disputes over wages owed, housing provision—and to
organize the entrainment of groups of labourers, whose rail fares to the
Gezira would be reduced, even waived.[84]

The government and the Syndicate, then, were increasingly desperate
to ensure a free flow of labour, particularly Westerner labour, to the
Gezira scheme during the depression. Foremost among the deterrents to

[77] 'Translation of an article published in "El Rai El Aam" Issue no 975 dated 2nd
July 1948', describing a speech by Arthur Gaitskell, Manager SPS Ltd, SAD 418/3/210.
[78] Culwick, *Human Factor*, 12.
[79] Duffield, 'Hausa and Fulani', 119–20.
[80] 'Note on Labour in the Gezira Irrigation Scheme (Both Sudan Plantations Syndicate
and Kassala Cotton Company Concession Areas) for the Season 1931/1932: With Special
Reference to the Picking Season', 15 July 1932, p. 71, BNP 1/20/125.
[81] Commissioner Gezira Area, Note, 26 Jan. 1932, p. 60, BNP 1/47/338.
[82] Emphasis his: O'Brien, 'Agricultural Labor', 174 n. 33.
[83] Ibid. 169–70.
[84] Duffield, 'Hausa and Fulani', 120–1; O'Brien, 'Agricultural Labor', 170–1.

Westerner labourers heading to the Gezira were the schistosomiasis quarantine stations at Kosti and Dueim. Mai Wurno, the Fulani noble who founded the Maiurno settlement near Sennar and helped to recruit and organize Nigerian labour for work in the Gezira, 'once said that his kinsmen may prefer to return to Nigeria rather than pass through the Kosti quarantine'.[85] Amid continuing concern about labour supply, the Syndicate urged the government in 1933 to lift the quarantines. The Central Sanitary Board decided to close the quarantine stations on 31 March 1934.

While it is tempting to read this as a straightforward question of the need to preserve a flow of cheap labour overriding all health considerations, further analysis reveals a more complicated and interesting situation. This was not simply a matter of profit-conscious, disease-insensitive Syndicate and political officials ignoring doctors' pleas for the maintenance of quarantine, but nor was it one of doctors slavishly serving the capitalist interests of the colonial state of which they were part. Undoubtedly the Syndicate applied pressure to obtain its desired outcome. At the decisive Central Sanitary Board meeting on 8 November 1933, the Board noted that one of the three main objections to the quarantines was 'that they acted as a deterrent to labour for the Gezira'. Dr Robert Archibald, WTRL director, 'emphasized that the quarantines were a definite deterrent to labour for the Gezira, and for that reason alone should be abolished as soon as possible'. Here was clear evidence of the extent to which doctors identified with the economic aims of the scheme. But there were also 'medical' considerations. At a cost of £400–800 per year, the stations only provided partial protection for the Gezira: 'a large proportion of Westerners' evaded them, or fled before completing the course of treatment, which was two to four weeks in length, extremely toxic, and carried unpleasant side-effects. As shown in Table 4.4, the decreasing number of people examined and the falling percentage of infected people who were actually cured suggested that the quarantines were becoming less and less effective. Lifting the quarantines was also a decision about medical administration. The Central Sanitary Board observed that the stations hindered the medical work of the districts in which they were located and that their existence may have been one cause of the unpopularity of the Suakin quarantine for pilgrims returning from Mecca, considered crucial in protecting Sudan from epidemic disease. The new SMS director felt that as

---

[85] Isam Ahmad Hassoun, ' "Western" Migration and Settlement in the Gezira', *SNR* 33 (1952), 69.

TABLE 4.4. *Kosti and Dueim quarantine statistics*

|  | 1927 | 1928 | 1929 | 1930 | 1931 | 1932 | 1933 |
|---|---|---|---|---|---|---|---|
| Examined | 10,921 | 19,402 | 16,375 | 27,261 | 12,205 | 8,319 | 6,055 |
| Infected | 1,067 | 3,820 | 2,937 | 4,582 | 2,072 | 1,170 | 1,045 |
| Infected as % of examined | 9.8% | 19.7% | 17.9% | 16.8% | 17.0% | 14.1% | 17.3% |
| Cured | 1,067 | 3,625 | 2,332 | 4,075 | 1,706 | 903 | 600 |
| Cured as % of infected | 100% | 94.9% | 79.4% | 88.9% | 82.3% | 77.2% | 57.4% |

*Sources*: *RSMS 1927*, 14; *RSMS 1928*, 18; *RSMS 1929*, 13; *RSMS 1930*, 22; *RSMS 1931*, 14; *RSMS 1932*, 12; *RSMS 1933*, 7; 259th meeting CSB, 8 Nov. 1933, p. 344, CIVSEC 44/8/36.

the medical organization was now advanced enough to find and treat infected Westerners in the irrigated area, the time was right for closing the quarantines, always intended as a temporary measure.[86] It was left to the Commissioner for the Gezira area, a political official, to express the clearest concern about the health consequences of this step: 'The population of the Gezira already suffers from endemic malaria, which is partly accountable for the lethargy and lack of stamina of a fair proportion of tenants. If to this will be added Bhilharzia [*sic*], the situation will undoubtedly grow worse and the outlook for the future will be gloomy in the extreme.'[87]

One of the conditions of the quarantine closure was that £300 be allotted to move certain 'Fellata' villages.[88] The aim was to move all temporary villages at least 300m from the nearest canal, a distance intended to be far enough away from the canal to prevent fouling, but close enough to provide a domestic water supply. In 1934, ninety-four of a proposed 102 temporary Westerner settlements were forcibly relocated to permanent, specially laid out sites. The residents were 'now settled in orderly, simply-designed villages, giving access to light and air . . .' The wholesale move of existing permanent villages was considered difficult, but a start was made in forbidding new building on the canal side of villages and in providing new lay-outs to a small number of such villages.[89] Residents of relocated villages were compensated for their old houses. The lifting of the quarantines was followed not only by relocation of

[86] 259th meeting CSB, 8 Nov. 1933, pp. 344–5, CIVSEC 44/8/36.

[87] 24 Oct. 1933, quoted in Gruenbaum, 'Health Services', 162.

[88] The other was that the question of quarantine be reconsidered yearly in the light of the results of the annual bilharzia survey. See 259th meeting CSB, 8 Nov. 1933, p. 345, CIVSEC 44/8/36.

[89] *RSMS 1934*, 9, quote 50.

Westerner villages, but also an 'intensified recruitment of settler groups', who were offered free transport, cash subsidies, and building materials. Sites for new and relocated villages, which had to be approved by the senior medical inspector, were chosen in part for their access to fuel and building materials, and to small plots of land on which residents could cultivate *dura*.[90] Relocation continued slowly throughout the 1930s: in 1936, there were at least 102 Westerner villages, housing 3,659 labourers, whose sites were not approved by the medical authorities.[91]

In her assessment of the decision to lift the quarantines, Gruenbaum has written that 'the fear of changes in disease patterns which the settlement of Westerners might effect was not sufficient to inhibit the settlement policy, seen as important in assuring a supply of agricultural labor'.[92] This is, to some extent, true, but it misses the more important point that doctors did not view Westerner settlement as incompatible with schistosomiasis control. On the contrary, from 1930 onward, the SMS maintained that only village reorganization and sanitary improvements offered a lasting solution to the schistosomiasis problem. From the opening of the scheme, the SMS had placed a great deal of emphasis on destroying snails by drying out canals and by treating canal water with molluscicides, in the hope of creating an environment in which schistosomiasis could not be transmitted, regardless of people's behaviour. But snail destruction was never the panacea that the SMS had hoped for. The 1932 annual report declared: 'It is important to realise that this continued struggle to keep thousands of miles of canals free from infection is a tour de force and cannot be indefinitely maintained. A permanent natural solution must be arrived at.' Building public latrines between the villages and neighbouring canals and providing a proper village layout so that each house had its own yard and its own latrine constituted this permanent solution.[93]

Such an approach aimed to provide the infrastructure that would facilitate changes in tenant and labourer personal habits. Attempts to regulate these habits in the absence of infrastructure had not worked well. The Grand *Mufti*, Sudan's highest expert in Islamic law, issued a *fetwa* (legal opinion) at the request of the government, forbidding bathing, urination, and defaecation in or near canals; this was particularly intended to target

[90] O'Brien, 'Agricultural Labor', 156.
[91] 'Casual Labour Programme. Settlement of Villages. A. Existing Villages Not Approved by Medical Authorities', 11 Jan. 1936, and other correspondence in BNP 1/44/325.
[92] Gruenbaum, 'Health Services', 162.
[93] *RSMS 1932*, 10.

ritual bathing after excretion. The *fetwa* was distributed in the late 1920s along with an illustrated pamphlet describing the transmission of schistosomiasis, propaganda supplemented by health instruction classes in schools. Public notices erected next to canals were backed up by regulations making these actions punishable offences.[94] While such regulations imply the exertion of considerable power over the behaviour of tenants and labourers, they were rarely enforced: it seems likely that the government and the Syndicate were reluctant to risk alienating tenants and labourers over sanitary matters when their cooperation on agricultural production was the priority. In 1930, the SMS started building deep pit or auger bore latrines 'close to the canals at points near villages which are liable to fouling'; by the end of the year, 183 latrines were in place and were apparently being 'freely used'. The SMS also encouraged wealthy Sudanese to build latrines in their private compounds, as an example to others. The ultimate aim was to have a latrine in every private compound, preventing contamination of the canals and decreasing the incidence of dysentery and other water-borne diseases as well as schistosomiasis. But villages had been allowed to grow up 'without properly defined streets or regular and adequate compounds'. Before private latrines could be sunk, proper compounds had to be demarcated. Recognizing that reorganization into the ideal village lay-out and expenditure of money on private latrines were unlikely during the depression, the SMS proposed to start with a 'systematic survey of every village, marking out with permanent marks, the ultimate "lay-out" which is to be conformed to in any new building or reconstruction'.[95] The financial crisis of the depression meant that village surveying and latrine building proceeded very slowly: 'The present poverty of the people and the financial difficulties of the Government combine to hinder the execution of these very necessary sanitary improvements.'[96]

Far from being a health risk, settling Westerners, and reordering existing settlement, were seen as ways of controlling schistosomiasis, even before the quarantines were lifted. From the point of view of the medical authorities, the problem with Westerners was not their presence, but the fact that they were unsettled: 'These westerners are, for the most part, a vagrant population. They are difficult to control or to detain for treatment. They are dirty, ignorant, irresponsive to propaganda and disobedi-

[94] Humphreys, 'Vesical Schistosomiasis', 247; *RSMS 1927*, 13; R. J. Smith, 'Handing-Over Note Tabat Sub-Division, Sudan Irrigation Department', [Apr. 1931], SAD 500/16/37.
[95] *RSMS 1930*, 16, 62.     [96] *RSMS 1931*, 12.

ent to regulations. They are the main factor in the infection of the canals.'[97] They did not settle in permanent villages under headmen, but rather moved independently throughout the irrigated area, working in the same place for three or four days, making temporary accommodation, and then moving a few miles on.[98] Attempts to prescribe village development, particularly for Westerners, started in 1931, well before the quarantines were lifted: a 'large West African village' located on the edge of one canal was 'moved further from the canal and properly laid out' and public latrines were installed. The SMS then decided to direct village extensions away from canals and prevent Westerners from settling close to the canals.[99] Settled Westerners were easier for medical personnel to locate, monitor, and treat. Economically convenient, permanent Westerner settlements would also help to reduce the crime that occurred between the cleaning and the picking of cotton and during the off-season: the unsettled male Westerners thought responsible would be easier to trace and control and more likely to bring out women, thought to be a pacifying influence.[100] The emphasis on Westerner settlement after the lifting of the quarantines marked a continuity, rather than a change, in medical policy. Settlement was pursued, and the quarantines lifted, because both strategies simultaneously spoke to medical, social, and economic concerns, expressed by doctors, political officials, and Syndicate inspectors.

If medical policy targeted Westerners, medical discourse contributed to the making of the category of 'Westerner', and both reflected and reinforced the Fellata ideology and the Takari identity that have been described by Mark Duffield. 'Fellata' was initially a term of Fulani self-ascription. But in the course of the interaction between Sudanese and the large number of Westerners who migrated to Sudan during the colonial period, it became, in the Niles region which includes the Gezira, a term of derision used to describe all Westerners. Fellata is not a racial term, but refers to a group defined by, and disdained for, its association with menial manual labour, such as cotton-picking. It started out referring to Nigerians, only to expand to include people from Chad and Darfur as they became an increasingly significant part of the colonial labour market in the late 1920s and early 1930s. Characteristics associated with Fellata resonate with those used to describe other minority groups: 'although often

[97] Ibid.     [98] Humphreys, 'Vesical Schistosomiasis', 244.

[99] *RSMS 1931*, 12.

[100] 'Note on Labour in the Gezira Irrigation Scheme (Both Sudan Plantations Syndicate and Kassala Cotton Company Concession Areas) for the Season 1931/1932: With Special Reference to the Picking Season', 15 July 1932, pp. 57–8, BNP 1/20/125; Commissioner, Gezira to Governor, BNP, 13 June 1932, pp. 190–1, BNP 1/47/338.

acknowledged as hardworking, [they] are regarded as dirty, disease-ridden and fond of poor food'; they are thought to be 'shifty and con-spiratorial'.[101] Duffield considers the 'Fellata' ideology to be primarily a popular Sudanese ideology. It designates Westerners as migrants and foreigners, and negates the importance of manual labour to the Sudanese economy by denying political, social, and economic standing to those who perform it. The colonial attitude, according to Duffield, was different: '"Fellata" were a hardworking, peaceable and honest folk and a useful addition to Sudan's labour force.'[102] Hausa settlers reproduced this colo-nial view in creating a 'Takari' (their self-chosen label) identity, which tried to counteract the 'Fellata' ideology by emphasizing their thrift, diligence, resourcefulness, hard work, piety, and moral superiority, in contrast to the Sudanese around them.[103]

On the basis of the foregoing discussion about quarantine and settle-ment, I would suggest that the colonial view was more equivocal than Duffield acknowledges. The governor of Blue Nile province looked forward in 1933 to the 'complete absorption and "Nigerianisation" of the decadent Arabs of the Central Sudan by the more virile immigrant race',[104] a positive assessment of Westerner fitness shared by Gezira malariologist Dr Joseph Bryant, whose views are discussed more fully below. But as we have seen, colonial doctors and political officials also viewed Westerners, particularly unsettled men from Chad and Darfur and impoverished pilgrims, as diseased and disorderly. In its focus on Westerners, the obvious outsiders, as the main culprits in relapsing fever epidemics and in the transmission of schistosomiasis, government medical policy both helped to create, and succumbed to, the Fellata ideology. We are left to reconcile these two very different, yet co-existent, assessments of health status. Each undoubtedly served an ideological purpose. Label-ling Westerners as disease carriers seemed to correspond with the facts; provided an identifiable infected group towards which resources could be directed and against which quarantines could be erected; allowed the colonial government, like local Sudanese, to deny the centrality of foreign labour to the colonial economy through stigmatization; and conformed to the apparently universal human preference for blaming the outsider for disease transmission. Labelling Westerners as healthy and fit seemed to correspond with the fact of their hard work; served to denigrate the 'weak'

[101] Duffield, 'Fallata', 130.
[102] Duffield, 'Hausa and Fulani', 141.
[103] Ibid. 132–41.
[104] Governor, BNP to Civil Secretary, 29 July 1933, quoted in Duffield, 'Hausa and Fulani', 126.

Arabs with whom they were compared, consistent with a divide and rule policy; and recognized the centrality of foreign labour to the colonial economy, supporting the government policy of promoting Westerner settlement. Contradictory stereotypes about Westerner health spoke to different, though not always contradictory, concerns within the colonial government. The key to reconciling these two assessments empirically is poverty. Poverty made Westerners migrants and made them susceptible, in physical and environmental terms, to disease infection. The perception of Westerners as fit and virile emerged from their reputations as hard workers, rather than from any scientific measures of health status. Westerners may have worked hard in part to promote their Takari identity in face of the Fellata labelling. But they also worked hard, and were therefore seen as fit, because they were poor and dependent on wage labour for survival.

## RACIAL RESPONSIBILITY

No single group was targeted as the primary carrier of malaria. But in describing malarial infection and prescribing preventive and curative measures, doctors imparted views on the physique and personal responsibility of the different labouring groups in the Gezira, revealing and reinforcing perceptions of the nature and culture of different races. In so doing, they participated in the colonial process of classifying and ordering Sudan and its peoples. Such views were mainly the province of the designated expert, the Gezira malariologist, a medical inspector seconded to work under the WTRL director in the wake of the 1927 epidemic on the 'study of mosquito breeding and other factors affecting the incidence of malaria in this area'.[105] (Such an arrangement of course provides further evidence that the WTRL and the SMS continued to collaborate in spite of the organizational debates outlined in Chapter 2.)

Taking prophylactic and therapeutic quinine and sleeping under mosquito nets were personal responsibilities that the SMS saw as crucial to malaria control, particularly in the wake of the late 1920s epidemics. Quinine was distributed liberally and free of charge by sanitary hakims, and by the malariologist during the annual malaria survey, while mosquito nets were distributed to tenants, on payment, through the Syndicate offices on pay days; in 1928, more than 20,000 nets were distributed in this way.[106] According to Gezira malariologist Dr Joseph Bryant (1929–31),

[105] *RSMS 1927*, 70.
[106] Annual Report for the Period January 1st. to December 31st, 1928 [BNP], p. 3, BNP 1/27/201; Annual Report of the Gezira Malariologist, 12 June 1930, 10; *RSMS 1927*, 69.

writing in 1930, it was the variation in willingness to assume these personal responsibilities, as well as other lifestyle choices, that resulted in the differential impact of malaria on the different communities in the Gezira. Far from invoking a biological notion of racial immunity, Bryant appealed to cultural difference in commenting on the levels of malaria and the effectiveness of prevention among the British, the educated Sudanese, the ordinary Sudanese, and the West Africans. This is consistent with the shift in colonial understandings of racial immunity that Warwick Anderson describes for the late nineteenth and early twentieth centuries, from the view that indigenous populations had hereditary immunity to tropical diseases, to the position that the insanitary culture of these races made them particularly susceptible to disease.[107]

In spite of heavy rains, malaria had not been nearly as widespread among British officials (government employees and Syndicate inspectors) as expected during the 1929–30 season. This was due to their realization of the 'disastrous effect of fever on themselves and the devastating effect on the native villages which provide the labour for cultivation', and their resulting 'unceasing war against the domestic mosquito'. British officials were taking appropriate measures to protect themselves: using mosquito nets and mosquito boots, keeping their mosquito wiring in good repair, treating their servants and other Sudanese who lived near their houses with SMS-issued prophylactic quinine and plasmochine.[108] While malaria was widespread among educated Sudanese clerks and translators, they usually presented themselves for treatment early on. But Bryant criticized their frequent failure to finish the course of treatment out of fear that quinine would cause impotence, a belief that he described as 'universal' among Sudanese; in the case of another 'bad spell', he suggested that the 'effendia' be paraded publicly to ensure that they took their quinine. The seclusion of their wives, moreover, meant that treatment reached only half of this community. Despite the fact that the 'popular policy is to refrain from what is falsely called intrusion into the family life of the native', Bryant urged that educated Sudanese, as government employees and public servants, be made aware of their responsibilities for malaria control in their families.[109]

Bryant's overall view of the 'natives' or ordinary Sudanese was ex-

[107] Warwick Anderson, 'Immunities of Empire: Race, Disease, and the New Tropical Medicine, 1900–1920', *Bulletin of the History of Medicine*, 70 (1996), 94–118.

[108] Quotes from Annual Report of the Gezira Malariologist, 12 June 1930, 5; see also *RSMS 1930*, 60.

[109] Annual Report of the Gezira Malariologist, 12 June 1930, 5–6.

tremely negative: he effectively blamed them for their high levels of infection with malaria. He argued at one point that much ill health in the British community was due to the Gezira environment, specifically the wearing effect of repetitive work and of the monotonous landscape:

The dead level unbroken skyline and the never varying alternation of lubia, cotton durra and fallow numbers along roads and canals all exactly alike. The sameness of the diurnal drive round the block. The same orders as to hishing, watering etc. to the same none too intelligent native, in many cases in [*sic*] the cause, quite indirectly, of much chronic ill health.

He notices little and consequently has little to think about until, for absence of a better subject for thought, he starts to think about himself. We have here the germ of neurasthenia set in a suitable medium for the full development of the syndrome.[110]

This was a modern variant on the nineteenth-century theory of white degeneration in the tropics, with psychological deterioration leading to chronic illness;[111] Bryant's solution to this was hobbies, reading, clubs, and outside amusements. But while he recognized that irrigation increased the incidence of malaria, there was no link to hard agricultural work in a water-ridden environment when it came to analysing the position of ordinary Sudanese. 'Unhappily', wrote Bryant, 'the people themselves are the main obstacles to the control of malaria.' Infection emerged from the 'nature' of the Sudanese:

Naturally lazy, it is difficult enough to get them to cultivate their land properly, much less look after their health or that of their families.

One cannot help but being struck by the improvident attitude of the native who is too apathetic to change his usual maiment [*sic*] for something warmer, or to spend less on women and eat a little better in the cold weather. He is an unproductive person with little imagination.[112]

Perhaps unsurprisingly, Sudanese employed by or working with the colonial state—police, domestic servants, sheikhs, *omdas*—asked for and used mosquito nets. But 'Whether the average native will ever recognize the anopheline as the vector of malaria or realize the appalling effects of the malaria on his family is doubtful, or whether the average native provided with a mosquito net can be induced to sleep under it instead of on it, is

[110] Ibid. 4–5.
[111] Anderson, 'Immunities of Empire', 97–105; Warwick Anderson, 'Disease, Race, and Empire', *Bulletin of the History of Medicine*, 70 (1996), 64–5; Mark Harrison, '"The Tender Frame of Man": Disease, Climate, and Racial Difference in India and the West Indies, 1760–1860', *Bulletin of the History of Medicine*, 70 (1996), 79–81, 85–9.
[112] Annual Report of the Gezira Malariologist, 12 June 1930, 7.

again doubtful.' Bryant had little time for Sudanese views of nets as 'irreligious' or to be avoided because of their association with prostitutes. But despite his pessimism, he supported public health education about the benefits of netting and thought much could be gained if prominent Sudanese led by example.[113]

While Westerners were at this time being condemned for infection with schistosomiasis, medical observation on malaria promoted the positive colonial attitude toward Westerners described by Duffield. Here was a full elaboration of the mythology of the fit Westerner, whose labour was so crucial to the operation of the Gezira scheme: 'Their stature, the muscular development of many, and the magnificent chests and shoulders of not a few dwarf in development and vigour the weed manhood of the arab village.' This physical superiority was not considered inherent, but was attributed by some to a diet containing more meat and protein-rich corn. Casual observation suggested that West Africans had lower splenomegaly rates, which Bryant traced to their superior physiques, and to the smoky fires around which they gathered each night, which kept away mosquitoes.[114] Bryant also pointed to living conditions in villages generally as favourable to the spread of malaria: 'cool, dark, badly ventilated' huts, some crowded with 'ophthalmic children and mangey, helminth infested dogs, sheep . . .' and often malarious people, were ideal for harbouring mosquitoes.[115] These observations did not, however, translate into a new approach to malaria control based on housing and nutritional reform. While the SMS was obviously willing to intervene in the lives of Sudanese to the point of using police to forcibly assemble them for malaria surveys, intervention much beyond that point seems to have been considered too costly in terms both of money and of the goodwill required for the operation of the scheme. Bryant's report was not a blueprint for action, but it does provide insight into the racial perceptions which were influencing, and being influenced by, doctors in the Gezira.

## CONCLUSION

The Sudan government undertook a distinctly colonial project of social, economic, and geographical transformation in the Gezira, carving the landscape into tenancies and canals, and remaking the way that people lived and worked. The Gezira was distinctive territory, in terms of its physical appearance, the system of production that it harboured, and its

---

[113] Annual Report of the Gezira Malariologist, 12 June 1930, 9.
[114] Ibid. 8.    [115] Ibid. 10–11.

economic and political importance. It is easy to see why the Sudan government laid such great weight on protecting that territory from diseases that would thrive in the irrigated environment and that could ultimately undermine the scheme's operation. Consistent with a political economy of health analysis, irrigation in the Gezira carried health costs. The medical service was ultimately unable to prevent the entrenchment of schistosomiasis in the scheme, and an increase in the incidence of malaria.

Economic considerations in a sense underlay the entire medical enterprise in the Gezira. No one promoted disease control in the Gezira for its own sake or out of a particular concern for the health of individual labourers; all involved agreed that disease control mattered because uncontrolled infection could cripple the scheme. But even in this area of capitalist production, economic factors were never all-determining: medical factors, including disease etiology, preconceptions about disease epidemiology, and the availability of medical technology such as drugs and vector-killing chemicals, all shaped the SMS's disease control efforts. Indeed in the Gezira, the relationship between medicine and capital was much more complicated than has sometimes been assumed. Debates over disease control show a diversity of opinion among doctors, political officials, and management agents about how best to balance the need to prevent disease infection against the need to ensure the scheme's cheap and efficient operation. Colonial doctors in this case were not always mere slaves to the capitalist project, but nor were they always fierce advocates of preventive medicine.

Disease control in the Gezira was an attempt to order its environment. Quarantines aimed at Westerners, sophisticated snail and mosquito destruction, (comparatively) widespread availability of treatment drugs, and a (comparatively) dense concentration of medical facilities and personnel were all intended to make the Gezira into an infection-free environment, and where they did not erect actual physical boundaries to the Gezira, certainly served to underline the divide between the irrigated area and the rest of Sudan. Village relocation, latrine building, and regulations against fouling canals aimed to inculcate sanitary habits and create communities that conformed to British notions of cleanliness. Medical knowledge helped to order the colonized population in the Gezira, though not without contradiction, into the diseased and the fit, the stigmatized and the valued, by reflecting and reinforcing the ideologies developed about Westerners and colonial labour hierarchies more generally.

But even in this man-made colonial space, there were limits to the extent to which people could be ordered, regulated, and controlled for medical purposes. Medical and sanitary services were relatively plentiful, but lacking in absolute terms: more dispensaries, more staff, more latrines, and piped water supplies were all considered too expensive, particularly during and after the depression. There were serious problems with the planning for and the actual operation of the Gezira medical organization. Ambitious though its efforts were, the medical service was never quite equal to the task of disease control within the complex, enormous, and expanding Gezira scheme. Ultimately, the need for a mobile, cheap labour force always provided a check on how intrusive disease control measures could be. Life in the Gezira had been remade primarily in the name of agricultural production, and enforcement of medical measures could not be permitted to interfere too greatly with tenant and labour cooperation with the agricultural regime. By contrast, in the sleeping sickness areas of southern Sudan, discussed in the next chapter, indigenous lifestyles were remade primarily in the name of disease control, a project made possible by the region's economic and political marginalization.

# 5

# *Sleeping Sickness and the Ordering of the South*

This chapter looks at disease control in a part of Sudan that was arguably the Gezira's polar opposite. Located at the heart of the country, the Gezira was economically vital, politically stable, and administered by civilian medical and political personnel. It was an environment ordered, although never completely, by colonialism and capitalism. Sleeping sickness appeared on a physical frontier. The tsetse fly that transmitted the disease was confined to an economically insignificant and politically unstable region that was extremely remote from Khartoum, where political officials were either serving or former military men and where, as discussed in Chapter 2, military doctors provided civil medical services until well into the inter-war period. Pacification, rather than administration, was the priority in this area for the first two decades of colonial rule; it was considered a wild, primitive environment. The Gezira mattered to the Sudan government because of its productive capacity. These remote parts of southern Sudan mattered because of sleeping sickness: during the first decade of the twentieth century, epidemics raging in neighbouring countries prompted doctors to search for locally infected cases in Sudan, only found in the next decade.

From this context, completely different from the Gezira, but equally colonial, this chapter argues, as did Chapter 4, that political, economic, geographical, and epidemiological factors were crucial in shaping disease control efforts in Sudan. The inclusion of epidemiological factors here is important. In his comparative study of sleeping sickness control in Uganda, the Belgian Congo, and Tanganyika, Michael Worboys traces the British emphasis on the fly, the Belgian emphasis on humans and human movement, and the German emphasis on the trypanosome, to the expert scientific advice provided to these colonial states, to 'colonial structures and policies', and to the interaction between the two.[1] The fact that

---

[1] Michael Worboys, 'The Comparative History of Sleeping Sickness in East and Central Africa, 1900–1914', *History of Science*, 32 (1994), 89–102; see also Michael Worboys, 'British Colonial Medicine and Tropical Imperialism: A Comparative Perspective', in G. M. van

the British in Sudan adopted elements of all three approaches may challenge Worboys's certainty that tsetse fly control was the characteristic
British tactic, but ultimately supports his view that the colony, rather than
the tropics, is the decisive unit when analysing disease control: in this
sense we are quite right to speak of 'colonial', rather than 'tropical',
medicine. The Sudan case bears out the importance of Worboys's influencing factors, but also demonstrates that he is wrong to discount completely the influence of epidemiological/material conditions.[2] The spatial
conception of sleeping sickness in Sudan cannot be traced to the advice of
Liverpool School experts, who introduced it in the Belgian Congo and
Northern Rhodesia;[3] indeed the Sudan case is notable for its lack of
consultation of outside experts. Such a conception emerged in part from
the apparent absence of locally acquired sleeping sickness cases in southern Sudan before 1910, and was strengthened when the beginnings of
Sudan's epidemics were consistent with a theory of outside introduction.
Epidemiological/material conditions such as the limited extent of Sudan's
*Glossina palpalis* belt, and its location along an international border, had
a significant impact on Sudan's approach to disease control.

As with schistosomiasis in the Gezira, then, an epidemiological baseline
of apparent non-infection, a defined territory to which possible infection
was restricted, and an identifiable set of infected immigrants encouraged
a spatial understanding of disease and an emphasis on the need to protect
territory, rather than particular individuals, from infection. Such protection was attempted through the hardening of boundaries, between
countries, and between people and tsetse flies. Regulations controlled
movement across international borders with Uganda, the Belgian Congo,
and the French Congo; a massive relocation effort aimed at preventing the
spread of infection by separating people from tsetse flies; confinement of
infected people to fly-free isolation camps and settlements was implemented not so much to cure them as to prevent them from infecting flies,
and therefore other people.

This chapter also argues, as Maryinez Lyons has argued for the Belgian
Congo,[4] that it was largely through sleeping sickness research and control
that the Sudan government came to know, order, and administer the
affected areas of southern Sudan. Sleeping Sickness Commission research
expeditions and mass medical examinations brought military doctors, and

---

Heteren, A. de Knecht van Eekelen, and M. J. D. Poulissen (eds.), *Dutch Medicine in the
Malay Archipelago, 1816–1942* (Amsterdam: Rodopi, 1989), 153–67.

[2] Worboys, 'Comparative History', 98–9.
[3] Ibid. 94, 96.          [4] Lyons, *Colonial Disease*.

by extension the colonial state, out of colonial enclaves and into the lives of local people. Operating on a physical frontier, sleeping sickness doctors were also working on a frontier of knowledge where little was known about local peoples and their natural environments. Mapping—of tsetse flies, rivers, villages, and geographical landmarks—was the crucial preliminary to disease control, and provided intelligence about little known territory. Disease control measures also modified that territory, ordering the southern Sudanese environment and people in the name of public health and civilization, by clearing watering places, moving people onto newly-cut roads, creating and reinforcing international and internal boundaries, and disciplining all residents of sleeping sickness areas through regular medical inspections, and infected people and their families in isolation camps and settlements. Such ordering rarely went uncontested, however. Doctors found their work both defining, and being structured by, Sudanese attitudes towards the government. Sudanese hostility towards a government established in name but not in fact meant that some early sleeping sickness expeditions were extremely tentative, while others were indistinguishable from punitive military patrols. This chapter, in other words, highlights the extreme exertions of state power and the extreme tenuousness of state control that simultaneously characterized the colonial situation. At times, the chapter shows medicine in Sudan at its most intrusive and coercive, but it continually highlights the limits of colonial power: understaffed and underfunded, the colonial state could never completely control people inside and outside the sleeping sickness areas, and it could never block the colonial borders, international and district, that Africans were determined to cross.

Sleeping sickness doctors, then, assumed administrative roles, and their work was inherently political. In this context, the categories of 'medical' and 'political' seem to dissolve into one another. This did not mean, however, that political officials suddenly became irrelevant, or that sleeping sickness control received universal, even adequate, government backing, as post-World War I understaffing and a lack of administrative support for the first relocation effort make clear. Though doctors often acted in a manner identical to political officials, they still saw their political counterparts as fulfilling a different function, and one necessary and complementary to their own.

This chapter is loosely chronological, progressing from early research expeditions, through the imposition of strict measures to eradicate the epidemics, to the eventual embrace of tsetse fly control in the late 1930s. I begin, however, with a discussion of the possible origins of Sudan's

sleeping sickness epidemics. If colonialism cannot yet be straightforwardly blamed for the start of these epidemics, the chapter does show that
sleeping sickness control measures, specifically relocation, carried social,
political, agricultural, health, and possibly environmental, costs, and that
the disease itself had a high mortality rate.

## THE ORIGINS OF THE EPIDEMICS

There is considerable debate in the historical literature about what caused
the sleeping sickness epidemics that ravaged East and Central Africa
beginning at the turn of the century. The standard colonial explanation,
still invoked today, was that the process of colonial conquest and the
ensuing establishment of peace overcame isolation imposed by inter-tribal
warfare to increase communications, spreading sleeping sickness into new
areas where it had a devastating impact. Soldiers, labourers, and traders
carried *Trypanosoma gambiense* from old endemic foci in West Africa and
on the lower reaches of the Congo into the interior of the continent. The
outbreak of sleeping sickness in Busoga, Uganda, along the shores of Lake
Victoria in 1896, detected in 1901, is traced by this account to Sudanese
soldiers serving Emin Pasha, or to the Africans staffing Stanley's Emin
Pasha relief expedition. The presence of sleeping sickness in East Africa
caused by *Trypanosoma rhodesiense*, deemed to be a new disease when first
identified in Rhodesia in 1908, is similarly attributed to importation.[5]
Research demonstrating that pre-colonial African societies were not as
isolated as colonial officials had assumed, that Africans in the nineteenth
century had for example engaged in local and long distance trade, has
undermined, but not altogether discredited, this account.

The environmental explanation also considers the advent of colonialism
as decisive, but in emphasizing the complex ecology of sleeping sickness—involving humans, domestic and wild animals, trypanosomes and
tsetse flies—rejects the outside introduction hypothesis as too simplistic.
The most famous proponent of this viewpoint was John Ford, who argued
that late nineteenth-century ecological disasters and colonial policy upset
the environmental control established by pre-colonial African societies.
This control depended on ensuring light, regular infection of humans and
animals by tsetse flies which provided them with some immunity to

[5] A. J. Duggan, 'An Historical Perspective', in H. W. Mulligan (ed.) with W. H. Potts,
*The African Trypanosomiases* (London: George Allen & Unwin, 1970), pp. xliii–xlvii; Lyons,
*Colonial Disease*, 72; John Ford, 'Early Ideas about Sleeping Sickness and their Influence on
Research and Control', in E. E. Sabben-Clare, D. J. Bradley, and K. Kirkwood (eds.), *Health
in Tropical Africa During the Colonial Period* (Oxford: Clarendon Press, 1980), 30.

trypanosomiasis.[6] As James Giblin observes, Ford's views—particularly his emphasis on immunity and his contention that *gambiense* and *rhodesiense* sleeping sickness are simply clinical variants of the same disease—are controversial, but the evidence from northeastern Tanzania marshalled by Giblin appears to support Ford's position.[7] For those of us who follow the scientific orthodoxy in distinguishing between the *gambiense* and *rhodesiense* forms, Ford's emphasis on animals and patterns of land use seems most appropriate for the study of *T. rhodesiense*, a parasite primarily of animals, transmitted by *Glossina morsitans*, among other tsetse flies, for which humans are only incidental hosts; the presence of *G. morsitans* is directly related to the presence of bush belts that provide the habitat for the game on which it feeds. While animal reservoirs such as hartebeests and domesticated pigs have been recorded for *T. gambiense* in West Africa, such reservoirs seem to be less important for this trypanosome in Central Africa.[8] *Gambiense* sleeping sickness in our region operates on a man–fly–man cycle. It is transmitted primarily by *Glossina palpalis*, which has a localized habitat, along rivers in gallery forests on the edge of the savannah, where the fly feeds on small animals and humans using the water.

Maryinez Lyons's recognition of these epidemiological differences is part of the reason that her ecological approach to *gambiense* sleeping sickness in the Belgian Congo looks very different from Ford's analysis. Lyons, like Ford, emphasizes the ecological disruption of the late nineteenth century, but she does not link this disruption to expanded fly belts or to Africans losing control of their environment; given the particular habits of *G. palpalis*, such a link would probably not be convincing. The core of Lyons's argument is that the colonial conquest and the economic exploitation of the Congo by the Belgians forced Africans into closer contact with *G. palpalis*, unleashing epidemic sleeping sickness. Even as medical authorities sought to control the epidemic, colonial taxes continued to force Africans into the gallery forest habitat of the fly to collect rubber.[9] In his reinterpretation of the Busoga epidemic, Thorsten Körner

[6] John Ford, *The Role of the Trypanosomiases in African Ecology: A Study of the Tsetse Fly Problem* (Oxford: Clarendon Press, 1971).

[7] James Giblin, 'Trypanosomiasis Control in African History: An Evaded Issue?', *Journal of African History*, 31 (1990), 59–80.

[8] D. H. Molyneux, 'African Trypanosomiasis', *Clinics in Tropical Medicine and Communicable Diseases*, Dec. 1986, 537–43; P. E. C. Manson-Bahr and D. R. Bell, *Manson's Tropical Diseases*, 19th edn. (London: Baillière Tindall, 1987), 70–1, 1454.

[9] Lyons, *Colonial Disease*. On Lyons's engagement with Ford's ideas, see Giblin, 'Trypanosomiasis Control', 68–9.

adopts an environmental approach closer to Ford's. Körner argues first
that contrary to colonial and ensuing assumptions, this was an epidemic of
*rhodesiense* rather than *gambiense* sleeping sickness. He then argues that
the epidemic was due to the modification of the Uganda environment by
the loss of domestic animals to rinderpest, increased communication and
mobility, and changing patterns of farming, fishing, and settlement.[10]
Implicit in the environmental explanation is the view that sleeping sickness existed in East and Central Africa before these epidemics occurred at
the turn of the century.

    The general picture for southern Sudan appears to be consistent with
the environmental explanation. As in much of East and Central Africa,
outsiders disrupted patterns of life during the nineteenth century. Commercial companies of Arab traders from the 1850s onward set up *zaraib*
(armed camps) in the south, from which they could collect slaves and
ivory; the Turco-Egyptian administration took over these posts in the
1870s.[11] During the 1880s and 1890s the Mahdists occupied, in some cases
very briefly, parts of what became Bahr-el-Ghazal and Mongalla provinces. Under the terms of the Anglo-Congolese Treaty of 1894, the
British leased the Lado Enclave to King Leopold of Belgium for the
duration of his reign, so from 1897 onward, forces from the Congo Free
State started moving into that area.[12] Finally Anglo-Egyptian forces appeared in the Bahr-el-Ghazal from 1900 onward to prevent Leopold from
achieving dominance in the region.[13] Rinderpest and contagious bovine
pleuro-pneumonia affected the Lado Enclave in particular in the 1890s.[14]
It is tempting to follow R. O. Collins in his characterization of southern
Sudan as a 'devastated and unhappy land' at the start of the twentieth
century:[15] certainly the nineteenth century had seen conflict between
invaders, between southern Sudanese societies, and between invaders and

---

[10] Thorsten Körner, 'Sleeping Sickness—A Case Study of Environmental History in
Uganda since the late Nineteenth Century', Magisterarbeit (Universität Hannover, 1995);
see also T. Koerner, P. de Raadt, and I. Maudlin, 'The 1901 Uganda Sleeping Sickness
Epidemic Revisited: A Case of Mistaken Identity?', *Parasitology Today*, 11 (1995), 303–6.
[11] Douglas H. Johnson, 'Recruitment and Entrapment in Private Slave Armies: The
Structure of the *Zara'ib* in the Southern Sudan', *Slavery & Abolition*, 13 (1992), 162–73.
[12] R. O. Collins, *The Southern Sudan, 1883–1898: A Struggle for Control* (New Haven:
Yale University Press, 1962), 123, 156–65.
[13] R. O. Collins, *Land Beyond the Rivers: The Southern Sudan, 1898–1918* (New Haven:
Yale University Press, 1971), 14–15.
[14] Kjell Hødnebø, 'Cattle and Flies: A Study of the Cattle Keeping in Equatoria Province,
the Southern Sudan, 1850–1950', Hovedoppgave i historie varen (University of Bergen,
1981), 28–34.
[15] Collins, *Land*, 46.

southern Sudanese societies. But such a generalization ignores the patchiness of outside penetration and the resilience of some southern Sudanese societies. In the immediate vicinity of stations or *zaraib*, traders and/or officials ruled, enlisting local Africans for porterage and construction work, extracting grain, cattle, and ivory, and raiding for slaves either for trade or for labour within the camp. But the fact that Africans increasingly moved away from these posts to avoid such exactions indicates that the disruption to indigenous agricultural production was extremely local.[16]

Pinpointing the cause of the epidemics in southern Sudan is not my main aim in this chapter, partly because while I can highlight disruption in the areas in which sleeping sickness epidemics occurred,[17] I do not have the specific local evidence, written or oral, to draw explicit links between such upheaval and the outbreak of disease.[18] On the basis of the evidence available to me, it is hard to make a convincing case for the intensification of man–fly contact due to environmental upheaval. In Tembura, the worst disruption occurred almost forty years before the outbreak of epidemic sleeping sickness in 1918, as shown in Table 5.1, and we have as yet little indication that this disruption caused lasting change in the way of life of the local inhabitants, the Azande. Belgian officials recorded sleeping sickness cases in the Lado Enclave in 1907; Captain R. J. C. Thompson of the EAMC testified in 1913 that the disease had been endemic in the Enclave, which reverted to Sudan in June 1910, for 'about 15 years'.[19] This means that the epidemic occurred soon after the consolidation of conquest, but again we lack the specific local information required to build up a picture of subtle shifts in intricate ecological relationships. Even where upheaval occurred and resulted in the abandonment of land, helping the encroachment of *G. morsitans*, it is hard to see how this would start an epidemic transmitted by *G. palpalis*. In Sudan, in contrast to the Belgian Congo, there was no punitive taxation driving Africans into the habitat of *G. palpalis*: the levying of direct taxes started only in 1910.[20] None of this means that an environmental explanation should be ruled out, only that it cannot yet be adequately substantiated. The alternative, colonial

---

[16] Johnson, 'Recruitment', 170; Collins, *Southern Sudan*, 14.

[17] See Bell, 'Medical Research', 181–3.

[18] On the importance of such evidence and how it might change our understanding of southern Sudanese history, see Douglas H. Johnson, 'The Future of the Southern Sudan's Past', *Africa Today*, 28 (1981), 33–41.

[19] Captain R. J. C. Thompson, 14 Nov. 1913, *Minutes of the Evidence Taken by the Departmental Committee on Sleeping Sickness* (London: Eyre & Spottiswoode for HMSO, 1914), 93.

[20] Collins, *Land*, 233–4.

TABLE 5.1. *Sleeping sickness admissions by district, 1911–1940*

| Year | Yei | Kajo Kaji | Nimule | Tembura | Yambio |
|------|-----|-----------|--------|---------|--------|
| 1911 | 268 | | | | |
| 1912 | 140 | | | | |
| 1913 | 139 | | | | |
| 1914 | 24 | | | | |
| 1915 | 17 | 187 | 6 | | |
| 1916 | 21 | 197 | 14 | | |
| 1917 | 14 | 95 | 4 | | |
| 1918 | 32 | 42 | 2 | 255 | |
| 1919 | 15 | 63 | 8 | 621 | |
| 1920 | 32 | 54 | 2 | 192 | |
| 1921 | 24 | 31 | 12 | 656 | |
| 1922 | 7 | 68 | 35 | 434 | |
| 1923 | 3 | 5 | 4 | 839 | 4 |
| 1924 | 0 | 82 | 9 | 276 | 14 |
| 1925 | 0 | 10 | 9 | 203 | 6 |
| 1926 | 0 | 3 | 0 | 79 | 0 |
| 1927 | 1 | 0 | 18 | 49 | 3 |
| 1928 | 1 | 0 | 0 | 26 | 2 |
| 1929 | 0 | 0 | 0 | 18 | 0 |
| 1930 | 0 | 0 | 0 | 37 | 1 |
| 1931 | 0 | 0 | 0 | 61 | 1 |
| 1932 | 0 | 0 | 0 | 49 | 14 |
| 1933 | 1 | 0 | 0 | 70 | 12 |
| 1934 | 4 | 6 | 0 | 20 | 2 |
| 1935 | 1 | 10 | 0 | 80 | 0 |
| 1936 | 0 | 8 | 0 | 142 | 0 |
| 1937 | 2 | 23 | 0 | 63 | 1 |
| 1938 | 0 | 4 | | 106 | 0 |
| 1939 | 0 | 6 | | 103 | 0 |
| 1940 | 0 | 0 | | 80 | 0 |

*Sources*: *RSMS 1926*, 20; *RSMS 1937*, 19; *RSMS 1942*, 12.

explanation is not particularly convincing either: the idea that sleeping sickness epidemics in Sudan were simply the logical outcomes of the disease's spread northeastward across Africa[21] is too unproblematic given the complex ecology of the disease.

Since we cannot make a judgement on how these epidemics started, we are left to analyse what Sudan doctors and officials thought, what influenced their thinking, and how that thinking structured control measures. They embraced the importation theory, believing that sleeping sickness was brought into the Lado Enclave by Belgian Congolese soldiers and

---

[21] Duggan, 'Historical Perspective', p. xlvi.

Ugandan porters, and into Zandeland by Sudanese soldiers returning from the French Congo and by French Congolese refugees. While this view made them typical of their colonial counterparts elsewhere in colonial Africa, it was not, as will become clear, adopted blindly.


## THE SLEEPING SICKNESS COMMISSION

The outbreak of major epidemics of sleeping sickness in Uganda in 1900–2 and the Congo Free State in 1903–4 provided tropical medical experts with the opportunity to demonstrate the power of their new discipline. By 1903, the work of Castellani and Bruce for the second Royal Society Commission on Sleeping Sickness to Uganda had established that the disease was caused by a trypanosome, *T. gambiense*, carried by the tsetse fly, *G. palpalis*.[22] The existence of epidemics in neighbouring colonies, as well as the interest of Andrew Balfour, turned Sudan government attention towards the frontier territory in southern Sudan which it was in the process of pacifying. Balfour soon established that animal trypanosomiasis, transmitted by *G. morsitans*, was widespread in southern Sudan.[23] But early expeditions sent to find human trypanosomiasis cases and map *G. palpalis* belts failed: neither Dr Sheffield Neave, WRL travelling naturalist and pathologist, nor Captain E. D. W. Greig, of the Indian Medical Service and the Royal Society Commission, found cases of sleeping sickness or *G. palpalis* during tours in 1904 and 1905.[24] The first recorded sighting of *G. palpalis* in Sudan was along the Mvolo Road near Meridi in 1905, by military doctor Major H. A. Bray. Bray also reported a February 1905 encounter with an Arab from Kordofan, who warned of much sleeping sickness in Zemios, Congo Free State, fifteen days trek from Tembura.[25] In response to these findings, Governor-General Wingate followed the metropolitan pattern and established the Sudan Sleeping Sickness Commission, composed of Balfour, Principal Medical Officer G. D. Hunter, and Captain George Dansey-Browning of the EAMC. The Commission mandate was, in effect, to push back the

[22] On the unravelling of the etiology of sleeping sickness, see Lyons, *Colonial Disease*, 68–71; John J. McKelvey, *Man Against Tsetse: Struggle for Africa* (Ithaca, NY: Cornell University Press, 1973), 71–83.
[23] Andrew Balfour, 'Trypanosomiasis in the Anglo-Egyptian Sudan', *Edinburgh Medical Journal*, 18 (1905), 202–12.
[24] *Second RWRL*, 10; E. D. W. Greig, 'Summary of Report Number VI of the Sleeping Sickness Commission of the Royal Society; Report on Sleeping Sickness in the Nile Valley', *JRAMC* 5 (1905), 582–6.
[25] *Second RWRL*, 30–1.

frontier of medical knowledge about Sudan and about sleeping sickness by undertaking:

1. To ascertain the distribution of various species of tsetse flies or other biting flies in the Sudan.

2. To ascertain if the disease at present exists in Sudan territory. If so, to determine the exact areas—and to what extent the distribution of the disease coincides with the presence of the tsetse or other flies in these areas.

3. A systematic investigation of the blood and lymph glands of a population in an infected district.

4. A thorough and complete research into the character of its disease, especially as regards its origin and spread.[26]

The Commission sent a series of military doctors to southern Sudan to carry out this brief between 1906 and 1910.[27] Although they examined thousands of Sudanese, they found only a handful of sleeping sickness cases and none that was unequivocally locally acquired.

Without clinical cases of sleeping sickness, the Commission's work focused primarily on tsetse flies, becoming increasingly absorbed by the habits, habitat, and distribution of *G. palpalis*, which they soon found along most watercourses in the extreme southern Sudan. The absence of local cases reinforced the colonial instinct to blame disease on foreigners: Commission doctor Captain Howard Ensor believed that sleeping sickness would probably enter Sudan from the Congo Free State; his successor, Captain R. G. Anderson, emphasized the threat from the Lado Enclave, where cases were already known to be occurring.[28] But the ambitious measures recommended by Ensor, Anderson, and the Commission to prevent spread within Sudan, and to stop infection from the outside—a ban on the introduction of porters from Uganda, the Lado Enclave, and the Belgian Congo, medical examination of African passengers on steamers at Mongalla, regulation of trade routes by international agreement, the appointment of a medical officer specifically to oversee these measures—were not implemented.[29] It would seem that with limited

[26] *Second RWRL*, 10.

[27] Captain George Dansey-Browning, 1906; Captain Howard Ensor, eleven months in 1907–8 in the border regions of the Bahr-el-Ghazal; Captain R. G. Anderson, five months in 1908–9 on the boundary between the Bahr-el-Ghazal and the Lado Enclave; Captain C. M. Drew, 1909–10 in the western Bahr-el-Ghazal.

[28] H. Ensor, 'Report on Investigations Carried out in the Bahr-el-Ghazal Province on Behalf of the Sudan Sleeping Sickness Commission, 1907–1908', *JRAMC* 12 (1909), 394–6; R. G. Anderson, 'Final Report of the Sudan Sleeping Sickness Commission, 1908–1909', *JRAMC* 16 (1911), 206–7.

[29] 'The Anglo-Egyptian Sudan and Sleeping Sickness', *BSSB* 1 (1909), 346; Ensor, 'Report', 397–401.

resources and an uncertain political situation, the government decided against spending more money on a disease that did not seem to be clinically expressed within its territory.

But when the medical officer at Raga, western Bahr-el-Ghazal, reported a sleeping sickness case in a merchant from the French Congo in September 1909, and a second case was diagnosed in October, the government introduced control measures swiftly. These measures were consistent with a spatial conception of sleeping sickness that regarded Sudan as uninfected territory, in contrast to the French Congo, where, enquiry revealed, epidemic sleeping sickness was raging.[30] The Commission sought to bolster the international border as a barrier to disease spread by regulating cross-border movement. Inspection posts placed along the main trade routes at Biri, Sabun, and Said Buldas were staffed by local policemen, who turned most porters away at the border, and directed merchants and all other permitted travellers toward quarantine camps at Deim Zubeir and Raga, where they were held until a medical officer was satisfied that they were free from infection. To monitor refugees and runaway slaves who travelled through the forest to avoid government posts, officials urged local chiefs to bring all new village arrivals to a post for inspection; at least one sleeping sickness case was detected in this way.[31] To prevent spread, extensive clearing designed to reduce man–fly contact was carried out around quarantine camps and inspections posts, and along roads and river banks.

The disease continued to be regarded as foreign: while Captain C. M. Drew, despatched from Khartoum in December 1909 to survey the potentially infected area, found plenty of *G. palpalis* and examined over 1,400 local residents, the only sleeping sickness he saw was in the two men from the French Congo. Local chiefs knew all about the disease in the French Congo, but said they had never heard of it occurring in their own people. Drew concluded that 'there is no Sleeping Sickness amongst the natives of the Western District', but emphasized the danger to the area.[32] The cases at Raga, combined with the impending takeover of the Lado Enclave, prompted the government to allocate an additional £1,000 to prevent human carriers from spreading infection in the east. A medical officer was stationed at Darago Post on the Yei river to inspect Africans

[30] 'Anglo-Egyptian Sudan', *BSSB* 2 (1910), 77.
[31] C. M. Drew, 'Sudan Sleeping Sickness Commission. Report on the State of the Western Bahr el Ghazal and the Liability of this District to an Invasion of Sleeping Sickness from French Congo', *SIR*, no. 197, Dec. 1910, appendix, 9–10.
[32] Ibid. 7–8.

coming in from the Lado Enclave, while the medical officer at Mongalla covered the Nile route by examining Africans from the Lado Enclave and Uganda.[33]

When the Anglo-Egyptian government took over the Lado Enclave from the Belgians on 16 June 1910, in the kind of land exchange and border change that occurred frequently during the colonial period, it inherited an epidemic of sleeping sickness: the Belgians had taken little action against the disease in this area, now part of Mongalla province.[34] After an initial fly and case survey by Major C. Mackenzie, the medical member of the transfer commission, Syrian medical officers Nesib Baz and Adib Haddad, and Captain R. J. C. Thompson established Yei as sleeping sickness campaign headquarters in late 1910, implementing measures virtually identical to those adopted in the western Bahr-el-Ghazal: mapping of fly and sleeping sickness areas; clearance of fly-infested areas near Yei and Kagelu; confinement of sleeping sickness cases to isolation camp; and regulation of movement and trade, particularly across Enclave and international borders.[35]

The epidemic in the Lado Enclave provided scientists in Sudan with new material for study and therefore new ways of contributing to the wider pool of medical knowledge about sleeping sickness. There was a new purpose to mapping tsetse flies. On touring the Lado District for the first six months of 1911, H. H. King, WTRL entomologist, found that the Yei river from Bufi to Yei and many streams throughout the Enclave harboured *G. palpalis*.[36] Research into human trypanosomiasis was now high on the WTRL's agenda and was built into the work of the Yei isolation camp. Captain W. B. Fry, the WTRL's first protozoologist, and Captain H. S. Ranken, posted as bacteriologist to the Yei camp, arrived in Sudan from work investigating sleeping sickness chemotherapy for the Royal Society Commission. Fry and Ranken found granules extruding from trypanosomes from Yei and elsewhere, which they concluded signalled a point in the trypanosomal life cycle after which the parasite would disappear from the blood.[37] Ranken administered and studied the effec-

[33] 'Anglo-Egyptian Sudan', *BSSB* 2 (1910), 77; Anderson, 'Final Report', map opposite 204.

[34] Lyons, *Colonial Disease*, 118.      [35] *Fourth RWTRL*, vol. A, 34–40.

[36] Harold H. King, 'Observations on the Occurrence of Glossina in the Mongalla Province of the Anglo-Egyptian Sudan', *Bulletin of Entomological Research*, 3 (1912), 89–93.

[37] W. B. Fry, 'A Preliminary Note on the Extrusion of Granules by Trypanosomes', *Proceedings of the Royal Society*, series B, 84 (1911), 79–80; W. B. Fry and H. S. Ranken, with a Note on Methods by H. G. Plimmer, 'Further Researches on the Extrusion of Granules by Trypanosomes and on their Further Development', *Proceedings of the Royal Society*, series B, 86 (1913), 377–93.

tiveness of different drug treatments, finding that metallic antimony was safe and effective used alone and in conjunction with other drugs.[38] In 1914, A. J. Chalmers and Captain W. R. O'Farrell, Fry's successor, showed that the Yei epidemic was caused by the same trypanosome as those in Uganda and the Belgian Congo.[39]

Most of this research had direct consequences for control measures: King's mappings showed where infection might spread; Fry and Ranken's work structured treatment; and if Chalmers and O'Farrell had found that the Yei trypanosome had been different from those causing epidemics in foreign countries, sleeping sickness doctors would have had to rethink their aim of protecting Sudan from outside infection. Ranken's recall for war duty in Europe, where he was killed, ended the most directly relevant line of work, however, as his successor, Captain B. H. H. Spence, concentrated on control measures rather than drug treatments.[40] The WTRL's wartime research into trypanosomiasis was precisely the kind of work that could be performed with limited staff and at a great distance from the sleeping sickness area: Chalmers and O'Farrell extended their 1914 paper to show that *T. gambiense* Dutton 1902 was the causal agent for sleeping sickness in Uganda, the Belgian Congo, Principe, the Gambia, and the Lado, while Chalmers intervened in the involved European debates on trypanosome nomenclature and classification.[41] This was very much aimed, like the earlier Commission research, at a wider international community whose methods it used, but it had little to offer men in the field. Trypanosomiasis research waned and veered away from the needs of practice at the same time as practitioners found control measures dominating their work.

## CROSS-BORDER MOVEMENT

Doctors in Sudan held porters from Uganda and the Belgian Congo responsible for introducing the disease to the region. Although sleeping sickness infection was actively occurring within the Lado Enclave, trade was restricted to Rejaf and Loka and foreign human porters were denied

[38] H. S. Ranken, 'A Preliminary Report on the Treatment of Human Trypanosomiasis and Yaws with Metallic Antimony', *Proceedings of the Royal Society*, series B, 86 (1913), 203–18.
[39] A. J. Chalmers and W. R. O'Farrell, 'Sleeping Sickness in the Lado of the Anglo-Egyptian Sudan', *JTMH* 17 (1914), 273–84.
[40] Spence to Mother, 10 Jan. 1915, SAD 852/1/2.
[41] A. J. Chalmers and W. R. O'Farrell, 'Measurements of Dutton and Todd's Gambia Strain of *Trypanosoma Gambiense* Dutton 1902', *JTMH* 19 (1916), 189–94; A. J. Chalmers, 'The Classification of Trypanosomes', *JTMH* 21 (1918), 221–4.

entry to Sudan.[42] In 1913, the government outlawed private transport altogether, mandating that merchants use government carts under police convoy on the Rejaf–Libogo road; the road was declared closed save to government and army officials, merchants with trading licences, Belgian Congo officials, people with special permits from the Sleeping Sickness Commission, and up to two servants for each of the above.[43] Sudan's first Public Health Ordinance (1912) enshrined a spatial approach to sleeping sickness by allowing the governor-general to designate territories within and without Sudan as 'infected areas' for sleeping sickness, and to regulate movement into and within Sudan's infected areas.[44] Sleeping sickness regulations for Mongalla and Bahr-el-Ghazal provinces implicitly designated Uganda, the Belgian Congo, and the French Congo as infected areas, and particularly targeted foreigners as disease carriers. Anyone who had, within the previous six months, been in Uganda, the Belgian Congo, or an infected part of Mongalla, anyone who wished to go north from Uganda, the Belgian Congo, or Mongalla, and anyone in a vessel in Sudan waters that bordered on Mongalla, could be examined for sleeping sickness by the medical officer. All new arrivals from Uganda by land or boat were required to report to Mongalla for a medical examination. The medical officer could decide to send infected residents of Uganda and the Belgian Congo back to their home countries.[45] The Bahr-el-Ghazal regulations stipulated much the same, adding that anyone entering the province from Uganda, the Belgian Congo, the French Congo, or Mongalla province was required to do so at Yambio, Raga, or Meridi, and to be medically examined.[46] The maximum punishment for the breach of any of these regulations was a £10 fine or a six-month prison sentence, or both. Such regulations were attempting to create borders, to give physical and legal force to the lines often arbitrarily drawn by colonial powers on maps and in so doing, assign nationalities—Sudanese, Ugandan, Belgian Congolese—to peoples who had in many cases previously identified themselves as being part of the same ethnic groups.

Regulations aimed at stopping cross-border movements were nonetheless extremely difficult to enforce, particularly when borders split ethnic

[42] 'Anglo-Egyptian Sudan', *BSSB* 3 (1911), 474, 476.

[43] 'Public Health Ordinance, 1912. Rejaf-Libogo Road Transport Regulations, 1913', *SGG*, no. 239, 28 July 1913, 857.

[44] 'Public Health Ordinance, 1912', part X, *SGG*, no. 228, 31 Dec. 1912, 24.

[45] 'Public Health Ordinance, 1912. Mongalla Province. Sleeping Sickness Regulations, 1913', *SGG*, no. 231, 7 Mar. 1913, 764–7.

[46] 'Public Health Ordinance, 1912. Bahr el Ghazal Province. Sleeping Sickness Regulations, 1913', *SGG*, no. 283, 30 June 1913, 844–7.

groups in two. The Kakwa, Nilo-Hamites divided between the West Nile district of northwestern Uganda and the Yei district of southern Sudan, provide a case in point. Fearing the spread of sleeping sickness from Sudan into Uganda—the stereotype of foreign infection worked both ways—the governor of Uganda proposed in the early 1910s that a five-mile wide strip of land be cleared between the Sudanese and the Ugandan Kakwa. People were forcibly moved to one side or the other, but the strategy was soon abandoned: there was a shortage of land on which to resettle and a lack of personnel meant that the border area was impossible to police. A series of orders-in-council were then passed, each shifting the Sudan–Uganda boundary with the aim of preventing sleeping sickness spread. In this case, sleeping sickness not only reinforced, but was a crucial determinant in setting, international boundaries. The Kakwa meanwhile resisted the efforts of colonial governments to restrict cross-border movement, refusing to abandon their system of shifting cultivation, which had historically involved moving north and south of what had become the border. The sleeping sickness epidemic actually heightened the need to cross the border, as Kakwa in Uganda travelled to Sudan to 'visit sick and bereaved relations' and Kakwa in Sudan travelled to Uganda to visit ancestral graves, the rainmakers concentrated there, and the shrine of Kakwa supreme deity Nguleso. From the perspective of Kakwa in Sudan, the sleeping sickness epidemic would only end if they crossed the border and appeased these sacred spirits. They were emboldened to do so by the Water of Yakan, a liquid produced by rainmakers that was believed 'to confer immunity from death or disease', to protect against arrest, and if sprinkled over an individual's body, to turn bullets fired at that person into water.[47] Sleeping sickness regulations created and reinforced international boundaries, but the extent to which they could render those boundaries impermeable would always be limited by the lack of government personnel and the determination of African communities in border areas to maintain the cross-border activities and connections crucial to their ways of life.

Border impermeability was also constrained by the actions of colonial governments. Cross-border movements during the war made the southern Bahr-el-Ghazal the primary focus of sleeping sickness control in Sudan, partly because the Sudan government made Sudanese breach the

[47] Ade. Adefuye, 'The Kakwa of Uganda and the Sudan: The Ethnic Factor in National and International Politics', in A. I. Asiwaju (ed.), *Partitioned Africans: Ethnic Relations across Africa's International Boundaries, 1884–1984* (London: C. Hurst, 1984), 53, 56–7, quotes 57, 53, respectively.

border in defence of the colonial system. In March 1916, in order to help French and Belgian forces quell a revolt by the Zande chief Bangazene, fifty men of the Tembura Equatorial Company, and 800 Sudanese volunteers crossed into French Equatorial Africa from Tembura district, passing through an area heavily infected with sleeping sickness. Periodic medical inspections of Tembura residents were therefore instituted following the force's return on 25 March. Captain B. H. H. Spence reported in 1918 that these soldiers, once dispersed, had 'provoked . . . the appearance of a large number of cases' but by November 1916, examinations of 3,882 people had failed to uncover a single case of sleeping sickness.[48] In April 1916, Dr Cuthbert Christy, who toured the Nile–Congo watershed as an outside expert in 1915–16, warned that people were moving uncontrollably between an infected area of the Belgian Congo and Yambio district; in May, he reported that hundreds of people were moving from the French Congo into Tembura district.[49] Christy recommended the complete closure of the border to Tembura district, a measure dismissed as impractical by both P. M. Larken, the inspector (political official) and E. M. Parsons Smith, the senior medical officer, who instead suggested that only those carrying passes issued by the local medical officer should be allowed to cross the border.[50] French Congolese continued to cross the border regardless—Spence described the flow as continual from September 1916 through at least the spring of 1917—and it was these immigrants who were labelled by later accounts as the 'chief source' of sleeping sickness infection.[51] If borders imposed by colonial powers were often arbitrary, Africans nonetheless recognized that they separated the territory of more and less punitive colonial regimes. The emigration of thousands of Africans, mostly Azande, from the French Congo into Sudan was partly their response to the French authorities' imposition of a heavy rubber tax intended to meet wartime requirements; Larken also blamed the 'uncontrolled free hand' given to French Senegalese soldiers in the French Congo. According to Spence, the governor-general was warned in May 1917 that this immigration constituted a serious public health risk.

[48] E. M. Parsons Smith, SMO, 'Sleeping Sickness Report:—Tembura District', 29 Nov. 1916, pp. 3, 6, MONGALLA 1/6/40, NRO; B. H. H. Spence, Annual Report on Sleeping Sickness for 1918, excerpts in Andrew Balfour, E. van Campenhout, Gustave Martin, and A. G. Bagshawe, *Rapport provisoire sur la tuberculose et la maladie du sommeil en Afrique Équatoriale* (Société des nations, Organisation d'hygiène, 1924), 105.

[49] Ibid.

[50] E. M. Parsons Smith, 'Remarks on Dr Christy's Final Report', 29 Nov. 1916, p. 13, MONGALLA 1/6/40.

[51] G. K. Maurice, 'The History of Sleeping Sickness in the Sudan', *SNR* 13, part II (1930), 219; Spence, Annual Report, 105.

Larken appealed for the immigrants to be allowed to stay, and when his request was denied, sent in a second appeal with his resignation. In August 1917, the governor-general decreed that the immigrants were political refugees and were therefore allowed to remain.[52] The exact sequence of these events remains unknown, but the trade-off between political and health considerations seems clear: keeping Larken, an experienced official committed to the Azande, in post during the war, at a time when the government was facing serious personnel shortages, was worth the risk of an epidemic in a border area remote from Khartoum. The Sleeping Sickness Commission's decision that same month to despatch a doctor to Tembura to organize sleeping sickness control promised to reduce the risk. When Dr Nesib Baz arrived from Mongalla in March 1918, he found sixty sleeping sickness cases within the first week, and 250 within six months; more than 90 per cent of the first 207 cases were found in immigrants from French territory. Baz followed the Yei model and singlehandedly carved out a camp at the head of the Maminza stream in which he segregated all sleeping sickness patients.[53]

## NEGOTIATING INSPECTIONS

Whether intentionally or not, the control measures employed for the Yei and Tembura outbreaks extended government control over these parts of southern Sudan. Such control was never absolute, and with few colonial personnel and poor infrastructure, never could be. As we saw with the Kakwa, as will be explored further below, and as Kirk Hoppe has argued for sleeping sickness control in Uganda, the power of the colonial state was always circumscribed by African action.[54] The negotiated nature of sleeping sickness inspections makes clear that the work of sleeping sickness doctors helped to define, and was structured by, southern Sudanese attitudes towards medical procedures and towards the government. But the fact that doctors assumed administrative roles did not necessarily mean that they always received administrative support for their actions.

Like schistosomiasis and malaria surveys in the Gezira, sleeping sickness inspections became first a sporadic, then a routine part of life in the

[52] Tembura Report 1924, p. 62, MONGALLA 1/6/40; Spence, Annual Report, 106; P. M. Larken, 'Notes on the Azande of Tambura and Yambio, 1911–1932', in T. A. T. Leitch (ed.), *Zande Background* (Nzara: Equatorial Projects Board, 1955), 52.
[53] Spence, Annual Report, 106; Tembura Report 1924, p. 62, MONGALLA 1/6/40.
[54] Kirk Arden Hoppe, 'Lords of the Fly: Colonial Visions and Revisions of African Sleeping-Sickness Environments on Ugandan Lake Victoria, 1906–61', *Africa*, 67 (1997), 86–105.

affected parts of southern Sudan. The doctor, on a trek of anywhere from a few days to several months, sent ahead word of his impending arrival to the local chief, with instructions that his people be assembled for 'parade'. During the inspection, the doctor palpated the cervical (neck) glands of all present and those showing enlarged glands, the characteristic Winterbottom's sign for sleeping sickness, went to one side. During the initial Commission tours, if such gland enlargement could be explained by another infection, the examination went no further.[55] Once the epidemics had started, it seems that the doctor, perhaps more confident politically and more cautious medically, took a blood specimen and performed a gland puncture on each person with enlarged glands. The highly painful and intrusive lumbar puncture, which was routinely used for diagnosis in the Belgian Congo, does not seem to have been part of the standard diagnostic procedure in Sudan.[56] If after a thorough microscopic examination, trypanosomes were found in the blood or lymph, or the red blood cells tested positive for auto-agglutination, or if the case was clinically advanced, arrangements were made, usually through the chief, to send the infected individual to the nearest isolation camp.[57]

The extent to which southern Sudanese cooperated with these inspections depended largely on local attitudes towards the government and their medical procedures. When the first Commission doctors toured, the Sudan government was in the process of settling its authority on southern Sudan. The southern Bahr-el-Ghazal was contested territory: the Belgians maintained posts in the region from 1904 to 1907. A 1905 British patrol had killed chief Yambio and thus broken the power of the strongest Zande kingdom, but the other Zande chiefs remained unsettled, trying to play the two governments off against each other, and to maintain authority despite the Sudan government's attempts to restrain their power.[58] Commission tours helped to extend government authority, and were undoubtedly closely identified with political and military power: doctors sometimes accompanied the inspector on trek and always travelled with an armed escort. But the insecurity of the local situation constrained doctors' activities and meant that these were in some ways highly tentative expeditions. In 1907–8, Ensor found that the chiefs around Yambio, Wo, Gindu, Bekki, and N'Doruma's Post were 'anything but well disposed' towards

[55] Drew, 'Sudan', 7.

[56] Lyons, *Colonial Disease*, 80, 84, 145–6, 184.

[57] On sleeping sickness inspections in the 1930s, see Cruickshank, *Kindling Fire*, 58–63.

[58] Collins, *Land*, 113–29, 169–73.

the Sudan government. He described his tour in these areas as 'practically useless, as far as getting in touch with the natives is concerned, as the people for the most part avoided me as much as possible.'[59] Ensor found only four *palpalis* areas between Rikita's Post and Meridi, he explained, because as he was the first Sudan government official to travel through this region, he was 'obliged to adopt every precaution *en route*': he did not consider it 'safe to leave camp or the line of march in search of palpalis', as 'one could not be certain what one's reception by the natives might be'.[60] His was a military expedition, but Ensor acknowledged its vulnerability and was at pains not to offend the local population: when five people with enlarged cervical glands refused to have their glands punctured, 'for obvious reasons no pressure was applied to induce them to submit to it'.[61]

The initial cooperation of Yei district inhabitants—none of Dr Yusef Derwish's first patients resisted having their glands punctured—was possibly due to their preference for the new Anglo-Egyptian administration over the previous Belgian one: Mackenzie reported at the time that the tribes had 'the greatest faith in the English'.[62] But the situation was not static. The inspector and the senior medical officer were well-received when they toured in 1911 among the Kaliko, considered to be 'by far the least advanced in civilization of any of the tribes belonging to the [Yei river] district'.[63] By late 1914, however, some Kaliko had killed one of Spence's messengers; during an inspection, a sub-chief had threatened one of Spence's men with what turned out to be poison-covered arrows; another messenger had been greeted with a cut stalk of ripe sesame and told 'if you will send as many soldiers as there are grains in this sesame we will fight them'.[64] Spence's inspections in this area were indistinguishable from government patrols, as he used his powers as a second-class magistrate to enforce good turn-outs: in the territory of Chief Aluma, a Kaliko chief, men whose wives were hiding received six lashes; absent village chiefs were sent to Yei as prisoners. He made a brutal public example of one Kaliko village where the chief hid and only twenty of the seventy

[59] Ensor, 'Report', 392.    [60] Ibid. 379.

[61] Ibid. 390; see also H. Ensor, 'A Day's Work on the Sudan Sleeping Sickness Commission', *JRAMC* 23 (1914), 33.

[62] 'Anglo-Egyptian Sudan', *BSSB* 3 (1911), 89.

[63] P. M. Dove, 'Report on Tour through Kakwa and Kaliko Country, Lying West of River Yei and South of the Yei-Aba Automobile Road', *SIR*, no. 205, Aug. 1911, appendix A, 8.

[64] Spence to Father, 31 Dec. 1914, SAD 852/1/2.

inhabitants appeared for inspection: 'The chief is my prisoner, my men are searching the bush, all the huts have been burnt and the whole village moved in closer to Aluma as it was too far away from his influence.'[65]

In Tembura district and the border areas of the southern Bahr-el-Ghazal in 1916, by contrast, Parsons Smith and Larken took a much more conciliatory approach, informed by both political and practical considerations. Zande responses, in other words, shaped medical practice. Zande chiefs at this time continued to resist the government, firm in the quite reasonable belief that it was not permanent but would disappear like the Egyptians, the French, and the Belgians before it.[66] Government officials recognized that they were at a distinct disadvantage when it came to assembling and inspecting the Azande, for they lived in homesteads scattered throughout the forest, which made it easy for them to disappear when warned of an impending inspection. Parsons Smith considered that in this context, 'any question of force would be at once fatal', regarding the 'employment of kindness' as the only way to win Zande 'confidence and trust'. He and Larken bought cooperation through the liberal distribution of salt and beads and the promise of money for those who appeared at examinations. Since his use of gland punctures during a 1915 inspection had turned out to be extremely unpopular—according to Larken, all deaths that had occurred in the district since had been attributed to a spell cast by the doctor—Parsons Smith abandoned this diagnostic method, relying solely on blood examinations.[67]

Doctors came to regard their ability to examine all local inhabitants regularly as decisive if they were to prevent sleeping sickness from spreading. Institutionalizing this kind of regular mass examination required that the doctors know who the local inhabitants were, who ruled them, and where they lived, and that infrastructure make them reasonably accessible. The doctors started from a baseline of almost complete ignorance: when Spence joined Baz at Tembura in August 1918, there was, according to G. K. Maurice, 'no moderately accurate census of the people, no map of any value, no knowledge of the internal tribal organization, nor any lists of important men. There were only two roads in the district . . .'[68] It was for this reason that investigating the geographical, social, and political make-up of the district was so important. In mapping the epidemic, Baz

[65] Spence to Mother, 15 Dec. 1914, SAD 852/1/1–2.

[66] Collins, *Land*, 219; *SIR*, no. 293, Dec. 1918, 4.

[67] E. M. Parsons Smith, SMO, 'Sleeping Sickness Report:—Tembura District', 29 Nov. 1916', pp. 3–6, quotes 4, MONGALLA 1/6/40.

[68] Maurice, 'History', 220.

and Spence, a Fellow of the Royal Geographical Society, mapped and ordered Zandeland, following on from the mapping and descriptive work done by early Commission doctors and by Christy during his trek along the Nile–Congo divide.[69] Spence's maps of Tembura, Yambio, and Mindi districts became the backbone of the official map of the southern Bahr-el-Ghazal.[70] Spence modified these areas as he mapped them: old paths were abandoned, while new roads intended to improve communications and avoid tsetse areas were cut. A working party of fifty men built dams to allow the road to pass over streams and cleared vegetation from around the resthouses they built.[71] Spence was delighted to be trekking along the 'untraversed and unmapped country' along the Nile–Congo watershed and to be enforcing the watershed as international boundary:

. . . today I found 2 more villages on the Congo side; the first I destroyed and sent the people into the Sudan; the second I burned and made the head man a prisoner and chased the rest back into the Sudan. He lied fluently and I found him out so he will get 6 months. Tomorrow I hear I will find a lot of Belgian subjects living on our side; they will make a rapid journey back to where they belong.[72]

Sleeping sickness doctors remade and reordered the landscape in the name of disease control and colonial administration.

The fact that sleeping sickness work had administrative consequences did not, however, mean that it was universally supported by local officials or by Khartoum. The severe understaffing of the sleeping sickness campaign in Tembura—only two doctors were assigned to inspect the district and run the camp—demonstrated a lack of complete support on the part of the central government. Disease and the punishing pace of work began to take its toll on the doctors, and started to undermine control efforts. Spence left in September 1919 because of malaria; his successor died three days after his arrival. When district inspections, suspended for a year in the absence of a second doctor, resumed in October 1920, the roads had grown over and an epidemic was raging. By the end of 1921, with the epidemic showing no signs of abating, medical and political officials agreed on a policy of relocating the Azande from their homes in the forest, where they obtained water from tsetse fly-infested streams, onto roads near communal watering places that could more easily be kept fly-free.

[69] Cuthbert Christy, 'The Nile–Congo Watershed', *Geographical Journal*, 50 (1917), 199–216.
[70] Spence to Mother, 18 Feb. 1919, SAD 852/1/9; Spence to Mother, 16 May 1920, SAD 852/1/10.
[71] Spence to Mother, 28 Dec. 1918, SAD 852/1/8.
[72] Spence to Mother, 2 Mar. 1919, SAD 852/1/9.

Although backed by the governor, the district commissioner's order to the Azande to move in 1922 fell on deaf ears. Many headmen adopted an 'attitude of passive resistance', while some chiefs claimed not to know where the sites were located; those who tried to enforce the order found that their people deserted them. Attendance at inspections dropped off. Confronted by an often impassable Tembura district, Baz and Captain G. K. Maurice turned to the apparently uninfected districts of Yambio and Meridi, in an attempt to prevent the disease from spreading to the north and east.[73] In his annual report, filed in September 1922, Maurice emphasized that although they might be containing the disease, they were unable to extinguish it at its centre. Only one-third of the population in Tembura district had been relocated. Insufficient medical and administrative staff made regular inspections virtually impossible; more effective cooperation was needed between the two sets of officials.[74] In the wake of Maurice's report, the principal medical officer threatened to withdraw his small staff of doctors if they were not given adequate administrative and financial support.[75]

## THE SOCIAL COSTS OF RELOCATION

The threat worked: almost immediately, the government approved an escalation of state penetration into southern Sudanese societies in sleeping sickness areas and provided the resources to accomplish it. New sleeping sickness regulations, effective 15 December 1922, granted considerable administrative powers to the sleeping sickness senior medical officer. Subject to the approval of the governor, he could now order the removal of any villages 'so situated as to facilitate the spread of sleeping sickness'; place any village in which sleeping sickness was epidemic in quarantine; order chiefs to clear brush from river banks and drinking places within their territories; and frame local rules regarding carriers and the use of roads for infected areas. The regulations reconfirmed the closed character of the sleeping sickness area and escalated the restriction and monitoring of movement into, out of, and within infected areas.[76] A new assistant district commissioner for Tembura district alone arrived in March 1923. Financial approval was given for an increase in medical staff, which from June 1923 to April 1924 swelled to seven, before decreasing to four in

---

[73] Maurice, 'History', 222–5, 227–8.
[74] Tembura Report 1922, pp. 55–6, MONGALLA 1/6/40.
[75] Lt. Col. G. K. Maurice, 'Sleeping Sickness', SAD 627/7/8.
[76] 'Public Health Ordinance, 1912. Sleeping Sickness Regulations, 1922', *SGG*, no. 405, 15 Dec. 1922, 1693–6.

August 1924; except for Maurice, all of the doctors were Syrian. The new political interest was manifested in Spence's return to southern Sudan in February 1923 at the behest of the governor-general, to investigate the state of the sleeping sickness organization. The strategy for a coordinated administrative and medical attack on the epidemic emerged from his conference with Maurice, the district commissioner, and the governor.[77]

Relocation remained the centrepiece of control efforts; in contrast to the depopulation strategy adopted in Uganda, which was conceived and presented as a temporary measure,[78] it was always intended to be permanent. Azande in Tembura district were forced to move onto roads, newly cut 'along the watersheds as far as possible so that streams were avoided or crossed at right angles'; river crossings and watering places were cleared of bush.[79] The concentration of population in Tembura was completed by the end of 1924. Relocation was implemented that same year as a precautionary measure in Meridi, and in neighbouring Yambio district, where sleeping sickness was still minimal. Since speed was less important, Larken moved the Azande in Yambio into villages of 1,000 people, centred around grassy streams where little clearing would be required, linked by uninhabited roads.[80] With the concentration of people complete, the medical staff settled into a pattern of monthly inspections in heavily infected areas, with inspections every two to three months elsewhere. Census lists in hand, medical officers travelled by bicycle, motorbike, and eventually car throughout the newly ordered districts. This examination ritual became a routine part of Zande life and continually reasserted the authority of the Sudan government regime over the Zande people.

Contemporary views held that relocation was either good for the Azande[81] or had little effect on them.[82] A brief survey of the short- and long-term stresses brought by relocation—the social costs of disease control, rather than the social costs of production discussed in Chapter 4— demonstrates that neither assessment is accurate. Relocation brought upheaval to the Zande way of life, not least by changing a pattern of settlement that reflected the Zande political organization and system of agricultural production. The Azande lived in isolated family homesteads

---

[77] Maurice, 'History', 229.
[78] Hoppe, 'Lords of the Fly', 89, 99.
[79] A. R. Hunt and J. F. E. Bloss, 'Tsetse Fly Control and Sleeping Sickness in the Sudan', *TRSTMH* 39 (1945), 47.
[80] Maurice, 'History', 236; Tembura Report 1924, pp. 66–70, MONGALLA 1/6/40.
[81] Tembura Report 1924, p. 66, MONGALLA 1/6/40.
[82] E. E. Evans-Pritchard, *Witchcraft, Oracles and Magic among the Azande* (Oxford: Clarendon Press, 1937), 15.

in savannah forest near streams, usually on fertile soil immediately above the gallery forest. A few close kin often lived nearby; paths connected individual homesteads to that of the sub-chief, whose court was in turn connected to that of the provincial governor, which was linked to the court of the king. For nine months of the year, the Azande were farmers; during the other three months, hunting, fishing, repairs, and building were their main occupations. They farmed a wide range of crops—eleusine, cassava, maize, ground-nuts, simsim—in the land that they cleared around their homes, following a shifting cultivation. Azande moved their fields and their homes according to the advice of their oracles, whom they consulted on major and minor matters, the most important of which was *benge*, a poison oracle. They were not unaccustomed to moving their homes, often suddenly, in response to repeated misfortune, the death of a family member, or crop failure.[83]

In this case the sudden move was caused by government threats administered through chiefs. When the 1 April deadline arrived in Tembura and many people had still not moved, the chiefs were gathered together and instructed to send their deputies out to burn down the remaining huts. The inhabitants were permitted to remove their possessions and grain stores before burning, but the fierce message had the intended effect. According to Maurice, most of the move was accomplished without incident once the superiority of governmental and chiefly force had been demonstrated. Resisters included 500–600 people who fled to Yambio district and were relocated in 1925, but in fact there was less opposition than expected.[84] The government scheduled the move so that it would be complete before the onset of the rainy season, but the timing must have brought nutritional trauma. In studying the Azande in the late 1940s, G. M. Culwick identified a 'marked stress period in April–May when the hardest work coincides with the lowest energy intake, and people lose weight and feel overburdened'. The clash of domestic and field duties that created this stress period would have been exacerbated by the hard work

---

[83] E. E. Evans-Pritchard, *The Azande: History and Political Institutions* (Oxford: Clarendon Press, 1971), 168–71; G. M. Culwick, *A Dietary Survey among the Zande of the Southwestern Sudan* (Khartoum: Agricultural Publications, 1950), 23, 27–31; André Singer, 'Ethnography and Ecosystem: A Zande Example', in André Singer and Brian V. Street (eds.), *Zande Themes: Essays Presented to Sir Edward Evans-Pritchard* (Oxford: Basil Blackwell, 1972), 6; P. De Schlippe, *Shifting Cultivation in Africa: The Zande System of Agriculture* (London: Routledge & Kegan Paul, 1956), 192–4; Evans-Pritchard, *Witchcraft*, 260.

[84] Tembura Report 1924, 65–6, MONGALLA 1/6/40.

involved in building a new home and clearing fields; if communication with the old homestead was poor or the grain stores had been destroyed, food scarcity would also have been a problem. Relocation in the 1920s probably caused the same kind of nutritionally 'hard, lean year' that Culwick observed following the second relocation of the Azande in the 1940s, for the cotton-growing Zande scheme.[85]

Relocation interfered with the Zande system of agriculture, pushing Azande to be fixed and therefore accessible, rather than shifting, cultivators. Fields and homes had to be within sight of the road and under a forest conservation ordinance, cultivation within 150 yards of a stream was forbidden, leaving Azande with a much reduced choice of cultivable land; in Yambio district, houses had to be more than 400 yards from the water.[86] The move of homes and crops away from water often meant a shift from the rich forest soils bordering river valleys to poorer savanna soils. According to De Schlippe, the most serious consequence of this move was the delay in cultivation and reduction in yields of early maize, which 'must have without doubt increased considerably the nutritional strain in June'.[87]

Like the settlement of Westerners in the Gezira, relocation was shaped by political as well as medical considerations and had socio-political consequences. In the pre-colonial period, the institution of chief was stronger among the Azande than among any other southern Sudanese society. While the British claimed to be ruling through traditional leaders, the first two decades of this century saw a drastic limitation of the powers of Zande chiefs. As elsewhere in colonial Africa, colonial officials undermined the authority of chiefs by intervening in local affairs: by dismissing chiefs who would not consent to alien rule, by removing chiefs' right to punish their subjects severely, by providing legal protection to women and changing standards of moral behaviour, by imposing peace that ended Zande expansion and internal territorial rivalries, by curtailing trade and access to arms, and by dealing directly with the population to obtain labour. Tembura started to lose control of recently conquered peoples in his territory: Balanda, Bongo, and Golo left to settle and work in and around

[85] Culwick, *Dietary Survey*, quotes 8, 9, respectively; see also De Schlippe, *Shifting Cultivation*, 179, 195–6.

[86] Hunt and Bloss, 'Tsetse Fly Control', 47; Conrad Reining, *The Zande Scheme: An Anthropological Case Study of Economic Development in Africa* (Evanston, Ill.: Northwestern University Press, 1966), 101; Larken, 'Notes on the Azande', 58.

[87] De Schlippe, *Shifting Cultivation*, 227–9, quote 228.

Wau in 1907. Once ruled by Yambio alone, Yambio district was by the end of the First World War divided into twenty-six chieftainships.[88]

Conrad Reining views relocation as a restoration of chiefly power and therefore as a break with the past.[89] Certainly the government appeared to be supporting chiefly authority through relocation: chiefs and sub-chiefs were assigned sections of road, and made responsible for the clearing of roads and stream crossings and the maintenance of public facilities such as bridges, roads, and rest houses in their territory.[90] Inhabitants of Yambio district were moved into villages, rather than onto roads, in part because a 'long string of houses would be more difficult for the headman to supervise than a closer concentration of huts'. But the new patterns of settlement also granted government officials easy access to ordinary Azande—'I could see more of them than had been possible before', enthused Larken—which, while facilitating direct administration, further undercut the position of chiefs.[91] The western district commissioner, J. E. T. Phillipps, wrote:

In Tambura there was, as far as one could see, in January 1925, no vestige of an idea among the Chiefs of their responsibility to Government for even the most elementary duties of administration of their countries, much less any conception of indirect rule . . . Justice, roads, bridges, Rest Houses, and Sleeping Sickness orders were being carried out by officials and their police by 'direct action' on the people and little advantage was being taken of the prestige of the ruling caste of the conquering race, who impressed one as being ignorant of and bewildered as to their position vis-à-vis the Government.[92]

Central to the role of Zande chiefs was the control of magic and witchcraft, to which most misfortune was attributed, and the protection of their subjects from witches. The emasculation of chiefs, to which relocation contributed, weakened the socio-political mechanism for dealing with witchcraft, creating considerable social insecurity. Relocation also heightened Zande fear of adultery and witchcraft by forcing people to live in close proximity to their neighbours; natural cover, grass screens, and cassava hedges were used in vain attempts to restore privacy. During the inter-war period, the number of witch-doctors increased, with their proliferation eventually leading to a loss of confidence in their abilities;

[88] Collins, *Land*, 164–73; Reining, *Zande Scheme*, 17–22, 39–67; Johnson, 'Criminal Secrecy', 184–5, 190–1.
[89] Reining, *Zande Scheme*, 19–20.
[90] Maurice, 'History', 229.
[91] Larken, 'Notes on the Azande', quotes 58, 57, respectively.
[92] Quoted in Collins, *Land*, 170.

Azande increasingly turned to secret societies to mediate gender relations and for protection from witchcraft.[93] Thus relocation fuelled wider socio-political dislocation. In Yambio district, it also created unforeseen health problems: concentrating people into villages caused such a high incidence of dysentery that in 1930, officials broke up some villages, relocating residents once more, to spaced plots along roads.[94]

In the Lado district of Mongalla, resettlement may have had other environmental consequences. Cattle could not survive in twentieth-century Zandeland because of the presence of *G. morsitans*; the evidence suggests that this was not a recent encroachment and that the Azande had never been cattle-keepers.[95] Communities in the Lado area, where villages were relocated along roads during the 1910s and 1920s to prevent the spread of sleeping sickness,[96] kept cattle. Kjell Hødnebø has argued that when the Fajelu, Kakwa, Kaliko, and Makaraka were moved onto roads, the area between the Kuku plateau and the Rejaf–Yei road was opened up to game. According to Hødnebø, the resulting spread of the tsetse fly *G. morsitans*, which transmits animal trypanosomiasis, was the 'main factor' in the destruction of local cattle stocks.[97] These are bold conclusions, which can in fact only be regarded as unconfirmed hypotheses until a more systematic study that uses oral sources can be conducted.[98]

## THE CAMP/SETTLEMENT SYSTEM

Relocation onto roads and into villages carried social, political, agricultural, and health costs, and involved a marked state intervention into southern Sudanese lives. But it was in the sleeping sickness camps and settlement that state control over southern Sudanese was at its most powerful, direct, and prolonged. The only comparable medical institutions in northern Sudan were the various quarantine stations and delousing posts discussed in Chapter 4. Detention at these stations ranged from one day to a maximum of a month. Detention in the sleeping sickness camps and settlement lasted years and frequently ended in death.

The feeding system distinguished the camp from the settlement. At the

---

[93] Johnson, 'Criminal Secrecy', 187–92; Larken, 'Notes on the Azande', 57; Culwick, *Dietary Survey*, 15.

[94] *RSMS 1930*, 45.

[95] Evans-Pritchard, *Witchcraft*, 17.

[96] *SIR*, no. 203, June 1911, 4; 'Anglo-Egyptian Sudan', *BSSB* 3 (1911), 474; *RSMS 1925*, 20; *RSMS 1926*, 18.

[97] Hødnebø, 'Cattle and Flies', 95–7, 130, 137.

[98] I owe this observation to Douglas H. Johnson, personal communication, 15 Mar. 1996.

Yei camp, opened in January 1911, and the Nimule and Kajo Kaji camps, opened in 1915, the government was responsible for feeding patients. In Tembura, where the Maminza camp required Tembura and Yambio districts to supply increasingly large quantities of grain, this system proved too costly and too dangerous in the event of bad rains to be sustainable. In response to this problem and to the camp's general un-popularity, Baz and 669 patients established Source Yubo settlement in February 1920. Patients and their uninfected families were admitted to the twenty square mile, tsetse fly-free settlement and were expected to build huts and grain stores and cultivate crops on their own land, on average five acres under cultivation per patient. Source Yubo was soon self-supporting; the government provided food only for severely ill pa-tients and for new arrivals during their first six months.[99]

Isolation in the camp/settlement followed on from the spatial concep-tion of sleeping sickness. The point was to protect outside territory by separating infected people from uninfected people and tsetse flies, as much as to cure individual illness through chemotherapy, as Spence's reply to a patient complaining about a shortage of atoxyl reveals: 'When a patient says "Why do you bring me here and then give me no medicine?" it is not easy to answer him. As a matter of fact the answer he gets is that he is not here for his own sake but for that of the uninfected people of the District.'[100] The first treatment available for trypanosomiasis, from 1906 onward, was atoxyl, a toxic arsenical today used only for the prophylaxis and treatment of enteric infections in pigs and as a growth-promoting agent. The danger with atoxyl was that doses of 1g could atrophy the optic nerve and produce blindness.[101] Two years of atoxyl injections was none-theless the standard treatment at Source Yubo. Administrative and labour considerations were as important as medical ones in structuring treat-ment. In 1919, Spence introduced a programme of weekly intramuscular injections of 50 cgms (5ccs) of atoxyl: 1g doses had produced debilitating side-effects such as 'gastric and enteric pains & diarrhoea' that left pa-tients unable to work the day after their injections; the previous ten-day injection cycle had proved difficult to administer, and had disrupted the routine of working parties.[102] But side-effects are not mentioned in reports

[99] Tembura Report 1919, p. 41; Tembura Report 1924, pp. 63, 76; Tembura Report 1926, p. 108, MONGALLA 1/6/40.

[100] Tembura Report 1919, p. 43, MONGALLA 1/6/40.

[101] James E. F. Reynolds, *Martindale: The Extra Pharmacopoeia*, 30th edn. (London: The Pharmaceutical Press, 1993), 118; 'Chemo-Therapy of Trypanosomiasis', *BSSB* 1 (1908), 35.

[102] Tembura Report 1919, p. 42, MONGALLA 1/6/40.

after 1919 and there are no comments on blindness caused by treatment, which reached 30 per cent in pre-World War I Belgian Congo lazarets.[103]

An assessment of the effectiveness of treatment is handicapped by a lack of data; as in the Gezira, self-monitoring was not the strong point of this disease control effort. The principal medical officer called, post-war, for more sleeping sickness researchers, attributing the lack of research since Ranken's death to a shortage of funds and staff.[104] Sleeping sickness doctors in Tembura, who echoed their chief's appeal, did not have the spare time: 'The epidemic has been too acute and the Staff too limited to allow much time for the study of the medical aspect. It has been necessary to devote every effort to the control of the epidemic.'[105] Research seemed all the more important when a case referred to Archibald at the WTRL in 1922 turned out to be caused by *T. rhodesiense*, rather than the standard *T. gambiense*.[106] The vector for the former, *G. morsitans*, was 'practically universal' in Bahr-el-Ghazal and Mongalla provinces. If all the cases in Tembura were in fact caused by *T. rhodesiense*, the principal medical officer feared 'an immense conflagration'. But Archibald's proposed visit to Tembura in 1923 to investigate the matter does not seem to have materialized.[107] The epidemic did not spread across southern Sudan, and the view that *T. gambiense* was the primary causal agent continued to predominate, as Archibald and Riding made clear in their discussion of a second *T. rhodesiense* case in 1926.[108] Rats inoculated with gland juice from newly admitted cases continued to be sent from Source Yubo to the WTRL,[109] but the above two cases marked the extent of the WTRL's inter-war research into human trypanosomiasis; WTRL attention, as we have seen, was focused on northern Sudan, primarily the Gezira. Control, in contrast to research, had come to define Sudan's approach to the disease: when a Foreign Office official suggested in 1925 that the Sudan government establish a trypanosomiasis research laboratory in the south,

[103] Lyons, *Colonial Disease*, 120.

[104] Report by PMO, EA on Sleeping Sickness for the Year Ending 30 Sept. 1919, p. 6; Report by PMO, EA on Sleeping Sickness for the Year Ending 30 Sept. 1922, p. 46, MONGALLA 1/6/39.

[105] Quote from Tembura Report 1924, p. 76; see also Tembura Report 1922, p. 56, MONGALLA 1/6/40.

[106] R. G. Archibald, '*Trypanosoma Rhodesiense* in a Case of Sleeping Sickness from the Sudan', *ATMP* 16 (1922), 339–40.

[107] Report by PMO, EA on Sleeping Sickness for the Year Ending 30 Sept. 1922, p. 46, MONGALLA 1/6/39.

[108] R. G. Archibald and Douglas Riding, 'A Second Case of Sleeping Sickness in the Sudan Caused by *Trypanosoma Rhodesiense*', *ATMP* 20 (1926), 166.

[109] Tembura Report 1926, p. 84, MONGALLA 1/6/40.

Colonel B. Biggar, principal medical officer of the SDF, explained that Sudan had 'always specialized in the application of our knowledge to field work, and the control of sleeping sickness from the epidemiological standpoint'.[110]

The most systematic tabulations of the effectiveness of treatment that we have come from Derwish's 1921 report and his 1923 presentation to the Royal Society of Tropical Medicine and Hygiene. At Yei camp, the most effective treatment programme was a combination of antimony and atoxyl, with a death rate of 17.4 per cent among the twenty-three treated cases, ninety-three months after the end of their treatment. The death rates for all other treatments were generally between 40 and 60 per cent.[111] Though of course not all deaths were from sleeping sickness, death rates overall were very high. Between 1911 and 1921, 50 per cent of people admitted to the Yei camp died. Between 1918 and 1924, 28 per cent of people admitted to the camp/settlement at Tembura died. Of the 3,746 cases admitted to Source Yubo between 1918 and 1931, 53 per cent had died by the end of 1931.[112]

Discharge was irregular. To be discharged from Yei, patients had to have been under observation for five years and free from all symptoms for three years.[113] By March 1921, 222 people (30.6 per cent of total admissions) had been discharged since the camp's inception. Sleeping sickness regulations continued to rule the lives of discharged patients: they were required to report to Yei three times a year for an examination and apparently did so willingly; on this basis, six were readmitted to the camp as relapsed in 1921. Discharged patients were required to live in fly-free areas and to prevent them from taking employment which might result in reinfection, adult male discharged patients were exempted from paying poll tax.[114] The first 334 discharges from Source Yubo were made in 1922; all had undergone treatment for between two and four years. The discharged patients returned to their villages, were examined every three months, and were given a short course of atoxyl. By 1924, 62 (18.6 per

[110] Biggar to J. Murray, Egyptian Section, FO, 26 July 1925, p. 21A, CIVSEC 44/10/44.
[111] J. Dervish, discussion following Clement C. Chesterman, 'Tryparsamide in Sleeping Sickness', *TRSTMH* 16 (1923), 411–14; Sleeping Sickness Annual Report of Yei Camp & of Work Done in Yei River District. Oct. 1920 to Sept. 1921, p. 20, CIVSEC 44/9/42.
[112] Sleeping Sickness Annual Report of Yei Camp & of Work Done in Yei River District. Oct. 1920 to Sept. 1921, pp. 5–6, CIVSEC 44/9/42; Tembura Report 1924, pp. 78–9, MONGALLA 1/6/40; *RSMS 1931*, 28.
[113] Report by PMO, EA on Sleeping Sickness for the Year Ending 30 Sept. 1919, p. 6, MONGALLA 1/6/39.
[114] Sleeping Sickness Annual Report of Yei Camp & of Work Done in Yei River District. Oct. 1920 to Sept. 1921, pp. 5–6, CIVSEC 44/9/42.

cent) of those discharged had been readmitted showing signs of the disease.[115]

The camps and the settlement were created for medical purposes but they were also part of the wider administrative and cultural project of the Sudan government in the south. With the same contradictions that emerged during relocation, Source Yubo was theoretically run by indirect rule: on arrival, patients chose one of five, later seven, headman divisions; each division was in turn broken down into sections of men, women and girls, and boys, supervised by a headman, headwoman, and headboy, respectively. The position of division headman, intended to provide the 'first link of responsibility between the medical staff and the patients', was awarded to men who were prominent in their home communities and was largely a ceremonial post. The men, women, and boys who acted as section heads paraded their section for work in the morning and reported on the status of their section at settlement headquarters each day at 1pm. The weekly routine turned the settlement into a large-scale model village in which discipline, hard work, and respect for authority were supposedly inculcated in all residents. Patients in advanced stages of the disease did not have to work and were cared for in hospital. Most of the week, fit patients were occupied tending their own crops. To pay for their treatment, all patients were required to work for the settlement one half day per week; uninfected residents contributed ten days of labour to the settlement each year. Each division performed its communal work on a different day; to avoid disrupting domestic duties, women and men from the same division started working at different times. Communal work included the enormous task of clearing the ten miles of streams that ran throughout the settlement, constructing buildings, making charcoal for the blacksmith, and cultivating communal crops; the 140 *terebai* (a perversion of the French word *travailleur*, usually Azande from the French Congo) employed by the settlement also helped with these tasks. On Saturday, medicine day, the different sections assembled at different times to receive their injections and their ration of salt. Doctors examined uninfected residents once a month. To meet material needs and to spread the discipline of wage labour, the doctors exploited existing Zande technical and craft skills and introduced them to others. By 1929, a carpenter shop, a blacksmith's shop, a basket-making enterprise, and a cane chair factory which supplied chairs to a Khartoum firm employed over fifty men: 'It is undoubtedly better to have in constant employment many boys

---

[115] Tembura Report 1924, p. 77, MONGALLA 1/6/40.

& young men, who would, otherwise be getting into mischief—they are being turned into craftsmen earning a steady wage, and are no longer the young scallywags they once were.'[116]

If the move to the camps and settlement brought upheaval similar to relocation, if treatment was toxic and ineffective, mortality rates high, discharge unreliable, and life within highly disciplined, why did people stay?[117] According to Derwish, there were no significant desertions from Yei after 1911–12, when seven people left. The peak of desertions in Tembura came in 1919 when 149 people left the Maminza camp; once the settlement was functioning, the number of desertions subsided from ninety-nine in 1920 to twenty in 1924. By September 1926, 4,477 people were living at Source Yubo, 61 per cent of whom were not infected by sleeping sickness; two years later, the total had risen to just under 6,000, nearly 10 per cent of the total population of the district.[118] While doctors may have exaggerated the level of patient contentment, there is, Maminza aside, no record of mass desertions as occurred in the Korhogo and Séguela segregation villages in Côte d'Ivoire in 1912 and 1916, of riots like those at the prison-style lazaret at Ibembo, Belgian Congo in 1909–10, or of African protest that treatment did not cure resulting in abandonment, as at the Kaniamkago sleeping sickness settlement in Kisii, Uganda.[119]

Government and chiefly coercion obviously played a role in compelling people to stay. But if the thousands resident at Source Yubo had wanted to leave, perhaps flee across the border, it is hard to see how the small medical staff and the *terebai* could have stopped them. This was perhaps the fundamental contradiction of the colonial situation: even when colonial medical power was at its most apparently coercive, it was in fact extraordinarily weak, ultimately dependent on the consent of African patients. There are several possible reasons why the camp/settlement

[116] Tembura Report 1929, quotes 105, 108, MONGALLA 1/6/40; Maurice, 'History', 238–9.

[117] Space constraints prevent me from discussing southern Sudanese perceptions of sleeping sickness. Lyons, *Colonial Disease*, 169–76, discusses Zande understandings of disease in the context of a wider discussion (162–98) about African responses to sleeping sickness control for which see also Luise White, 'Tsetse Visions: Narratives of Blood and Bugs in Colonial Northern Rhodesia, 1931–9', *Journal of African History*, 36 (1995), 219–45 and Hoppe, 'Lords of the Fly', 86–105.

[118] Sleeping Sickness Annual Report of Yei Camp & of Work Done in Yei River District. Oct. 1920 to Sept. 1921, p. 7, CIVSEC 44/9/42; Tembura Report 1924, p. 79; Tembura Report 1926, p. 83, MONGALLA 1/6/40; *RSMS 1928*, 9.

[119] D. Domergue, 'La Lutte contre la trypanosomiase en Côte d'Ivoire, 1900–1945', *Journal of African History*, 22 (1981), 65; Lyons, *Colonial Disease*, 122, 193–4; Harvey G. Soff, 'Sleeping Sickness in the Lake Victoria Region of British East Africa, 1900–1915', *African Historical Studies*, 2 (1969), 265.

system was tolerated, perhaps even liked, during the 1910s and 1920s. The settlement in particular was large and each patient had access to land; once relocation and regular sleeping sickness inspections had been instituted in the wider district, there was less of a difference in the lifestyle and the level of state monitoring between the settlement and the outside. Admission to the camp/settlement did not mean a severance of all family ties or an end to all outside contact. Despite the burden of added rationing, wives of male patients were allowed to accompany their husbands to Yei camp in order to cook for them. Patients who had undergone a course of drug treatment and who seemed well were permitted to return to their village for a short visit of up to a month; they could receive visitors without restrictions.[120] The 205 patients given one month's leave from Kajo Kaji camp in March 1924 all returned voluntarily.[121] The settlement system was predicated on the presence of uninfected family members who would help with cultivation and food preparation. Doctors at Source Yubo organized a weekly market day so that merchants from the French Congo could trade their goods in the parade ground. At Yei, the steady food supply, with its regular salt and sugar, probably constituted as strong a motive as any for remaining in the camp. Crop yields were consistently good at Source Yubo, to the extent that some people outside asked to be allowed to settle there; patients were often given food surpluses from communal crops, which could be eaten or used for trade. The introduction of foreign vegetables such as onions, cabbage, and tomatoes proved popular and increased the range of foods in the Zande diet. Although Zande men in the settlement could no longer hunt, the doctors shot game to provide meat for residents.[122] Going into the settlement could increase the standard of living of patients and their families. The settlement system was considered so successful that it was adopted for leprosy control in sleeping sickness areas: an adjoining settlement was opened for lepers at Source Yubo and in 1929, the Sudan medical service opened the Li Rangu leprosy settlement near Yambio.[123] But the camp/settlement system was not tolerated indefinitely.

---

[120] *RFACS 1912*, ii. 412; 'Sudan Sleeping Sickness Commission', *Tropical Diseases Bulletin*, 5 (1915), 296; Captain C. M. Drew, 9 Dec. 1913, *Minutes of the Evidence Taken by the Departmental Committee on Sleeping Sickness* (London: Eyre & Spottiswoode for HMSO, 1914), 162.

[121] Report by PMO, EA on Sleeping Sickness for the Year Ending 20 Sept. 1924, p. 72, MONGALLA 1/6/39.

[122] Tembura Report 1926, p. 83; Tembura Report 1929, pp. 104–6, MONGALLA 1/6/40; *RSMS 1925*, 22.

[123] Cruickshank, 'The Birth', 183–8; *RSMS 1930*, 29–31.

While the medical service annual report declared in 1927 that sleeping sickness was 'under complete control',[124] admissions at Tembura and Yambio refused to drop to zero in the late 1920s and early 1930s, as Table 5.1 indicates. In 1932, the medical service identified dispensaries run by local Sudanese as the future of sleeping sickness control: dispensaries would provide medical intelligence, treatment closer to home, general medical care, and would remove the taint of compulsion from the entire exercise.[125] The existing control system continued as the dispensaries were slowly built, but it was considered to have outlived its usefulness in 1936, when 142 cases were admitted to Source Yubo. All came from the seemingly uncontrollable area next to the frontier, where tsetse flies were plentiful and cross-border movement was constant, in spite of government regulations. Sleeping sickness already cost £17,000 per year;[126] redoubling enforcement efforts would require additional, costly staff. It would also retard the development of native administration and interfere with economic development, finally a possibility: plans were already underway for the cotton-growing venture in Yambio district that would become the Zande scheme after the Second World War.[127] The reality was, moreover, that the Azande had lost patience after nineteen years of monthly inspections, stream clearing, and isolation. The confinement of cultivation to a comparatively restricted area under relocation had led, since at least 1933, to overcropping and soil exhaustion. People had started moving their fields, and sometimes even their homes, away from the roads.[128] Inspection attendance had fallen off and even Source Yubo had acquired a bad name. At unacceptably high social, economic, and political cost, the status quo was failing to eradicate sleeping sickness.

At the beginning of 1937, the medical service decided to restore Zande confidence and to aim at sleeping sickness control, rather than eradication, by relaxing the frequency of inspections; by treating infected people in hospital for three months and then discharging them to their homes under observation; by working as much as possible through trained Sudanese auxiliaries; and above all, by destroying tsetse flies. The first attempt to create a safe environment in which behaviour did not matter, by clearing watering places to destroy the tsetse fly habitat, had been 'largely unsuccessful, costly and burdensome'; the strategy of reducing human–fly con-

---

[124] *RSMS 1927*, 32.      [125] *RSMS 1932*, 32.      [126] *RSMS 1926*, 22.

[127] Robert O. Collins, 'Pounds and Piastres: The Beginnings of Economic Development in the Southern Sudan', *Northeast African Studies*, 5 (1983), 54–61.

[128] *RFACS 1933*, 90; Hunt and Bloss, 'Tsetse Fly Control', 47; De Schlippe, *Shifting Cultivation*, 20.

tact was similarly deemed a failure. The new policy was to catch flies over the circumscribed areas—around villages, at watering places—where most infection occurred.[129] Implementation of this block clearing method for tsetse fly control started in 1938.[130]

## CONCLUSION

Confined by the habitat of *G. palpalis* to the southern border belt, sleeping sickness in Sudan never took the toll in human lives that it did in neighbouring countries. Between 1911 and 1940, reported cases in Sudan numbered 6,281. The mortality rate of between 30 and 50 per cent was devastating, but this was not a human disaster on the scale of the 1896–1910 Busoga epidemic in Uganda, estimated to have killed 250,000 people, or even the epidemic in Tanganyika, which killed 11,500 of 23,000 sleeping sickness patients between 1922 and 1946.[131]

Sleeping sickness nonetheless had a profound impact on Sudan. Research expeditions and disease control measures ordered the environment and the people of the extreme south, extending government authority and bringing social, political, and environmental upheaval. Sleeping sickness shows colonial medical power at its most forceful: burning huts to create borders, relocating thousands of people from their forest homes onto roads, confining infected people to camps and settlements where treatment was caustic, discharge irregular, and mortality extremely high. But it also shows the extremely tenuous hold that an underfunded and undermanned colonial state had on this part of southern Sudan. It could not stop cross-border movement, did not dare in some places to perform gland punctures, at least once failed in its efforts to relocate the Azande, and depended on Sudanese consent for the persistence of the camp/settlement system.

Perhaps more than anywhere else in Sudan, doctors in sleeping sickness areas assumed administrative and political roles. If the boundary between medicine and politics seemed to disappear at times, it never dissolved completely for the doctors themselves, who appealed for more political officials to be posted to sleeping sickness areas to support them. Such support—indeed, the wider support of the colonial administration—was

[129] Information on the re-evaluation and the new system from [G. K. Maurice], 'A Note on the Problem of Sleeping Sickness in the Sudan', [approx. 15 Mar. 1937], pp. 540–50, quote p. 546; 'Supplementary Note Embodying Some Details Affecting Sleeping Sickness Control', p. 553 CIVSEC 44/8/36; *RSMS 1936*, 26; *RSMS 1937*, 20.

[130] *RSMS 1938*, 25.

[131] Körner, 'Sleeping Sickness', 60; McKelvey, *Man Against Tsetse*, 154–5.

not, however, guaranteed to them simply because they had assumed political roles, as the under-resourcing of the Tembura campaign in the late 1910s and early 1920s attests.

At every stage, the political, economic, and geographic context—in particular, this region's marginality—shaped sleeping sickness research and control measures. So did material and epidemiological conditions: the timing of Sudan's epidemics, their confinement to the border region, and the limited extent of Sudan's *G. palpalis* belt played a significant role in the creation of the spatial, territorial conception of sleeping sickness that dominated medical thinking in Sudan throughout this period. Only when the results were conclusively ineffective medically and too costly in social, political, and economic terms, did the medical administration relent from its policy of maintaining boundaries between areas of infection and non-infection and between people and tsetse flies. The distinctiveness of Sudan's approach to sleeping sickness control, and the importance of these conditions in shaping it, reinforce Worboys's point that colonialism, and therefore colonial medicine, had many and changing forms. But the 'colonial' was not the only influence on medicine in Africa in the inter-war period, as the next chapter explains.

# 6

# *The International Construction of Yellow Fever*

This chapter highlights a new and important international dimension to medical research and disease control in Africa, born of the very specific conditions of the inter-war period. The linking of metropole and periphery that defined empire, and European concerns about the spread of diseases out of the tropics, meant that colonial medicine had always been to some extent international. Pre-1914 sleeping sickness conferences and conventions on maritime trade and quarantine were 'international' in the sense that they involved some of the Europeans powers, and perhaps their Asian and African colonies. The inter-war period, however, saw the emergence of a new set of actors and a new set of global health concerns. The First World War generated a new commitment to international health organizations, in which European countries of course played leading roles. But, reflecting the growing importance of the United States on the international stage, the conception, funding, and execution of international health initiatives during the inter-war period depended largely on the American Rockefeller Foundation, the world's premier medical philanthropy.[1]

The new international actor faced a changing international context. Countries had long been contending with the removal of geographical barriers to the spread of disease, but the start of commercial air travel in the inter-war period globalized disease concern, specifically about the spread of yellow fever, in an unprecedented manner. Countries that had long seen themselves as safe from yellow fever infection now found themselves under threat from distant countries to which they had been previously unconnected. Air travel ignored conventional national borders. New barriers to disease spread therefore had to be erected. The international sanitary convention on aerial navigation (ISC), administered through the *Office international d'hygiène publique*, was one attempt at addressing this new situation.[2] The International Health Division (IHD) of the

---

[1] Weindling (ed.), *International Health Organisations*.

[2] The Rome agreement mandating the creation of an *Office international d'hygiène publique* was signed in 1907. The *Office* was constituted in 1909; its mission was to collect from, and

Rockefeller Foundation made the ISC meaningful. Providing medical techniques, funding, personnel with international experience of yellow fever, and considerable intellectual enthusiasm, the IHD mapped yellow fever endemicity worldwide, and was at the forefront of research into yellow fever.

No one had any idea that yellow fever occurred as far east in Africa as Sudan until 1933, when the disease's previous biological existence was discovered during the IHD's Africa-wide immunity survey. Tests revealed that the disease had been present in parts of southern Sudan as recently as the late 1920s, but no doctor could recall ever having seen a clinical case. While the precise meaning of the test results and the actual status of yellow fever in Sudan were debated during the 1930s, the Sudan government undertook the control measures demanded by its international obligations, and in collaboration with the IHD and British scientists, conducted yellow fever research. Sudan's strange 'non-experience' of this disease finally culminated in the largest yellow fever epidemic ever recorded in Africa, the Nuba Mountains epidemic of 1940. This episode resolved important scientific debates by providing the first documented, clinical expression of yellow fever in East Africa and the first strains of East African yellow fever virus.

By any estimate, yellow fever in Sudan before 1940 counted for an insignificant amount of sickness and death. The international community and the Rockefeller Foundation invented the yellow fever problem in Sudan and made yellow fever research and prevention a priority for the Sudan government, though they could never completely determine the form such research and control would take. The Foundation's yellow fever project in Africa was almost exclusively research work,[3] in contrast to Latin America, where it undertook major yellow fever eradication

disseminate to, member nations information about public health and esp. infectious/quarantinable diseases, such as plague, yellow fever, cholera, and smallpox (Fraser Brockington, 'The World Health Organization (WHO)', in B. A. Wortley (ed.), *The United Nations: The First Ten Years* (Manchester, 1957), 133). After 1923, the *Office* affiliated with the Health Organization of the League of Nations, based in Geneva. However, while the LNHO became a dynamic body concerned to promote health rather than simply to discourage the spread of disease, the *Office* remained a conservative organization that distributed information and enforced sanitary conventions (Martin David Dubin, 'The League of Nations Health Organisation', in Weindling (ed.), *International Health Organisations*, 56–80).

[3] On the IHD's inter-war shift away from building up local and national health organizations and from field-based work, towards the advancement of scientific knowledge through laboratory research, in which the African yellow fever work played a crucial role, see John Farley, 'The International Health Division of the Rockefeller Foundation: The Russell Years, 1920–1934', in Weindling (ed.), *International Health Organisations*, 203–21.

campaigns, administered by authoritarian sanitary bureaucracies that often clashed with the local populace.[4] In both places, however, the IHD directed resources at yellow fever out of all proportion to the disease's impact on local health. In both places, local resistance to the global goal—whether by the general population or a government—was regarded by the IHD and its allies as selfish and irresponsible.[5] Luise White has described the post-war smallpox eradication campaign in Africa as the 'triumph of global humanitarian concerns at the expense of local sovereignty and local humanitarian concerns'. Armed with technology, funding, and missionary zeal, the World Health Organization 'acted as a sovereign body', crossing national boundaries, ignoring national health priorities and needs, even undermining national sovereignty.[6] Sudan's experience of yellow fever, and inter-war yellow fever campaigns in Latin America, show that this was not an entirely new phenomenon. Of course, in the inter-war period, international health organizations such as the *Office* were nothing like as powerful as the post-war WHO, nor were inter-war yellow fever research and mosquito control efforts in Africa anything like as aggressive as the smallpox campaign. But in their emphasis on the disease dangers facing the global community because of air travel, their backing by international health organizations, their reliance on sophisticated medical technology, and their dependence on well-funded personnel pursuing a single disease across all borders in the name of the greater good, the inter-war yellow fever efforts can be seen as a forerunner of the smallpox campaign, and as the beginning of a new international medicine.

This chapter also provides an extreme example of medical activity depending on laboratory analysis. Yellow fever research and preventive

[4] Steven C. Williams, 'Nationalism and Public Health: The Convergence of Rockefeller Foundation Technique and Brazilian Federal Authority during the Time of Yellow Fever, 1925–1930', 23–51, and Armando Solórzano, 'The Rockefeller Foundation in Revolutionary Mexico: Yellow Fever in Yucatan and Veracruz', 52–71, in Marcos Cueto (ed.), *Missionaries of Science: The Rockefeller Foundation and Latin America* (Bloomington: Indiana University Press, 1994); Ilana Löwy, 'What/who should be Controlled: Opposition to Yellow Fever Campaigns in Brazil, 1900–1939', in Bridie Andrews and Andrew Cunningham (eds.), *Western Medicine as Contested Knowledge* (Manchester: Manchester University Press, 1997); Armando Solórzano, 'Sowing the Seeds of Neo-imperialism: The Rockefeller Foundation's Yellow Fever Campaign in Mexico', *International Journal of Health Services*, 22 (1992), 529–54.
[5] See e.g. discussion later in this chapter, and the attitude towards Peruvian workers striking against yellow fever control measures in 1921 quoted in Marcos Cueto, 'Sanitation from Above: Yellow Fever and Foreign Intervention in Peru, 1919–1922', *Hispanic American Historical Review*, 72 (1992), 21.
[6] Luise White, 'The Needle and the State: Immunization and Inoculation in Africa. Or, The Practice of Unnational Sovereignty', paper presented to the Workshop on Immunization and the State, Delhi, India, 16–17 Jan. 1997, quotes from 13, 16, respectively.

measures in Sudan were prompted not by the diagnosis of clinical illness, but by the detection of immunity, and therefore past exposure to yellow fever virus, in human blood through the mouse protection test. But the authority of the laboratory was not absolute. The international medical community challenged the integrity of this test, and the precise meaning of its results, for a range of reasons. The test detected yellow fever infection in places such as Sudan where clinicians had never diagnosed the disease and where medical orthodoxy held it did not exist. This called into question the professional judgement of most doctors in Africa, particularly the clinicians on the ground in the affected area; resentment at being told by outsiders, and Americans no less, of the disease situation in one's own colony may have encouraged scepticism about the test results. Accepting the IHD interpretation of the test results meant accepting the political implications of yellow fever being a health threat in a much wider area than previously thought and taking precautions against its spread via air travel; this was frightening and costly. Perhaps most crucially, until 1940, no yellow fever virus could be isolated from the area in which the protection test signalled that infection was occurring. The controversy surrounding the protection test was a controversy about defining the 'medical', about what could legitimately be called 'medical' knowledge. This chapter argues that the medical community in the interwar period policed the boundary between accepted and illegitimate medical knowledge—in this case knowledge generated by a new medical technology—using medical, political, and professional considerations, including those outlined above.

The emphasis placed on isolating the yellow fever pathogen to vindicate the protection test—and to identify yellow fever as such in Africa throughout the inter-war period—reinforces at one level Andrew Cunningham's argument that the 'laboratory revolution in medicine' immediately transformed the identity of infectious disease from one that was symptom-based to one that was cause-based.[7] But this chapter also demonstrates, contrary to Cunningham, and perhaps paradoxically, that even within the laboratory and even among scientists embracing a cause-based view of disease, the identity of yellow fever continued to depend on a careful reading of symptoms. The difficulty in isolating yellow fever virus, which disappears from the bloodstream within three to six days of infection, meant that diagnosis in Sudan continued to depend on a careful consideration of a patient's clinical history, and post-mortem, an examina-

[7] Cunningham, 'Transforming Plague', 209–44.

tion of the liver in search of the characteristic yellow fever necrosis. Even where isolation of the virus was possible, the fact remained that yellow fever virus, unlike Cunningham's plague bacillus, was too small to be seen using inter-war microscopes: indeed, viruses were defined as a category in the inter-war period by their non-cultivability, filterability, and invisibility.[8] The virus was 'isolated' by injecting infected blood into a laboratory animal and seeing if that animal developed clinical yellow fever. An analysis of symptoms therefore remained paramount, even in identifying the pathogen.

The chapter explores these themes through a chronological discussion, starting with the immunity survey and culminating in the 1940 epidemic.

## INTERNATIONAL CONCERN AND THE IMMUNITY SURVEY

African research in general, and the Sudan case in particular, were central to a major shift in the scientific understanding of yellow fever. It was Carlos Finlay, a Cuban doctor, who in 1881 first hypothesized that the female *Aedes aegypti* mosquito transmitted yellow fever; his theory was investigated and confirmed by the work of the US Army Yellow Fever Commission in Cuba at the turn of the century.[9] According to the scientific orthodoxy of the mid-1920s, yellow fever was an urban disease, carried from human to human by this one species of domestic mosquito; there were no other carriers, nor were there any animal reservoirs. Eradicating yellow fever in West Africa was the primary aim of the Rockefeller Foundation's International Health Board (from 1927, the IHD) Yellow Fever Commission when it arrived in Lagos, Nigeria in 1925. Before eradication could be attempted, however, the fever associated with jaundice in West Africa had to be shown to be the same disease as yellow fever in the Americas.[10] The Commission therefore sought to isolate from African cases of yellow fever *Leptospira icteroides*, the spirochete identified in 1918 as the yellow fever pathogen by Hideyo Noguchi, a respected bacteriologist at the Rockefeller Institute of Medical Research. When

---

[8] Ton van Helvoort, 'History of Virus Research in the Twentieth Century: The Problem of Conceptual Continuity', *History of Science*, 32 (1994), 186.

[9] Nancy Stepan, 'The Interplay between Socio-Economic Factors and Medical Science: Yellow Fever Research, Cuba and the United States', *Social Studies of Science*, 8 (1978), 397–423.

[10] West Africa Annual Report 1925, p. 3, box 214, series 3, Record Group (RG) 5, Rockefeller Foundation Archive (RFA), Rockefeller Archive Center (RAC), North Tarrytown, New York.

Commission members failed to isolate *L. icteroides* from typical clinical cases, they decided that there was 'probably some distinct difference between the organisms of the two kinds of yellow fever' and began to intensively study West African fever as an 'unknown infection'.[11] Human yellow fever virus was first isolated in susceptible rhesus monkeys by Commission scientists at Lagos in 1927.[12] Noguchi travelled to West Africa to defend his theory before dying of yellow fever in May 1928 but it was increasingly clear that he had been wrong: the causal organism for yellow fever was a filterable virus, not a spirochete that could be cultured. Once American virus had been isolated, cross-immunity tests conducted by IHD scientists in New York and others definitively established the single identity of the two diseases.[13]

Using the susceptible monkey and building on the assumption, confirmed by their own experiments, that exposure to the virus brought permanent immunity to the disease, IHD doctors developed in 1928 a protection test to detect the past presence of yellow fever. Yellow fever virus and a person's blood serum were injected into a rhesus monkey. If the monkey was not killed by the virus, it must have been 'protected' from infection by yellow fever immune bodies present in the human serum; the person in question must have been infected, at some point, by yellow fever, making for a positive test. If the monkey died of yellow fever, the test result was negative: the serum offered no immunity. By 1929, IHD Drs H. Beeuwkes, J. H. Bauer, and A. F. Mahaffy were using this technique to delimit zones of yellow fever endemicity in West Africa.[14]

The existence of this protection test provided a vital tool precisely at the time when international health bodies were considering how to address the health threats arising from the newly dawning age of commercial

---

[11] West Africa Annual Report 1926, quotes pp. 25, 26, box 214, series 3, RG 5, RFA, RAC.

[12] Adrian Stokes, Johannes H. Bauer, and N. Paul Hudson, 'Experimental Transmission of Yellow Fever to Laboratory Animals', *American Journal of Tropical Medicine*, 8 (1928), 103–64.

[13] Max Theiler and Andrew Watson Sellards, 'The Immunological Relationship of Yellow Fever as It Occurs in West Africa and in South America', *ATMP* 22 (1928), 449–60; N. C. Davis, 'Studies on South American Yellow Fever II: Immunity of Recovered Monkeys to African Virus', *Journal of Experimental Medicine*, 49 (1929), 985–91; W. A. Sawyer, S. F. Kitchen, Martin Frobisher, Jr., and Wray Lloyd, 'Relationship of Yellow Fever of the Western Hemisphere to That of Africa and to Leptospiral Jaundice', *Journal of Experimental Medicine*, 51 (1930), 493–517.

[14] Henry Beeuwkes, J. H. Bauer, and A. F. Mahaffy, 'Yellow Fever Endemicity in West Africa, with Special Reference to Protection Tests', *American Journal of Tropical Medicine*, 10 (1930), 305–33.

air travel.[15] In their abbreviation of travel time, airplanes removed one of the natural physical barriers to the spread of disease, allowing infectious people to travel from an endemic area to a non-infected area without showing symptoms. In the case of yellow fever, infected mosquitoes trapped in planes also threatened to spread the disease. India and other Asian countries were particularly concerned: while yellow fever was unknown in these regions, kept away by geographical barriers, *Aedes aegypti* bred locally. It was thought that only one infected traveller or mosquito brought in by plane was needed to act as lethal spark for an epidemic among Asian populations, all non-immune. Many believed that because of air travel, the world was 'approaching what might prove to be one of the major disasters of mankind, to wit, the spread of yellow fever via Africa to Asia'.[16]

The international sanitary convention on aerial navigation drafted by the *Office international d'hygiène publique* aimed at preventing this disaster, but debate surrounded the draft ISC. The leading members of the *Office*, Britain and France, found themselves pulled between concern for the health of their colonies, many of which were members in their own right of the *Office*, and the interests of their fledgling airline industries. The most contentious question was how to handle planes arriving in yellow fever-free areas from endemic centres. One camp favoured stringent regulations: in late 1930 for example, India and the Dutch East Indies, both yellow fever-free, 'prohibited the landing of any aeroplanes coming from areas which can be considered endemic'. A second camp, not wanting to ruin the airplane industry, preferred only to go as far as the facts warranted in making regulations.[17] But what were the facts? Aerodromes could not be placed outside endemic areas and appropriate precautions could not be taken against flights travelling from endemic areas if the exact delimitations of those areas remained unknown. The *Office* decided in

[15] British-owned Imperial Airways surveyed the Cairo to Cape route in late 1929 and early 1930. Service to Mwanza, Tanganyika, which included passenger service to Khartoum, started on 28 Feb. 1931. Between London and Cape Town, an eleven-day mail service started on 20 Jan. 1932 and passenger service began on 27 Apr. 1932. The first flight connecting West Africa with the main north–south route left Khartoum on 9 Feb. 1936; on 15 Oct. 1936, this service was extended to Lagos (R. E. G. Davies, *A History of the World's Airlines* (London: Oxford University Press, 1964), 180–2).

[16] Dr Fred Soper, cited in P. Mitchell, 'Note of Conversation with Mr. D. Newbold, Civil Secretary of the Sudan on 9.9.41', 11 Sept. 1941, p. 590, CIVSEC 44/5/27. Identical concerns had been voiced about the opening of the Panama Canal, prompting William C. Gorgas's yellow fever eradication work in the Canal Zone from 1904 onwards.

[17] G. K. Strode to F. F. Russell, 7 Jan. 1931, folder 782, box 84, series 100 O, RG 1.1, RFA, RAC.

October 1930 to undertake a yellow fever survey to locate endemic areas; it approached the Rockefeller Foundation 'to undertake the technical management and organization of these investigations'.[18] At a meeting in Paris in February 1931, and later in a formal letter, F. F. Russell, head of the IHD, notified the *Office* that the division 'would do everything possible to assist' in its epidemiological researches. The help proferred followed standard Rockefeller Foundation procedure in aiming at the eventual technical self-sufficiency of the countries assisted. The IHD would train colonial service doctors to conduct protection tests. Until colonial governments had the resources to perform the tests themselves, the IHD would conduct them in its yellow fever laboratory in New York, opened in the Rockefeller Institute of Medical Research in 1928. The survey would initially be confined to Africa.[19]

The timing of the request was fortuitous, for American researchers had only just developed a mouse protection test which—cheaper, more efficient, and more sensitive than the monkey test—made such an extensive survey possible. In 1930, Dr Max Theiler of Harvard Medical School showed that white mice were susceptible to yellow fever virus injected intracerebrally;[20] while Theiler then developed an intracerebral mouse protection test, it was the intraperitoneal test developed by IHD Drs Wilbur A. Sawyer and Wray Lloyd that was used for the African survey.[21] The specimens that started arriving in New York in May 1931 were collected from West Africa, since yellow fever was known, and thought to exist, only on that part of the continent. But growing vehemence on all sides at the *Office* about the danger from air travel, and the failure of the early stages of the survey to clear up confusion about the extent of the disease meant that by late 1932, the survey was extended to the Belgian Congo.[22] Yellow fever did not appear to travel beyond Central Africa, but once surveying in the Belgian Congo had started, it was logical to begin

---

[18] O. Velghe, President of the Permanent Committee of the International Office for Public Hygiene to [President of the Rockefeller Foundation], 31 Dec. 1930, folder 782, box 84, series 100 O, RG 1.1, RFA, RAC.

[19] Excerpt from G. K. Strode diary, 20 Feb. 1931; quote from Russell to Dr Hugh Cumming, 17 Apr. 1931, folder 782, box 84, series 100 O, RG 1.1, RFA, RAC.

[20] Max Theiler, 'Studies on the Action of Yellow Fever Virus in Mice', *ATMP* 24 (1930), 247–72.

[21] W. A. Sawyer and Wray Lloyd, 'Use of Mice in Tests of Immunity Against Yellow Fever', *Journal of Experimental Medicine*, 54 (1931), 533–55; Kenneth C. Smithburn, 'Immunology', in G. K. Strode (ed.), *Yellow Fever* (New York: McGraw-Hill, 1951), 177–81.

[22] George Abt, Directeur de l'Office to Russell, 4 July 1932; Russell to Velghe, 25 July 1932; Sawyer to Russell, 8 Aug. 1932; H. Beeuwkes to Russell, 31 Oct. and 23 Dec. 1932, folder 784, box 84, series 100 O, RG 1.1, RFA, RAC.

thinking about East and Southern Africa. The Anglo-Egyptian Sudan and neighbouring countries first came under discussion at the *Office* as areas 'in which it is thought that yellow fever has never existed but would be capable of becoming epidemic if it were introduced'.[23] East Africa needed to be protected itself and guarded as a buffer zone for India.[24] The possibility that the region was already infected with yellow fever was not considered.

The IHD cultivated the British government, in part because it saw London as the gateway to influencing the entire British empire; relations, as a result, were warm.[25] It is therefore unsurprising that when the IHD sought to extend the African survey, it turned to the Colonial Office. Dr Sawyer, director of the IHD laboratory division, attended the Pan-African Health Conference, organized by the Health Organization of the League of Nations at Cape Town in November 1932, as an invited 'neutral' expert, so-termed because he had no position to defend in the ongoing debate over the ISC, since he did not come from a country where yellow fever existed, nor from one which feared invasion.[26] In Europe before the conference and in Cape Town, Sawyer made arrangements first with Dr Stanton, medical adviser to the Colonial Office, and then with colonial doctors for extending the immunity survey into British East and Southern African territories. A new collaborator of the IHD, Dr G. M. Findlay of the Wellcome Bureau of Scientific Research in London, served as middleman for the survey. At the joint cost of the Rockefeller Foundation and the Colonial Office, Findlay visited the IHD yellow fever laboratory in New York in the autumn of 1932, in order to learn techniques for the preparation and administration of IHD yellow fever vaccine. Back in London, he started vaccinating Britons destined for West Africa.[27] For the expanded survey, colonial doctors sent sera in specially distributed venules to Findlay in London, who organized transshipment of the specimens to New York. The results of tests performed at the IHD

[23] 'Office Session of April–May 1932 Report of the Yellow Fever Committee', folder 403, box 36, series 4, RG 5, RFA, RAC.

[24] Sawyer, 'Diary of Attendance at South African Yellow Fever Conference, and of Trip to and from Conference, 1932–1933', 1 Nov. 1932, folder 777, box 84, series 100 O, RG 1.1, RFA, RAC.

[25] Donald Fisher, 'The Rockefeller Foundation and the Development of Scientific Medicine in Great Britain', *Minerva*, 16 (1978), 20–41; Donald Fisher, 'Rockefeller Philanthropy and the British Empire: The Creation of the London School of Hygiene and Tropical Medicine', *History of Education*, 7 (1978), 129–43.

[26] Dr L. Rajchmann to Russell, 17 June 1932; Dr Frank Boudreau to Strode, 29 July 1932, folder 776, box 84, series 100 O, RG 1.1, RFA, RAC.

[27] Correspondence in folder 116, box 11, series 4, RG 5, RFA, RAC.

laboratory were sent to Findlay, who forwarded them to the relevant colonial chief medical officer; the colony or the Colonial Office paid for the ampoules and their transportation.[28]

The prompt arrival of specimens from the Anglo-Egyptian Sudan at the New York laboratory in April 1933 came as a 'pleasant surprise'.[29] Though Sudan had been mentioned in the new immunity survey plans, its administration by the Foreign Office left it outside the jurisdiction of the Colonial Office officials who were in closest touch with the IHD, and it had not been represented in Cape Town. The specimens appeared after Sir George Buchanan, senior medical officer at the British Ministry of Health and president of the *Office* from 1932, forwarded Sawyer's request to the director of the Sudan medical service.[30] Sudan turned out to be far more important than anyone had anticipated. The results on fifty-seven specimens tested from Wau and Rumbek, Bahr-el-Ghazal were 'quite startling': 42 per cent of the specimens tested positive for immunity against yellow fever.[31] Yellow fever virus had been present in Sudan within the lifetime of the individuals tested.

These results radically transformed the disease landscape. IHD scientists were astonished but excited, and eager to plan new investigations in Sudan, which contained the easternmost frontier of yellow fever infection in Africa.[32] The senior Sudan government doctors and political officials sitting on the Central Sanitary Board focused immediately on the political and legal implications of the test results. A member in its own right of the *Office* from 1927, Sudan had decided in May 1933 to accede to the ISC, finally signed at the Hague on 12 April 1933.[33] The test results forced a re-evaluation of Sudan's position. While little was required of non-infected countries, the ISC stipulated that countries with endemic regions take steps to prevent the spread of yellow fever to non-infected areas; these consisted primarily of ensuring that people could not be infected at aerodromes in areas endemic for yellow fever. The cost of such measures was of considerable concern to a colonial government still struggling with

[28] Sawyer, 'Diary of Attendance at South African Yellow Fever Conference, and of Trip to and from Conference, 1932–1933', 25 Oct. 1932, folder 777, box 84, series 100 O, RG 1.1, RFA, RAC.
[29] Sawyer to Findlay, 26 Apr. 1933, folder 785, box 84, series 100 O, RG 1.1, RFA, RAC.
[30] Sawyer to Sir George Buchanan, 28 Apr. 1933, folder 785, box 84, series 100 O, RG 1.1, RFA, RAC.
[31] Quote from Sawyer to Beeuwkes, 14 July 1933; results from Sawyer to Atkey through Findlay, 13 June 1933, folder 786, box 85, series 100 O, RG 1.1, RFA, RAC.
[32] Sawyer to Findlay, 14 July 1933, folder 786, box 85, series 100 O, RG 1.1, RFA, RAC.
[33] Correspondence, pp. 1–22, CIVSEC 44/1/5; Secretariat to Chancery, 27 May 1933, p. 77, CIVSEC 44/6/33.

depression retrenchment, which found itself at the crossroads of African north–south and east–west air routes.

To clarify Sudan's yellow fever position and its obligations once the ISC came into effect, the Central Sanitary Board ordered the collection of further serological specimens by WTRL staff and SMS doctors, under Archibald's direction.[34] The first set of additional collections, analysed in November 1933, demonstrated that the initial results were not anomalous: four (15 per cent) of twenty-seven specimens from Kosti, White Nile province, and seven (7 per cent) of 107 sera from Upper Nile and Mongalla provinces tested positive.[35] But the Central Sanitary Board found what it had been seeking in these results. The ISC required notification to the *Office* and special precautions at aerodromes only if yellow fever existed clinically or biologically. The major Imperial Airways aerodromes in southern Sudan were at Malakal and Juba, where one (2 per cent) of fifty and six (11 per cent) of fifty-five specimens had tested positive. But the sole positive at Malakal was in an adult, and although children were tested, none of the positives at Juba was found in people below the age of 12. Yellow fever therefore did not exist 'at present on the main air routes' and there was 'no objection' to acceding to the ISC. While the Central Sanitary Board recognized that the terms of the ISC might put the government to considerable expense and inconvenience in the event of a yellow fever outbreak, the Sudan government sent the instrument of accession to the Hague early in 1934.[36]

In certain quarters of the international medical community, the Sudan results led to 'a good deal of anxiety':[37] they contradicted the long-held view that yellow fever did not occur in East Africa, they were at odds with the clinical record in Sudan, where no doctor had diagnosed yellow fever since the start of Anglo-Egyptian rule, and they had potentially grave consequences for air travel and Asian countries. At the yellow fever commission of the *Office*, a group of doctors including Surgeon-General Boyé, director of the French colonial health services, questioned the specificity and the significance of the protection test. Did a positive protection test really mean that the person in question had suffered

---

[34] 257th meeting of the CSB, 18 July 1933, pp. 333–4, CIVSEC 44/8/36.

[35] Sawyer to Archibald via Findlay, 6 Nov. 1933; Sawyer to Archibald through Findlay, 24 Nov. 1933, folder 787, box 85, series 100 O, RG 1.1, RFA, RAC.

[36] E. D. Pridie to Civil Secretary, 24 Dec. 1933, quotes p. 99; Extract from the minutes of the 260th meeting of the CSB, 18 Dec. 1933, p. 100; Acting Governor-General, Sudan to Acting High Commissioner, Egypt, 4 Jan. 1934, p. 101, CIVSEC 44/6/33.

[37] Strode diary (Excerpt from), 22 Nov. 1933, folder 787, box 85, series 100 O, RG 1.1, RFA, RAC.

previously from human yellow fever? They wondered if the yellow fever virus caused some 'other local or general disease' that scientists ought to be looking for in the region. Perhaps, they suggested, the test detected a modified or attenuated strain, analogous to cowpox, that immunized in the absence of 'real' yellow fever.[38] These doctors were questioning whether the protection test was a valid medical technique, and whether the results produced by it should be considered as accepted medical knowledge. Despite the apparent dominance of the laboratory, clinical evidence, medical preconceptions about disease epidemiology, fear of policy and health implications, and professional and imperial rivalries were among the factors that policed the boundary between legitimate and illegitimate medical knowledge. The IHD had in fact taken great care with the protection test methodology. Each serum sample was tested on six mice[39] and sera from countries such as Canada where yellow fever was thought never to have existed were tested from 1931 onward in order to show that false positives occurred in less than 1 per cent of tests. Sawyer strongly defended the specificity of the test, but readily conceded that there was much that the test could not tell them.[40]

All parties agreed on the need for more clinical, serological, and pathological research, to answer these questions about the test and to clarify the status of yellow fever in East and Central Africa. Dr T. F. Hewer, WTRL bacteriologist, eagerly continued his collection of sera and corresponded with the IHD doctors in New York, who considered him a 'live wire'.[41] Results of tests on these new sera revealed that significant pockets of yellow fever existed in southern and western Sudan: positive tests were found in the south at Rumbek (3 per cent), Amadi (6 per cent), Wau (10 per cent), Li Rangu (13 per cent), and Yubo (14 per cent); in Darfur at Geneina (5 per cent), Zalingei (6 per cent), and El Fasher (24 per cent); and in the Nuba Mountains at Dilling (16 per cent).[42] Age group testing suggested that the disease had been present between six and thirty years ago, depending on the town. No immunity was found in El Obeid; earlier tests had shown no immunity in Wad Medani and the one positive uncov-

[38] Colonel S. P. James to Sawyer, 20 Nov. 1933, folder 787, box 85, series 100 O, RG 1.1, RFA, RAC.
[39] For the full test procedure, see Sawyer to Atkey through Findlay, 13 June 1933, folder 786, box 85, series 100 O, RG 1.1, RFA, RAC.
[40] Sawyer to James, 5 Jan. 1934, folder 788, box 85, series 100 O, RG 1.1, RFA, RAC.
[41] Sawyer to Beeuwkes, 14 July 1933, folder 786, box 85, series 100 O, RG 1.1, RFA, RAC.
[42] Loring Whitman to Archibald, 31 May 1934, folder 790, box 86, series 100 O, RG 1.1, RFA, RAC.

ered in Khartoum was traced to the Nuba Mountains.[43] Dr E. D. Pridie, director of the SMS, thought that the distribution of immunity was determined by the routes taken by West African pilgrims to reach Mecca,[44] but this comment marked the extent of Westerner targeting for yellow fever. In the event, the character of the disease meant that such targeting would have been unproductive: the rapid disappearance of yellow fever virus from the blood meant that pilgrims infected in West Africa were either dead or immune by the time they reached Sudan on foot, and therefore not in a position to pass on the disease.

Since this feature of the virus also made it hard to isolate, only the characteristic pathological changes of the liver wrought by the disease constituted a firm diagnosis. Medical inspectors in southern and western Sudan were accordingly instructed to report suspicious cases of febrile jaundice and to obtain, wherever possible, liver specimens from all cases of fatal acute febrile illness of less than ten days' duration. This was to be accomplished with IHD-donated viscerotomes, apparatus which allowed doctors to obtain a liver specimen without opening up a corpse, useful in areas such as southern Sudan where people objected to post-mortems.[45]

In June–July 1934, two cases of yellow fever, one from Juba and one from Wau, were diagnosed by SMS doctors on the basis of liver specimens. Although the civil secretary's representative pointed out that the ISC was not yet in force and that complying with it would be costly, the Central Sanitary Board took immediate action to prevent the disease from spreading to other countries and to ensure that the Imperial Airways route via Sudan would not have to be closed down. Bahr-el-Ghazal and Mongalla provinces were declared infected under the Public Health Ordinance of 1924; the *Office* was notified. The Board closed Bahr-el-Ghazal to all aircraft traffic and made Juba and Malakal aerodromes anti-amaryl.[46] The latter meant removing the threat of acquiring yellow fever from the area around the aerodrome by ridding it of mosquitoes, providing mosquito-proof accommodation for travellers in transit, and ensuring that the nearest human habitation was at a distance beyond the flight range of

[43] T. F. Hewer, 'Yellow Fever in the Anglo-Egyptian Sudan', *Lancet*, 1 Sept. 1934, 496–7; Sawyer to Archibald through Findlay, 24 Nov. 1933, folder 787, box 85, series 100 O, RG 1.1, RFA, RAC.
[44] Cited in W. A. Sawyer and Loring Whitman, 'The Yellow Fever Immunity Survey of North, East and South Africa', *TRSTMH* 29 (1936), 405.
[45] Medical Officer, Fasher to Director, WTRL, 23 Aug. 1934, R. G. Archibald Leave File, NMRLL; Hewer, 'Yellow Fever', 498; E. R. Rickard, 'The Organization of the Viscerotome Service of the Brazilian Cooperative Yellow Fever Service', *American Journal of Tropical Medicine*, 17 (1937), 163–90.
[46] 265th meeting CSB, 24 July 1934, p. 366, CIVSEC 44/8/36; *RSMS 1934*, 72.

*Aedes aegypti* (two kilometres). Massive and rapid relocation resulted: the more than one thousand people living in the 'native lodging area' at Juba aerodrome were evacuated within two days of the order being issued; all buildings, numbering some 571 huts, were disinsectized and moved to three new villages within three months.[47] Consulted about the liver specimens, Findlay confirmed the Wau diagnosis, but the Juba case turned out not to be yellow fever.[48] This episode demonstrated the great difficulty of diagnosing yellow fever in Sudan and established the Sudan government's pattern of acting with extreme caution when faced with potential cases.

Eager to see a yellow fever laboratory opened in Sudan from the time of the first test results,[49] IHD interest in such a project was heightened by the closing of its Lagos laboratory in April 1934. At an unofficial meeting at the British Ministry of Health in early July 1934, Findlay and others agreed that if possible, further research should be undertaken at a field laboratory in Sudan, under the direction of Archibald, aimed particularly at isolating yellow fever virus from this 'silent area'. Isolating virus would vindicate the protection test, thereby silencing sceptics such as the French, who had again questioned the test at the spring *Office* meeting, and 'greatly strengthen[ing] the hands of those who wish to take administrative action'.[50] The Wau and Juba cases only intensified scientific and political interest in the Sudan situation.

The IHD's cultivation of WTRL bacteriologist Hewer, who in the autumn of 1934 spent six weeks in New York and Toronto learning about yellow fever at IHD expense, did not, alas, bear fruit.[51] Archibald helped to arrange Hewer's trip,[52] but he was not interested in the proposals for building a yellow fever laboratory at Wau drafted by Hewer and Sawyer in New York. Archibald suggested building the laboratory farther south, at Fort Portal, Uganda and also opposed building any laboratory in Sudan until another immunity survey was done. He recommended that Hewer try to isolate the virus by experimenting with a few rhesus monkeys while on trek. Hewer was dismissive of this 'travelling circus of monkeys' proposal but his resolution to continue with research in Sudan as best he

[47] Governor, Mongalla to Financial Secretary, 1 Dec. 1934, pp. 160–1, CIVSEC 44/4/ 26.

[48] Findlay to Sawyer, 23 Aug. 1934, folder 116, box 11, series 4, RG5, RFA, RAC; 268th meeting CSB, 10 Sept. 1934, p. 376, CIVSEC 44/8/36.

[49] Sawyer to Findlay, 14 July 1933, folder 786; Sawyer to James, 5 Jan. 1934, folder 788, box 85, series 100 O, RG 1.1, RFA, RAC.

[50] Findlay to Russell, 6 July 1934, folder 791, box 86, series 100 O, RG 1.1, RFA, RAC.

[51] Sawyer Memorandum to Russell, 1 Oct. 1934; Hewer to Sawyer, 8 Nov. 1934, folder 149, box 14, series 4, RG 5, RFA, RAC.

[52] Archibald to Sawyer, 1 May 1934, folder 149, box 14, series 4, RG 5, RFA, RAC.

could soon flagged.[53] Still in London in May 1935 because of illness, he had 'very discouraging news of the Sudan': 'I gather that the director of the Medical Service does not intend to take any really active steps in the investigation. They are pursuing a curious "laissez-faire" course . . .' Hewer resigned his Sudan appointment.[54] Findlay attributed the lack of progress to Archibald 'putting up a passive opposition to anything being done in the Bahr el Ghazal in the investigation of yellow fever'.[55]

Archibald had sound reasons for such a stance. The Sudan government in general and Archibald in particular had been wary of yellow fever research involving virus since the receipt of the first test results. In July 1933, Archibald observed that his Khartoum laboratories could not handle yellow fever virus because of their proximity to the civil hospital and their lack of mosquito-proof rooms; the Central Sanitary Board supported his recommendation that the import into Sudan of yellow fever virus or any modification of it be prohibited.[56] Both Findlay and Sawyer knew that this had become government policy. They were inclined to see personal considerations behind Archibald's position. Findlay suggested that Archibald was perhaps 'a little bit ruffled' by the discovery of yellow fever in 'his' territory; Sawyer thought that he might have unwittingly offended Archibald by dealing directly with the junior Dr Hewer over protection tests.[57] The reality was, however, that intensive and costly research into yellow fever, a disease barely present in Sudan, if it existed at all, was not a priority in a country where, to take an example raised in Chapter 4, financial cuts had in 1933 ended research into the far more pressing matter of malaria in the Gezira. Moreover, building another laboratory was simply not feasible at a time when the WTRL organization was, as we saw in Chapter 3, being summarily dismembered, and responsibility for bacteriological research was being passed from Archibald to the director of the SMS.

## PREVENTING SPREAD AND
## RESUMING RESEARCH

The failure of the Sudan government to pursue the IHD-prescribed research path did not mean that it was not concerned about yellow fever. Although it had doubts about the precise meaning of the test results, the

[53] Hewer to Sawyer, 27 Nov. 1934, folder 149, box 14, series 4, RG 5, RFA, RAC.

[54] Hewer to Sawyer, 16 May 1935, folder 149, box 14, series 4, RG 5, RFA, RAC.

[55] Findlay to Sawyer, 1 June 1935, folder 387, box 35, series 4, RG 5, RFA, RAC.

[56] 257th meeting CSB, 18 July 1933, p. 334, CIVSEC 44/8/36.

[57] Findlay to Sawyer, 5 Mar. 1934, folder 116, box 11, series 4, RG 5; Sawyer to Findlay, 20 Mar. 1934, folder 789, box 85, series 100 O, RG 1.1, RFA, RAC.

SMS acted as if the positive test results definitely signalled yellow fever infection. For the rest of the decade, it pursued measures designed to track yellow fever, cut off its supposed transmission cycle, and prevent its spread, primarily in order to satisfy government obligations to the international community. Yellow fever research resumed, in collaboration with Findlay and with the IHD, but never involving the laboratory study in Sudan of yellow fever virus.

Margaret Humphreys has argued 'that yellow fever provided the main fuel for the growth of public health' in the late nineteenth-century southern United States.[58] One could similarly argue that, although it was far from being the most pressing local health problem, yellow fever fuelled the extension of sanitary services to the towns of southern Sudan. In July 1934, in the wake of the first test results, special Sudanese sanitary officers were posted to Juba, Malakal, and Wau, all of which housed aerodromes, in order to oversee anti-mosquito measures and to assemble mosquito brigades.[59] As the first and only town in which yellow fever had been diagnosed, Wau became an object of particular interest. A comprehensive scheme drawn up in 1935 to reduce mosquito breeding in the stagnant *khor* (water course) that ran through the town, and to move people and trees away from its swampy edges, was considered most valuable as a prophylactic against malaria. But yellow fever made the scheme's implementation more urgent: 'It is important,' wrote the SMS director, 'to wipe out yellow fever from the only known endemic centre in the Sudan.'[60] Mosquito control for the purposes of yellow fever prevention became one of the defining projects for the cadre of trained Sudanese sanitary personnel and the public health wing of the SMS, developed, as we saw in Chapter 2, during the 1930s. While the 1920s scientific orthodoxy was being overturned—rural epidemics in early 1930s South America had revealed an epidemiologically distinct form of the disease, so-called jungle yellow fever, which occurred in the absence of *Aedes aegypti* and which passed only accidentally from animals (mainly monkeys) to man[61]—Sudan's preventive measures remained based on the classical transmission cycle. *Aedes aegypti* surveys conducted by Sudanese

[58] Margaret Humphreys, *Yellow Fever and the South* (New Brunswick, NJ: Rutgers University Press, 1992), 11.

[59] E. D. Pridie, 'Faits récents concernant la fièvre jaune dans le Soudan Anglo-Égyptien, en particulier la lutte contre les moustiques', *BOIHP* 28 (1936), 1293.

[60] Pridie to Financial Secretary, 12 May 1935, p. 185; see also District Commissioner, Central District to Governor, Bahr-el-Ghazal, 5 Jan. 1935, pp. 173–4; Governor, Bahr-el-Ghazal to Civil Secretary, 20 Mar. 1935, p. 179, CIVSEC 44/4/26.

[61] G. K. Strode, 'The Conquest of Yellow Fever', in Strode (ed.), *Yellow Fever*, 24–6.

sanitary personnel started in approximately twenty towns in 1935.[62] Such surveys mapped the distribution of the yellow fever vector, while their removal of larvae served as one of the main means of yellow fever prophylaxy. In the interests of scientific certainty, starting in 1937, all suspected *Aedes* larvae were bred out locally and sent to the SMS medical entomologist for identification.[63] By 1938, over five million annual inspections in forty towns produced 1,861 specimens of *Aedes aegypti* from 125 collections.[64] Surveys of this kind in endemic areas had been urged by officials at the Pan-African Medical Congress in Johannesburg in 1935 and at the May 1936 meeting of the *Office*,[65] and Sudan's annual findings were duly relayed to the latter body.

The Sudan government was scrupulous in its obedience to the ISC. All aircraft landing at or taking off from frontier aerodromes in Sudan were inspected and disinsectized. By 1938, this procedure had been centralized at Khartoum, except when planes made a night stop near the frontier. Inspections numbered 2,372 in 1938, and as from 1934 to 1937, no aedine mosquitoes were in fact found. Passengers entering Sudan from areas endemic for yellow fever were also 'inspected': on penalty of six-day quarantine, they were required to produce a 'certificate stating that they [had] not been exposed to the risk of infection by yellow fever during the previous six days'.[66]

Reporting of suspicious cases of febrile jaundice continued throughout the late 1930s, but between 1933 and 1939, only sixty-five liver specimens were analysed.[67] This small number reflects the fact that Sudanese did not go to hospitals for fever and also highlights the comparatively small scale of the actual clinical problem with which the SMS was dealing: 'fevers of uncertain origin' rarely constituted more than 3 per cent of total admissions to hospitals and dispensaries, and more than 3 per cent of total deaths.[68] After the Wau case, the only other seriously suspicious specimen

---

[62] Pridie, 'Faits récents', 1292–5; *RSMS 1935*, 32.

[63] E. D. Pridie, 'Distribution et incidence d'*Aedes aegypti* au Soudan Anglo-Égyptien en 1937', *BOIHP* 30 (1938), 1973, 1978.

[64] 'Distribution et incidence de l'*Aedes aegypti* au Soudan Anglo-Égyptien en 1938', *BOIHP* 31 (1939), 1588–9.

[65] Under Secretary of State, Colonial Office to Under Secretary of State, Foreign Office, 11 May 1936, p. 196; Extract from Short Summary of May 1936 Session of the Office International [by O. F. H. Atkey], p. 192, CIVSEC 44/4/26.

[66] Quote from *RSMS 1938*, 35; see also H. Richards, 'Rapport sur la déinsectisation des aéronefs à l'aérodrome de Khartoum', *BOIHP* 30 (1938), 563–7.

[67] R. Kirk, 'Some Observations on the Study and Control of Yellow Fever in Africa, with Particular Reference to the Anglo-Egyptian Sudan', *TRSTMH* 37 (1943), 129.

[68] *RSMS 1931* through *RSMS 1938*.

emerged in December 1935 from Malakal. According to Findlay, the man's liver slides were 'extraordinarily suggestive of yellow fever and had they come from a case in West Africa or one with a more suggestive clinical history, I should have little hesitation in saying that they were from a case of yellow fever'. In spite of the suggestive histology, the SMS annual report declared that it was 'extremely doubtful' that the disease was yellow fever.[69] This case highlighted the extreme uncertainty of yellow fever diagnosis, even with the tools of a cause-based scientific medicine at hand: even if histories and specimens could be secured, a clinical history had to be squared with the pathological analysis of a liver specimen, as well as with the preconceptions about geography held by the scientists involved.

Despite the debate that surrounded both the Wau and Malakal diagnoses,[70] the SMS erred on the side of caution and behaved as if the Malakal case was definitely yellow fever. The victim had fallen ill sixteen days after his arrival in Malakal, following a four-day journey from his home in Eliri, Nuba Mountains. Since the sanitary officials could find no *Aedes aegypti* in Malakal at the time of the man's illness, it seemed possible that he had been infected at home.[71] Dr Robert Kirk, Hewer's successor as WTRL bacteriologist, accordingly collected blood samples in the Nuba Mountains in 1936 and sent them to Findlay for testing. The results were again striking: protection ranged from 10 per cent in Heiban to a staggering 79 per cent (of thirty-eight sera) in Kau. Local inquiry revealed that there was no history of jaundice 'or any other suggestive clinical condition' at Kau; a dispensary was established in the village to try to obtain a thorough medical history of the region.[72] The Nuba Mountains became the focus of yellow fever research in Sudan: in early 1937, Findlay visited the area with Dr E. S. Horgan, SMS assistant director for laboratory services, to collect sera from people and animals. The further 515 human sera analysed in 1937–8 confirmed the earlier findings, and moreover, suggested that the virus was currently active: in contrast to the 1936 survey, the percentage of positives among children under the age of 10 in the Kau area was very high. There was other evidence of current infection: the protection test of N. L. Corkill, a British doctor, switched from negative in the autumn of 1936 to positive in February 1937 after he

[69] *RSMS 1935*, 74.

[70] R. Kirk, 'Notes on Yellow Fever', *SNR* 34 (1953), 51.

[71] H. A. Crouch, 'Note on the Yellow Fever Situation in Malakal, Upper Nile Province, Sudan', 26 Mar. 1938, p. 392, CIVSEC 44/1/5.

[72] *RSMS 1936*, 77.

suffered a febrile attack in Kau that left him bedridden for five days; unlike previous bouts of fever, this one did not respond to the anti-malarial atebrin.[73] Infection seemed active in Malakal as well. Two jaundice cases that occurred in October 1937 were later diagnosed as yellow fever on the basis of a switch from a negative protection test early in the course of illness to positive during convalescence. Although the *Aedes* index in the town seemed 'far too low for any outbreak to occur', the 'possibility of infection of sporadic cases' could not be excluded, and once the results had been received in early 1938, Malakal aerodrome was made anti-amaryl.[74] Other evidence pointed to active infection: in 1933, only one (2 per cent) of fifty sera from Malakal tested positive, and it was from an adult; in 1938, twenty-one (18 per cent) of 114 sera protected, including a sample from a 5-year-old child. The extension of the immunity survey to the Fung area in 1937–8 pushed the eastern frontier of yellow fever immunity beyond the White Nile to the Sudanese-Abyssinian border when 14 per cent of 132 sera collected from towns such as Roseires and Kurmuk tested positive.[75] But the absence of both a clinical condition and a causal agent—Findlay's efforts to isolate virus in the Nuba Mountains were unsuccessful[76]—continued to undermine the test results.

Farther south, the IHD was also proving unable to solve the East African yellow fever puzzle. It finally got its yellow fever laboratory in 1936: the Yellow Fever Research Institute at Entebbe, Uganda, opened in the buildings of the closed Human Trypanosomiasis Institute, was a joint venture between the Uganda government and the IHD, and was built along the lines initially proposed for a Sudan laboratory. The Uganda government provided a laboratory, residence quarters, and £5,000 annually for three years; the IHD provided three yellow fever experts and paid their salaries and travel expenses. While these men continued to report to the IHD in New York, the Institute fell administratively under the jurisdiction of the director of medical services of Uganda.[77] As in Sudan,

---

[73] G. M. Findlay, R. Kirk, and F. O. MacCallum, 'Yellow Fever and the Anglo-Egyptian Sudan: Distribution of Immune Bodies to Yellow Fever', *ATMP* 35 (1941), 125–9.

[74] Quotes from E. D. Pridie, 'Note', 28 Jan. 1938, p. 388, CIVSEC 44/1/5; 290th meeting CSB, 24 Feb. 1938, p. 632, CIVSEC 44/8/36.

[75] G. M. Findlay, discussion following Fred L. Soper, 'Yellow Fever: The Present Situation (October 1938) with Special Reference to South America', *TRSTMH* 32 (1938), 323–4; Findlay, Kirk, and MacCallum, 'Yellow Fever', 131–3.

[76] 'Renseignements récents sur la fièvre jaune reçus au cours des neufs mois finissant le 30 septembre 1937', *BOIHP* 30 (1938), 49.

[77] Annual Report for 1936 Paris Office–IHD Section 4: Uganda YFRI, pp. 9–10, box 241, series 3, RG 5, RFA, RAC.

yellow fever was clinically unknown in Uganda, but some sera had tested positive. When the Institute's director, Dr A. F. Mahaffy, started research work in early 1937, it was expected that the initial task of isolating the yellow fever virus from Ugandans would be accomplished by the end of the year.[78] What was believed to have been a small hurdle grew into a major stumbling block. To improve its chances of isolating the virus, the Institute cast its net more widely. It started a study of labourers building a road into the forest in Bwamba country, who were working under conditions identical to those in which jungle yellow fever had been discovered in South America; this became the Institute's main field project until 1940. It also started a field study in southern Sudan.[79]

This study was built partly on the friendly relations that the IHD had fostered with the SMS. Dr F. L. Soper, director of the IHD yellow fever laboratory in Brazil, stopped in at Khartoum on his way back from the Johannesburg Congress in 1935; Kirk and Horgan met Mahaffy while on leave in London in 1936; Sawyer and Dr G. K. Strode, head of the European office of the IHD in Paris, visited Khartoum and Malakal in early 1938.[80] Pridie had declared his willingness to cooperate with the new Institute in June 1936, but he had stipulated that all Rockefeller Foundation research programmes be approved by him and be carried out in conjunction with the SMS; this was both to give the IHD the benefit of SMS local knowledge and to safeguard SMS research priority.[81] With Pridie's consent the IHD started a preliminary survey in April and May 1938, in order to choose a suitable area for study. The 200 sera collected from seven localities showed a particularly high concentration of immunity around Meridi; field studies to locate and test suspicious cases began in Yubo, Meridi, and Juba in September, with headquarters at Juba. The twelve suspect cases that surfaced around Juba were all negative for yellow fever; the scarcity of dispensaries and hospitals and the fact that most southern Sudanese rarely sought medical treatment for fever compounded the usual difficulties in finding suspicious cases.[82] Southern Sudanese cooperation with the IHD doctors was variable. Notification of

---

[78] Semi-Annual Report for 1937 Paris Office–International Health Division, vol. i, pp. 1–2, box 241, series 3, RG 5, RFA, RAC.

[79] Annual Report for 1937 Paris Office–IHD Section III Uganda–YFRI, pp. 13–14, box 242, series 3, RG 5, RFA, RAC.

[80] A. F. Mahaffy Diary 1935–7, 28 Apr., 16 Sept. 1936, box 41; W. A. Sawyer Diary 1938, 28 Feb., 1, 16 Mar. 1938, box 55, RG 12.1, RFA, RAC.

[81] For Director, SMS to Civil Secretary, 9 June 1936, p. 200, CIVSEC 44/4/26.

[82] Semi-Annual Report for 1938 Paris Office–IHD, vol. ii, pp. 316, 325–6, box 242; Annual Report for 1938 Paris Office–IHD Section I, box 243, series 3, RG 5, RFA, RAC.

the doctors' arrival prompted all children and some adults at one village near Juba to disappear into the bush, while at one point along the Yei–Meridi road, the local chief greeted the doctors with a newly built grass hut and a parade of sick people.[83] Sleeping sickness inspections near Source Yubo offered a convenient vehicle for systematically identifying cases of fever and procuring blood specimens, as did the labour camp established for building the Meridi–Yei road; the IHD coupled sera collection with the distribution of quinine and aspirin, and simple medical treatment.[84] According to one district officer in Tanganyika, the collection of blood specimens for the yellow fever immunity survey gave rise to African stories of European vampires seeking African blood,[85] but precisely what southern Sudanese made of such collections remains hidden.

The IHD was less concerned with local cooperation than with the fact that these investigations produced few positive tests, and no virus. Work in the area was suspended in December 1938 and staff shortages meant that it was never resumed. The closing of the unsuccessful mouse colony at Juba in June 1939 marked the end of field work in Sudan.[86] Still in search of the elusive virus, the IHD closed the Bwamba station in June 1940 and started an investigation in the Belgian Congo the following month.[87]

By the beginning of the Second World War, then, only one case of yellow fever in Sudan had actually been confirmed by histopathological examination of the liver, although a handful of others had been diagnosed on the basis of mouse protection tests. Research had revealed the distribution of yellow fever immunity in humans, and to a lesser extent in animals, and of *Aedes aegypti*, and had highlighted the presence of febrile jaundice of unknown origin.[88] But without an isolated virus, the status of yellow fever within Sudan, and of the protection test, remained uncertain. Senior SMS doctors clearly doubted the existence of classical yellow fever within their territory: in 1935, according to Soper, 'All were loath to believe that

[83] A. F. Mahaffy Diary 1938–40, 11, 22 Nov. 1938, box 41, RG 12.1, RFA, RAC.

[84] A. F. Mahaffy Diary 1938–40, 20, 23 Sept., 22–3 Nov. 1938, box 41, RG 12.1, RFA, RAC.

[85] Luise White, 'Cars Out of Place: Vampires, Technology, and Labor in East and Central Africa', *Representations*, 43 (1993), 46 n. 46.

[86] A. F. Mahaffy Diary 1938–40, 15 Mar. 1938–29 June 1939, box 41, RG 12.1, RFA, RAC.

[87] Yellow Fever Research Institute. Entebbe, Uganda. Semi-Annual Report January–July, 1940, pp. 2, 11, box 244, series 3, RG 5, RFA, RAC.

[88] R. Kirk, 'Attempts to Demonstrate Leptospirosis in the Northern Sudan', *TRSTMH* 31 (1938), 667–70.

cases of yellow fever could occur without being discovered by the health service.' They attributed the positive tests to a mild strain or to another harmless virus.[89] In 1939, Pridie suggested that an attenuated form of yellow fever or a similar disease which gave positive protection tests existed in Sudan, on the grounds that 'It is unlikely that the Sudan Medical staff could miss cases of a disease which is always in mind and which is readily diagnosed by the Nigerian and F.E.A. [French Equatorial Africa] authorities.'[90] Though it quietly questioned the meaning of the test results, the Sudan government did not use the conflict between clinical experience and test evidence to avoid action. It collaborated with the IHD, on its own terms, and protected other countries by scrupulously meeting its international obligations under the ISC. Anti-*Aedes* measures, executed in towns by Sudanese sanitary personnel, were expected to eliminate any internal yellow fever threat, but the SMS seemed to regard any such threat as remote.

## THE NUBA MOUNTAINS EPIDEMIC

When the explosive epidemic that the IHD had been promising came, it nearly passed all the interested parties by: it was in fact an almost entirely reconstructed event. Even at the end of our period, the colonial government's ability to know when major disasters were occurring in some parts of the country, never mind address them, remained extremely limited. The Central Board of Public Health, successor to the Central Sanitary Board, first learned of 'an obscure outbreak with some symptoms suggestive of yellow fever' in the Eastern Jebels of the Nuba Mountains in October 1940.[91] The Sudanese assistant medical officer at Kauda, Ahmed El Araki, notified the touring district commissioner of the epidemic on 20 September. El Araki was certain that the disease resembled an epidemic of jaundice which he had observed while working in Gulfan in 1934, which Kirk during earlier investigations had told him was yellow fever. The Board sent a team of Kirk, two other British doctors, and a Sudanese laboratory assistant to investigate. As far as Kirk could tell, the epidemic had actually started in May. The delay in the official detection

[89] John Duffy (ed.), *Ventures in World Health: The Memoirs of Fred Lowe Soper* (Washington, DC: Pan American Health Organization, Pan American Sanitary Bureau, Regional Office of the WHO, 1977), 146.

[90] Pridie, 'Note on the Application in the Anglo-Egyptian Sudan of the Provisions of the International Sanitary Convention for Aerial Navigation for the Control of Yellow Fever', 12 Feb. 1939, p. 458, CIVSEC 44/1/5.

[91] Pridie to Governor, El Obeid, 22 Oct. 1940, p. 320, CIVSEC 44/4/26.

of the epidemic was due to the poverty of communications with and within the remote region of the Nuba Mountains during the rainy summer season, and to government preoccupation with the possibility, and then the actuality, of Italian invasion from Abyssinia: Italian forces occupied border towns in Kassala, Fung, and Upper Nile provinces in July and bombed Khartoum in August.[92] Although two of the SMS team fell immediately ill with the prevailing disease and transport was difficult, Horgan announced on 4 November that according to pathological analysis of liver specimens conducted in the SMS laboratories in Khartoum, the disease was indeed yellow fever; experimental, immunological, and epidemiological confirmation followed.[93]

In conjunction with the provincial authorities, the Central Board of Public Health created a sanitary cordon over an area much wider than that actually infected in order to prevent the disease from spreading to the Sudanese, British, and crucially, Indian troops travelling through Sudan; the standard treatment of rest, aspirin for relief of pain, and sugar was administered to as many cases as possible.[94] But the epidemic was dying out, because the rainy season had ended and the pools of stagnant water littering the ground were drying up. Sudanese assistant medical officers briefly trained to gather information and to recognize cases reconstructed the history of the epidemic, and its demise.[95] According to their findings, cases numbered more than 15,000 and deaths over 1,600 from the beginning of the epidemic to the end of November; in December, seventy-seven cases and twenty deaths were reported and by the end of the month, the disease seemed confined to the Tagoi Hills, in the north of the region. The last case was reported on 1 February 1941; a total of 20,000 cases and 2,000 deaths was eventually considered a conservative estimate.[96]

It is difficult to capture the intellectual excitement induced in the

[92] Daly, *Imperial Sudan*, 129–33.
[93] Account of the discovery of the epidemic from Kordofan Province Monthly Diary, Nov. 1940, p. 7, CIVSEC 57/13/48; R. Kirk, 'An Epidemic of Yellow Fever in the Nuba Mountains, Anglo-Egyptian Sudan', *ATMP* 35 (1941), 68–9, 76. On the Gulfan outbreak, see R. Kirk, 'Nouvelles recherches sur la fièvre jaune au Soudan Anglo-Égyptien', *BOIHP* 28 (1936), 2344.
[94] On control measures, see correspondence, pp. 320–88, 417–30, CIVSEC 44/4/26, and CBPH meeting minutes, pp. 907–40, CIVSEC 44/8/37; on treatment, see Kirk, 'Epidemic', 92–3.
[95] A. F. Mahaffy Diary 1938–40, 15 Nov. 1940, box 41, RG 12.1, RFA, RAC.
[96] Report on the Progress of the Yellow Fever Epidemic in the Nuba Mountains, 27 Nov. 1940, p. 367; Notes for inclusion in Civil Secretary's monthly letter for Dec. 1940, pp. 445–6, CIVSEC 44/4/26; H. A. Crouch, 'Memorandum on Yellow Fever in the Anglo-Egyptian Sudan with Special Reference to the Measures Adopted for the Control of the Disease', 2 Nov. 1941, p. 668, CIVSEC 44/1/6.

PLATE 3. 'If it were no for the war . . .': A. F. Mahaffy, Robert Kirk, and D. J. Lewis in the Nuba Mountains. (Courtesy of the Rockefeller Archive Center.)

doctors by the epidemic. Kirk's comment (in his Scottish accent) to T. R. H. Owen, the local district commissioner, that 'if it were no for the war, this epidemic wad be juist grrrand' gives some sense of their delight.[97] As Owen rightly observed, 'for the specialist an epidemic like this, which has killed its thousands, is a glorious field day'.[98] Mahaffy joined Kirk and SMS medical entomologist D. J. Lewis in the Nuba Mountains

[97] T. R. H. Owen, Memoirs: 'Sudan Days', SAD 769/11/64. This was the fulfillment of Hewer's earlier desire: 'They seem to be having an epidemic on the Gambia—I wish we cd [could] get one in the Sudan!' (Hewer to Sawyer, 30 Nov. 1934, folder 149, box 14, series 4, RG 5, RFA, RAC).
[98] Owen to Mother, 23 Nov. 1940, SAD 414/10/99–102.

on 20 November. Armed with six mosquito-proofed boxes of mice, his sole aim was to find the virus and so the start of dry weather concerned him: 'My only worry now is that I will be too late.' Assisted by Sudanese assistant medical officers, Kirk and Mahaffy took to the hills in order to find the increasingly rare new cases whose blood they could collect in the hope of finding the virus. IHD Dr K. C. Smithburn made a flying visit in late November to collect some of the inoculated mice and ferry them back to Entebbe.[99]

When Mahaffy passed through Uganda en route to a hastily assembled conference on yellow fever in Nairobi on 9–10 December, it looked as though two of the mouse groups might produce strains of yellow fever virus. At the conference, all the colonial medical officials were converts. Test results were never questioned as the discussion focused on protecting East Africa in the 'present emergency': Sudan's experience suggested that large epidemics might occur in other 'silent areas'. Mahaffy contrasted the atmosphere after his presentation to that following his speech to a British Medical Association meeting two years previously: 'Many then present, who questioned [the protection test's] specificity said to me today "well Mahaffy we know now that you people were backing the right horse." '[100] The two virus strains isolated provided the definitive evidence. As he watched the two groups of mice come down with the symptoms of yellow fever, Smithburn wrote: 'Naturally this gave great joy to all concerned as the quest of Y.F. virus in East Africa has been most elusive.'[101]

It is instructive to contrast briefly this view of the epidemic as 'grrrand' scientific event with what confronted the Nuba communities who experienced the disease. The Nuba were sedentary, 'animist' farmers who for the most part still lived in the isolated hilltop and hillside villages to which their ancestors had taken in the eighteenth century to protect themselves from invading Baggara Arabs, Muslim nomadic cattle owners who still dominated the plains in 1940. People started falling ill and dying at Tira Limon in May; the start of illness coincided with the onset of the rains,

[99] A. F. Mahaffy Diary 1938–40, 6–30 Nov. 1940, quote 12 Nov. 1940, box 41; K. C. Smithburn Diary 1939–40/1942–4, 23–8 Nov. 1940, box 57, RG 12.1, RFA, RAC.

[100] A. F. Mahaffy Diary 1938–40, 4 Dec. 1940, quote 9 Dec. 1940, box 41, RG 12.1, RFA, RAC. See also 'Record of the Proceedings, Conclusions and Recommendations of the Conference . . . on Yellow Fever held at Nairobi, Kenya . . .', pp. 389–416, CIVSEC 44/4/26.

[101] K. C. Smithburn Diary 1939–40/1942–4, 1 Dec. 1940, box 57, RG 12.1, RFA, RAC. On the isolation of the virus, see A. F. Mahaffy, T. P. Hughes, K. C. Smithburn, and R. Kirk, 'The Isolation of Yellow Fever Virus in the Anglo-Egyptian Sudan', *ATMP* 35 (1941), 141–8.

which lasted from May until October. The disease came on suddenly, with 'fever, severe headache, pains in the neck, loins and legs, often with vomiting'. It did not last long: the patient was 'either dead or out of danger inside a week'.[102]

The fact that epidemics of cerebrospinal meningitis had ravaged the area throughout the 1930s meant that large-scale sudden illness and death were not new to the Nuba. However, Kirk among others insisted that yellow fever with its 10 per cent death rate caused more panic among the Nuba than meningitis with its 70 per cent mortality.[103] In retrospect, Owen suggested that the Nuba did not fear meningitis unduly because as 'a recurrent scourge', it was 'understood and even expected as a periodic evil'. With no previous experience of yellow fever, they could only respond with terror to an unfamiliar plague.[104] This is not to say that the Nuba lacked accounts of the disease's origin. In Tira Limon, the epidemic was thought to be caused by the opening of a SMS dispensary by an assistant medical officer. According to Nuba beliefs, a man capable of curing disease could also cause disease. A deputation of Tira Limon chiefs called on the *mamur* at Talodi in August demanding the immediate removal of the dispensary, because 'ever since its construction, deaths ha[d] increased'.[105] The dispensary was duly closed. Some Nuba clearly linked the epidemic to what they had heard about the war: 'Well informed circles in the Eastern Jebels hold a theory that the Yellow fever virus was brought by storks from Germany.'[106] In part of the Moro hills, a long and severe dust storm that occurred in early 1940, unleashed by the irresponsibility of a member of the wind-controlling Ludar clan, was believed to have caused the epidemic.[107] According to Findlay, the Nuba turned to a variety of remedies for yellow fever, including the breaking of a raw egg on a patient's teeth, followed by the pouring of the yolk and white down his throat; the drinking of ardeib pods crushed and soaked in boiling water; the ingestion of the bitter juice and pulp of an unripe gourd.[108]

---

[102] Kirk, 'Epidemic', 83.

[103] Ibid. 75. On meningitis, see Gerald W. Hartwig, 'Cerebrospinal Meningitis in the Sudan', in K. David Patterson and Gerald W. Hartwig, *Cerebrospinal Meningitis in West Africa and Sudan in the Twentieth Century* (Los Angeles: Crossroads Press, 1984), 35–69.

[104] T. R. H. Owen, Memoirs: 'Sudan Days', SAD 769/11/63.

[105] Kordofan Province Monthly Diary, Aug. 1940, p. 3, Sept. 1940, p. 4, CIVSEC 57/13/48.

[106] Kordofan Province. Yellow Fever. Monthly Diary—Dec. 1940, p. 429, CIVSEC 44/4/26.

[107] S. F. Nadel, *The Nuba: An Anthropological Study of the Hill Tribes in Kordofan* (London: Oxford University Press, 1947), 205.

[108] Findlay, 'Memorandum on Yellow Fever in Africa', [1941], p. 764, CIVSEC 44/5/27.

Like all epidemics, this one had serious social consequences. Deaths among the Nuba required elaborate ritual, careful allocation of the deceased's property, and new marriages between widows and their deceased husbands' relatives.[109] Men and women and rich and poor alike came down with the disease; even *meks* (chiefs) died. Only the very young and in some cases, the very old, were left unscathed. Sickness and death among the fittest made it difficult for some communities—for example in Tira and Otoro—to tend and harvest their crops.[110] Famine, a visitor of 'sinister regularity' to the Nuba Mountains,[111] threatened. The strict system of quarantine and movement control within and around the infected area was only in place for a comparatively short time, namely from the end of October until January. But these control measures, which included the closure of markets, compromised people's ability to compensate for deprivation through local trade. Still, while much hardship may have gone unrecorded, by December when most crops had been harvested, the governor commented that grain was 'generally plentiful though some areas such as Kalogi, Werni and Kau will need some assistance later on'.[112]

By all accounts, the Nuba willingly cooperated with the authoritarian control measures—enforced by every available policeman, native administration employee, even schoolmasters, with severe punishment for breaking the sanitary cordon[113]—because the disease caused such widespread panic. Among the Arabs living in the plains, to whom yellow fever did not spread, the force of the police and the support of local leaders were crucial to securing compliance with the cordon.[114] As the epidemic abated, the fear of disease which had ensured cooperation lost its hold. Merchants, labourers, and peasants seeking to sell their produce began to press for the lifting of restrictions; Baggara Arabs became anxious about moving to find water for their cattle. The Kordofan governor pressed for the lifting of quarantine measures, while district commissioner Owen, using lorry drivers vaccinated with Rockefeller Foundation 17D vaccine, made alternative arrangements for producers and merchants to get their cotton and gum arabic to market. The infected area was reduced at the end

[109] See Nadel, *Nuba*, 119–24, 129–31, for rules of widowhood and inheritance among the Heiban and the Otoro.

[110] Kirk, 'Epidemic', 80–1; Kordofan Province Monthly Diary, Oct. 1940, p. 3, CIVSEC 57/13/48; Owen to Mother, 5 Nov. 1940, SAD 414/11/92–4.

[111] Nadel, *Nuba*, 50.

[112] Kordofan Province Yellow Fever Monthly Diary—Dec. 1940, p. 429, CIVSEC 44/4/26.

[113] Owen to Mother, 5 Nov. 1940, SAD 414/11/92–4; Owen to Father, 29 Nov. 1940, SAD 414/11/103.

[114] Owen to Father, 14 Nov. 1940, SAD 414/11/95–8.

of December to the Eastern Jebels and further in mid-January to the Tagoi Hills, from which the sanitary cordon was finally lifted following vaccination of all 1,300 residents of Tagoi jebel.[115]

Part of my intention in trying to reconstruct a Nuba view is to emphasize that the epidemic not only looked like, but in fact was, a very different episode depending on where an individual was located. The doctors regarded the epidemic primarily as a source of virus, not, as the Nuba did, as a source of illness, death, and social dislocation. If the doctors regarded the local experience and understanding of the epidemic as essentially irrelevant, they were nonetheless dependent on Nuba for accounts of the epidemic's progress and for physical evidence. If the medical investigation and the Nuba social crisis seemed to co-exist without intersecting, there were crucial points at which the quest of doctors for scientific material conflicted sharply with Nuba priorities. Unable to win local approval for autopsies, Kirk required police protection to obtain the five viscerotome liver specimens on which the yellow fever diagnosis was based; he secured the first of them by interrupting a funeral, seizing the body, and punching the liver with the viscerotome.[116]

But for all the narrow, pathogen obsession of the medical investigators, their interpretation of the epidemic considered a very broad range of influencing factors. In addressing how the epidemic began, the favoured notion of outside introduction was quickly dismissed: the epidemic started at a time when the Nuba Mountains were entirely inaccessible except on foot or animal; Tira Limon, where the epidemic began, was and always had been particularly isolated. The epidemic had to have started internally. Protection tests indicated virus activity over decades. Old Nuba men recalled a similar disease appearing during the Mahdia.[117] Kirk unearthed evidence that suggested that the virus had been active in the Nuba Mountains even earlier: Sudanese soldiers from Darfur and Kordofan, including Nuba, who served in Napoleon III's army in Mexico in 1863–7, did not succumb to the fever that felled French troops.[118] The

[115] Owen to Father, 29 Nov. 1940, SAD 414/11/103–6; Owen to Mother, 13–14 Jan. 1941, SAD 414/12/1–4; Governor, Kordofan, 'Kordofan Quarantine Control Measures', 2 Jan. 1941, pp. 418–19, CIVSEC 44/4/26; 304th CBPH meeting, 22 Dec. 1940, p. 923; 305th CBPH meeting, 13 Jan. 1941, p. 929, CIVSEC 44/8/37. On the development of vaccines, see Max Theiler, 'The Virus', in Strode (ed.), *Yellow Fever*, 44–6.
[116] 'Record of the Proceedings, Conclusions and Recommendations of the Conference . . . on Yellow Fever held at Nairobi, Kenya . . .', p. 404, CIVSEC 44/4/26; A. F. Mahaffy Diary 1938–40, 20 Nov. 1940, box 41, RG 12.1, RFA, RAC; Eric Pridie, 'Travels in Peace and War', unpublished memoir, 1968, SAD 720/7/32.
[117] Kirk, 'Epidemic', 77.
[118] R. Kirk, 'The Sudanese in Mexico', *SNR* 24 (1941), 111–30.

longtime presence of the virus in the area did not, however, explain why
the epidemic had started precisely when and where it did within the
region. Kirk considered the possibility that famine-like conditions influenced the severity of the epidemic, but he found no useful pattern.
Plagues of locusts meant that the 1938 and 1939 harvests were very poor,
leaving people in some parts of the Eastern Jebels on the verge of famine
conditions in 1940 until the new grain arrived. But the granaries were full
in Tira Limon, and the hungriest areas were not the areas that suffered
most severely from the epidemic. In Kirk's account, want of grain probably played its most significant role in helping to spread the disease.
Residents of Um Gabralla, an area which suffered badly from poor harvests, seem to have become infected when they travelled to Tira Limon in
search of food; they then spread the disease to Kororak and Um Dorein,
also well-off grain depots. Kirk expected the disease to be most severe in
the communities in which earlier surveys showed the lowest immunity,
but this did not explain why Moro, with 20 per cent positives pre-
epidemic, rather than Tira, Otoro, and Shwai, with virtually no positives,
suffered so severely. Rainfall in 1940 was average, although the possibility
that the mosquitoes in the area had reached a population-cycle peak could
not be dismissed altogether. The decline in the epidemic was more
straightforward, due to the disappearance of mosquitoes after the end of
the rains.[119]

The study of the disease vector yielded the greatest epidemiological
insights. The delay in notification of the epidemic meant that entomological conditions during most of the 1940 rainy season went uninvestigated;
Lewis studied mosquitoes during the 1940 dry season and the 1941 rainy
season on the assumption that conditions had not changed radically, and
then performed transmission experiments at the Entebbe Institute. Researchers had initially attributed disease transmission to *Aedes aegypti*
bred in the jars and gourds used to fetch and store water within Nuba
huts. But Lewis's work revealed a very low *Aedes aegypti* index.[120] Targeted by sanitary surveys since the mid-1930s, *Aedes aegypti* probably
played a very small role in yellow fever transmission during this epidemic.
Lewis identified *Aedes vittatus* as the most important vector, a mosquito
that bred mainly in the numerous rock holes, produced by grinding
sesame for oil, located on the hill slopes near Nuba huts. Abundant and
active fliers *Aedes taylori* and *Aedes furcifer* were also significant vectors.

[119] Kirk, 'Epidemic', 73, 77–9.
[120] D. J. Lewis, 'Mosquitoes in Relation to Yellow Fever in the Nuba Mountains, Anglo-
Egyptian Sudan', *ATMP* 37 (1943), 69–71.

The epidemic may have started in Moro because it was the only place in the Nuba Mountains where *Aedes vittatus* bred during the dry season; Moro also showed a higher *Aedes aegypti* index than other areas, probably due to its larger, and therefore less frequently emptied, water storage pots. While noting that there were 'great local variations' in rainfall, and that he had 'no direct evidence whether any species of mosquito was unusually abundant in 1940', Lewis thought that the timing of the epidemic may have been due to the fact that the rainfall recorded for May in a town near the Moro Hills was 'the second highest in 26 years and nearly twice the average'. The predominance of *Aedes* mosquitoes and the positioning of houses on the hills in close proximity to their breeding places accounted for the 'rapid and extensive spread of the outbreak'. Lewis remarked that control of yellow fever would be easier when, encouraged by government-enforced security, more Nuba moved down into the cleared plains, 'far from the principal haunts of *A. vittatus*'.[121]

The scientific articles published on the epidemic painstakingly described the characteristics of the land, climate, fauna, and population in the Nuba Mountains, correctly observing that local social and economic conditions were changing fairly rapidly. But the scientists did not seem to make the connection between these changing conditions and their analysis of the epidemiology of yellow fever. Lewis did not wonder, for example, if the Nuba moves downward that had already occurred during the 1920s and 1930s had disrupted long-stable local ecology sufficiently to trigger an epidemic. During the inter-war period, the Sudan government had forcibly resettled 'more recalcitrant tribes such as Tira, Otoro, Nyimang and Koalib'; down-migration in the Moro hills started later, in the late 1930s.[122] Had such moves intensified man–mosquito contact among those who remained in the hills? Had the clearing of bush and forest in the foothills and plains brought Nuba into contact with monkeys carrying yellow fever virus? Leaving aside the precise timing of the epidemic outbreak, the Nuba had, under colonialism, generally come into more frequent contact with outsiders, including: the plain-dwelling Arabs, who spent some of their year in Upper Nile Province, where immunity surveys indicated yellow fever infection was current; ex-slaves from similar regions, who settled near some Nuba villages; and West Africans, who provided labour for cotton cultivation in the Nuba Mountains. Had this contact introduced a new source of virus to the area? More and more

---

[121] Lewis, 'Mosquitoes', 73–5.
[122] David Roden, 'Down-migration in the Moro Hills of Southern Kordofan', *SNR* 53 (1972), 86.

Nuba men were engaging in waged labour in towns in order to raise money for their brideprice; had they brought virus with them when they returned home? Had the introduction of rain-grown cotton provided more sheltered moist breeding grounds for yellow fever's insect vectors and brought Nuba labourers into contact with them? What impact had changes in diet, due perhaps to the demise of wild game, had on disease susceptibility? The significance of these factors remains hidden, in large part because the medical researchers did not investigate links between ecology, patterns of production, and disease.[123]

The Nuba Mountains epidemic nonetheless marked a substantial breakthrough for the scientists researching yellow fever. The epidemic of clinical cases and the isolated pathogen validated the protection test, and the medical knowledge produced by it. An East African form of yellow fever was finally identified and studied. Crucially, the epidemic demonstrated that the scientific confusion that had surrounded the positive protection tests in the absence of clinically recognizable cases was absolutely appropriate: many cases of yellow fever in Sudan were in fact very mild or even sub-clinical. According to Kirk, 'The "typical case" of yellow fever as observed in this epidemic bore little resemblance to the text-book descriptions of the disease. It was, in fact, merely a "three-day fever." In sporadic cases of this type clinical diagnosis would be well-nigh impossible.'[124] Even with personnel scouring the district for short febrile illnesses, post-epidemic immunity surveys in Heiban, Otoro, and Tira suggested that the number of cases recorded—8,808—was only a fraction of the number of people—23,710—actually immunized. Although Kirk conceded that the latter figure was based on 'largely speculative' calculations and could not 'be regarded as in any way accurate', it suggested that many cases were missed and/or that many people experienced sub-clinical infections.[125] The ongoing difficulty in diagnosing yellow fever was amply illustrated in the Tagoi Hills, the area to which the epidemic was believed to be confined by January 1941. Although *Aedes aegypti* mosquitoes were locally abundant and the symptoms suggested yellow fever, the disease was later identified as relapsing fever.[126] To Findlay, this

---

[123] On the interaction between ecology and patterns of production and historical changes in Nuba communities, see Leif O. Manger, 'Traders, Farmers and Pastoralists: Economic Adaptations and Environmental Problems in the Southern Nuba Mountains of the Sudan', in D. H. Johnson and D. M. Anderson (eds.), *The Ecology of Survival: Case Studies from Northeast African History* (London: Lester Crooks, 1988), 155–72.

[124] Kirk, 'Epidemic', 103.     [125] Ibid. 99–100.

[126] G. M. Findlay, R. Kirk, and D. J. Lewis, 'Yellow Fever and the Anglo-Egyptian Sudan: The Differential Diagnosis of Yellow Fever', *ATMP* 35 (1941), 149–64.

reinforced the impossibility of diagnosing yellow fever on clinical grounds alone: every country where yellow fever was endemic or likely to be introduced required adequate laboratory facilities for diagnosis.[127]

The difficulties encountered in explaining the previous immunity and the epidemic in the Nuba Mountains in fact showed that the problem of understanding yellow fever in East Africa, particularly its endemiology and epidemiology, had only just begun. While this was not a classical epidemic—urban, man–mosquito transmission, *Aedes aegypti* as vector —it did not seem to fit the jungle yellow fever model, predicated on a monkey–mosquito–man cycle. The Nuba Mountains were clearly rural, but monkeys were 'by no means common'.[128] Although Findlay's Africa-wide analysis of monkey sera had shown immunity in 23 per cent of ninety-two monkeys, none of the wild animals from Kau—monkeys, squirrels, rats, lizards, bats, mongoose—that he tested in 1937 produced positive sera. Findlay did find positive results in domestic animals in Kau—cows, pigs, and dogs—but the specificity of the test in these animals was questionable since positive test results had also been found in domestic animals from non-endemic areas.[129] Even if there was a local animal reservoir, how was the virus sustained, given the rapid immunization process in both humans and animals, the short lifespan of mosquitoes, and their almost complete disappearance during the dry season?[130] What triggered an epidemic in such a setting? How should yellow fever control proceed? IHD experience in South America in the 1930s had already shown that rural eradication was unrealistic.[131] For all the universalization of medical knowledge about yellow fever and of laboratory technique, understanding the disease still required a careful analysis of local conditions that had yet to be undertaken in most of Africa.

[127] Findlay, 'Memorandum on Yellow Fever in Africa', [1941], pp. 763–4, CIVSEC 44/5/27.

[128] Findlay, Kirk, and MacCallum, 'Yellow Fever', 137.

[129] G. M. Findlay and F. O. MacCallum, 'Yellow Fever Immune Bodies in the Blood of African Primates', *TRSTMH* 31 (1937), 105; *RSMS 1937*, 72; Findlay, Kirk, and MacCallum, 'Yellow Fever', 138.

[130] Findlay, 'Memorandum on Yellow Fever in Africa', [1941], p. 770, CIVSEC 44/5/27. Research has since shown that mosquitoes can maintain yellow fever virus through generations by transovarial transmission; the capacity of eggs of all *Aedes* species to survive prolonged desiccation preserves virus through the dry season (World Health Organization, *Prevention and Control of Yellow Fever in Africa* (Geneva, 1986), 22, 24).

[131] Marcos Cueto, 'The Cycles of Eradication: The Rockefeller Foundation and Latin American Public Health, 1918–1940', in Weindling (ed.), *International Health Organisations*, 232–4.

## CONCLUSION

The story of yellow fever in Sudan shows a new international medicine emerging and making its mark on an individual country. International concern about the spread of yellow fever by airplane, channelled through international health organizations, combined with the IHD's ongoing preoccupation with yellow fever and its newly available mouse protection test to produce the immunity survey, the results of which placed yellow fever firmly on the Sudan government's agenda. The international sanitary convention on aerial navigation, and the inability to resolve the puzzle that was the Sudan situation, kept it there.

My emphasis on the international dimension is not meant to obscure the continued importance of colonial relationships; 'international' medicine and 'colonial' medicine were not mutually exclusive. Nor do I wish to suggest that international initiatives necessarily overrode national (or colonial) sovereignty. The Rockefeller Foundation was in many respects an international agency, and certainly in Africa, in contrast to Latin America, it appeared to be a neutral third party, with no vested political and economic interests. Pursuing its international agenda did, however, depend on collaborative relationships with the British government, many of its colonial administrations in Africa, and researchers such as Findlay at the Wellcome Bureau and Hewer of the SMS. International medicine in this context served as a reinforcement, rather than a negation of the colonial system. Highlighting the contrasts between Sudan and Uganda, and between French and British attitudes to the protection test, yellow fever also supports the argument, made in Chapter 5, that different colonialisms produced different approaches to disease control and that precisely because of its emphasis on the colony, 'colonial medicine' is an apposite term. Pressure from Britain undoubtedly encouraged Sudan's compliance with the ISC and its cooperation with the Rockefeller Foundation, though over the matter of the laboratory, Sudan showed a determination to go its own way. It is, however, true that the imperialism of interest in this story is not that of mother countries controlling colonial governments, or of colonial officials exerting influence over colonized populations; indeed the lack of engagement with, and concern about, Sudanese people is one of the striking features of the yellow fever investigation. The overpowering imperialism in this chapter is that of self-confident medical researchers pursuing their chosen problem around the world, ignoring all national boundaries in order to push back the frontiers of medical knowledge.

Their findings did not go uncontested. Some members of the international medical community refused to simply accept the protection test as a valid medical technique or the results produced by it as legitimate medical knowledge as long as these were at odds with clinical experience and medical orthodoxy, carried serious and costly consequences for disease control, and crucially, remained unsupported by an isolated pathogen. The clinical cases and the isolated virus from the Nuba Mountains epidemic legitimized the protection test as a technique that produced knowledge that could safely be labelled 'medical' and 'scientific'. The emphasis on isolating the virus reinforces Cunningham's contention that the rise of germ theory and of the laboratory made the pathogen the central source of disease identity. But the contested diagnoses of the 1930s also demonstrate the continued importance of clinical histories and of pathological evidence in identifying yellow fever. Even within a pathogen-centred, laboratory-based world, isolating the virus frequently proved impossible. When the isolation of the virus did occur, it depended on the expert analysis of symptoms expressed in laboratory animals. It is however clear that in the mouse protection test, medical science had a technique that changed the definition of disease. By reading past infection from people's blood, the test helped to further sever disease identity from the experience of people actually feeling unwell. The 1930s preventive measures against yellow fever were unique in Sudan's colonial medical history for being driven not by any past or current illness, but by the laboratory reconstruction of past viral activity.

Like the two previous chapters, this one has highlighted those factors constraining the medical enterprise in colonial Sudan and limiting the power of imperialistic scientific medicine. The yellow fever investigation in Sudan in the 1930s was comparatively well-equipped, well-funded, and well-publicized; medical and political officials across the country were watching for the disease. And yet when the epidemic came, it was only detected at a very late stage, and in spite of a thorough, wide-ranging investigation, could only be partially understood. While the initial diagnosis of the epidemic by a Sudanese assistant medical officer seemed a vindication of the dispensary system, the epidemic was in fact only one more reminder that as late as 1940, the colonial government's grasp of the activities and peoples of parts of Sudan remained extremely weak. Yellow fever shows characteristically colonial conditions—small numbers of trained personnel, poor transportation and communication (particularly during the rains), the physical and political remoteness of rural areas, the paucity of government medical facilities, and the mistrust and selective use of those facilities by indigenous communities—combining to seriously limit what scientific medicine, even at its most technically outstanding, could accomplish. The difficulties of providing medical services to rural areas figure prominently in the next chapter, which discusses a very different form of colonial medicine.

# 7

# *Midwifery Training and the Politics of Female Circumcision*

Training Sudanese midwives and supervising all midwifery practice constituted a distinctive enterprise for the Sudan medical service. As the
discussion so far has made clear, much of colonial medicine in Sudan
focused on studying insect vectors, isolating pathogens in laboratories,
and protecting territory from infection, to the increasing exclusion of
concern about individual people and their understandings of health and
disease; yellow fever provides the extreme example. In articles in the
*Reports of the Wellcome Tropical Research Laboratories* and in the occasional piece in *Sudan Notes and Records*, doctors expressed at least an
intellectual interest in traditional healing. But aside from pre-1914 efforts
to use traditional *hallaqs* (sanitary barbers) as vaccinators and registrars of
births, the medical department never legitimized male Sudanese healers
(such as *fikis* (religious healers) or *basirs* (bone-setters)) by either regulating their practice or seeking to incorporate it into the state medical system.
By contrast, the Midwifery Training School or MTS, opened in
Omdurman in 1921, recognized traditional practitioners as agents who
could be reformed: it sought to create a class of modern, trained Sudanese
midwives, out of, and in rivalry to, an entrenched class of traditional
midwives known as *dayas*.[1] Such a transformation required constant and
explicit engagement with Sudanese people, and their cultural norms
about gender roles and intimate practices such as childbirth and female
circumcision.

My analysis here relies heavily on the papers of Mabel E. Wolff,
founding matron of the MTS and her sister, Gertrude L. Wolff, who first
arrived in Sudan to train nurses.[2] Throughout the chapter, the name

---

[1] The strategy of training traditional midwives was also used in colonial Malaya and
India; the similarities between training in Sudan and Malaya are particularly striking. See
Lenore Manderson, 'Women and the State: Maternal and Child Welfare in Colonial Malaya,
1900–1940', in Valerie Fildes, Lara Marks, and Hilary Marland (eds.), *Women and Children
First: International Maternal and Infant Welfare, 1870–1945* (London: Routledge, 1992),
154–77; Geraldine Forbes, 'Managing Midwifery in India', in Engels and Marks (eds.),
*Contesting Colonial Hegemony*, 152–72.

[2] M. E. Wolff: Matron MTS, 1920–9; Inspectress of Midwives, 1930–7. G. L. Wolff:

PLATE 4. Mabel and Gertrude Wolff and the MTS staff, 1937. (Courtesy of the University of Durham Library.)

'Wolff' alone designates Mabel, whose voice dominates their collective papers. My first argument is that the interaction between traditional and Western medicine, and between Sudanese and British cultures engendered by midwifery training and practice in the colonial context, was highly complex and constantly being negotiated. Even when colonial medicine appeared aggressively didactic—with for example its British representatives in a classroom lecturing illiterate Sudanese women—it rarely involved a straightforward imposition of Western medical and cultural views on an indigenous society. This is not a new insight of course, but the Wolff papers allow us to go some way towards disentangling the complexity of these interactions, showing where and why cultural accommodations were quite explicitly made.[3]

To argue that the boundaries between Western and traditional medi-

Matron, Omdurman Women's Hospital and Principal, Nursing Training School, 1925–30; Matron MTS, 1930–7.

[3] On the exaggerated divisions and the often blurred lines between Western and indigenous medicine, and on the overstatement of the hegemonic power of Western medicine in a similar context, see Catherine Burns, 'Reproductive Labors: The Politics of Women's Health in South Africa, 1900 to 1960', Ph.D. thesis (Northwestern University, 1995), chs. 1, 3, and 6.

cine, and Sudanese and British cultures, seem extremely fluid in the
context of midwifery is not, however, to say that the Wolff sisters saw
them as such. Like their doctor colleagues who trained Sudanese medical
students, they believed themselves to be replacing harmful and superstitious indigenous practice with Western scientific medicine. They placed
the responsibility for maintaining the standards and practices of Western
midwifery firmly on trained midwives: cleanliness, respectable behaviour,
subordination to superior medical authority, proper use and maintenance
of equipment and supplies, and crucially, use of the semi-reclining position for delivery, defined the Western midwife, and could not be compromised. Trained midwives who failed to keep these standards were
cautioned and eventually struck off the roll. Respectability was central to
the identity and the practice of the inter-war Western midwife; to the
Wolff sisters, far from compromising the integrity of Western medicine,
accommodating Sudanese views on what made a woman respectable
strengthened Western medicine and made its transfer to another culture
possible. Similarly, their tolerance of the work of untrained *dayas* did not
mean that the Wolff sisters approved of traditional methods. Theirs was a
pragmatic stance, born of the weaknesses of the government licensing
system, and it did not deflect them from their ultimate goal of eliminating
*dayas* through training.

The MTS marked the first and most successful attempt to train Sudanese women as medical practitioners, and joined girls' education and
nursing as the areas in which British and Sudanese women took leadership
roles under the colonial government. My second argument, however, is
that while midwifery training incorporated the Wolff sisters and Sudanese
midwives into the work of the colonial state, they remained to some extent
marginalized within that state, denied authority, status, and remuneration.[4] This was not entirely a function of the colonial context; midwives in
early twentieth-century Britain faced similar problems.[5] In Sudan, such
difficulties emerged primarily from the very feature that made doctors
willing to incorporate traditional practitioners into this form of Western
medicine, and no other: the low status of midwifery as an occupation
within both British and Sudanese communities, on account of the class
and gender of the midwives, and the nature and location of midwifery

[4] On the marginalization of European women who worked as teachers, nurses, and
political officials in Nigeria, see Helen Callaway, *Gender, Culture, and Empire: European
Women in Colonial Nigeria* (Basingstoke: Macmillan, 1987), 83–162.

[5] Sarah Robinson, 'Maintaining the Independence of the Midwifery Profession: A Continuing Struggle', in Jo Garcia, Robert Kilpatrick, and Martin Richards (eds.), *The Politics
of Maternity Care: Services for Childbearing Women in Twentieth-Century Britain* (Oxford:
Clarendon Press, 1990), 61–91.

work. This chapter, then, provides the most vivid support for the argument first made in Chapter 2, that hierarchies of gender, race, occupation, and class disciplined the medical service's employment of non-European personnel.

In addressing the government's handling of the controversial matter of female circumcision, the chapter also provides evidence of the rigid boundary sometimes drawn between medicine and politics in Sudan. This was a professional boundary, with political officials deciding that because of its religious significance, female circumcision was a political, rather than a medical problem, for which there must ultimately be a political solution. But it was also a heavily gendered boundary. While the Wolff sisters and Sudanese trained midwives constantly confronted community politics, about this issue and others, central government policy on female circumcision was high politics, a sphere which in Sudan did not welcome women.

## THE CONTEXT

The *daya* had long been a fixture in northern Sudanese communities because of the widespread practice of pharaonic female circumcision. Although this practice pre-dated the advent of Islam in Sudan, over time it had become closely identified with religion. But as Ellen Gruenbaum observes, and as the work of Janice Boddy has demonstrated, 'The practice is deeply embedded in the cultures of northern Sudanese ethnic groups, exhibiting symbolic significance far deeper than its religious associations or other conscious rationales.'[6] Performed on pre-pubescent girls, usually aged between 5 and 10, the pharaonic form of circumcision involves the excision of all external genitalia (clitoris, labia minora, labia majora) and infibulation, the stitching together of the outer labia, resulting in almost complete vaginal occlusion by scar tissue, leaving a single, small opening through which both urine and menses pass. The *daya* performed the initial circumcision and reinfibulated women after childbirth. The fact of infibulation meant that no birth could go unattended: a midwife had to be present to cut open the mother to allow the infant to emerge safely from the womb.

Pharaonic circumcision made midwives socially indispensable, then, but their work also made them socially problematic. Susan Kenyon's

---

[6] Ellen Gruenbaum, 'Reproductive Ritual and Social Reproduction: Female Circumcision and the Subordination of Women in Sudan', in O'Neill and O'Brien (eds.), *Economy and Class*, 309. See also Janice Boddy, 'Womb as Oasis: The Symbolic Context of Pharaonic Circumcision in Rural Northern Sudan', *American Ethnologist*, 9 (1982), 682–98; Boddy, *Wombs and Alien Spirits*, esp. 47–75, 100–6.

characterization of Sudanese midwifery in the 1980s resonates with the
evidence from the colonial period. She observes that the reputations of
Sudanese midwives are somewhat 'tarnished' because their work gives
them special knowledge and freedom from the usual social constraints on
women, for example the ability to go out alone late at night:

> Certainly midwives seem more controversial in the Sudan than any other occupa-
> tional group . . . Criticisms of midwives seem to have less to do with their job
> performance or with demands for payment, than with the nature of the job itself.
> It is as if their involvement with sexuality, and particularly female sexuality, is at
> once reassuring and threatening.[7]

It may also be, to borrow from other contemporary work, that midwives
were regarded ambivalently because of their position as both preservers
(in their role as infibulators) and breachers (in their role as deinfibulators
during birth) of bodily enclosures. Boddy argues that bodily orifices
are the focus of considerable tension in northern Sudanese rural culture:
while the vaginal opening is intimately linked with fertility and children,
it also leaves women vulnerable to the invasion of *jinn* (spirits) attracted
to genital blood, which may possess her or even render her sterile. Their
work also exposes midwives to different types of blood, a substance
that again is regarded either positively or negatively depending on the
context.[8]

There are limits to how far contemporary evidence can be projected
back into the past. The tensions that Kenyon identifies for the 1980s, for
example, were probably at least partial consequences of the training
started in the 1920s, which exaggerated the apartness of midwives. But the
requirement of an unconventional lifestyle, and the association with female sexuality and fertility, seem to have been defining and problematic
features of midwifery as a practice in the Sudanese context throughout
this century, whether the practitioners were trained or untrained. Such
associations seem to have been particularly troubling when the midwife
was young and unmarried. As we will see later, it was in the intersection
of unconventionality, sexuality, marital status, and age that social anxiety
around midwifery was produced.

Exceptionally among British colonies in Africa, where missionaries
usually ran maternal and infant health initiatives,[9] the MTS was a govern-

---

[7] Kenyon, *Five Women of Sennar*, 97–8.
[8] Boddy, *Wombs and Alien Spirits*, 100–6, 248–50.
[9] Vaughan, *Curing Their Ills*, 56, 66–71; Carol Summers, 'Intimate Colonialism: The
Imperial Production of Reproduction in Uganda, 1907–1925', *Signs*, 16 (1991), 799–807.

ment enterprise. Unfortunately, the patchiness of Sudan government records between 1918 and 1924 means that the origins of the MTS are obscure. According to Mabel Wolff, the MTS owed its foundation to the initiative of Molly Crowfoot, wife of Sudan's director of education. Horrified by a female circumcision and a birth that she had witnessed, Crowfoot successfully lobbied Dr E. S. Crispin, director of the Sudan medical department, to establish a midwifery training school, and recommended Wolff to be the founding matron.[10] This account is believable given the small, unbureaucratized, colonial elite that existed in Khartoum at the time, but it seems fair to speculate that other factors figured in Crispin's decision.

Like other colonial governments, the Sudan government had been preoccupied with the apparent underpopulation of the country since the start of the Condominium in 1899; the mortality caused by the influenza epidemic in 1918–19 could only have heightened concern.[11] The Gezira irrigation scheme, scheduled to open in the mid-1920s, and Sudan's general economic development, required an ample supply of fit labourers; this depended in the long term on high fertility and safe reproduction. Crispin may also have seen the initiation of midwifery training as a logical consequence of the newly acquired civilian status of the medical department. Under civilian control, the department would start providing services to the truly civilian population of Sudanese women and children. Indeed, the foundation of the MTS seems to have been part of a wider government initiative to reach out to Sudanese women, one that may reflect the inter-war development of intense concern about maternal health and child welfare worldwide.[12] The Girls' Training College opened in Omdurman at virtually the same time as the MTS, in order to expand educational provision by training Sudanese girls to be schoolmistresses.[13] The exact role of these socio-economic and

[10] M. E. Wolff, 'Some Notes on the Sudan', 1952, SAD 582/10/16. See also Obituary of Grace Mary Crowfoot, *Palestine Exploration Quarterly*, SAD 582/8/82–3.

[11] *RFACS 1914/1919*, 134; *SIR*, no. 296, Mar. 1919, 2–3, and no. 297, Apr. 1919, 3–4.

[12] Fildes, Marks, and Marland (eds.), *Women and Children First*. For British concern, see Anna Davin, 'Imperialism and Motherhood', *History Workshop Journal*, 5 (1978), 9–66; Jane Lewis, *The Politics of Motherhood: Child and Maternal Welfare in England, 1900–1939* (London: Croom Helm, 1980).

[13] The parallels between the early development of midwifery training and of girls' education are marked. Systematic girls' education was also pioneered by two sisters who had previously worked in Egypt, Dorothy and Dora Evans. Only five students enrolled for the first teaching session at the GTC in 1921 and accommodations were made in order to persuade Sudanese families to send their daughters to the school. High walls were provided around the GTC compound, each pupil was accompanied by a female chaperone, and to enhance their damaged marriage prospects, schoolmistresses who had taught for four or

institutional factors remains unclear, but we do know that by 1919, funds had been provided for a maternity school and construction of the building was underway, and that Mabel Wolff joined the medical department on 26 November 1920.[14]

The Wolff sisters were from a modest background: their father was working as a clerk for a shipping firm in Port Tewfiq, Egypt when Gertrude Lucy and Mabel Elsie were born on 18 July 1886 and 16 October 1890, respectively.[15] They grew up in Egypt, became fluent in Arabic, and trained as nurse-midwives, apparently in Britain.[16] Mabel Wolff arrived in Sudan from Fayoum, Upper Egypt, where she and Gertrude, with some interruption for war nursing at Alexandria, had spent the previous seven years successfully running a dispensary for poor children and then a midwifery training school.[17]

Like the short-lived attempts at training and registering *dayas* under-taken by some doctors in Sudan before the First World War,[18] the MTS began as an urban project. Wolff's work initially focused on the town of Omdurman, but the beginnings were not auspicious. Her Egyptian Arabic initially proved little use in communicating with Sudanese women and she found it difficult to convince anyone to enroll: none of the *dayas* could understand what a young woman with no children of her own could possibly teach them about Sudanese childbirth.[19] But Wolff persuaded four women to start training in January 1921, and began to overcome local opposition by demonstrating that she could deliver healthy babies and keep mothers healthy in the weeks following delivery. By the end of 1921, Wolff had trained ten women, started a session with a further eight pupils, and had been permitted to hire her first Sudanese staff midwife: Gindiya Saleh, a 38-year-old widow who assisted with teaching, helped to secure

more years were paid a bonus on marriage equivalent to one month's salary for every year of service. See Ina Beasley, *Before the Wind Changed: People, Places and Education in the Sudan*, ed. Janet Starkey (Oxford: Oxford University Press, 1992), 345–9.

[14] *RFACS 1914/1919*, 135; Sudan government, *Quarterly List*, July 1923, 7.

[15] Birth certificates of G. L. Wolff and M. E. Wolff, General Register Office, St Catherine's House, London.

[16] Bente Torsvik, 'Receiving the Gifts of Allah: The Establishment of a Modern Mid-wifery Service in the Sudan 1920–1937', Hovedoppgave i Historie hosten (University of Bergen, 1983), 7. M. E. Wolff passed the Central Midwives Board examination, and was admitted to the Midwives Roll in 1916 (*The Midwives Roll, 1917* (London, 1917), 1755). Nothing further is known about their training.

[17] SAD 579/2/1–37.

[18] *RFACS 1904*, 63; *RFACS 1906*, 643; *RFACS 1908*, 234; *Provisional Regulations of the Sudan Medical Department* (Khartoum: El Sudan Press, 1910), 8–9.

[19] E. M. Kendall, 'A Short History of the Training of Midwives in the Sudan', *SNR* 33 (1952), 42.

the future of the MTS by persuading Omdurman women to use its services.[20] Throughout the 1920s, Wolff expanded her project first to the towns of northern Sudan, then to more rural areas. From 1923 onwards, she did so through annual tours of inspection, which allowed her to oversee all midwifery work, to meet the women who would be her students' clients, and to choose potential pupils, who would train in Omdurman and then return home to work.[21] The vast majority of these pupils were, and remained, illiterate.

## RECRUITMENT, TRAINING, AND LICENSING

Wolff's accommodation with Sudanese culture started with recruitment. That midwives should be women was uncontroversial.[22] Like other nursing matrons throughout Britain and the empire, Wolff laid great weight on finding 'respectable' women to train.[23] She wanted to ensure that trained midwives would be embraced by their communities on return from training and more generally, to improve the low status of midwifery among British and Sudanese. Since Sudanese and British concerns about marital status, class, and age differed, Sudanese and British notions of respectability did not always coincide. The profile that evolved of the ideal MTS candidate—a fit married woman, of good moral character and

[20] M. E. Wolff, Speech to Committee of Guild Service, SAD 579/3/24–9; Annual Report MTS 1921, 20 Oct. 1921, SAD 579/3/15; Second Report 1921, 29 Jan. 1922, SAD 579/3/21–2; Crispin to M. E. Wolff, 6 Nov. 1921, SAD 579/3/17; MTS Trained Midwives Register, SAD 579/8/1–40; M. E. Wolff, 'M.T.Sch. History', n.d., SAD 580/2/14–15.

[21] The first student from Northern province enrolled in 1922, from Blue Nile and Kordofan provinces in 1924, White Nile province in 1925, Kassala in 1929, Darfur in 1930, and Upper Nile province in 1933 (MTS Trained Midwives Register, SAD 579/8/1–40).

[22] No attempts were made to incorporate the occasional male midwife into the training system, although the evidence suggests that nothing was done to discourage such men from practising. Male midwifery in Sudan seems to have been hereditary and to have emerged from the care of animals. See Midwives Inspection Sheets Kordofan Province contd 1929–30, SAD 580/5/34; Dr J. B. Christopherson, 'Medical and Surgical Customs in the Sudan', 29 Mar. 1908, SAD 407/6/18.

[23] On the importance of the 'respectability' and 'moral character' of nurses in the modernization of nursing from the mid-Victorian period onward, see Anne-Marie Rafferty, *The Politics of Nursing Knowledge* (London: Routledge, 1996), 9–41; Shula Marks, *Divided Sisterhood: Race, Class and Gender in the South African Nursing Profession* (London: St Martin's Press, 1994), 31–2; Pat Holden, 'Colonial Sisters: Nurses in Uganda', in Pat Holden and Jenny Littlewood (eds.), *Anthropology and Nursing* (London: Routledge, 1991), 67–83. Moral values were particularly vital when auxiliary medical personnel were African: on Uganda and the Belgian Congo, see Lyons, 'Power', 204, and Summers, 'Intimate Colonialism', 803–6.

popular in her village, between the ages of 20 and 30[24]—was a compromise between the preferences of Wolff and of Sudanese communities. Wolff had for example wanted to train some young, single women to be professional, career midwives, but discovered that midwives who were too independent, and too 'athletic' in their movements, were labelled '*dakarieh*' (sexual pervert or lesbian) by their home communities, particularly if they were 'young, unattached, and sufficiently interested in [their] work to refuse mens' advances'.[25] A clear expression of Sudanese concern about the sexual nature of midwifery work, this may also have been a demonstration of generational conflict: such labelling may have been a means by which older women conveyed their displeasure at having their control over infibulation and the birth process challenged.[26] Wolff's emphasis on the pre-existing popularity of pupil midwives and on young pupils being married grew out of this Sudanese reaction. Wolff gave preference, where possible, to *dayas* and to the daughters of *dayas*,[27] in order to eliminate traditional rivals and to conform to the Sudanese custom of passing midwifery practice from mother to daughter. About half of the pupils who trained between 1921 and 1934 had prior midwifery experience when they started training. As this discussion suggests, age was central to the construction of respectability. While Wolff wanted women young enough to be shaped by her teaching, most *dayas* were older and for all midwives, age implied experience and demanded some community respect. So while the average age of pupils dropped from 50.9 in 1921 to 38.7 in 1925, it never fell much below the high thirties thereafter. The age range in each class remained large between 1921 and 1934; most women who trained were between 20 and 60 years old.[28]

According to Wolff, as the MTS became better known, the initially strong disapproval of husbands began to wane, and more and younger married women were able to train.[29] Husbands' disapproval mattered. Wolff worked within existing gender relations, even as she modified them

---

[24]  M. E. Wolff to Director, SMS, 27 Oct. 1928, SAD 582/1/34; M. E. Wolff to Medical Inspector, BNP, 14 Nov. 1928, SAD 582/1/40.

[25]  Annual Report MTS 1931, SAD 581/1/28; see also Midwives Inspection Sheet 1931 BNP, SAD 580/6/3 and M. E. Wolff, Ref-letter received from Mr Newbold—30/5/32, SAD 582/6/14–17.

[26]  On generational conflict over initiation among Meru women, see Lynn M. Thomas, '"*Ngaitana* (I will circumcise myself)": The Gender and Generational Politics of the 1956 Ban on Clitoridectomy in Meru, Kenya', *Gender and History*, 8 (1996), 338–63.

[27]  'Notice Regarding the Training of Midwives', SAD 580/3/6–7.

[28]  Prior experience and ages from MTS Trained Midwives Register, SAD 579/8/1–40.

[29]  Annual Report MTS 1931, SAD 581/1/28–9.

through training, by requiring the approval of the relevant man (spouse or relative) before a woman was allowed to train. As married women came to be more sought after as recruits, changes were made to facilitate their training. In 1934, with the MTS located in new, larger premises, the medical service decided to allow each pupil to bring up to three children below the age of 12 with her to the MTS, and made financial provision for their travel.[30] Caring for these children became part of the training course as each pupil in turn became the weekly 'mother', in charge of children's meals, bathing, and recreation.[31]

Social background was another determinant of respectability. Women of 'slave type', namely southern Sudanese settled in the north, were scrupulously avoided as pupil midwives, because of their low social status.[32] Although we have no systematic breakdown of the family origins of the trained midwives, it is clear that Wolff recruited a significant minority of women who were married, or related, to men in positions of authority: some were traditional leaders within or without the native administration structure, while others were medical auxiliaries. Wolff involved those same male Sudanese leaders in the recruitment process, seeking official backing and guaranteed local acceptance for her trained midwives. By 1932, each prospective pupil required 'a signed letter from the Omdah & Sheikhs stating she is a woman of good morals & character & approved of by the villagers & women especially'.[33]

Educated, literate women remained a small minority of Sudanese trained midwives throughout the inter-war period, particularly as one could be a 'better class' woman without being educated. Provision for girls' education, both government and missionary, was poor in inter-war Sudan,[34] and the problematic nature of midwifery work meant that it was not a vocation that most educated girls and/or their families on their behalf aspired to.[35] The bias against nursing training, for which literacy

---

[30] N. Macleod for Director, SMS to M. E. Wolff, 21 Apr. 1934, SAD 582/4/31. While some children had accompanied their mothers to the MTS during the 1920s (Inspectress of Midwives to Obstetric Surgeon and Gynaecologist, 31 Aug. 1937, SAD 580/2/2), the scattered evidence suggests that before 1934, pupil midwives were not encouraged to bring their children with them (M. E. Wolff to Senior Medical Officer, BNP, 31 Dec. 1928, SAD 582/1/48; Midwives Inspection Sheets 1930 Eastern Kordofan, SAD 580/5/44).

[31] M. E. Wolff, 'Some Notes on the Sudan', 1952, SAD 582/10/19.

[32] M. E. Wolff to G. L. Wolff and Mother, 2 Nov. 1928, SAD 582/7/12.

[33] M. E. Wolff to All, 12 Nov. 1932, SAD 582/7/52.

[34] Lilian M. Sanderson, 'Some Aspects of the Development of Girls' Education in the Northern Sudan', *SNR* 42 (1961), 92–9.

[35] See e.g. Kendall, 'Short History', 46.

was considered more important, but which involved menial work in a hospital in the presence of unfamiliar men, was even greater.[36] Government policy, as we will see below, enhanced the attractions of teaching over midwifery. If educated women were going to work outside the home during the inter-war period, becoming a schoolteacher was the most respectable option from the Sudanese perspective.

Wolff's lecture notes show that trained midwives were provided with 'modern' equipment and drugs, and were schooled to a high level in anatomy and disease causation.[37] Initially three months long, the residential training course was lengthened to six months in 1924 to raise standards.[38] In contrast to India, where the training of traditional midwives was hampered by the choice of English as the language of instruction, all teaching was in Arabic.[39] The illiteracy of the vast majority of pupils made the MTS extremely unusual among colonial training schools in Africa and elsewhere, where literacy was normally a prerequisite. It meant that all lessons had to be memorized and that the identity of medicines had to be learned through texture, colour, and smell. Demonstration and practice on dolls, on the cases that each pupil was required to attend in Omdurman, and on a model pelvis complete with deliverable foetus, reinforced lessons. Wolff used whatever materials were at hand in her teaching: episiotomies were practised on old rubber tyres before they were performed on delivering women. Meeting the course requirements demanded considerable technical skill: the successful pupil had seen twenty cases, delivered twenty under supervision, and passed oral and practical examinations administered by senior British doctors. The 1930 examination consisted of fourteen questions including: explain/demonstrate how to take a temperature and pass a catheter; under what conditions should you send for help or send the patient to the hospital? (Correct answer: prolapsed cord, adherent placenta, abnormal presentation, convulsions.)[40]

---

[36] Inspection of Midwives 1927, SAD 579/5/48; M. E. Wolff, Personal Interview with Director SMS January 1928, SAD 582/1/2; M. E. Wolff, 'Midwives Inspection Tour Report 1928', 7 Jan. 1929, SAD 582/1/49–53. From 1927, between five and eight women graduated each year as nurses from the two-year course at the Nursing Training School in Omdurman.

[37] M. E. Wolff, 'Lectures in English', [n.d. but probably 1936–7], SAD 581/5/1–84; Midwifery Training School—Omdurman, 'Syllabus', SAD 581/5/79–80.

[38] Kendall, 'Short History', 45; Annual Report MTS 1923, SAD 579/4/12.

[39] Forbes, 'Managing Midwifery', 168, 171.

[40] 'Midwives Examination Questions—1930', SAD 581/5/82. Training details from M. E. Wolff, 'Lectures in English', SAD 581/5/1,5; J. S. Fairbairn, 'Midwifery Service in the Sudan', [1936], SAD 581/4/1; 'Methods of Teaching' photo album, 1930s, SAD 583/

Wolff's lectures reveal some of the negotiations between Sudanese and British cultures involved in midwifery training. An amalgam of scientific teaching and moral preaching, the lectures laid out her beliefs in terms intended to appeal to Sudanese women. In her opening lecture, Wolff declared that only a 'moral, trustworthy, conscientious and truthful' midwife could be relied upon 'to carry out the teachings of her training'. Here was an attempt to cultivate the respectability that would improve the status of midwifery in both British and Sudanese communities, a respectability that Wolff disciplined by punishing any behaviour that she considered immoral during training.[41] Lectures spelled out that cleanliness, required in all aspects of the midwife's life (clean hands, nails, home, husband, children, and work), would keep away disease-causing microbes, thereby preventing puerperal fever; students were taught how to sterilize their equipment and to wash their hands frequently. But 'cleanliness' was as much a moral state as a physical phenomenon: 'You must remember that in midwifery there are two or more lives dependent on your skill and care, each baby you help from darkness to the light of Day, is a gift from God and you should be at all times worthy to receive it.'[42] While this lesson sounds Christian in tone, the depiction of the infant as a gift from God was as much Sudanese and Islamic as British and Christian in inspiration. It resonated with local custom, according to which midwives were not necessarily paid for delivering babies, since such work earned divine reward.[43]

This blending of moral and hygienic ideas, and this appeal to Sudanese values, blur any quick division between Western and indigenous medicine. For Sudanese clients, the most marked difference came in the delivery position. During a traditional Sudanese delivery, a woman gave birth in a semi-upright position, over a hole dug in the ground for the afterbirth, hanging on to the *habl* or rope tied to the ceiling.[44] A Western

6/1–66; Alexander Cruickshank, 'The Midwives' Training School and the Development of a Midwifery Service in the Sudan During the Anglo-Egyptian Condominium, 1899–1956', in Deborah Lavin (ed.), *The Condominium Remembered*, Proceedings of the Durham Historical Records Conference 1982, vol. ii (Centre for Middle Eastern and Islamic Studies, University of Durham, 1993), 133.

[41] One student was dismissed for her 'immoral conduct': M. E. Wolff to Director, Medical Department, 19 Feb. 1924, SAD 589/4/20; M. E. Wolff to Leonard Bousfield, 3 Mar. 1924, SAD 579/4/21.

[42] M. E. Wolff, 'Lectures in English', SAD 581/5/18, quotes 7.

[43] M. E. Wolff to Director, SMS, 17 Jan. 1929, SAD 581/1/11–13; see also M. E. Wolff, 'Some Notes on the Sudan', 1952, SAD 582/10/17.

[44] For a fuller description of Sudanese childbirth and the ritual around it, see Anne Cloudsley, *The Women of Omdurman: Victims of Circumcision* (London, 1981), 107–23.

delivery meant that the woman gave birth in a semi-reclining position on top of a mackintosh sheet which covered the bed or ground beneath. The mackintosh and the *habl* served as mutually exclusive, rival symbols and their importance was not lost on Sudanese women: children delivered by trained midwives became known as *ibn* or *bint al mashamma*, son or daughter of the mackintosh.[45] The most visible marks of the newly trained midwife were her white uniform and her tin midwifery box, which contained her equipment and supplies.[46] The importance of these new status symbols to their trained rivals was quickly assimilated by some *dayas*, who adopted similar uniforms and created their own midwifery boxes, some empty, some containing iodine and other drugs. This occurred to such an extent that the 1931 annual report of the MTS recommended that untrained midwives not be permitted to use boxes and thereby pose as trained midwives.[47]

In general, however, Wolff adopted a reasonably accommodating posture towards *dayas*, knowing that to ban their practice would be ineffective and unpopular. Both she and medical service director O. F. H. Atkey, agreed that the ultimate aim was to eliminate traditional practitioners through training, but that in the meantime, the state should seek to know and control *dayas* through annual inspections and licensing.[48] Around the world, licensing, coupled with training, was the mechanism for introducing standards into midwifery: registration of midwives started in Britain in 1902, in Malaya in 1917, and in India in the mid-1930s.[49] Legislation passed in 1924 made it mandatory for all practitioners of midwifery in Sudan to hold a government licence and to renew that licence annually.[50] Wolff urged, and Atkey agreed, that licences be withheld from those

---

[45] Annual Report MTS 1926, SAD 581/1/2. On the *habl*, see also A. E. Lorenzen to Director, SMS, 25 Mar. 1934, SAD 582/4/25; M. E. Wolff to Director, SMS, 8 Apr. 1934, SAD 582/4/26.
[46] For a complete listing of the contents of the midwifery box, see 'Trained Midwives Equipment', n.d., SAD 580/3/8–12.
[47] Annual Report MTS 1931, SAD 581/1/29. See Inspection Dongola Province— Merowe District, Hagga Gamal Hessein Ali, 9 Nov. 1932, SAD 580/6/43; Inspection Upper Nile Province Malakal, 21 Nov. 1932, Kaka Ahmed Ali, SAD 580/6/40; M. E. Wolff, 'Midwives Inspection 1931', 1932, SAD 582/2/73.
[48] See e.g. Annual Report MTS 1926, SAD 581/1/2; M. E. Wolff to Medical Inspector, El Obeid, 25 Apr. 1927, SAD 579/5/40.
[49] Robinson, 'Maintaining the Independence', 64–5; Lenore Manderson, 'Blame, Responsibility and Remedial Action: Death, Disease and the Infant in Early Twentieth Century Malaya', in Norman G. Owen (ed.), *Death and Disease in Southeast Asia: Explorations in Social, Medical and Demographic History* (Singapore: Oxford University Press, 1987), 265; Forbes, 'Managing Midwifery', 167.
[50] 'Public Health Ordinance 1924', section 18, *SGG*, no. 438, 25 July 1924, 2054.

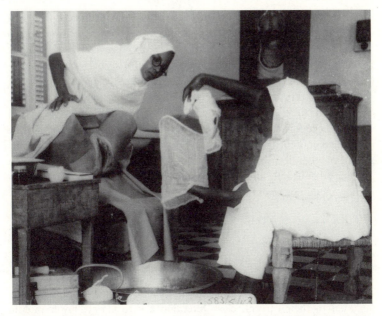

PLATE 5. A midwifery student examines the placenta from the 'reclining' model pelvis; note the mackintosh sheet underneath. (Courtesy of the University of Durham Library.)

midwives who were very old and blind (and thus dangerous), and also that no young, inexperienced woman be licensed or allowed to practise until she had undergone training: once equipped with a licence, young women were much less willing to train.[51] Such stipulations were only of value, however, if political and medical officials ensured that unlicensed women did not practise.[52]

On tour, Wolff found that doctors, midwives, and other officials were ignorant of the law and that the licensing system functioned extremely poorly. Rather than travel to government stations to obtain or renew licences, many *dayas* simply denied practising. In some areas by the early 1930s, licences were annually collected for renewal, but in the resulting confusion, they were often lost, torn, or wrongly renewed. Some trained

[51] M. E. Wolff to Governor, Kordofan, 7 Dec. 1925, SAD 579/5/10; M. E. Wolff to Director, SMS, 7 Jan. 1929, SAD 582/1/55; Atkey to M. E. Wolff, 15 Jan. 1929, SAD 582/1/56; M. E. Wolff to Senior Medical Inspector, BNP, 12 Apr. 1929, SAD 582/1/62; M. E. Wolff to Senior Medical Inspector, Berber, 13 Dec. 1933, SAD 582/3/47–8.

[52] Annual Report MTS 1931, SAD 581/1/29–30.

midwives had their special licences replaced by ordinary ones and some midwives were charged for licences they never received. Such difficulties emerged partly from the decision, enshrined in the Public Health Ordinance 1924, to allow only provincial governors, on the recommendation of the provincial medical officer of health, and not the Wolff sisters, who were annually inspecting all practising midwives, to issue licences. In 1925, when two governors authorized Wolff to issue and endorse licences in their names, Atkey informed her that she was in infringement of the law.[53] Despite Wolff's repeated appeals for a rationalization of the licensing system, the law appears to have remained unchanged. Virtually all *dayas* were tolerated, in part because the licensing law could not be enforced.

## MARGINAL PRACTICES

The refusal to grant the Wolff sisters the right to license in part reflects and reveals their marginalization within the medical service, as well as their generally problematic status within colonial Sudan. Their gender, devotion to their careers, clear intention not to marry, lower middle class background, and low status work focused on Sudanese women made them highly unusual in Sudan's masculine, upper middle class, colonial society.[54] British preconceptions about the low status of midwives generally were reflected in government policy. Sudanese women schoolteachers were paid more than Sudanese staff midwives, who also performed a teaching role. During term, these women (three in 1930, six by 1937) taught midwifery classes and accompanied students to cases; out of term, they kept the MTS open for antenatal work, coached midwives in the field, and helped with inspections. When travelling on official business, schoolteachers received second-class railway warrants. Until 1934, to Wolff's great distress, staff midwives were required to travel third class, in more crowded, less private carriages, in the presence of unfamiliar men, not the sort of setting considered suitable for the

---

[53] M. E. Wolff to Director, SMS, 17 Nov. 1925, SAD 579/5/8. On licensing, see also 'Report on Inspection of Midwives', 5 Jan. 1926, SAD 579/5/15–16; Inspection of Midwives 1927, SAD 579/5/47; Atkey to Governor, 15 Jan. 1929, SAD 582/1/57; M. E. Wolff to MOH through Director, SMS, 2 Dec. 1932, SAD 582/3/20.

[54] Even Sudan political service wives had difficulty adjusting to the masculine culture: see Rosemary Kenrick, *Sudan Tales: Recollections of Some Sudan Political Service Wives* (Cambridge: Oleander, 1987).

kind of women—respectable, educated if possible—whom the Wolffs were trying to recruit.[55]

Sudanese midwives occupied an ambiguous position with respect to the colonial state. The government funded and ran training,[56] and licensed and supervised midwives, but this was not, strictly speaking, a government midwifery service. Trained midwives did not appear on the medical service staff lists, and crucially, they were not paid a government salary. They were expected to support themselves, as *dayas* did, on fees paid to them for deliveries and circumcisions. This was not easy, since many Sudanese viewed midwifery as charitable work which brought divine reward after death rather than material benefit in life. Wolff recorded very small cash payments, ranging from 5 to 100 Pt as fees for a delivery. In addition, the midwife would ideally receive grain, dates, fat, scents, and portions of any animal sacrificed in celebration. But in poor communities, Wolff emphasized, the midwife received either a small payment in kind or nothing at all. The trained midwife faced significantly higher expenses than her untrained rivals, since she had to maintain her equipment and supplies, issued at cost from the medical store, out of her own earnings: Atkey believed firmly that trained midwives would take less care with their equipment if replacements were issued free of charge. The added expense, along with local hostility, meant that some midwives came to regard their training as a handicap.[57]

The British and Sudanese model of midwifery as private practice, which was cheap for the state, predominated throughout the inter-war period. But perhaps as the difficulties in providing rural, trained midwifery services became clearer to the urban-based medical service, some of the measures recommended by Wolff to improve the position of trained

[55] M. E. Wolff to Director, SMS, 10 Mar. 1933, SAD 582/3/28; N. Macleod for Director, SMS to M. E. Wolff, 21 July 1934, SAD 582/4/40. See also M. E. Wolff to G. L. Wolff, Mother, and Evelyn, 28 Oct. 1932, SAD 582/7/45–6; M. E. Wolff to Director, SMS, 16 June 1932, SAD 582/3/4.

[56] During training, the government provided free accommodation, bedding, and uniforms and a 60 Pt/month allowance which pupils paid into a messing fund. The 90 Pt/month allowance initially paid to all pupils during training was stopped during the 1930s: enough women could be found to train and the government was by this time feeding and clothing pupils' children as well. See M. E. Wolff to Dr MacDowell, 13 Apr. 1929, SAD 582/1/63; M. E. Wolff, 'A Few Notes on our Management of Staff Teacher Midwives etc.', 31 Aug. 1937, SAD 580/2/11–12.

[57] M. E. Wolff to Director, SMS, 17 Jan. 1929, SAD 581/1/11–13; M. E. Wolff to Director, SMS, 1 Dec. 1932, SAD 582/3/19; MOH to M. E. Wolff, 7 Apr. 1921, SAD 579/3/13; Inspection of Midwives 1927, SAD 579/5/47–8; Atkey to M. E. Wolff, 6 Nov. 1930, SAD 582/2/39.

midwives were gradually implemented. In 1929, the medical service
started paying a small, monthly hardship stipend of 60 Pt/month
to trained midwives working in the poorest areas (approximately one-
quarter of the total trained) and a stipend to three Omdurman midwives
who worked as MTS district midwifery teachers.[58] When financial hardship among trained midwives persisted, Atkey followed another of
Wolff's recommendations in asking governors in 1933 to pressure Sudanese male leaders into ensuring better payment to trained midwives.[59] By
1937, trained midwives were finally receiving free replacements of equipment and supplies and that same year, the idea of paying a salary to trained
midwives was under consideration.[60] That, however, is where the idea
remained. To improve the supervision offered to trained midwives, Atkey
started sending lists of the local trained midwives to each of his doctors in
1930, instructing them to see the midwives once a month and check their
supplies;[61] Wolff had long done this herself. Small stipends and pressure
for increased supervision marked the institutional recognition that greater
attempts needed to be made to incorporate the growing cadre of trained
midwives into the Sudan medical service.

But overall, and particularly in rural areas, the financial position and
supervision of trained midwives remained poor. Trained midwives had
difficulty throughout the inter-war period in obtaining replacement drugs
and renewing their equipment. Dispensaries and hospitals were often far
away, and the doctors and medical auxiliaries who ran these institutions
had other priorities; they did not always consider the needs of trained
midwives when they made their supply requisitions.[62] The system also
discounted the difficulty that rural Sudanese women, socialized not to
deal publicly with unfamiliar men, had in demanding assistance from
male British doctors and even more so from male Sudanese medical
auxiliaries.[63] In this context, the two-month long annual inspections that
each Wolff sister conducted quickly became all-important, but large dis-

---

[58] F. D. Rugman for Financial Secretary to Director, SMS, 3 Mar. 1929, SAD 582/1/58;
Annual Report MTS 1929, SAD 581/1/8.
[59] Annual Report MTS 1932, SAD 581/1/49; Atkey to Governor, 14 Feb. 1933, p. 6,
KASSALA 2/122/512, NRO.
[60] E. D. Pridie, 'Description sommaire de l'instruction et de l'organisation des sages-
femmes au Soudan Anglo-Égyptien', *BOIHP* 29 (1937), 1933; undated later note on G. L.
Wolff to Director, SMS, Inspection Tour of Midwives 1929–30, SAD 580/5/10–11.
[61] Atkey to M. E. Wolff, 20 Feb. 1930, SAD 582/2/17; Atkey to Medical Inspector, 29
Apr. 1930, SAD 582/2/31.
[62] M. E. Wolff to Medical Inspector, Atbara, 1 Jan. 1927, SAD 579/5/38; M. E. Wolff to
Director, SMS, 1 June 1928, SAD 582/1/9; Annual Report MTS 1935, SAD 581/2/26–8.
[63] M. E. Wolff to All, 3 Dec. 1932, SAD 582/7/56–8.

tances and time constraints meant that not all trained midwives could be inspected each year. In her 1935 report, Wolff put the matter starkly: 'With regard to the work of the Rural trained midwives, unless steps are taken for more frequent inspection and supervision, with better facilities for issuing them the necessary drugs, dressings and equipment, than is possible at present, the work cannot help becoming retrogressive and unfortunately this is already apparent in some places.'[64] By 'retrogressive', Wolff meant that trained midwives forgot their lessons, gave up maintaining their boxes, and effectively reverted to being *dayas*. Brief postgraduate refresher courses at the MTS, started in 1932, were designed to counter this tendency.[65] But the underlying problems of inadequate supervision and financial hardship went unresolved.

In Wolff's eyes, however, these problems did not excuse trained midwives from failing to live up to the standards of their training. At the same time as she urged better support, she also asked doctors not to show any 'leniency' towards trained midwives, as it set a bad example, and requested that she be informed of 'any negligence, malpractice or misdemeanour'.[66] During inspection tours, the Wolff sisters examined trained midwives' hands and nails to ensure that they were clean and neat, and boxes and equipment, particularly nail brushes, to ensure that they were clean and well-used; accompanied the midwives to cases; and tested them to see how well they remembered their lessons. For *dayas*, also visited during inspections, it was enough to be fit, sighted, and not too dangerous if they expected to continue their practice.[67] For trained midwives, the standard was much higher. Unsatisfactory performance—which included having an unused, dirty box, reverting to *habl* deliveries, unreliability and unpopularity, and immoral behaviour—resulted in strong cautions, temporary or permanent suspension of their hardship stipend, and eventually, cancellation of their licence, repossession of their midwifery box, and removal of their name from the MTS roll.[68] Between 1921 and 1934, the licences of thirteen trained midwives (6 per cent) were cancelled for

[64] Annual Report MTS 1935, SAD 581/2/26–7.
[65] Annual Report MTS 1932, SAD 581/1/47; Annual Report MTS 1933, SAD 581/1/55; M. E. Wolff to Director, SMS, 9 Mar. 1933, SAD 582/3/29.
[66] M. E. Wolff to Medical Inspector, Atbara, 1 Jan. 1927, SAD 579/5/38.
[67] See e.g. Midwives Inspection Sheet, Kordofan Province Contd, 1929, SAD 580/5/34, 36.
[68] See e.g. Howad Mohammed Omar Hassan, Abu Zabad Dec. 1930, Midwives Inspection Sheet, SAD 580/5/20; Midwives Inspection Sheet 1931–2 White Nile province Contd: Amna Salah Bakhit, SAD 580/6/16, Zeinab Mohamed Nour, SAD 580/6/19; Annual Report MTS 1933, SAD 581/1/56.

malpractice.[69] With or without the support of the colonial state, trained midwives were the standard bearers of Western scientific medicine in Sudanese communities, and the Wolff sisters disciplined their personal and professional conduct accordingly.

Sudanese responses to trained midwives were mixed, ranging from wholehearted embrace to outright public opposition. Without oral evidence, it is hard to know why pregnant Sudanese women, and the female relations and friends who participated in their circumcisions and deliveries, decided to use the services of trained midwives. The Wolff papers suggest that the personality and social standing of the trained midwife, her ability as demonstrated in difficult cases, the influence of her untrained rivals, and the dynamic of community politics, gender and generational, all mattered.

Trained midwifery was confined almost exclusively to northern Sudan in this period. Of the 243 midwives trained from 1921 to 1935, only three were from Upper Nile province and none at all were from the two other southern provinces of Mongalla and Bahr-el-Ghazal.[70] Trained midwifery was most firmly established in the Three Towns area of Khartoum, Khartoum North, and Omdurman. By 1927, there were twenty-one trained midwives working in Omdurman, where only one untrained midwife was still practising.[71] Preventing untrained midwives from practising was much easier within this capital region, with its concentration of medical institutions and the presence of the Wolff sisters. Interest in the MTS was such that starting in 1932, applicants from the Three Towns and Tuti Island had to pay a fee of 360 Pt to enroll as pupil midwives.[72]

The embracing of the new midwifery by the Sudanese political elite in the Three Towns was crucial in boosting the position of the MTS.[73] As head of the Khatmiya *tariqa* (*sufi* brotherhood), Sayyid ʿAli al-Mirghani was one of the three most prominent leaders of Sudanese popular Islam

---

[69] Midwives Trained 1921–34, SAD 581/2/8.
[70] MTS Trained Midwives Register, SAD 579/8/1–40.
[71] Annual Report MTS 1927, SAD 581/1/4.
[72] Annual Report MTS 1933, SAD 581/1/54–5.
[73] Cruickshank, 'Midwives' Training School', 135. Consider the favourable review granted the MTS in 'A Visit to the Midwifery Institution Omdurman', 6 July 1937, by Magboul El Sayed El Awad, Omda [headman] of Omdurman, SAD 581/4/8–10. In Nyasaland, 'progressive' men backed Western midwifery (Megan Vaughan, 'Health and Hegemony: Representation of Disease and the Creation of the Colonial Subject in Nyasaland', in Engels and Marks (eds.), *Contesting Colonial Hegemony*, 193–4); in India by the 1930s, support for Western midwifery had become one of the hallmarks of progress among middle-class Indian men and women (Forbes, 'Managing Midwifery', 152–72).

and wielded considerable economic and political power. At the heart of
the 'collaborative establishment', he was knighted during the First World
War and led a delegation of Sudanese notables to London in 1919.[74] The
fact that his three children (the first born in 1926) by his wife Fatmah,
including his long-awaited son and heir, were delivered by M. E. Wolff,
assisted by a trained midwife, sent a powerful message of approval to the
people of the Three Towns and to his followers in northeastern Sudan.[75]
But the MTS also catered specifically to the poor women of Omdurman.
Between March 1933 and May 1937, the MTS Maternity Fund provided
over fifty women, who were either MTS patients or under the care of a
trained midwife, with gifts of food, supplies, and/or cash, before and after
delivery.[76]

During the 1930s, state medical provision for women in towns expanded to include antenatal and child welfare clinics. The MTS started
northern Sudan's first antenatal clinic in 1932 and by 1938, there were at
least fourteen antenatal and child welfare clinics in major northern Sudanese towns, and two in southern Sudan.[77] Trained midwives worked in
conjunction with these clinics, most of which were run by British nurses;
in smaller towns such as Rufaʿa, trained midwives started their own, more
modest clinics.[78] To persuade initially sceptical Sudanese women that
antenatal exams were worthwhile, the Wolffs and their staff midwives
invoked a cooking metaphor: with a pregnancy as with a cooking pot on
the fire, a good cook did not let the food burn, but inspected it periodi-
cally. Antenatal exams became another birthing ritual, known as *kashf el
halla* or checking the pot.[79] Annual attendances at the Khartoum province
clinics almost doubled between 1934 and 1936, from 5,325 to 9,085, and
in 1938, 71 per cent of pregnant women in Omdurman attended a clinic
for an examination.[80]

While the prescription of modern childcare methods seems to have
become more important at the clinics during the 1940s,[81] the MTS and the

[74] Niblock, *Class*, 52, 105–6, 174, 178–80; Daly, *Empire*, 122–3, 165–6, 280, 286, 394–5.
[75] M. E. Wolff, 'Midwives Inspection Tour Report 1928', 7 Jan. 1929, SAD 582/1/49–
53); Antenatal clinic card for Sherifa Sayeda El Maghrani (Fatmah), SAD 745/1/25–6.
[76] Maternity Fund Book 1933, SAD 580/8/1–53.
[77] Annual Report MTS 1932, SAD 581/1/46; *RSMS 1933*, 75; *RSMS 1934*, 61; *RSMS
1938*, 62; *RFACS 1929*, 126.
[78] M. E. Wolff to Senior Medical Inspector, Abu Usher, through Senior Medical
Inspector, BNP, 5 Mar. 1934, SAD 582/4/24.
[79] Annual Report MTS 1932, SAD 581/1/46.
[80] *RSMS 1934*, 61; *RSMS 1936*, 62; *RFACS 1938*, 73.
[81] Marjorie Hall and Bakhita Amin Ismail, *Sisters under the Sun: The Story of Sudanese
Women* (London: Longman, 1981), 89.

Sudan medical service do not seem to have taken the kind of intervention-
ist approach to birthspacing, infant feeding, and infant welfare work seen
elsewhere in colonial Africa and colonial south-east Asia.[82] Antenatal vis-
its, which included a test for protein in the urine and a thorough physical
examination, seem to have been the priority at the clinics during the
1930s. Consistent with Wolff's emphasis on the importance of diet to the
health of the pregnant mother and her child, milk was distributed to
women as they waited.[83] This limited evidence suggests that at the beginning of such an initiative, in a country where infibulation was so widespread, the danger of delivery overshadowed most other concerns, hence
the emphasis on the training of birth attendants and on the uncovering of
potential problems during antenatal exams. Female circumcision was a
crucial determinant of midwifery training and practice.

## THE POLITICS OF FEMALE
## CIRCUMCISION

Despite the close links between midwifery and female circumcision, and
despite the existence of the MTS, the colonial government never viewed
female circumcision as a midwives' issue. While most British officials
regarded pharaonic circumcision as a practice that psychologically and
physiologically harmed young girls, that probably lowered the birthrate,
and probably increased maternal mortality, the government did not even
view female circumcision primarily as a medical issue. Female circumcision was always first and foremost a politically explosive matter of 'native
policy' for a government whose top political priorities included avoiding
any provocation of fundamentalist Islamic groups.[84] Senior government
officials knew, as did Sudanese Islamic leaders, that the Quran did not
prescribe or even condone pharaonic circumcision. But the close identification of circumcision with Islam made the government loathe to make
any intervention without the confirmed backing of Sudanese religious and
political leaders and educated elites.

As midwives, as educators of midwives, and as the government officials
concerned with the reproductive health of Sudanese women, the Wolff

---

[82] Nancy Rose Hunt, ' "Le Bébé en brousse": European Women, African Birth Spacing
and Colonial Intervention in Breast Feeding in the Belgian Congo', *International Journal of
African Historical Studies*, 21 (1988), 401–32; Manderson, 'Women and the State', 163–4;
Lenore Manderson, 'Bottle Feeding and Ideology in Colonial Malaya: The Production of
Change', *International Journal of Health Services*, 12 (1982), 597–616.

[83] M. E. Wolff, 'Lectures in English', SAD 581/5/34–5, 37–9; see also 'Methods of
Teaching' photo album, 1930s, SAD 583/6/42–4, 47.

[84] Daly, *Empire*, 250, 388–95.

sisters had considerable knowledge of, and informed opinions about, the practice of female circumcision. But their position on the subject, which provides further evidence of their willingness to accommodate Sudanese custom, had little influence on the policy debate. The Sudan government defined female circumcision as a political issue; discussion of government policy about this issue was therefore the province of senior, male, political officials. As this boundary was drawn between medicine and politics, even male doctors found themselves marginalized from the discussion. As medical personnel, as midwives, and as women, the Wolff sisters had no place in the political sphere to which government policymaking on circumcision was confined.

The topic of female circumcision generated intense discussion and information gathering among senior officials at three junctures in the inter-war period. In 1924 and 1930, no action resulted and interest subsided; though it took some time, the resurrection of the topic in 1936 helped to lead to a propaganda campaign against circumcision, and the 1946 law banning pharaonic circumcision. The first entries in the Sudan government file on female circumcision make clear that although medical personnel were seen as useful sources of information, the subject was perceived as a political matter from the start. The file opens in 1924 with a memo from a doctor describing the different operations and a note from the director of intelligence, urging government backing for the movement among 'intelligent natives' to stop the custom.[85] The civil secretary and the governor-general quickly ruled out the possibility of governors and district commissioners issuing anti-circumcision propaganda, on the grounds that this would be 'unwarrantable interference'. Descriptive information about circumcision was, however, sent to all governors.[86] Sudanese religious leaders similarly eliminated the option of issuing a *fetwa* and/or administrative order against pharaonic circumcision on the grounds that it would incite opposition.[87]

Here, as at other points in the inter-war period, political officials raised the possibility of a medical strategy for eliminating female circumcision. The governor-general and his private secretary quickly identified medical department staff as apparently apolitical vehicles for educating Sudanese about the harms of female circumcision without causing offence. They decided that medical staff in hospitals and dispensaries should use serious

[85] E. A. Grylls, Medical Inspector to Director of Intelligence, 17 Feb. 1924, p. 1; 'Circumcision of Women', n.d., pp. 4–4A, CIVSEC 44/2/12.

[86] Private Secretary to Civil Secretary, 25 Feb. 1924, p. 9; quote from note by H. A. MacMichael for Civil Secretary, 23 Feb. 1924, p. 8, CIVSEC 44/2/12.

[87] C. A. Willis to Civil Secretary, 18 Mar. 1924, p. 14, CIVSEC 44/2/12.

cases to point out the disadvantages of pharaonic circumcision, though precisely to whom remains unclear. The training of Sudanese doctors and assistant medical officers would highlight the 'undesirability of the custom'. Dr Atkey further felt that the two most promising 'lines of attack' were the establishment of the Nursing Training School, which opened in 1925, and improvement in midwifery standards.[88] While rhetoric about a medical strategy was convenient, however, it soon became clear that the government had no intention of providing the resources that would make such an approach viable. When a provincial governor proposed in 1925 that 'an appreciable amount' of the £500,000 Stack indemnity be spent on maternity hospitals, nurses, and midwives, with the specific aim of combating female circumcision, the item was kept off the agenda of the relevant meeting for procedural reasons, and was never raised again.[89]

Government officials seemed to be saying that, as a political matter, female circumcision was simply too important to be left in the hands of mere, apolitical, doctors and midwives. Government failure to take any explicitly 'political' action in fact left the issue entirely to midwives, the only state-affiliated personnel who were engaging regularly with Sudanese women and their reproduction. Wolff's strategy was twofold. She preached emphatically against pharaonic female circumcision to her midwives and to the women and men she met on inspections, and she taught a modified form of it. Her lectures against the practice deftly invoked the religion that seemed to support it: 'You say that "higat Allah Sherif" (God knows best) but you do not act as if you believed this, by your practice of mutilation, for by doing the Circumcision and after-birth operations you are attempting to improve on what God has created.' Knowing that a prohibition on circumcision would be ineffective and ill-received, Wolff then taught her pupils a modified form of pharaonic circumcision; in severity, this lay somewhere between sunna circumcision (a term of variable definition which in this context meant excision of the clitoris and the labia minora), and full pharaonic. Her aim was to reduce the complications of circumcision, by making it into a safer operation, with a smaller wound and less infibulation, performed under

[88] Private Secretary to Civil Secretary, 25 Feb. 1924, p. 9; quote from Atkey to Private Secretary through Civil Secretary, 1 Mar. 1924, p. 11, CIVSEC 44/2/12.
[89] Agenda for Northern Governors' Meeting 1925, p. 17; Civil Secretary to Governor, Kassala, 29 Dec. 1924, p. 18, CIVSEC 44/2/12. The fact that Atkey was on the record as saying that he believed female circumcision had a small impact on the infant mortality rate when compared with malaria and venereal disease did not help this initiative. None of the Stack indemnity went to nursing, midwifery, or women's health.

hygienic conditions, with a sharp razor, and with the benefit of vigilant after-care.[90] When a newly circumcised girl died in Omdurman in 1926, Wolff appealed to the medical officer of health in Khartoum to make an example of the case, since the girl's parents were Coptic Christians, and therefore not circumcising for religious reasons. No official action was taken, but Wolff henceforth forbade trained midwives working in Omdurman from performing full pharaonic circumcisions, and required that they keep a register of all circumcisions performed, which she used to check up on cases.[91]

When J. A. Gillan, governor of Kordofan, reopened the subject of female circumcision in February 1930, with his concern about its spread among the Nuba, H. A. MacMichael, the civil secretary, declared that 'the time has now come when definite action should be taken'.[92] Immediate legislation and direct propaganda by district commissioners were still out of the question. MacMichael's 'action' was contingent on the backing of, and would operate through, Sudanese religious leaders. J. L. Maffey, the governor-general, viewed female circumcision 'mainly at this stage' as 'a political & not a medical question', and wanted government to 'remain in the background'.[93] Such a strategy was complicated by the arrival in April 1930 of a questionnaire developed by an unofficial, all-party, parliamentary committee, headed by the Duchess of Atholl, inquiring into the status of women and children throughout the Crown colonies.[94] Along with Eleanor Rathbone, Atholl brought the controversy over clitoridectomy in Kenya to the centre of British politics in 1929–31.[95] Perhaps wary of similar publicity, Sudan's secretary for education and health pointed to education and midwifery training as the means adopted for discouraging female circumcision when he met Atholl in London in July 1930. He added that he would have no objection to her announcing this publicly. Here again we see midwifery being paraded as the acceptable face of government intervention into female circumcision. He also told her of the plan to approach Sudanese religious leaders and notables, but confided

[90] M. E. Wolff, 'Lectures in English', SAD 581/5/13.
[91] M. E. Wolff to MOH, Khartoum, 21 Mar. 1926, SAD 579/5/21; M. E. Wolff to MOH, Khartoum, 7 Apr. 1926, SAD 579/5/22.
[92] Gillan to SEH, 3 Feb. 1930, pp. 19–22; MacMichael, 'Memorandum', 10 Feb. 1930, p. 23, CIVSEC 44/2/12.
[93] Maffey, Feb. 1930, p. v, CIVSEC 44/2/12.
[94] Acting High Commissioner to Maffey, 24 Apr. 1930, p. 41; J. C. Wedgwood and Katharine Atholl to Henderson, Home Office, 1 Apr. 1930 and Suggested Questions for Circulation [from same], pp. 42–5, CIVSEC 44/2/12.
[95] Susan Pedersen, 'National Bodies, Unspeakable Acts: The Sexual Politics of Colonial Policy-Making', *Journal of Modern History*, 63 (1991), 647–80.

that a public announcement of this strategy would embarrass the government greatly. With Atholl's cooperation secured, communications with her thereafter proceeded formally, through the Foreign Office.[96] The government's continuing determination to avoid outside intervention in its delicate political situation was evident in 1933, when M. E. Wolff drafted a paper on midwifery in Sudan for submission to the Congress on Social Hygiene of the British Social Hygiene Council. Senior government officials balked at the large section she included on female circumcision, fearing a 'crusade' against them by individuals such as Atholl if the paper were presented. When Wolff was told that she could submit the paper only with the offending section omitted, she withdrew the paper altogether.[97]

The first step in the execution of MacMichael's carefully guarded plan, a meeting in which the legal secretary would discuss a report on female circumcision written by Atkey with the Grand *Qadi* (head Islamic religious judge), finally took place in 1931, one year after it was first proposed. The Grand *Qadi* reaffirmed that pharaonic circumcision was not required by Islamic law, but when he consulted other religious leaders, he found that they considered 'the issue of a fetwa absolutely impossible', for they thought 'this form of circumcision a good thing for the people'.[98] The later stages of MacMichael's strategy, all dependent on the issue of such a *fetwa*, were abandoned.[99] The government still hoped that educated Sudanese, particularly doctors and medical students, would lead a campaign of quiet propaganda against pharaonic circumcision. But the government seemed to doubt its own rhetoric on the apolitical face of medicine. When medical student Abdel Rahman El Atabani submitted an article calling for the abolition of pharaonic circumcision to *al-Hadara* in August 1930, senior officials feared a backlash against such a piece appearing in a government-supported newspaper, and invoked their right of censorship to delay its publication.[100]

The government's insistence on acting only with guaranteed Sudanese support was heightened by watching the 'female circumcision contro-

[96] J. G. Matthew, SEH, to MacMichael, 31 July 1930, pp. 65–7; Maffey to Matthew, 7 Aug. 1930, p. 68; Matthew to Duchess of Atholl, 12 Aug. 1930, p. 69, CIVSEC 44/2/12.
[97] Various commentaries 6–20 Mar 1933, pp. 175–7, CIVSEC 44/2/12; M. E. Wolff to Hans Vischer, 2 Apr. 1933, SAD 582/8/20.
[98] B. H. Bell, 'Grand Kadi re female circumcision', 7 Feb. 1931, pp. 81–2, CIVSEC 44/2/12.
[99] For this strategy, see MacMichael, 'Memorandum', 10 Feb. 1930, pp. 25–6; Maffey to Acting High Commissioner, 8 May 1930, pp. 47–9, CIVSEC 44/2/12.
[100] By the time the article had finally appeared in Feb. 1931, government officials rather hoped that it would spark some Sudanese anti-circumcision reaction which they could build on, but it in fact failed to create 'any notable stir' ('Female Circumcision: Government's

versy' that escalated in Kenya in 1928–30;[101] newspaper clippings about
the murder and apparent circumcision of a woman missionary in Kenya in
January 1930 were duly placed in the Sudan government file.[102] Information on anti-circumcision legislation obtained from the Kenya government was nonetheless regarded as 'helpful & valuable' and possibly as
providing a model for how to proceed in southern Sudan.[103] Following the
failure to obtain the *fetwa*, the government turned to the spread of circumcision to 'pagan areas'. In southern Sudan, where female circumcision was
not indigenous but imported, local government officials threatened those
involved in the practice with prosecution for causing 'hurt' under the
Sudan penal code; several convictions, resulting in imprisonment, were
secured. But no such active measures were planned for arabicized parts of
Fung province and the Nuba Mountains, where circumcision was becoming more popular: fearing protest by Arab Sudanese, the government
preferred to leave any initiatives to the native courts.[104]

In northern Sudan, action waited on public opinion. Atkey's 1930
report on female circumcision had declared that the 'paramount affliction
of women in the Sudan is labour as conducted by untrained midwives',
identifying the remedy as 'the progressive displacement of these women
by adequately trained midwives'; he seemed to regard untrained midwives
as a greater danger than pharaonic circumcision. He accordingly argued
for more administrative and medical support to be provided to trained
midwives, support he attempted to provide through his instructions to

Cognizance of the Problem', 29 Dec. 1937, p. 205). See 'An Article on Female Circumcision
by Abdel Rahman el Atabani, Submitted for Publication in the Hadara, Translation', 19
Aug. 1930, p. 71; R. K. Winter to His Excellency (Legal Secretary), 21 Aug. 1930, pp. ix,
xxi, CIVSEC 44/2/12.

[101] See Maffey, 6 Dec. 1930, p. xv, CIVSEC 44/2/12. The Kenya government's 1925
policy of encouraging Local Native Councils to promote less extreme circumcisions had
been overtaken by an aggressive missionary campaign against clitoridectomy; the Kikuyu
Central Association condemned such interference in local custom, redoubling support for
this female initiation rite, and Kikuyu left the church in droves. See Charles H. Ambler,
'The Renovation of Custom in Colonial Kenya: The 1932 Generation Succession Ceremonies in Embu', *Journal of African History*, 30 (1989), 147–50; Thomas, ' "Ngaitana" ',
341–3.

[102] 'Murdered Missionary in Kenya', *The Times*, 18 Feb. 1930; 'Native Unrest in Kenya',
*The Times*, 27 Feb. 1930, pp. 29A–B, CIVSEC 44/2/12.

[103] MacMichael to Legal Secretary, 16 Feb. 1931, p. xxvi, CIVSEC 44/2/12.

[104] Winter, 'Circumcision of Women in Pagan Areas. Summary of Information Supplied
by Governors', Nov. 1931, pp. 169–74; Governor, Fung, 'Report on Female Circumcision
Southern District Fung Province', 1 June 1931, pp. 147–9; MacMichael to Governor, Fung,
10 June 1931, pp. 150–1, CIVSEC 44/2/12. For examples of convictions, see District
Commissioner, Yirrol to Governor, Malakal, 15 Nov. 1936, p. 195, CIVSEC 44/2/12;
J. G. S. Macphail, District Commissioner, Shilluk, to Governor, Upper Nile Province, 29
Jan. 1938, SAD 762/6/32.

medical inspectors, discussed earlier.[105] In 1931 in a letter to Wolff, he called for improved standards among trained midwives and for a strong stand against the unmodified pharaonic operation. But like other government officials who invoked the work of the MTS when questioned about female circumcision, he never grasped the pressures operating on midwives, trained and untrained, to continue performing the full pharaonic operation.[106] Midwives' clients demanded the full pharaonic form, and circumcisions could bring large fees, crucial to the trained midwife trying to make a living without a government salary.

Wolff proposed exploiting this incentive structure, arguing that only recognized, licensed midwives (trained or untrained) should be permitted to perform circumcisions. In this manner, at least some control could be exercised over the operators.[107] Such control would be greater in the case of trained midwives, who were for example disciplined for performing circumcision operations other than the one they had been taught.[108] Eventually, of course, the sets of trained and licensed midwives would be identical. Wolff's proposal, as she later explained, would ensure the cooperation of licensed midwives: if it was illegal for anyone other than a licensed midwife to circumcise, it would be in the licensed midwife's own interest to report any illegal operators, since this would be stealing work assigned to her (and income guaranteed to her).[109] As a sympathetic district commissioner observed, such a system could only work with strong support from doctors and local leaders; otherwise, the result would be no convictions and alienation of licensed midwives from their clientele.[110] Given that adequate state support could not be provided for normal midwifery services and licensing procedures and that the government was determined to proceed cautiously on female circumcision, it is unsurprising that this medicalizing measure was never implemented.

[105] Atkey, 'Female Circumcision in the Sudan', 7 Apr. 1930, p. 39, CIVSEC 44/2/12.
[106] Atkey to M. E. Wolff, 26 Jan. 1931, SAD 582/2/48. This lack of understanding persists today: Ellen Gruenbaum, 'The Movement Against Clitoridectomy and Infibulation in the Sudan: Public Health Policy and the Women's Movement', *Medical Anthropology Newsletter*, 13 (1982), 5, 10.
[107] M. E. Wolff, 'Female Circumcision in the Sudan', 19 Apr. 1932, SAD 582/8/14–16; M. E. Wolff, 'Addition to Annual Report 1933', SAD 582/3/51.
[108] Medical Inspector, Omdurman Civil Hospital to MOH, 25 July 1928, SAD 582/1/19; Acting MOH to Medical Inspector, Omdurman Civil Hospital, 26 July 1928, SAD 582/1/20.
[109] Draft of M. E. Wolff and G. L. Wolff to the editor of *The Times*, 21 Feb. 1949, SAD 582/8/57–8.
[110] Douglas Newbold to M. E. Wolff, 30 May 1932, SAD 582/6/10–12.

The third wave of administrative concern about female circumcision seems to have been prompted by a meeting of the Sudan branch of the British Medical Association, held on 9 March 1936, at which Dr D. R. Macdonald delivered his paper on 'Female Circumcision in the Sudan'.[111] The civil secretary and the governor-general attended, as did the Wolffs: even if under the protective covering of medicine, government officials were now at least willing to discuss female circumcision semi-publicly. But old patterns seemed to hold. Following the meeting, J. A. Gillan, now civil secretary, consulted Dr E. D. Pridie, the new SMS director. Pridie discussed female circumcision with the Wolff sisters, wrote to his senior medical inspectors for information, and identified two measures that could be taken at once: 'Improve & extend the midwifery service as fast as we can' and 'Propaganda of a <u>discreet</u> variety in schools'. The first point was dropped in subsequent correspondence as the civil secretary focused attention on the second measure.[112] While the Wolff sisters were asked for information, proposals to allocate more resources to midwifery, as ever, were not followed up. But the efforts of the Wolff sisters, far removed from this high political sphere, continued. According to Wolff's account, the dominance of trained midwives in Omdurman meant that when she and her sister retired in 1937, the majority of circumcisions being performed there were modified pharaonic.[113] But from 1938 onward, no female circumcision operation of any kind was taught at the MTS. Although the economic imperatives already mentioned meant that trained midwives continued to circumcise, Elaine Hills-Young, the new principal of the MTS, forbade her trained midwives from performing circumcisions of any kind.[114]

Despite Hills-Young's stance, government correspondence suggests that this third wave was set to peter out like the two previous ones. Two factors were different and determined that it did not. In 1938, Douglas Newbold, influential governor of Kordofan, pointed to a hardening of feeling against female circumcision among educated Sudanese and British political officials. He argued convincingly that with the support of educated Sudanese men, the government had an obligation to start leading

[111] D. R. Macdonald, 'Female Circumcision in the Sudan', 9 Mar. 1936, SAD 657/4/9–14.
[112] Interdepartmental correspondence, Apr. 1936, pp. xxxix–xli, CIVSEC 44/2/12.
[113] M. E. Wolff to Lady Huddleston, 14 Oct. 1946, SAD 582/8/35–6.
[114] Lilian Passmore Sanderson, *Against the Mutilation of Women* (London: Anti-Slavery Society and Ithaca Press, 1981), 79–80. Firmly abandoning the Wolff policy of accommodation, Hills-Young also stopped the licensing of untrained midwives (Draft of M. E. Wolff and G. L. Wolff to the editor of *The Times*, 21 Feb. 1949, SAD 582/8/57–8).

general public opinion against the practice.[115] As civil secretary (from November 1939), he established the Civil Secretary's Standing Committee on Female Circumcision.[116] The second factor was that this time the *Mufti* agreed to issue a *fetwa*. Declaring pharaonic circumcision a 'mutilation' which was therefore 'categorically forbidden', it appeared on 31 July 1939 in *al Nil* newspaper.[117] Department of education officials distributed the *fetwa* while on trek during the war,[118] but the public government campaign against pharaonic circumcision was launched in earnest on 1 March 1945, with the publication of a bilingual pamphlet authored by Sudanese and British doctors, with forewords by the governor-general, the *Mufti*, Sayyid ʿAli al-Mirghani, and Sayyid ʿAbd Rahman al-Mahdi (posthumous son of the Mahdi and al-Mirghani's arch-rival).[119] Sudanese support and the apolitical veneer of medicine clearly continued to be vital. The 1946 law prohibiting pharaonic circumcision, passed on the recommendation of the Sudanese men who constituted the Northern Sudan Advisory Council, proved unenforceable. But anti-circumcision propaganda continued to be disseminated in schools and on educational tours conducted by Sudanese staff midwives and schoolmistresses throughout the 1940s.[120]

Overall, this evidence suggests that during the inter-war period, medicine and midwifery only ever featured peripherally in the discussion of what was defined fundamentally as a political issue. The Wolff sisters were considered a useful source of information, and their apparently apolitical status sometimes made them convenient covers for inaction. But they had no role in the political sphere where decisions about government policy on female circumcision were being made. Political action depended on the political will of men, namely Sudanese religious leaders and senior British political officials.

## CONCLUSION

The poverty of inter-war maternal mortality data and the absence of a pre-MTS baseline mean that it is impossible to make a quantitative assessment of the school's achievements. While her account must be re-

---

[115] Douglas Newbold to Civil Secretary, 3 Nov. 1938, SAD 761/4/1–7.

[116] Beasley, *Before the Wind Changed*, 405 n. 48.

[117] Sanderson, *Against the Mutilation of Women*, 80–1.

[118] Beasley, *Before the Wind Changed*, 414.

[119] E. D. Pridie et al., *Female Circumcision in the Anglo-Egyptian Sudan* (Khartoum, 1945).

[120] Muddathir ʿAbd Al-Rahim, *Imperialism and Nationalism in the Sudan* (Oxford: Clarendon Press, 1969), 151–2; Sanderson, *Against the Mutilation of Women*, 81–95; Daud K. Abdalla, District Commissioner, Kassala to Governor, Kassala, 17 Sept. 1947, pp. 57–8, KASSALA 2/64/312; Beasley, *Before the Wind Changed*, 397 n. 36, 404–5.

garded with caution, Wolff wrote in 1928 that post-natal mothers had
become healthier since the opening of the MTS and that women attended
by trained midwives were more prolific.[121] In conjunction with the antenatal clinics, however, the most significant medical impact of the MTS may
have been in persuading Sudanese women to use state medical institutions. Admissions of 'non-European' women to hospital increased from
1,696 or 9 per cent of total admissions in 1925 to 28,975 or 30 per cent of
total admissions in 1936.[122]

Trained midwives served the colonial medical regime then, but occupied a marginal position within it. Wolff's efforts to recruit 'respectable'
women did not overturn British stereotypes of midwifery as a low status
occupation. Trained midwives were expected to operate ably at the bottom of the medical hierarchy, with comparatively little professional and
financial support. While midwives maintained their established position
as birth attendants, doctors staked out their medical authority over midwifery through administration, examinations, and legislation. Trained
midwives were trumpeted as the bearers of health and hygiene into Sudanese homes,[123] but their medical interventions were strictly circumscribed, limited to conditions connected to pregnancy and childbirth.[124]
Being able to recognize when cases should be referred to a higher medical
authority was one of the trained midwife's most important skills. While
the Wolff sisters had considerable latitude in choosing their teaching
methods, planning their curriculum, and defining their role in relation to
trained and untrained midwives, they too were constantly subordinated to
male authority, particularly in administrative and political matters. Of
course, colonial regimes were hierarchical, and male officials, Sudanese
and British, political and technical, junior and senior, were also constrained by male authority. Gender and occupational status compounded,
rather than simply created, difficulties around institutional autonomy for
the Wolff sisters. In areas such as the planning of inspection itineraries
and the issuing of licences, one might have expected a medical service
not particularly concerned about women's health to have allowed the
Wolff sisters final authority. But, and admittedly sometimes with the
consent of the Wolff sisters, trained midwifery—recruitment, training
examinations, licensing—depended to a remarkable degree on certifica-

[121] Annual Report MTS 1928, SAD 581/1/5.
[122] *RSMS 1925*, 29; *RSMS 1936*, 102. See *RSMS 1934*, 61 on the increase in hospital
deliveries following the opening of the clinics.
[123] Pridie, 'Description sommaire', 1932.
[124] See e.g. Senior Medical Inspector, BNP to Inspectress of Midwives, 16 Apr. 1934,
SAD 582/4/28.

tion by men. Sudanese and British men controlled the official, political realm in colonial Sudan and, most notably in the case of female circumcision, the Wolff sisters sometimes found themselves excluded from that realm altogether.

Midwifery training and practice in Sudan demonstrate that colonial medicine sometimes involved careful negotiation between the cultures of the colonizer and the colonized. Sudanese perceptions of midwifery as charitable work of a problematic sexual nature influenced Wolff's construction of respectability, recruitment patterns, and the standard of living experienced by trained midwives. Her lectures, her attitude towards licensing *dayas*, and her stance on circumcision show an accommodation with Sudanese culture, born of a personal preference for change through slow collaboration, and of the realization that the state had a limited ability to enforce unpopular measures. Such accommodation did not mean that Wolff regarded the midwifery practice she was teaching as any less scientific than, say, laboratory research. That she considered herself to be imparting Western scientific medicine to an unenlightened society without compromise is clear from the high standards that she set for trained midwives and the new childbirth rituals that she ensured they used.

Some rituals, however, were much more easily challenged than others. The association of circumcision with religion made it a political matter of the greatest sensitivity for a colonial government that was established by defeating the fundamentalist Khalifa. But in discussing female circumcision, political officials never came to terms with the financial pressures on midwives to continue the practice, nor did they ever take seriously the idea that the Wolff sisters had anything substantial to contribute beyond factual information. Rather, senior political officials viewed medicine and midwifery as convenient covers for inaction until the government was ready to undertake a public anti-circumcision campaign. In modifying midwifery practice, the Wolffs and the trained midwives became deeply involved in community and household politics. But these medical practitioners were thought to have no place in the high politics, domestic and international, implicated in the female circumcision question.

# 8

# *Conclusion*

Embroiled in the detail of medical training programmes and disease control efforts, it is easy to lose sight of the fact that the boundaries of colonial medicine in Sudan expanded in some very basic ways between 1899 and 1940. Driven by the ambition of its doctors and by the changing priorities of the colonial state, as discussed in Chapter 2, the medical administration literally and figuratively carved out new spaces in which to operate. In 1899, a tiny medical administration staffed exclusively by military personnel focused on preserving the health of European colonizers in colonial enclaves. By 1940, a much larger medical service manned by civilians accepted responsibility for addressing the medical needs of the Sudanese population throughout the entire country, even if, as we have seen, medical provision continued to be skewed towards particular regions. Initially confined to hastily thrown up hospitals in towns, and to any reasonably accessible place where epidemic disease struck, state medical activity by 1940 was centred in permanent hospitals, a dispensary network, antenatal and child welfare clinics, and a range of more unusual, though in some ways typically colonial, spaces, such as a leprosy settlement, a floating laboratory, and a floating hospital. While colonial doctors burned down some Sudanese homes in the name of disease control, colonial medicine had, in what was arguably its most radical undertaking, ventured peacefully into others through trained midwifery. The scope of medical activity had widened to include not only more effective control of epidemic disease, but also attempts to tackle endemic disease, manage childbirth, and actually start promoting health. Some of these ambitions were made possible by the availability of new medical therapies. In 1899, the colonial doctor seeking prevention and cure for infectious disease had a limited, though recently enlarged, arsenal at his disposal, confined mainly to smallpox and rabies vaccines, quinine, mercury for syphilis, and diphtheria anti-toxin, the full benefits of which were not necessarily available to patients in Sudan because of their high cost, frequent deterioration due to heat, and/or the country's remoteness. For uncurable conditions, purges of calomel and magnesium sulfate, emetics, syrups, and/or hot fomentations were still the standard therapeutic options.[1] By 1940, local laboratory facilities meant higher quality vaccines, and new chemotherapeutic weapons, if in some cases toxic, were at hand: salvarsan or novarsenobenzol for syphilis and yaws, atoxyl, tryparsamide, and Bayer 205 for sleeping sickness, antimony tartrate for schistosomiasis, plasmochine for malaria, and sulfa drugs, which greatly reduced mortality from cerebrospinal meningitis. New chemicals rendered mosquito and snail destruction more efficient. From a small number of Egyptian, Syrian, and British doctors, and more numerous untrained Sudanese personnel, the medical service had come to include Sudanese doctors and trained medical auxiliaries, as well as trained women, Sudanese and British, who worked as nurses and midwives.

Colonial medicine in 1940 no longer confronted, as it had in 1899, an essentially unknown territory, where the identity and location of countless peoples, never mind its diseases, remained a mystery; where the country's borders, if fixed on a map, remained indeterminate; and where the government in fact controlled only a fraction of the country's territory. By 1940, the colonial medical administration was in every way more integrated into the territory it defined as Sudan, which the colonial state for the most part finally controlled. Sudanese personnel had been incorporated into the medical service in a meaningful way; the disease, natural, and human landscapes had been mapped; and attempts to prevent infection had, if never completely, solidified the country's internal and external borders. But if, as I have argued, scientific research and disease control constituted vehicles through which the colonial government came to know and order its colonial territory, it is also clear that this remained a work in progress, even in 1940. The difficulties involved in supporting trained midwifery in rural areas and the extremely late notification of the Nuba Mountains epidemic are only two reminders that in this vast territory, poor communications and the priorities chosen in the context of scarce resources meant that government ability to know what was going on in certain parts of the country, never mind deal with health problems, still remained extremely limited. Throughout our period, extreme assertions of colonial power and aggressive interventions into people's lives—quarantines, relocation, sleeping sickness settlements, even attempts to change birthing practices—always coexisted with extremely tentative behaviour—reluctance to enforce sanitary regulations in the Gezira, to puncture cervical glands, and to take a public stance on the politically

[1] See e.g. Edward S. Crispin, *The Prevention and Treatment of Disease in the Tropics: A Handbook for Officials and Travellers Compiled Chiefly for the Use of Officials in the Sudan* (London: Charles Griffin and Company, 1912).

charged issue of female circumcision. Even the extreme assertions of power revealed colonial vulnerability, always traceable to the small size of the colonial presence. Lasting changes to lifestyle and behaviour depended on Sudanese consent, as demonstrated by the creation and eventual abandonment of the sleeping sickness settlement and the necessity of accommodating Sudanese opinions about respectability in the training of midwives.

Chronic underfunding, which I identified in Chapter 1 as a distinctively 'colonial' feature, meant that even in a country where outside investment was regarded warily, capital—in the form of Henry Wellcome, the Sudan Plantations Syndicate, the Empire Cotton Growing Corporation, even Imperial Airways—could have a significant impact, shaping institutions, research agendas, and the choice of disease control measures. While recognizing the importance of capital, or more broadly, economic interests, I have also argued that like political considerations, they were never the sole determinants of medical policy. Medical factors, including existing medical knowledge, epidemiological evidence, and local disease history, were essential in determining which diseases were addressed and in what way. So were the ambition and the interests of the doctors themselves: the projects of the Wellcome Tropical Research Laboratories, the early search for sleeping sickness cases, and above all the quest for the yellow fever virus were at least partly driven by the intellectual excitement of the doctors involved. The comments of William Byam, Basil Spence, G. K. Maurice, and Robert Kirk make clear that doctors in Sudan relished the challenges of working on physical frontiers and on the frontiers of medical knowledge.

Colonial medicine and science confronted many of the same situations and concerns faced by metropolitan medicine and science. Like their metropolitan counterparts, doctors in Sudan policed the boundary around medicine to ensure that the admission of questionable medical techniques and illegitimate medical practitioners did not dilute their professional prestige. But the particular colonial environment of Sudan influenced the permeability of professional boundaries and the way in which this policing occurred. The apparently higher professional prestige enjoyed by British doctors in Sudan, compared with European doctors in Belgian Congo, Uganda, South Africa, and India, seems to have made them less defensive, and therefore more willing to loosen professional boundaries to accommodate non-European and/or auxiliary personnel; such a move was of course also demanded by colonial political and economic considerations. This inclusiveness, as I argued in Chapters 2 and 7, was managed by the creation of internal, intersecting hierarchies of race, gender, class, and occupation. These hierarchies were to some extent a function of the professional division of labour in medicine generally, but the colonial context permitted, even demanded, greater rigidity to them. It laid particular stress on race and gender, and introduced, as we saw most acutely with midwifery, the distinctive influence of the indigenous population's views about what made suitable medical practitioners. The debate over the acceptability of the mouse protection test as a medical technique, discussed in Chapter 6, though an international one, was significantly shaped by the colonial context. Thin distribution of medical personnel and reluctant Sudanese patients meant that there was little clinical evidence of fever from the affected region, so decisions had to be made with comparatively little information; national professional rivalries sharpened because imperial pride was at stake. The division between research and practice which, as discussed in Chapter 3, so exercised both researchers and practitioners in Sudan, was a concern also shared by their counterparts in medicine and agriculture in Britain. But the institutional organization of research in Sudan and the dependence of the economy on one cash crop, both functions of the colonial context, greatly increased the stakes.

The colonial setting helped to blur the boundary between medicine and politics/administration in some cases, and solidify it in others. Doctors working in this colonial context always carried dual identities, as doctors and therefore members of a profession, and as employees of either the imperial army or the colonial government, and therefore administrative agents. The scarcity of colonial personnel further blurred the medical/political boundary by forcing doctors, particularly in remote areas, to assume multiple roles. As seen with sleeping sickness, however, doctors' assumption of administrative roles did not guarantee them administrative support, nor did it lessen doctors' own sense that administrative and medical personnel each performed different, if complementary, functions. Where the division between medicine and politics was most firmly drawn, during the debate over how to handle female circumcision, the importance of that division emerged directly from the colonial setting, that is from the perceived volatility of colonial politics, and the resulting political caution of a colonial government that had conquered a fundamentalist Islamic state.

It is of course possible to overstate the influence of the colonial context. Colonial doctors' apparent lack of interest in the patient experience of disease might, for example, be thought to be a reflection of their lack of respect for their 'primitive' colonized patients. But Sudan's history of yellow fever indicates that this disinterest may have had less to do with colonialism than with the increasing sophistication of laboratory medicine, which in its ability to read past infection from the blood shifted the definition of disease, making the experience of the patient, whoever she might be, less and less relevant. The case of yellow fever also points to ways in which colonial ties and settings were being transcended in the inter-war period, by air travel which globalized disease threat, and by an international medicine which responded to this new challenge by setting ambitious, global goals. Only fully dominant after the Second World War with the establishment of the WHO, this international medicine built on the methods of colonial medicine, adopting the military, campaign approach to disease control; promoting the provision of primary medical care through dispensaries manned by trained auxiliaries; and eventually seeking to incorporate traditional medical practitioners into Western medical administrations. Though both operated on frontiers of knowledge, international medicine, in its eagerness to cross international borders, was fundamentally at odds with the colonial medicine described in this book. For colonial medicine was ever preoccupied with creating a country, protecting a profession, and controlling disease by erecting and reinforcing boundaries, literal and figurative.

# BIBLIOGRAPHY

### ARCHIVAL SOURCES

*National Records Office, Khartoum*

CIVSEC, records of the Civil Secretary's department. Explicitly medical topics were filed under CIVSEC 44/

BNP, files concerning Blue Nile province

MONGALLA, files concerning Mongalla province

KASSALA, files concerning Kassala province

LANDS, records of the Department of Lands

*National Medical Research Laboratories Library, Khartoum*

Files on bilharzia and on the WTRL

*Wad Medani*

While I was in Khartoum, Dr Ahmed Abdel-Hameed, of the Faculty of Medicine at the University of the Gezira, kindly shared with me some documents that he had found in Wad Medani. I do not know their precise location.

Annual Report of the Gezira Malariologist, 12 June 1930

Untitled file containing WTRL correspondence on entomology

*Sudan Archive, University of Durham Library*

The papers of the following individuals and institutions have been particularly useful:

Andrew Balfour

J. F. E. Bloss

J. B. Christopherson

G. M. Culwick

H. B. McD. Farrell

Arthur Gaitskell

Gordon Memorial College trust fund

Elaine Hills-Young

E. Jane

Mary Macdonald

J. H. R. Orlebar

T. R. H. Owen

E. D. Pridie

R. J. Smith

F. R. Wingate
Mabel E. Wolff and Gertrude L. Wolff

*Rockefeller Archive Center, North Tarrytown, New York*
Rockefeller Foundation Archives

*Glaxo Wellcome Group Archive, Glaxo Wellcome Research and
Development, Greenford, Middlesex UB6 oHE*
Henry S. Wellcome personal letter books
Burroughs Wellcome & Company private letter books
HSW/Friends/Balfour Files 1–2

*Contemporary Medical Archives Centre, Wellcome Institute for
the History of Medicine, London*
Henry S. Wellcome papers

*London School of Hygiene and Tropical Medicine Library*
MSS FC:D1: Laboratory notebooks of Andrew Balfour
Balfour correspondence in Ross collection

*Public Record Office, London*
Various files in:
FO 78: Turkey including Egypt, 1895–1905
FO 141: Egypt, consular correspondence, 1896–1934

OFFICIAL PUBLISHED SOURCES

*Agricultural Research Work in the Sudan. Reports for the Season 1928–29 and the
  Programme for the Season 1929–30.*
*Annual Report of the Education Department*, 1928–30.
*The Gordon Memorial College at Khartoum, Report and Accounts to 31st December
  19...*, 1904–36.
*Provisional Regulations of the Sudan Medical Department* (Khartoum: El Sudan
  Press, 1910).
*Quarterly List* [of Sudan government personnel], 1914–52.
*Report, Kitchener School of Medicine 1924–1925.*
*Report by Her/His Majesty's Agent and Consul-General on the Finances, Administra-
  tion and Condition of Egypt and the Soudan*, 1899–1914.
*Report by His Majesty's High Commissioner on the Finances, Administration and
  Condition of Egypt and the Soudan*, 1914/1919, 1920.
*Report on the Finances, Administration and Condition of the Soudan*, 1921, 1925–34,
  1938.
*Report of the Sudan Medical Service for the Year...*, 1925–40. [Called *Report on*

*Medical and Health Work in the Sudan for the Year . . .* for part of this period.]
Sudan government, *Financial and Trade Statistics 1926–1938*.
*Sudan Government Gazette*, 1899–1939.
*Sudan Intelligence Reports*, 1906–25.

PRIMARY AND SECONDARY PRINTED SOURCES

ʿABD AL-RAHIM, MUDDATHIR, *Imperialism and Nationalism in the Sudan* (Oxford: Clarendon Press, 1969).

ABDEL-HAMEED, AHMED AWAD, 'The Wellcome Tropical Research Laboratories in Khartoum (1903–1934): An Experiment in Development', *Medical History*, 41 (1997), 30–58.

ABDELKARIM, ABBAS, 'Social Forms of Organization of Labour in the Sudan Gezira', School of Development Studies, University of East Anglia, discussion paper no. 171, Nov. 1984.

ADEFUYE, ADE., 'The Kakwa of Uganda and the Sudan: The Ethnic Factor in National and International Politics', in A. I. Asiwaju (ed.), *Partitioned Africans: Ethnic Relations across Africa's International Boundaries, 1884–1984* (London: C. Hurst, 1984), 51–69.

ALLAN, W. N., 'Irrigation in the Sudan', in J. D. Tothill (ed.), *Agriculture in the Sudan* (London: Oxford University Press, 1948), 593–631.

AL-SAFI, AHMAD, *Native Medicine in the Sudan: Sources, Concepts and Methods* (Khartoum: University of Khartoum, 1970).

AMBLER, CHARLES H., 'The Renovation of Custom in Colonial Kenya: The 1932 Generation Succession Ceremonies in Embu', *Journal of African History*, 30 (1989), 139–56.

ANDERSON, R. G., 'Medical Practices and Superstitions Amongst the People of Kordofan', *Third RWRL*, 281–322.

——'Final Report of the Sudan Sleeping Sickness Commission, 1908–1909', *JRAMC* 16 (1911), 200–7.

——'Some Tribal Customs in their Relation to Medicine and Morals of the Nyam-Nyam and Gour People Inhabiting the Eastern Bahr-el-Ghazal', *Fourth RWTRL*, vol. B, 239–77.

ANDERSON, WARWICK, '"Where Every Prospect Pleases and Only Man is Vile": Laboratory Medicine as Colonial Discourse', *Critical Inquiry*, 18 (1992), 506–29.

——'Disease, Race, and Empire', *Bulletin of the History of Medicine*, 70 (1996), 62–7.

——'Immunities of Empire: Race, Disease, and the New Tropical Medicine, 1900–1920', *Bulletin of the History of Medicine*, 70 (1996), 94–118.

'The Anglo-Egyptian Sudan and Sleeping Sickness', *BSSB* 1 (1909), 345–7.

'Anglo-Egyptian Sudan', *BSSB* 2 (1910), 77.

'Anglo-Egyptian Sudan', *BSSB* 3 (1911), 89, 473–6.

ARCHIBALD, R. G., '*Trypanosoma Rhodesiense* in a Case of Sleeping Sickness from the Sudan', *ATMP* 16 (1922), 339–40.

——and RIDING, DOUGLAS, 'A Second Case of Sleeping Sickness in the Sudan Caused by *Trypanosoma Rhodesiense*', *ATMP* 20 (1926), 161–6.

ARNOLD, DAVID, *Colonizing the Body: State Medicine and Epidemic Disease in Nineteenth-Century India* (Berkeley: University of California Press, 1993).

ATIYAH, EDWARD, *An Arab Tells His Story: A Study in Loyalties* (London: John Murray, 1946).

AUSTOKER, JOAN, 'Walter Morley Fletcher and the Origins of a Basic Biomedical Research Policy', in Austoker and Bryder (eds.), *Historical Perspectives*, 23–33.

——and BRYDER, LINDA (eds.), *Historical Perspectives on the Role of the MRC* (Oxford: Oxford University Press, 1989).

BAKER, COLIN, 'The Government Medical Service in Malawi, 1891–1974', *Medical History*, 20 (1976), 296–311.

BALFOUR, ANDREW, 'Trypanosomiasis in the Anglo-Egyptian Sudan', *Edinburgh Medical Journal*, 18 (1905), 202–12.

——and ARCHIBALD, R. G., *Review of Some of the Recent Advances in Tropical Medicine, Hygiene, and Tropical Veterinary Science, being a supplement to the Third Report of the Wellcome Research Laboratories at the Gordon Memorial College, Khartoum* (London: Baillière, Tindall & Cox for the Department of Education, Sudan Government, Khartoum, 1908).

————in collaboration with FRY, W. B., and O'FARRELL, W. R., *Second Review of Some of the Recent Advances in Tropical Medicine, Hygiene, and Tropical Veterinary Science, being a supplement to the Fourth Report of the Wellcome Tropical Research Laboratories at the Gordon Memorial College, Khartoum* (London: Baillière, Tindall & Cox for the Department of Education, Sudan Government, Khartoum, 1911).

BARBOUR, K. M., 'Population Shifts and Changes in Sudan Since 1898', *Middle Eastern Studies*, 2 (1966), 98–122.

BARNES, BARRY, *Scientific Knowledge and Sociological Theory* (London: Routledge & Kegan Paul, 1974).

BARNETT, TONY, and ABDELKARIM, ABBAS, *Sudan: The Gezira Scheme and Agricultural Transition* (London: Frank Cass, 1991).

BAYOUMI, AHMED, 'Medical Administration in the Sudan 1899–1970', *Clio Medica*, 11 (1976), 105–15.

——*A History of Sudan Health Services* (Nairobi: Kenya Literature Bureau, 1979).

BEASLEY, INA, *Before the Wind Changed: People, Places and Education in the Sudan*, ed. Janet Starkey (Oxford: Oxford University Press, 1992).

BECK, ANN, *A History of the British Medical Administration of East Africa, 1900–1950* (Cambridge, Mass.: Harvard University Press, 1970).

——'Medical Administration and Medical Research in Developing Countries: Remarks on their History in Colonial East Africa', *Bulletin of the History of Medicine*, 46 (1972), 349–58.

BECK, ANN, *Medicine, Tradition, and Development in Kenya and Tanzania, 1920–1970* (Waltham, Mass.: Crossroads Press, 1981).

BEEUWKES, HENRY, BAUER, J. H., and MAHAFFY, A. F., 'Yellow Fever Endemicity in West Africa, with Special Reference to Protection Tests', *American Journal of Tropical Medicine*, 10 (1930), 305–33.

BEINART, JENNIFER, 'The Inner World of Imperial Sickness: The MRC and Research in Tropical Medicine', in Austoker and Bryder (eds.), *Historical Perspectives*, 109–35.

BELL, HEATHER, 'Cleaning Up the Anglo-Egyptian Sudan: Water, Mosquitoes, and Venereal Disease, 1899–1914', paper presented to the Sudan Studies Association Conference, Boston, Mass., 20–23 Apr. 1994.

—— 'A Directory of Military and Civilian Doctors in Sudan', unpublished paper, 1997.

—— 'Medical Research and Medical Practice in the Anglo-Egyptian Sudan, 1899–1940', D.Phil. thesis (Oxford University, 1996).

BERNAL, VICTORIA, 'Cotton and Colonial Order in Sudan: A Social History with Emphasis on the Gezira Scheme', in Allen Isaacman and Richard Roberts (eds.), *Cotton, Colonialism, and Social History in Sub-Saharan Africa* (London: James Currey, 1995), 96–118.

BESHIR, M. O., *Educational Development in the Sudan* (Oxford: Clarendon Press, 1969).

BIRKS, J. S., 'Migration, a Significant Factor in the Historical Demography of the Savannas: The Growth of the West African Population of Darfur, Sudan', in *African Historical Demography* (Edinburgh, 1977), 195–210.

—— 'The Mecca Pilgrimage by West African Pastoral Nomads', *Journal of Modern African Studies*, 15 (1977), 47–58.

BLOSS, J. F. E., 'The History of Sleeping Sickness in the Sudan', *Proceedings of the Royal Society of Medicine*, 53 (1960), 421–6.

BODDY, JANICE, 'Womb as Oasis: The Symbolic Context of Pharaonic Circumcision in Rural Northern Sudan', *American Ethnologist*, 9 (1982), 682–98.

—— *Wombs and Alien Spirits: Women, Men and the Zar Cult in Northern Sudan* (Madison: University of Wisconsin Press, 1989).

BONNER, THOMAS NEVILLE, *Becoming a Physician: Medical Education in Britain, France, Germany, and the United States, 1750–1945* (Oxford: Oxford University Press, 1995).

BOUSFIELD, LEONARD, 'The Native Methods of Treatment of Diseases in Kassala and Neighbourhood', *Third RWRL*, 273–5.

—— *Sudan Doctor* (London: Christopher Johnson, 1954).

BROCKINGTON, FRASER, 'The World Health Organization (WHO)', in B. A. Wortley (ed.), *The United Nations: The First Ten Years* (Manchester: Manchester University Press, 1957), 130–49.

BRYDER, LINDA, 'Public Health Research and the MRC', in Austoker and Bryder (eds.), *Historical Perspectives*, 59–81.

BURNS, CATHERINE, 'Reproductive Labors: The Politics of Women's Health in South Africa, 1900 to 1960', Ph.D. thesis (Northwestern University, 1995).

BYAM, WILLIAM, *The Road to Harley Street* (London: Geoffrey Bles, 1963).

BYNUM, W. F., *Science and the Practice of Medicine in the Nineteenth Century* (Cambridge: Cambridge University Press, 1994).

CALLAWAY, HELEN, *Gender, Culture, and Empire: European Women in Colonial Nigeria* (Basingstoke: Macmillan, 1987).

CHALMERS, A. J., 'The Classification of Trypanosomes', *JTMH* 21 (1918), 221–4.

——and O'FARRELL, W. R., 'Sleeping Sickness in the Lado of the Anglo-Egyptian Sudan', *JTMH* 17 (1914), 273–84.

—— —— 'Measurements of Dutton and Todd's Gambia Strain of *Trypanosoma Gambiense* Dutton 1902', *JTMH* 19 (1916), 189–94.

'Chemo-Therapy of Trypanosomiasis', *BSSB* 1 (1908), 1–49.

CHRISTOPHERSON, J. B., 'Bilharzia Disease: The Sterilization of the Ova During the Course of Cure by Antimony (Tartrate)', *JTMH* 23 (1920), 165–7.

——and NEWLOVE, J. R., 'Laboratory and Other Notes on Seventy Cases of Bilharzia Treated at the Khartoum Civil Hospital by Intravenous Injections of Antimony Tartrate', *JTMH* 22 (1919), 129–44.

CHRISTY, CUTHBERT, 'The Nile–Congo Watershed', *Geographical Journal*, 50 (1917), 199–216.

CLOUDSLEY, ANNE, *The Women of Omdurman: Victims of Circumcision* (London, 1981).

CLYDE, DAVID F., *History of the Medical Services of Tanganyika* (Dar Es Salaam: Government Press, 1962).

COLLINS, R. O., *The Southern Sudan, 1883–1898: A Struggle for Control* (New Haven: Yale University Press, 1962).

——*Land Beyond the Rivers: The Southern Sudan, 1898–1918* (New Haven: Yale University Press, 1971).

——'The Sudan Political Service: A Portrait of the "Imperialists"', *African Affairs*, 71 (1972), 293–303.

——*Shadows in the Grass: Britain in the Southern Sudan, 1918–1956* (New Haven: Yale University Press, 1983).

——'Pounds and Piastres: The Beginnings of Economic Development in the Southern Sudan', *Northeast African Studies*, 5 (1983), 39–65.

COMAROFF, JEAN, 'The Diseased Heart of Africa: Medicine, Colonialism, and the Black Body', in Shirley Lindenbaum and Margaret Lock (eds.), *Knowledge, Power, and Practice: The Anthropology of Medicine and Everyday Life* (Berkeley: University of California Press, 1993), 305–29.

——and COMAROFF, JOHN, *Of Revelation and Revolution: Christianity, Colonialism, and Consciousness in South Africa*, i (Chicago: University of Chicago Press, 1991).

COOPER, FREDERICK, and STOLER, ANN LAURA (eds.), *Tensions of Empire: Colonial Cultures in a Bourgeois World* (Berkeley: University of California Press, 1997).

CRISPIN, EDWARD S., *The Prevention and Treatment of Disease in the Tropics: A Handbook for Officials and Travellers Compiled Chiefly for the Use of Officials in the Sudan* (London: Charles Griffin and Company, 1912).

CROMER, [Lord], *Modern Egypt*, ii (London: Macmillan, 1908).

CROSBY, A. W., *The Columbian Exchange: Biological and Cultural Consequences of 1492* (Westport, Conn.: Greenwood Press, 1972).

——'Hawaiian Depopulation as a Model for the Amerindian Experience', in Terence Ranger and Paul Slack (eds.), *Epidemics and Ideas: Essays on the Historical Perception of Pestilence* (Cambridge: Cambridge University Press, 1992), 175–201.

CRUICKSHANK, ALEXANDER, 'The Birth of a Leper Settlement—Li-Rangu, Equatoria', *SNR* 29 (1948), 183–8.

——*The Kindling Fire: Medical Adventures in the Southern Sudan* (London: Heinemann, 1962).

——*Itchy Feet—A Doctor's Tale* (Devon: Arthur H. Stockwell, 1991).

——'The Midwives' Training School and the Development of a Midwifery Service in the Sudan During the Anglo-Egyptian Condominium, 1899–1956', in Deborah Lavin (ed.), *The Condominium Remembered*, Proceedings of the Durham Historical Records Conference 1982, vol. ii (Centre for Middle Eastern and Islamic Studies, University of Durham, 1993), 129–42.

CUETO, MARCOS, 'Sanitation from Above: Yellow Fever and Foreign Intervention in Peru, 1919–1922', *Hispanic American Historical Review*, 72 (1992), 1–22.

——(ed.), *Missionaries of Science: The Rockefeller Foundation and Latin America* (Bloomington: Indiana University Press, 1994).

——'The Cycles of Eradication: The Rockefeller Foundation and Latin American Public Health, 1918–1940', in Weindling (ed.), *International Health Organisations*, 222–43.

CULWICK, G. M., *A Dietary Survey among the Zande of the Southwestern Sudan* (Khartoum: Agricultural Publications, 1950).

——'Social Change in the Gezira Scheme', *Civilisations*, 5 (1955), 173–81.

——*A Study of the Human Factor in the Gezira Scheme* (Barakat (reprint from 1955 original): Sudan Gezira Board and Sudan Rural Television Project, 1975).

CUNNINGHAM, ANDREW, 'Transforming Plague: The Laboratory and the Identity of Infectious Disease', in Cunningham and Williams (eds.), *Laboratory Revolution*, 209–44.

——and WILLIAMS, PERRY (eds.), *The Laboratory Revolution in Medicine* (Cambridge: Cambridge University Press, 1992).

DALY, M. W., *Empire on the Nile: The Anglo-Egyptian Sudan, 1898–1934* (Cambridge: Cambridge University Press, 1986).

——*Imperial Sudan: The Anglo-Egyptian Condominium, 1934–1956* (Cambridge: Cambridge University Press, 1991).

DAVIES, CELIA, *Gender and the Professional Predicament in Nursing* (Buckingham: Open University Press, 1995).

DAVIES, R. E. G., *A History of the World's Airlines* (London: Oxford University Press, 1964).

DAVIN, ANNA, 'Imperialism and Motherhood', *History Workshop Journal*, 5 (1978), 9–66.

DAVIS, N. C., 'Studies on South American Yellow Fever II: Immunity of Recovered Monkeys to African Virus', *Journal of Experimental Medicine*, 49 (1929), 985–91.

DAWSON, MARC H., 'Socio-economic and Epidemiological Change in Kenya: 1880–1925', Ph.D. thesis (University of Wisconsin-Madison, 1983).

—— 'The 1920s Anti-Yaws Campaigns and Colonial Medical Policy in Kenya', *International Journal of African Historical Studies*, 20 (1987), 417–35.

—— 'Socioeconomic Change and Disease: Smallpox in Colonial Kenya, 1880–1920', in Steven Feierman and John M. Janzen (eds.), *The Social Basis of Health and Healing in Africa* (Berkeley: University of California Press, 1992), 90–103.

DEACON, HARRIET, 'Cape Town and "Country" Doctors in the Cape Colony during the First Half of the Nineteenth Century', *Social History of Medicine*, 10 (1997), 25–52.

DEJAGER, TIMOTHY, 'Pure Science and Practical Interests: The Origins of the Agricultural Research Council, 1930–1937', *Minerva*, 31 (1993), 125–50.

DENOON, DONALD, *Public Health in Papua New Guinea: Medical Possibility and Social Constraint, 1884–1984* (Cambridge: Cambridge University Press, 1989).

DERVISH, J., discussion following CHESTERMAN, CLEMENT C., 'Tryparsamide in Sleeping Sickness', *TRSTMH* 16 (1923), 411–14.

DE SCHLIPPE, P., *Shifting Cultivation in Africa: The Zande System of Agriculture* (London: Routledge & Kegan Paul, 1956).

DIGBY, ANNE, ' "A Medical El Dorado?" Colonial Medical Incomes and Practice at the Cape', *Social History of Medicine*, 8 (1995), 463–79.

'Distribution et incidence de l'*Aedes aegypti* au Soudan Anglo-Égyptien en 1938', *BOIHP* 31 (1939), 1588–9.

DODGE, BAYARD, *The American University of Beirut: A Brief History of the University and the Lands which it Serves* (Beirut: Khayat's, 1958).

DOMERGUE, D., 'La Lutte contre la trypanosomiase en Côte d'Ivoire, 1900–1945', *Journal of African History*, 22 (1981), 63–72.

DOVE, P. M., 'Report on Tour through Kakwa and Kaliko Country, Lying West of River Yei and South of the Yei-Aba Automobile Road', *SIR*, no. 205, Aug. 1911, appendix A, 8–9.

DOYAL, LESLIE, with PENNELL, IMOGEN, *The Political Economy of Health* (London: Pluto, 1979).

DREW, C. M., 'Sudan Sleeping Sickness Commission. Report on the State of the Western Bahr el Ghazal and the Liability of this District to an Invasion of Sleeping Sickness from French Congo', *SIR*, no. 197, Dec. 1910, appendix, 7–12.

DUBIN, MARTIN DAVID, 'The League of Nations Health Organisation', in Weindling (ed.), *International Health Organisations*, 56–80.

DUFFIELD, MARK R., 'Hausa and Fulani Settlement and the Development of Capitalism in Sudan: With Special Reference to Maiurno, Blue Nile Province',

Ph.D. thesis (Centre of West African Studies, University of Birmingham, 1978).

—— *Maiurno: Capitalism & Rural Life in Sudan* (London: Ithaca Press, 1981).

—— 'Change among West African Settlers in Northern Sudan', *Review of African Political Economy*, 26 (1983), 45–59.

—— 'The Fallata: Ideology and the National Economy in Sudan', in O'Neill and O'Brien (eds.), *Economy and Class*, 122–36.

DUFFY, JOHN (ed.), *Ventures in World Health: The Memoirs of Fred Lowe Soper* (Washington, DC: Pan American Health Organization, Pan American Sanitary Bureau, Regional Office of the WHO, 1977).

DUGGAN, A. J., 'An Historical Perspective', in H. W. Mulligan (ed.) with W. H. Potts, *The African Trypanosomiases* (London: George Allen & Unwin, 1970), pp. xli–lxxxviii.

ELHASSAN, ABDALLA MOHAMMED, 'The Encroachment of Large Scale Mechanised Agriculture: Elements of Differentiation among the Peasantry', in Tony Barnett and Abbas Abdelkarim (eds.), *Sudan: State, Capital and Transformation* (London: Croom Helm, 1988), 161–79.

'Empire Cotton Growing Corporation 1921 to 1950', *The Empire Cotton Growing Corporation Review*, 28 (1951), 1–44.

ENGELS, DAGMAR, and MARKS, SHULA (eds.), *Contesting Colonial Hegemony: State and Society in Africa and India* (London: British Academic Press, 1994).

ENSOR, H., 'Report on Investigations Carried out in the Bahr-el-Ghazal Province on Behalf of the Sudan Sleeping Sickness Commission, 1907–1908', *JRAMC* 12 (1909), 376–401.

—— 'A Day's Work on the Sudan Sleeping Sickness Commission', *JRAMC* 23 (1914), 31–5.

EVANS-PRITCHARD, E. E., *Witchcraft, Oracles and Magic among the Azande* (Oxford: Clarendon Press, 1937).

—— *The Azande: History and Political Institutions* (Oxford: Clarendon Press, 1971).

FARLEY, JOHN, *Bilharzia: A History of Imperial Tropical Medicine* (Cambridge: Cambridge University Press, 1991).

—— 'The International Health Division of the Rockefeller Foundation: The Russell Years, 1920–1934', in Weindling (ed.), *International Health Organisations*, 203–21.

FEIERMAN, STEVEN, 'Change in African Therapeutic Systems', *Social Science and Medicine*, 13B (1979), 277–84.

—— 'Struggles for Control: The Social Basis of Health and Healing in Modern Africa', *African Studies Review*, 28 (1985), 73–147.

FENDALL, N. R. E., 'A History of the Yaba School of Medicine, Nigeria', *West African Medical Journal*, Aug. 1967, 118–24.

FILDES, VALERIE, MARKS, LARA, and MARLAND, HILARY (eds.), *Women and Children First: International Maternal and Infant Welfare, 1870–1945* (London: Routledge, 1992).

FINDLAY, G. M., discussion following SOPER, FRED L., 'Yellow Fever: The

Present Situation (October 1938) with Special Reference to South America', *TRSTMH* 32 (1938), 323–5.

——and MacCallum, F. O., 'Yellow Fever Immune Bodies in the Blood of African Primates', *TRSTMH* 31 (1937), 103–6.

——Kirk, R., and MacCallum, F. O., 'Yellow Fever and the Anglo-Egyptian Sudan: Distribution of Immune Bodies to Yellow Fever', *ATMP* 35 (1941), 121–39.

——Kirk, R., and Lewis, D. J., 'Yellow Fever and the Anglo-Egyptian Sudan: The Differential Diagnosis of Yellow Fever', *ATMP* 35 (1941), 149–64.

Fisher, Donald, 'The Rockefeller Foundation and the Development of Scientific Medicine in Great Britain', *Minerva*, 16 (1978), 20–41.

——'Rockefeller Philanthropy and the British Empire: The Creation of the London School of Hygiene and Tropical Medicine', *History of Education*, 7 (1978), 129–43.

Forbes, Geraldine, 'Managing Midwifery in India', in Engels and Marks (eds.), *Contesting Colonial Hegemony*, 152–72.

Ford, John, *The Role of the Trypanosomiases in African Ecology: A Study of the Tsetse Fly Problem* (Oxford: Clarendon Press, 1971).

——'Early Ideas about Sleeping Sickness and their Influence on Research and Control', in E. E. Sabben-Clare, D. J. Bradley, and K. Kirkwood (eds.), *Health in Tropical Africa During the Colonial Period* (Oxford: Clarendon Press, 1980), 30–4.

*Fourth Report of the Wellcome Research Laboratories at the Gordon Memorial College Khartoum*, vol. A—Medical (London: Baillière, Tindall & Cox for the Department of Education, Sudan Government, Khartoum, 1911).

*Fourth Report of the Wellcome Research Laboratories at the Gordon Memorial College Khartoum*, vol. B—General Science (London: Baillière, Tindall & Cox for the Department of Education, Sudan Government, Khartoum, 1911).

Fraser, Eileen, *The Doctor Comes to Lui* (London: Church Missionary Society, 1938).

Freidson, Eliot, *Profession of Medicine: A Study of the Sociology of Applied Knowledge* (New York: Harper and Row, 1970).

Fry, W. B., 'A Preliminary Note on the Extrusion of Granules by Trypanosomes', *Proceedings of the Royal Society*, series B, 84 (1911), 79–80.

——and Ranken, H. S., with a Note on Methods by Plimmer, H. G., 'Further Researches on the Extrusion of Granules by Trypanosomes and on their Further Development', *Proceedings of the Royal Society*, series B, 86 (1913), 377–93.

Gaitskell, Arthur, *Gezira: A Story of Development in the Sudan* (London: Faber and Faber, 1959).

Geison, Gerald L., *Michael Foster and the Cambridge School of Physiology: The Scientific Enterprise in Late Victorian Society* (Princeton: Princeton University Press, 1978).

Giblin, James, 'Trypanosomiasis Control in African History: An Evaded Issue?', *Journal of African History*, 31 (1990), 59–80.

Gooday, Graeme, 'Precision Measurement and the Genesis of Physics Teaching

Laboratories in Victorian Britain', *British Journal for the History of Science*, 23 (1990), 25–51.

GREIG, E. D. W., 'Summary of Report Number VI of the Sleeping Sickness Commission of the Royal Society; Report on Sleeping Sickness in the Nile Valley', *JRAMC* 5 (1905), 582–6.

GRUENBAUM, ELLEN RUTH, 'Health Services, Health, and Development in Sudan: The Impact of the Gezira Irrigated Scheme', Ph.D. thesis (University of Connecticut, 1982).

——'The Movement Against Clitoridectomy and Infibulation in the Sudan: Public Health Policy and the Women's Movement', *Medical Anthropology Newsletter*, 13 (1982), 4–12.

——'Reproductive Ritual and Social Reproduction: Female Circumcision and the Subordination of Women in Sudan', in O'Neill and O'Brien (eds.), *Economy and Class*, 308–25.

HALIM, AHMED ABDEL, 'Native Medicine and Ways of Treatment in the Northern Sudan', *SNR* 22 (1939), 27–48.

HALL, A. R., and BEMBRIDGE, B. A., *Physic and Philanthropy: A History of the Wellcome Trust 1936–1986* (Cambridge: Cambridge University Press, 1986).

HALL, MARJORIE, and ISMAIL, BAKHITA AMIN, *Sisters under the Sun: The Story of Sudanese Women* (London: Longman, 1981).

HARRISON, MARK, 'Tropical Medicine in Nineteenth-Century India', *British Journal for the History of Science*, 25 (1992), 299–318.

——*Public Health in British India: Anglo-Indian Preventive Medicine 1859–1914* (Cambridge: Cambridge University Press, 1994).

——' "The Tender Frame of Man": Disease, Climate, and Racial Difference in India and the West Indies, 1760–1860', *Bulletin of the History of Medicine*, 70 (1996), 68–93.

HARTWIG, GERALD W., 'Louse-Borne Relapsing Fever in Sudan, 1908–51', in Gerald W. Hartwig and K. David Patterson (eds.), *Disease in African History: An Introductory Survey and Case Studies* (Durham, NC: Duke University Press, 1978), 207–37.

——'Smallpox in the Sudan', *International Journal of African Historical Studies*, 14 (1981), 5–33.

——'Schistosomiasis in the Sudan', in K. David Patterson and Gerald W. Hartwig, *Schistosomiasis in Twentieth Century Africa: Historical Studies on West Africa and Sudan* (Los Angeles: Crossroads Press, 1984), 33–81.

——'Cerebrospinal Meningitis in the Sudan', in K. David Patterson and Gerald W. HARTWIG, *Cerebrospinal Meningitis in West Africa and Sudan in the Twentieth Century* (Los Angeles: Crossroads Press, 1984), 35–69.

HASSOUN, ISAM AHMAD, ' "Western" Migration and Settlement in the Gezira', *SNR* 33 (1952), 60–112.

HEADRICK, RITA, *Colonialism, Health, and Illness in French Equatorial Africa, 1885–1935*, ed. Daniel R. Headrick (Atlanta: African Studies Association Press, 1994).

HENDERSON, L. H., 'Prophylaxis of Malaria in the Sudan With Special Reference to the Use of Plasmoquine', *TRSTMH* 28 (1934), 157–64.

HEWER, T. F., 'Yellow Fever in the Anglo-Egyptian Sudan', *Lancet*, 1 Sept. 1934, 496–9.

HØDNEBØ, KJELL, 'Cattle and Flies: A Study of the Cattle Keeping in Equatoria Province, the Southern Sudan, 1850–1950', Hovedoppgave i historie varen (University of Bergen, 1981).

HOLDEN, PAT, 'Colonial Sisters: Nurses in Uganda', in Pat Holden and Jenny Littlewood (eds.), *Anthropology and Nursing* (London: Routledge, 1991), 67–83.

HOPPE, KIRK ARDEN, 'Lords of the Fly: Colonial Visions and Revisions of African Sleeping-Sickness Environments on Ugandan Lake Victoria, 1906–61', *Africa*, 67 (1997), 86–105.

HUMPHREYS, MARGARET, *Yellow Fever and the South* (New Brunswick, NJ: Rutgers University Press, 1992).

HUMPHREYS, R. M., 'Vesical Schistosomiasis in the Gezira Irrigated Area of the Sudan', *TRSTMH* 26 (1932), 241–52.

HUNT, A. R., and BLOSS, J. F. E., 'Tsetse Fly Control and Sleeping Sickness in the Sudan', *TRSTMH* 39 (1945), 43–58.

HUNT, NANCY ROSE, ' "Le Bébé en brousse": European Women, African Birth Spacing and Colonial Intervention in Breast Feeding in the Belgian Congo', *International Journal of African Historical Studies*, 21 (1988), 401–32.

HUSSEY, E. J. R., 'A Fiki's Clinic', *SNR* 6 (1923), 35–9.

ILIFFE, JOHN, *Africans: The History of a Continent* (Cambridge: Cambridge University Press, 1995).

JACYNA, L. S., 'The Laboratory and the Clinic: The Impact of Pathology on Surgical Diagnosis in the Glasgow Western Infirmary, 1875–1910', *Bulletin of the History of Medicine*, 62 (1988), 384–406.

JOHNSON, DOUGLAS H., 'The Future of the Southern Sudan's Past', *Africa Today*, 28 (1981), 33–41.

——'Criminal Secrecy: The Case of the Zande "Secret Societies" ', *Past & Present*, 130 (1991), 170–200.

——'Recruitment and Entrapment in Private Slave Armies: The Structure of the *Zara'ib* in the Southern Sudan', *Slavery & Abolition*, 13 (1992), 162–73.

KENDALL, E. M., 'A Short History of the Training of Midwives in the Sudan', *SNR* 33 (1952), 42–53.

KENRICK, ROSEMARY, *Sudan Tales: Recollections of Some Sudan Political Service Wives* (Cambridge: Oleander, 1987).

KENYON, SUSAN M., *Five Women of Sennar: Culture and Change in Central Sudan* (Oxford: Clarendon Press, 1991).

KING, HAROLD H., 'Observations on the Occurrence of Glossina in the Mongalla Province of the Anglo-Egyptian Sudan', *Bulletin of Entomological Research*, 3 (1912), 89–93.

KIRK, R., 'Nouvelles recherches sur la fièvre jaune au Soudan Anglo-Égyptien', *BOIHP* 28 (1936), 2340–5.

KIRK, R., 'Attempts to Demonstrate Leptospirosis in the Northern Sudan', *TRSTMH* 31 (1938), 667–70.

—— 'An Epidemic of Yellow Fever in the Nuba Mountains, Anglo-Egyptian Sudan', *ATMP* 35 (1941), 67–108.

—— 'The Sudanese in Mexico', *SNR* 24 (1941), 111–30.

—— 'Some Observations on the Study and Control of Yellow Fever in Africa, with Particular Reference to the Anglo-Egyptian Sudan', *TRSTMH* 37 (1943), 125–50.

—— 'Notes on Yellow Fever', *SNR* 34 (1953), 47–61.

KIRK-GREENE, A. H. M., 'The Sudan Political Service: A Profile in the Sociology of Imperialism', *International Journal of African Historical Studies*, 15 (1983), 21–48.

—— *The Sudan Political Service: A Preliminary Profile* (Oxford, 1982).

KOERNER, T., DE RAADT, P., and MAUDLIN, I., 'The 1901 Uganda Sleeping Sickness Epidemic Revisited: A Case of Mistaken Identity?', *Parasitology Today*, 11 (1995), 303–6.

KÖRNER, THORSTEN, 'Sleeping Sickness—A Case Study of Environmental History in Uganda since the late Nineteenth Century', Magisterarbeit (Universität Hannover, 1995).

KUBICEK, ROBERT V., *The Administration of Imperialism: Joseph Chamberlain at the Colonial Office* (Durham, NC: Duke University Press, 1969).

LARKEN, P. M., 'Notes on the Azande of Tambura and Yambio, 1911–1932', in T. A. T. Leitch (ed.), *Zande Background* (Nzara: Equatorial Projects Board, 1955), 1–68.

LASKER, JUDITH N., 'The Role of Health Services in Colonial Rule: The Case of the Ivory Coast', *Culture, Medicine and Psychiatry*, 1 (1977), 277–97.

LATOUR, BRUNO, 'Give me a Laboratory and I will Raise the World', in Karin Knorr-Cetina and Michael Mulkay (eds.), *Science Observed: Perspectives on the Social Study of Science* (London: Sage, 1983), 141–70.

LAWRENCE, CHRISTOPHER, 'Incommunicable Knowledge: Science, Technology and the Clinical Art in Britain, 1850–1914', *Journal of Contemporary History*, 20 (1985), 503–20.

LEWIS, D. J., 'Mosquitoes in Relation to Yellow Fever in the Nuba Mountains, Anglo-Egyptian Sudan', *ATMP* 37 (1943), 65–76.

LEWIS, JANE, *The Politics of Motherhood: Child and Maternal Welfare in England, 1900–1939* (London: Croom Helm, 1980).

LÖWY, ILANA, 'What/who should be Controlled: Opposition to Yellow Fever Campaigns in Brazil, 1900–1939', in Bridie Andrews and Andrew Cunningham (eds.), *Western Medicine as Contested Knowledge* (Manchester: Manchester University Press, 1997).

LYONS, MARYINEZ, *The Colonial Disease: A Social History of Sleeping Sickness in Northern Zaire, 1900–1940* (Cambridge: Cambridge University Press, 1992).

—— 'The Power to Heal: African Medical Auxiliaries in Colonial Belgian Congo and Uganda', in Engels and Marks (eds.), *Contesting Colonial Hegemony*, 202–23.

—— 'Foreign Bodies: The History of Labour Migration as a Threat to Public Health in Uganda', in Paul Nugent and A. I. Asiwaju (eds.), *African Boundaries: Barriers, Conduits, and Opportunities* (London: Pinter, 1996), 131–44.

MACDONALD, GILBERT, *In Pursuit of Excellence* (London: The Wellcome Foundation, 1980).

MCKELVEY, JOHN J., *Man Against Tsetse: Struggle for Africa* (Ithaca, NY: Cornell University Press, 1973).

MACLEOD, ROY M., 'Scientific Advice for British India: Imperial Perceptions and Administrative Goals, 1898–1923', *Modern Asian Studies*, 9 (1975), 343–84.

—— and ANDREWS, E. KAY, 'The Committee of Civil Research: Scientific Advice for Economic Development 1925–30', *Minerva*, 7 (1969), 680–705.

MAHAFFY, A. F., HUGHES, T. P., SMITHBURN, K. C., and KIRK, R., 'The Isolation of Yellow Fever Virus in the Anglo-Egyptian Sudan', *ATMP* 35 (1941), 141–8.

MANDERSON, LENORE, 'Bottle Feeding and Ideology in Colonial Malaya: The Production of Change', *International Journal of Health Services*, 12 (1982), 597–616.

—— 'Health Services and the Legitimation of the Colonial State: British Malaya 1786–1941', *International Journal of Health Services*, 17 (1987), 91–112.

—— 'Blame, Responsibility and Remedial Action: Death, Disease and the Infant in Early Twentieth Century Malaya', in Norman G. Owen (ed.), *Death and Disease in Southeast Asia: Explorations in Social, Medical and Demographic History* (Singapore: Oxford University Press, 1987), 257–82.

—— 'Women and the State: Maternal and Child Welfare in Colonial Malaya, 1900–1940', in Fildes, Marks, and Marland (eds.), *Women and Children First*, 154–77.

—— *Sickness and the State: Health and Illness in Colonial Malaya, 1870–1940* (Cambridge: Cambridge University Press, 1997).

MANGER, LEIF O., 'Traders, Farmers and Pastoralists: Economic Adaptations and Environmental Problems in the Southern Nuba Mountains of the Sudan', in D. H. Johnson and D. M. Anderson (eds.), *The Ecology of Survival: Case Studies from Northeast African History* (London: Lester Crooks, 1988), 155–72.

MANSON-BAHR, P. E. C., and BELL, D. R., *Manson's Tropical Diseases*, 19th edn. (London: Baillière Tindall, 1987).

MARKS, LARA, and WORBOYS, MICHAEL (eds.), *Migrants, Minorities and Health: Historical and Contemporary Studies* (London: Routledge, 1997).

MARKS, SHULA, *Divided Sisterhood: Race, Class and Gender in the South African Nursing Profession* (London: St Martin's Press, 1994).

—— and ANDERSSON, NEIL, 'Issues in the Political Economy of Health in Southern Africa', *Journal of Southern African Studies*, 13 (1987), 177–86.

MATHER, D. B., 'Migration in the Sudan', in R. W. Steel and C. A. Fisher (eds.), *Geographical Essays on British Tropical Lands* (London: George Philip, 1956), 115–43.

MATTHEWS, RODERIC D., and AKRAWI, MATTA, *Education in Arab Countries of the Near East: Egypt, Iraq, Palestine, Transjordan, Syria, Lebanon* (Washington, DC: American Council on Education, 1949).

MAURICE, G. K., 'The History of Sleeping Sickness in the Sudan', *SNR* 13, part II (1930), 211–45.

*Minutes of the Evidence Taken by the Departmental Committee on Sleeping Sickness* (London: Eyre & Spottiswoode for HMSO, 1914).

MOLYNEUX, D. H., 'African Trypanosomiasis', *Clinics in Tropical Medicine and Communicable Diseases*, Dec. 1986, 537–40.

MOULIN, ANNE MARIE, 'Patriarchal Science: The Network of the Overseas Pasteur Institutes', in P. Petitjean, Catherine Jami, and Anne Marie Moulin (eds.), *Science and Empires* (Boston: Kluwer Academic, 1992), 307–22.

—— 'The Pasteur Institutes between the Two World Wars. The Transformation of the International Sanitary Order', in Weindling (ed.), *International Health Organisations*, 244–65.

NADEL, S. F., *The Nuba: An Anthropological Study of the Hill Tribes in Kordofan* (London: Oxford University Press, 1947).

NEWMAN, CHARLES, *The Evolution of Medical Education in the Nineteenth Century* (London: Oxford University Press, 1957).

NIBLOCK, TIM, *Class and Power in Sudan: The Dynamics of Sudanese Politics, 1898–1985* (London: Macmillan, 1987).

O'BRIEN, JAY, 'The Formation of the Agricultural Labour Force in Sudan', *Review of African Political Economy*, 26 (1983), 15–34.

—— 'The Formation and Transformation of the Agricultural Labour Force in Sudan', in O'Neill and O'Brien (eds.), *Economy and Class*, 137–56.

O'BRIEN, JOHN JAMES, III, 'Agricultural Labor and Development in Sudan', Ph.D. thesis (University of Connecticut, 1980).

O'NEILL, NORMAN, and O'BRIEN, JAY (eds.), *Economy and Class in Sudan* (Aldershot: Avebury, 1988).

PACKARD, RANDALL M., 'Maize, Cattle and Mosquitoes: The Political Economy of Malaria Epidemics in Colonial Swaziland', *Journal of African History*, 25 (1984), 189–212.

—— *White Plague, Black Labor: Tuberculosis and the Political Economy of Health and Disease in South Africa* (Berkeley: University of California Press, 1989).

PATTERSON, K. DAVID, *Health in Colonial Ghana: Disease, Medicine, and Socioeconomic Change, 1900–1955* (Waltham, Mass: Crossroads Press, 1981).

PEDERSEN, SUSAN, 'National Bodies, Unspeakable Acts: The Sexual Politics of Colonial Policy-Making', *Journal of Modern History*, 63 (1991), 647–80.

PELIS, KIM, 'Pasteur's Imperial Missionary: Charles Nicolle (1866–1936) and the Pasteur Institute of Tunis', Ph.D. thesis (The Johns Hopkins University, 1995).

PETERKIN, A., JOHNSTON, WILLIAM, and DREW, R., *Commissioned Officers in the Medical Services of the British Army 1660–1960*, 2 vols. (London: Wellcome Historical Medical Library, 1968).

PETTY, CELIA, 'Primary Research and Public Health: The Prioritization of Nutrition Research in Inter-War Britain', in Austoker and Bryder (eds.), *Historical Perspectives*, 83–108.

PHILIPP, THOMAS, *The Syrians in Egypt 1725–1975* (Stuttgart: Franz Steiner Verlag Wiesbaden GMBH, 1985).

POWER, HELEN, 'Keeping the Strains Alive and More: Trypanosomiasis Research at the Liverpool School of Tropical Medicine's Laboratory in Runcorn', paper presented at the Wellcome Unit for the History of Medicine, Oxford, 22 Feb. 1996.

PRIDIE, E. D., 'Faits récents concernant la fièvre jaune dans le Soudan Anglo-Égyptien, en particulier la lutte contre les moustiques', *BOIHP* 28 (1936), 1292–7.

—— 'Description sommaire de l'instruction et de l'organisation des sages-femmes au Soudan Anglo-Égyptien', *BOIHP* 29 (1937), 1931–5.

—— 'Distribution et incidence d'*Aedes aegypti* au Soudan Anglo-Égyptien en 1937', *BOIHP* 30 (1938), 1973–8.

—— et al., *Female Circumcision in the Anglo-Egyptian Sudan* (Khartoum, 1945).

PROTHERO, R. MANSELL, *Migrants and Malaria* (London: Longmans, 1965).

RAFFERTY, ANNE-MARIE, *The Politics of Nursing Knowledge* (London: Routledge, 1996).

RANKEN, H. S., 'A Preliminary Report on the Treatment of Human Trypanosomiasis and Yaws with Metallic Antimony', *Proceedings of the Royal Society*, series B, 86 (1913), 203–18.

REINING, CONRAD, *The Zande Scheme: An Anthropological Case Study of Economic Development in Africa* (Evanston, Ill.: Northwestern University Press, 1966).

'Renseignements récents sur la fièvre jaune reçus au cours des neufs mois finissant le 30 septembre 1937', *BOIHP* 30 (1938), 45–53.

*Report of the Wellcome Research Laboratories at the Gordon Memorial College Khartoum* (Khartoum: Department of Education, Sudan Government, 1904).

REYNOLDS, JAMES E. F., *Martindale: The Extra Pharmacopoeia*, 30th edn. (London: The Pharmaceutical Press, 1993).

RHODES JAMES, ROBERT, *Henry Wellcome* (London: Hodder and Stoughton, 1994).

RICHARDS, H., 'Rapport sur la déinsectisation des aéronefs à l'aérodrome de Khartoum', *BOIHP* 30 (1938), 563–7.

RICKARD, E. R., 'The Organization of the Viscerotome Service of the Brazilian Cooperative Yellow Fever Service', *American Journal of Tropical Medicine*, 17 (1937), 163–90.

ROBINSON, SARAH, 'Maintaining the Independence of the Midwifery Profession: A Continuing Struggle', in Jo Garcia, Robert Kilpatrick, and Martin Richards (eds.), *The Politics of Maternity Care: Services for Childbearing Women in Twentieth-Century Britain* (Oxford: Clarendon Press, 1990), 61–91.

RODEN, DAVID, 'Down-migration in the Moro Hills of Southern Kordofan', *SNR* 53 (1972), 79–98.

SANDERSON, LILIAN, 'Some Aspects of the Development of Girls' Education in the Northern Sudan', *SNR* 42 (1961), 91–101.

SANDERSON, LILIAN PASSMORE, *Against the Mutilation of Women* (London: Anti-Slavery Society and Ithaca Press, 1981).

——and SANDERSON, NEVILLE, *Education, Religion & Politics in Southern Sudan, 1899–1964* (London: Ithaca Press, 1981).

SAWYER, W. A., and LLOYD, WRAY, 'Use of Mice in Tests of Immunity Against Yellow Fever', *Journal of Experimental Medicine*, 54 (1931), 533–55.

——and WHITMAN, LORING, 'The Yellow Fever Immunity Survey of North, East and South Africa', *TRSTMH* 29 (1936), 397–412.

——KITCHEN, S. F., FROBISHER, MARTIN, Jr., and LLOYD, WRAY, 'Relationship of Yellow Fever of the Western Hemisphere to That of Africa and to Leptospiral Jaundice', *Journal of Experimental Medicine*, 51 (1930), 493–517.

SCHRAM, RALPH, *A History of the Nigerian Health Services* (Ibadan: Ibadan University Press, 1971).

*Second Report of the Wellcome Research Laboratories at the Gordon Memorial College Khartoum* (Khartoum: Department of Education, Sudan Government, 1906).

SHAPIN, STEVEN, 'Discipline and Bounding: The History and Sociology of Science as Seen through the Externalism–Internalism Debate', *History of Science*, 30 (1992), 333–69.

SHAPIRO, KARIN A., 'Doctors or Medical Aids—The Debate over the Training of Black Medical Personnel for the Rural Black Population in South Africa in the 1920s and 1930s', *Journal of Southern African Studies*, 13 (1987), 234–55.

SINGER, ANDRÉ, 'Ethnography and Ecosystem: A Zande Example', in André Singer and Brian V. Street (eds.), *Zande Themes: Essays Presented to Sir Edward Evans-Pritchard* (Oxford: Basil Blackwell, 1972), 1–18.

SMITHBURN, KENNETH C., 'Immunology', in Strode (ed.), *Yellow Fever*, 165–228.

SOFF, HARVEY G., 'Sleeping Sickness in the Lake Victoria Region of British East Africa, 1900–1915', *African Historical Studies*, 2 (1969), 255–68.

SOLÓRZANO, ARMANDO, 'Sowing the Seeds of Neo-imperialism: The Rockefeller Foundation's Yellow Fever Campaign in Mexico', *International Journal of Health Services*, 22 (1992), 529–54.

——'The Rockefeller Foundation in Revolutionary Mexico: Yellow Fever in Yucatan and Veracruz', in Cueto (ed.), *Missionaries of Science*, 52–71.

SPAULDING, JAY, and BESWICK, STEPHANIE, 'Sex, Bondage, and the Market: The Emergence of Prostitution in Northern Sudan, 1750–1950', *Journal of the History of Sexuality*, 5 (1995), 512–34.

SPENCE, B. H. H., Annual Report on Sleeping Sickness for 1918, excerpts in Andrew Balfour, E. van Campenhout, Gustave Martin, and A. G. Bagshawe, *Rapport provisoire sur la tuberculose et la maladie du sommeil en Afrique Équatoriale* (Société des nations, Organisation d'hygiène, 1924), 104–9.

——'The Wadi Halfa Quarantine', *JRAMC* 43 (1924), 321–40.

SQUIRES, H. C., *The Sudan Medical Service: An Experiment in Social Medicine* (London: William Heinemann, 1958).

STEPAN, NANCY, 'The Interplay between Socio-Economic Factors and Medical Science: Yellow Fever Research, Cuba and the United States', *Social Studies of Science*, 8 (1978), 397–423.

STEPHENSON, R. W., 'Bilharziasis in the Gezira Irrigated Area of the Sudan', *TRSTMH* 40 (1947), 479–94.

STOKES, ADRIAN, BAUER, JOHANNES H., and HUDSON, N. PAUL, 'Experimental Transmission of Yellow Fever to Laboratory Animals', *American Journal of Tropical Medicine*, 8 (1928), 103–64.

STRODE, G. K. (ed.), *Yellow Fever* (New York: McGraw-Hill, 1951).

—— 'The Conquest of Yellow Fever', in Strode (ed.), *Yellow Fever*, 5–37.

STURDY, STEVE, 'The Political Economy of Scientific Medicine: Science, Education and the Transformation of Medical Practice in Sheffield, 1890–1922', *Medical History*, 36 (1992), 125–59.

'Sudan Sleeping Sickness Commission', *Tropical Diseases Bulletin*, 5 (1915), 296–7.

SUMMERS, CAROL, 'Intimate Colonialism: The Imperial Production of Reproduction in Uganda, 1907–1925', *Signs*, 16 (1991), 787–807.

SUTPHEN, MOLLY, 'Culturing Trust: Practitioners, Laboratory Medicine, and the Importance of Character in Hong Kong, 1902–1914', unpublished paper, Mar. 1997.

SWANSON, M. W., '"The Sanitation Syndrome": Bubonic Plague and Urban Native Policy in the Cape Colony, 1900–1909', *Journal of African History*, 28 (1977), 387–410.

TANSEY, E. M., 'The Wellcome Physiological Research Laboratories 1894–1904: The Home Office, Pharmaceutical Firms, and Animal Experiments', *Medical History*, 33 (1989), 1–41.

—— 'What's in a Name? Henry Dale and Adrenaline, 1906', *Medical History*, 39 (1995), 459–76.

—— and MILLIGAN, ROSEMARY C. E., 'The Early History of the Wellcome Research Laboratories, 1894–1914', in Gregory J. Higby and Elaine C. Stroud (eds.), *Pill Peddlers: Essays on the History of the Pharmaceutical Industry* (Madison: American Institute of the History of Pharmacy, 1990), 91–106.

TETTEY, CHARLES, 'A Brief History of the Medical Research Institute and Laboratory Service of the Gold Coast (Ghana) 1908–1957', *West African Medical Journal*, 9 (1960), 73–85.

THEILER, MAX, 'Studies on the Action of Yellow Fever Virus in Mice', *ATMP* 24 (1930), 247–72.

—— 'The Virus', in Strode (ed.), *Yellow Fever*, 39–136.

—— and SELLARDS, ANDREW WATSON, 'The Immunological Relationship of Yellow Fever as It Occurs in West Africa and in South America', *ATMP* 22 (1928), 449–60.

*Third Report of the Wellcome Research Laboratories at the Gordon Memorial College Khartoum* (London: Baillière, Tindall & Cox for the Department of Education, Sudan Government, Khartoum, 1908).

THOMAS, LYNN M., ' "*Ngaitana* (I will circumcise myself)": The Gender and Generational Politics of the 1956 Ban on Clitoridectomy in Meru, Kenya', *Gender and History*, 8 (1996), 338–63.

THOMAS, NICHOLAS, *Colonialism's Culture: Anthropology, Travel, and Government* (Oxford: Polity Press, 1994).

TIBAWI, A. L., 'The Genesis and Early History of the Syrian Protestant College', in Fûad Sarrûf and Suha Tamim (eds.), *American University of Beirut Festival Book* (Beirut: American University of Beirut, Centennial Publications, 1967).

TORSVIK, BENTE, 'Receiving the Gifts of Allah: The Establishment of a Modern Midwifery Service in the Sudan 1920–1937', Hovedoppgave i Historie hosten (University of Bergen, 1983).

TURSHEN, MEREDETH, 'The Impact of Colonialism on Health and Health Services in Tanzania', *International Journal of Health Services*, 7 (1977), 7–35.

——*The Political Ecology of Disease in Tanzania* (New Brunswick, NJ: Rutgers University Press, 1984).

VAN HELVOORT, TON, 'History of Virus Research in the Twentieth Century: The Problem of Conceptual Continuity', *History of Science*, 32 (1994), 185–235.

VAN HEYNINGEN, E. B., 'Agents of Empire: The Medical Profession in the Cape Colony, 1880–1910', *Medical History*, 33 (1989), 450–71.

VAUGHAN, MEGAN, *Curing their Ills: Colonial Power and African Illness* (Oxford: Polity Press, 1991).

——'Healing and Curing: Issues in the Social History and Anthropology of Medicine in Africa', *Social History of Medicine*, 7 (1994), 283–95.

——'Health and Hegemony: Representation of Disease and the Creation of the Colonial Subject in Nyasaland', in Engels and Marks (eds.), *Contesting Colonial Hegemony*, 173–201.

WARBURG, GABRIEL, *The Sudan Under Wingate* (London: Frank Cass, 1971).

WARNER, JOHN HARLEY, 'The Fall and Rise of Professional Mystery: Epistemology, Authority and the Emergence of Laboratory Medicine in Nineteenth-Century America', in Cunningham and Williams (eds.), *Laboratory Revolution*, 110–41.

WEINDLING, PAUL (ed.), *International Health Organisations and Movements 1918–1939* (Cambridge: Cambridge University Press, 1995).

WHITE, LUISE, 'Cars Out of Place: Vampires, Technology, and Labor in East and Central Africa', *Representations*, 43 (1993), 27–50.

——'Tsetse Visions: Narratives of Blood and Bugs in Colonial Northern Rhodesia, 1931–9', *Journal of African History*, 36 (1995), 219–45.

——'The Needle and the State: Immunization and Inoculation in Africa. Or, The Practice of Unnational Sovereignty', paper presented to the Workshop on Immunization and the State, Delhi, India, 16–17 Jan. 1997.

WILLIAMS, STEVEN C., 'Nationalism and Public Health: The Convergence of Rockefeller Foundation Technique and Brazilian Federal Authority during the Time of Yellow Fever, 1925–1930', in Cueto (ed.), *Missionaries of Science*, 23–51.

WORBOYS, MICHAEL, 'The Emergence of Tropical Medicine: A Study in the Establishment of a Scientific Specialty', in Gerard Lemaine, Roy MacLeod, Michael Mulkay, and Peter Weingart (eds.), *Perspectives on the Emergence of Scientific Disciplines* (Chicago: Aldine, 1976), 75–98.

—— 'Science and British Colonial Imperialism, 1895–1940', D.Phil. thesis (University of Sussex, 1979).

—— 'Manson, Ross and Colonial Medical Policy: Tropical Medicine in London and Liverpool, 1899–1914', in Roy MacLeod and Milton Lewis (eds.), *Disease, Medicine and Empire: Perspectives on Western Medicine and the Experience of European Expansion* (London: Routledge, 1988), 21–37.

—— 'British Colonial Medicine and Tropical Imperialism: A Comparative Perspective', in G. M. van Heteren, A. de Knecht van Eekelen, and M. J. D. Poulissen (eds.), *Dutch Medicine in the Malay Archipelago, 1816–1942* (Amsterdam: Rodopi, 1989), 153–67.

—— 'The Imperial Institute: The State and the Development of the Natural Resources of the Colonial Empire, 1887–1923', in John M. MacKenzie (ed.), *Imperialism and the Natural World* (Manchester: Manchester University Press, 1990), 164–86.

—— 'Vaccine Therapy and Laboratory Medicine in Edwardian Britain', in John V. Pickstone (ed.), *Medical Innovations in Historical Perspective* (London: Macmillan, 1992), 84–103.

—— 'The Comparative History of Sleeping Sickness in East and Central Africa, 1900–1914', *History of Science*, 32 (1994), 89–102.

World Health Organization, *Prevention and Control of Yellow Fever in Africa* (Geneva, 1986).

WRIGHT, PETER, and TREACHER, ANDREW, 'Introduction', in Peter Wright and Andrew Treacher (eds.), *The Problem of Medical Knowledge: Examining the Social Construction of Medicine* (Edinburgh: Edinburgh University Press, 1982), 1–22.

YAMBA, C. BAWA, *Permanent Pilgrims: The Role of Pilgrimage in the Lives of West African Muslims in Sudan* (Edinburgh: Edinburgh University Press, 1995).

ZEKI, HASSAN EFFENDI, 'The Healing Art as Practised by the Dervishes in the Sudan During the Rule of the Mahdi and of the Khalifa', *Third RWRL*, 269–72.

# INDEX

# *Index*

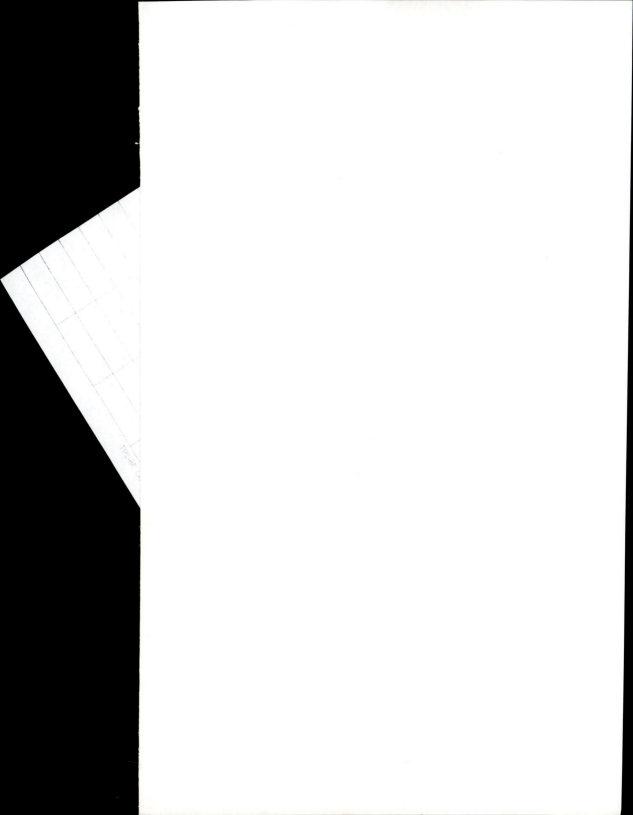